Integrating
Multiculturalism
and
Intersectionality
Into the
Psychology
Curriculum

Integrating Multiculturalism
and
Intersectionality
Into the
Psychology
Curriculum

STRATEGIES FOR INSTRUCTORS

Edited by
JASMINE A. MENA and KATHRYN QUINA

AMERICAN PSYCHOLOGICAL ASSOCIATION
Washington, DC

Published by
American Psychological Association
750 First Street, NE
Washington, DC 20002
https://www.apa.org

Order Department
https://www.apa.org/pubs/books
order@apa.org

In the U.K., Europe, Africa, and the Middle East, copies may be ordered from Eurospan
https://www.eurospanbookstore.com/apa
info@eurospangroup.com

Typeset in Meridien and Ortodoxa by Circle Graphics, Inc., Reisterstown, MD

Printer: Sheridan Books, Chelsea, MI
Cover Designer: Nicci Falcone, Gaithersburg, MD

Library of Congress Cataloging-in-Publication Data
Names: Mena, Jasmine A., editor. | Quina, Kathryn, editor.
Title: Integrating multiculturalism and intersectionality into the psychology curriculum : strategies for instructors / edited by Jasmine A. Mena and Kathryn Quina.
Description: Washington, DC : American Psychological Association, [2019] | Includes bibliographical references and index.
Identifiers: LCCN 2018049827 (print) | LCCN 2018051485 (ebook) | ISBN 9781433830082 (eBook) | ISBN 1433830086 (eBook) | ISBN 9781433830075 (pbk.) | ISBN 1433830078 (pbk.)
Subjects: LCSH: Psychology—Study and teaching. | Ethnopsychology. | Multiculturalism.
Classification: LCC BF77 (ebook) | LCC BF77 .I58 2019 (print) | DDC 150.71—dc23
LC record available at https://lccn.loc.gov/2018049827

http://dx.doi.org/10.1037/0000137-000

Printed in the United States of America

10 9 8 7 6 5 4 3 2 1

This work is dedicated to the memory of Phyllis Bronstein, who was the driving force behind the previous volumes (1989, 2003), along with three other authors: Janet M. Kulberg, Sondra Solomon, and Ethel Tobach. This volume reflects their vision and voice.

CONTENTS

CONTRIBUTORS

Kattalina Berriochoa, MPA, Doctoral Candidate, Department of Public Policy and Public Affairs, University of Massachusetts Boston

Su L. Boatright-Horowitz, PhD, Department of Psychology, University of Rhode Island, Kingston

Heather E. Bullock, PhD, Department of Psychology, University of California, Santa Cruz

Celeste M. Caviness, PhD, Behavioral Medicine and Addictions Research Group, Butler Hospital, Providence, RI

Connie S. Chan, PhD, Department of Public Policy and Public Affairs, University of Massachusetts Boston

Alice W. Cheng, PhD, Department of Psychology, Bridgewater State University, Bridgewater, MA

Lynn H. Collins, PhD, Department of Psychology, La Salle University, Philadelphia, PA

Nathan E. Cook, PhD, Department of Physical Medicine and Rehabilitation, Massachusetts General Hospital and Harvard Medical School, Boston

Florence L. Denmark, PhD, Psychology Department, Pace University, New York, NY; Department of Psychology, The City University of New York, Hunter College, New York

Andrea L. Dottolo, PhD, Department of Psychology, Rhode Island College, Providence

Halford H. Fairchild, PhD, Psychology and Africana Studies, Pitzer College, and the Intercollegiate Department of Africana Studies, Claremont, CA

Beverly J. Goodwin, PhD, Department of Psychology, Indiana University of Pennsylvania, Indiana

Kathleen S. Gorman, PhD, Department of Psychology, University of
Rhode Island, Kingston

Bergljot Gyda Gudmundsdottir, PhD, Breidholt Service Center,
Reykjavik, Iceland

Yvette Harps-Logan, PhD, Department of Psychology and Department
of Textiles, Fashion, Merchandising, and Design, University of
Rhode Island, Kingston

Camille J. Interligi, PsyD, Counseling Center, University of Pittsburgh,
Pittsburgh, PA

LaTrelle D. Jackson, PhD, ABPP, School of Professional Psychology,
Wright State University, Dayton, OH

Ashley E. Kasardo, PsyD, Carruth Center for Psychological and
Psychiatric Services, West Virginia University, Morgantown

Christopher Kilmartin, PhD, Department of Psychological Science,
University of Mary Washington, Fredericksburg, VA

Steven Kniffley, PsyD, ABPP, Spalding University Center for Behavioral
Health, Spalding University, Louisville, KY

Kate Miriam Loewenthal, PhD, Psychology, Royal Holloway University of
London, Egham, Surrey, England; New York University, London, England;
and Glyndwr University, Wrexham, Wales

Bernice Lott, PhD, Department of Psychology, University of Rhode Island,
Kingston

Kathleen A. Malloy, PhD, School of Professional Psychology, Wright
State University, Dayton, OH

Marisa E. Marraccini, PhD, School Psychology Program, School of
Education, University of North Carolina at Chapel Hill

Mala L. Matacin, PhD, Department of Psychology, University of Hartford,
West Hartford, CT

Kathy McCloskey, PhD, PsyD, ABPP-CL, Department of Psychology,
University of Hartford, West Hartford, CT

Maureen C. McHugh, PhD, Department of Psychology, Indiana University
of Pennsylvania, Indiana

Savannah McSheffrey, PhD, Rhode Island Hospital, Providence

Jasmine A. Mena, PhD, Department of Psychology, Bucknell University,
Lewisburg, PA

Gayle Skawen:nio Morse, PhD, School of Health Science, The Sage
Colleges, Troy, NY

Danielle R. Oster, PhD, The Buckley School, New York, NY

Andrea D. Poet, PsyD, Counseling and Psychological Services,
Pennsylvania State University, University Park

Brittney Poindexter, PhD, Department of Child and Adolescent Psychiatry
and Bradley Hasbro Children's Research Center, Providence, RI

Kathryn Quina, PhD, Department of Psychology, University of Rhode
Island, Kingston

Colleen A. Redding, PhD, Cancer Prevention Research Center, University
of Rhode Island, Kingston

Harriette W. Richard, PhD, Department of Social and Behavioral Sciences, Johnson C. Smith University, Charlotte, NC

Meghan Lamarre Rinaldi-Young, BS, Mental Health and Rehabilitation Counseling, Salve Regina University, Newport, RI

Alexandra Rutherford, PhD, Department of Psychology, York University, Toronto, Ontario, Canada

Stanley Sue, PhD, Clinical Psychology, Palo Alto University, Palo Alto, CA

Joseph E. Trimble, PhD, Department of Psychology, Western Washington University, Bellingham

Annemarie Vaccaro, PhD, Department of Human Development and Family Studies, University of Rhode Island, Kingston

Melba J. T. Vásquez, PhD, Vasquez and Associates Mental Health Services, Austin, TX

Kelli Vaughn-Johnson, MA, Department of Psychology, York University, Toronto, Ontario, Canada

Janeece R. Warfield, PsyD, School of Professional Psychology, Wright State University, Dayton, OH

Tammy Vargas Warner, PhD, Alan Shawn Feinstein College of Education and Professional Studies, University of Rhode Island, Kingston

Jacqueline S. Weinstock, PhD, Department of Leadership and Developmental Sciences, University of Vermont, Burlington

Lisa Weyandt, PhD, Department of Psychology, University of Rhode Island, Kingston

Lisa Whitten, PhD, Psychology Department, State University of New York, Old Westbury

Julie L. Williams, PsyD, ABPP, School of Professional Psychology, Wright State University, Dayton, OH

Miryam Yusufov, PhD, Dana Farber Cancer Institute, Harvard Medical School, Boston, MA

Mary Zahm, PhD, Department of Psychology, Bristol Community College, Fall River, MA

FOREWORD

Stanley Sue

Integrating Multiculturalism and Intersectionality Into the Psychology Curriculum: Strategies for Instructors, edited by Jasmine A. Mena and Kathryn Quina, is the most recent volume of the highly successful series of books on the teaching of diverse populations and cultural issues, including *Teaching a Psychology of People: Resources for Gender and Sociocultural Awareness* (1988) and *Teaching Gender and Multicultural Awareness: Resources for the Psychology Classroom* (2003) by Phyllis Bronstein and Kathryn Quina. Because I was invited to write forewords for two of the three books, I have an opportunity to reflect on changing issues in the field of multiculturalism and to compare the current version with the earlier versions.

The field has changed. First, in the past, multiculturalism and diversity issues were considered as peripheral or outside the mainstream of psychology. There is now greater acceptance of multiculturalism and diversity as an essential part of human existence. Although there are some who continue to regard a multicultural focus as a matter of "political correctness," people have increasingly adopted the view that human diversity should be recognized and respected. The change in these views is reflected in research on multiculturalism. Over the past 30 years, our knowledge about multiculturalism and diversity has increased dramatically. In the process, methods have emerged for studying different populations (e.g., quantitative, qualitative, and mixed method approaches) and small ethnic populations (e.g., improved sampling techniques), reducing reluctance to participate in research, and involving diverse communities in research and interpretation of findings. Thus, the field of psychology has benefited from multicultural research not only because of the new knowledge generated but also because the research has spawned innovative and expanded research approaches. What is the knowledge that should be conveyed, and what are the best approaches to teach multiculturalism to students? How can this knowledge be applied to or used in the lives of students? These are critical questions that must be addressed. Adding to the importance of these challenges in the teaching of multiculturalism is the continuing high student demand for psychology courses in general and multicultural and diversity courses in particular.

Second, the concepts of diversity and multiculturalism have become more inclusive. Ethnicity, race, gender, sexual orientation, religion, disability, and immigration are but some of the topics that are included in discussions of diversity and culture. But how can the inclusion be conceptualized or theoretically linked? That is, are diversity and multiculturalism simply a collection of different topics with the only commonality being "nonmainstream?" In the past, I would teach a course on ethnicity and race and give little coverage to other kinds of diversity. Now, it is important to discuss not only ethnicity and race but also different aspects of diversity (e.g., gender, social class, sexual orientation). Human beings are members of multiple groups (e.g., a woman who is heterosexual, who is Catholic). But rather than simply providing a list of our different group memberships, the task before us is to provide insights into the integration and interactions of various aspects of diversity. For example, the concepts of intersectionality and multiple identities have been used to conceptualize the different influences that affect our lives. Thus, in our approaches to teaching students about particular aspects of diversity (e.g., ethnicity and race), it is important to convey that human beings are a product of different groups and cultures and that these multiple memberships create complexity when dealing with self-identities, subjective experiences, and social status. How can this complexity be conveyed effectively to students? This is another important question.

Third, diversity and multiculturalism have always been associated with controversy and conflicts. For example, the genetic "superiority" of Whites over Blacks, the "abnormality" of being gay, and the "emotionality" of women are but some of the controversial claims that have been raised in the past. What has changed in the past 30 years is the overt polarity that has occurred not only in the United States but also worldwide. Immigration reform and isolationism (i.e., the philosophy that "America is for Americans") are particularly strong current controversies in the United States. Heated debates have occurred over the use of bathrooms by transgender persons, genocide and terrorism by religious extremists, police shootings involving African Americans, and so forth. Other countries are facing similar issues (e.g., trying to deal with the influx of Syrian refugees fleeing the war in their country). The pertinence of multiculturalism and diversity in all these controversies is apparent.

It is also important to realize that the controversial nature of these issues can make the classroom difficult to manage. Students may hold strong feelings and confront the teacher or classmates. Students themselves may experience personal conflicts. For example, in one class, a student who always felt she was racially unbiased became dispirited when she came to the realization that she was prejudiced and engaged in racial microaggressions. How do teachers deal with the difficult dialogues that can occur within and between students with different perspectives and experiences?

In summary, educators have several challenges: (a) to help students appreciate the new knowledge and strategies being used to study multiculturalism, (b) to encourage students to think critically about the intersections of different aspects of diversity, and (c) to enable students to gain insight into their values and perspectives and deal with different opinions and perspectives. This volume effectively deals with these challenges and serves as an important guide for teaching multiculturalism. It has something for everyone. For instructors of traditional psychology courses such as history of psychology, developmental psychology, and abnormal psychology, examples are provided about tactics to incorporate multiculturalism, including concrete teaching strategies, assignments, application of digital resources and technology, and the changing body of research and knowledge on diversity issues. For faculty members who teach specific courses on multiculturalism, the expanded definition of multiculturalism and newer concepts—such as intersectionality, multiple identities and perspectives, and microaggressions—are introduced and applied to students' lives. Finally, there are substantive discussions about ways of teaching controversial topics and engaging in difficult dialogues. The contributors, some of whom are among the most prominent in field, demonstrate their expertise and grasp of the issues.

This book is more than just a how-to manual. In the process of offering concrete suggestions for the education and training of students, it provides a sophisticated, up-to-date, and informative look at the field of multiculturalism.

FOREWORD

Florence L. Denmark

In recent years, the increased diversification of U.S. society has become evident. Today, opportunities for increased contact with other cultures and ways of life are more prevalent than ever before. As the world population continues to grow, the prospects for engaging with people whose customs and experiences differ from our own are virtually limitless. Population growth is fastest among ethnic and racial minority groups as a whole. As of July 1, 2011, more than half of children under 1 year of age belonged to ethnic and racial minority groups.[1] As our opportunities to work, learn, and associate with others from a multitude of backgrounds and traditions increase, we have a proportionally greater need to foster understanding of and respect for our similarities and differences.

Psychology is touted as a discipline devoted, in large part, to the study of human thought and behavior. In the past, however, psychological theory was based solely on the thoughts and behaviors of White males. The women's movement and the civil rights movement certainly played a role in broadening our horizons, and over the years, the realms of psychology have expanded to include women and men from different ethnic and racial backgrounds. Although psychology has paid increased attention to diverse individuals, studies of such individuals are often regarded as "special topics" in psychology. As educators, when we establish that the study of women or minorities belongs only in elective courses, we are sending an unfortunate message that such individuals will not be studied in mainstream psychology courses.

---

[1]U.S. Census Bureau. (2012). *Most children younger than age 1 are minorities, Census Bureau reports*. Retrieved from https://www.census.gov/newsroom/releases/archives/population/cb12-90.html

But psychology is the study of people, and all human beings on this earth fall into this category.

I believe that the importance of multicultural awareness should be paramount in psychology. Our cultural and ethnic backgrounds affect each of us in a multitude of ways, and it behooves all psychologists, especially those who work with students or clients of different nationalities, ethnicities, or lifestyles, to consider the impact of one's unique life experiences within the larger cultural context. Instructors and clinicians alike must remember that not all theories or treatment modalities will be equally effective when applied indiscriminately across all races and ethnicities.

In keeping with the growing need for students entering the field of psychology to develop multicultural skills and an appreciation for diversity, courses must be made relevant to include the experiences of all people. It is no longer sufficient for students to take a single class on gender, multiculturalism, or cross-cultural studies and, as a result, believe that they have gained a true understanding of their fellow human beings. Such issues should also be incorporated into each psychology course. In this spirit, the contributors have provided an integral book that will be helpful to all individuals studying psychology who are attempting to integrate recent sociocultural issues into a variety of courses and programs of study. Chapters not only discuss those groups traditionally considered in multicultural courses, such as African Americans, Latinxs, American Indians, and Asian Americans, but also include other diverse groups such as individuals with disabilities; elderly individuals; and lesbian, gay, bisexual, transgender, and queer (LGBTQ) people, who can sometimes be overlooked in such discussions. Authors provide not only information about social and cultural groups but also creative resources and projects by which such issues may be integrated into courses from the most basic introduction to psychology to graduate students' clinical experiences. This volume encourages instructors to review and select texts and materials with a critical eye, judging their relevance not only to one particular course but also to any class composed of members of a diverse society. Classroom techniques are suggested to encourage our students to gain an in-depth understanding of the different people in the world around them. *Integrating Multiculturalism and Intersectionality Into the Psychology Curriculum* is a wonderful resource for preparing students as well as faculty to be members of a growing and diverse international professional community.

As someone who benefited from the previous volumes, I am eager to make use of this new volume, which includes the most current ideas and materials on multiculturalism across the psychology curriculum. I encourage all psychology instructors to use this valuable resource.

ACKNOWLEDGMENTS

We thank Linda Malnasi McCarter, senior acquisitions editor, and the American Psychological Association for supporting our vision of transforming the psychology curriculum by meaningfully addressing multiculturalism and intersectionality. We also greatly appreciate the feedback provided by three anonymous reviewers and David Becker's editorial assistance. We are grateful to Miryam Yusufov for her excellent assistance with the supplemental website, which was supported by a University of Rhode Island Multicultural Enhancement Grant. Finally, we thank the contributors to this and previous volumes who have devoted themselves to the advancement of multicultural issues in psychology and related fields.

Integrating Multiculturalism
and
Intersectionality
Into the
Psychology
Curriculum

Introduction

Jasmine A. Mena and Kathryn Quina

The past 20 years have seen a proliferation of the multicultural psychology literature, and we now have a better appreciation for the importance of sociocultural factors and how they shape attitudes, cognitions, and behaviors. This expanding awareness has converged with demographic shifts in the United States, bringing an increased number of ethnoracial minority undergraduate and graduate students into psychology classrooms. Increased numbers of scholars from underrepresented groups seeking psychology degrees have increased awareness of the importance of multiculturalism and intersectionality across a wide swath of psychology.

The American Psychological Association (APA) has recognized that this new scholarship is relevant to research, practice, education, and organizational development and that multicultural awareness, knowledge, and skills are imperative to address the needs of today's society adequately (APA, 2017; see also Hall, 2014; Sue, 2013). Although this growth is exciting, incorporating this vast new theoretical and research literature into the psychology curriculum remains a challenge.

Taking on this challenge, the teacher–authors who contributed to this volume share their insights and strategies for achieving a psychology of and for the people. The chapters are intended to support educators in their quest to expand their courses to include multiculturalism and intersectionality and are geared for instructors, new or experienced, who wish to invigorate their teaching through new topics, resources, and pedagogical approaches to transform the psychology curriculum as well as culture-specific courses. Chapters include

http://dx.doi.org/10.1037/0000137-001
Integrating Multiculturalism and Intersectionality Into the Psychology Curriculum: Strategies for Instructors, J. A. Mena and K. Quina (Editors)

background knowledge and recent findings useful for instructor preparation as well as a plethora of practical recommendations, exercises, assignments, and activities that the authors have applied over their years of teaching from multicultural and intersectional perspectives. We understand that the strategies offered here can be intense and evocative for students and instructors. However, we believe that, with preparation, instructors can increase critical thinking and commitment to equity and justice among their students and at the same time make their courses more enjoyable.

STUDENT AND INSTRUCTOR VIEWPOINTS

Transforming the psychology curriculum to include multiculturalism and intersectionality may present new challenges for instructors and students alike. Take, for example, an experience I (JAM) had: I assigned a reaction paper to a reading that addressed the psychological toll of oppression and marginalization. A student turned in an incomplete paper indicating the exact page number where she stopped reading the article. A reasonable response might be a lower score and a note highlighting the values of commitment to learning and accountability to oneself and others. Would your response change if the student told you she interpreted the author's position (and, by implication, yours) as an affront to her worldview? On first introduction to these topics, students can have a negative reaction and may even believe that the lessons are one sided or that we have a personal agenda.

You may be wondering how I handled this scenario. I invited the student to speak with me in person. I validated her feelings of frustration, confusion, and even anger, given that she was grappling with racism, in the voice of a person oppressed, for the first time. I then asked her a series of questions for us to reflect on together, along the lines of, What is an individual act of racism? How is that different from structural barriers that claim "business as usual" yet cause harm? That only moved us forward part of the way. We leaped forward when I asked her to name an injustice in society that truly makes her mad. After we identified that injustice as sexual assaults, she was able to apply the same concept of structural oppression to the business as usual that allows for the obstinate continuation of violence against women. This difficult dialogue became a powerful teaching moment for both of us. Experiences like these compelled our authors to contribute to a community of instructors who are motivated but uncertain about how to transform their courses to address multiculturalism and intersectionality.

DEFINING MULTICULTURALISM AND INTERSECTIONALITY

We have adopted an inclusive perspective on multiculturalism and diversity that aligns with the APA's (2017) *Multicultural Guidelines: An Ecological Approach to Context, Identity, and Intersectionality*. The *Multicultural Guidelines* "consider contextual factors and intersectionality among and between reference group identities, including culture, language, gender, race, ethnicity, ability status, sexual orientation, age, gender identity, socioeconomic status, religion, spirituality, immigration status, education, and employment, among other variables" (p. 8). In addition to a broad and inclusive definition of multiculturalism, we have taken seriously the implications of Crenshaw's (1989) intersectionality theory, which takes special interest in the experiences unique to the "borderlands" of identities that are not always captured by a focus on single identities (Anzaldúa, 1987; Bowleg, 2012). As stated by Krieger (2012),

> After all, we are not one day White or a person of color, another day working class or a professional, still another day a woman or a man or transgendered, on yet another day straight or lesbian, gay, bisexual, or transgender, and yet another an immigrant versus native born. (p. 942)

Indeed, there are many dimensions and intersections of diversity that influence how people feel, think, and act. Today, most people accept that we are all cultural beings and that all encounters are multicultural. Beyond embracing diversity for the richness it adds to our lives, we acknowledge that underrepresented groups often experience oppression and marginalization; as such, throughout this book, we have taken special care to highlight the needs and strengths of marginalized groups.

CORE ASSUMPTIONS

Given the response to this book's two predecessors (Bronstein & Quina, 1988, 2003), we know that most educators want to transform their courses in line with multicultural recommendations. To that end, the authors in this volume have tried to introduce information and ideas that will make the process of transforming existing courses more accessible and help educators at varied levels of readiness feel more prepared to do so. We have been fortunate to find contributors who have incorporated the latest evidence as well as multicultural goals and outcomes into their teaching and practice.

The courses discussed in this book are not representative of the entire psychology discipline. We selected courses commonly considered core or foundational to the psychology curriculum, with a general focus on the undergraduate level. Similarly, the social and cultural minority groups we include are also the ones most commonly taught in psychology. In making these difficult decisions, we sought guidance from the *APA Guidelines for the Undergraduate Psychology Major, Version 2.0*, specifically Goal 2: Scientific Inquiry and Critical Thinking and Goal 3: Ethical and Social Responsibility in a Diverse World (APA, 2013; Dunn et al., 2010). Although our focus is primarily on undergraduate education, the background content in the chapters and the practical recommendations are generally applicable to graduate students, with minor modifications; some chapters address graduate curricula directly.

We chose the separate course model for the social and cultural groups because this approach has generated the largest literature base reporting positive outcomes (Rogers & O'Bryon, 2014). However, there are risks associated with focusing on any one group, including devaluation of minoritized groups and the instructors teaching these courses, who are often also minoritized, and a more limited reach to nonminoritized students (Denmark & Paludi, 2008). Broad infusion has been identified as a desirable alternative (Trimble, Stevenson, & Worell, 2004), and although we agree, we believe that there is still a need for concentrated information about specific underrepresented groups, both to inform stand-alone courses (e.g., Asian American Psychology) and increase awareness of the history and experiences of members of those groups. Thus, we have elected to continue the blended model adopted in Bronstein and Quina (1988, 2003), which includes both broad infusion in the curriculum as well as separate cultural groups. We hope that the informed educator will be able to present multicultural content not only as a single topic or focus—a separate section or a "special instance"—but also as a crucial way to increase students' knowledge about all people and help them become more consciously aware of themselves, "others," and the contexts that impact them.

We also respect varied approaches to understanding the psychological world. In the past decade, we have seen substantial increases in qualitative and mixed methods approaches to psychology, using phenomenological approaches that delve into the lived experience of participants. For example, Sevelius's (2013) qualitative interview research with transgender Women of Color revealed a context of oppression based on multiple social identities (gender identity and race) that was accompanied by psychological distress, a need for gender affirmation, and in high-risk contexts, sexual risk behavior. Qualitative methods provide richness and texture to psychological constructs, especially when seeking to understand the experiences of marginalized groups (Gergen & Gergen, 2000; Karnieli-Miller, Strier, & Pessach, 2009). We have included these alongside the more traditional quantitative methodologies, reflecting the range of ontological and epistemological stances identified throughout this volume.

Psychological research has often failed to account for human diversity at all levels of the research process (Parent, DeBlaere, & Moradi, 2013). The common practice of lumping "minorities" together for analyses is problematic because it obscures group differences. Some scholars have advocated for the eradication of the use of identity labels, such as race, in research because of the lack of shared conceptual definitions (Betancourt & López, 1993; Phinney, 1996). For example, Helms, Jernigan, and Mascher (2005) leveled this critique: "Equating race with racial categories gives scientific legitimacy to the conceptually meaningless construct of race, thereby perpetuating racial stereotypes and associated problems in society" (p. 27). Some of these scholars offer various substitutions, including using concepts such as values, customs, and traditions. Multicultural identities are complex; thus, a simple question about one's identity label often proves inadequate. Understanding the mechanisms behind the labels is more desirable, and it also makes room for the true heterogeneity within groups. It is equally problematic to ascribe to an individual the characteristics of a culture-sharing group. Recognizing these critiques, chapter authors have addressed within-group heterogeneity whenever possible, encouraging readers to consider the information about specific groups as common but not stereotypical. We hope the information we offer will, rather than provide all the answers, lead the reader to ask good questions.

Scholars have urged psychologists to embrace the responsibility that comes with the growth of multicultural psychology and intersectionality by incorporating it in classrooms, research, and service delivery (Cardemil, Moreno, & Sanchez, 2011; Leong, Comas-Díaz, Nagayama Hall, McLoyd, & Trimble, 2014; Sue & Sue, 2013). As psychology instructors, we can intentionally cultivate our multicultural teaching competencies by connecting with our motivation to learn, grow, and improve (Mena & Rogers, 2017). On the practical side, we believe you will find that incorporating these multicultural topics, exercises, and instructional strategies promotes greater awareness, critical thinking, and cultural competency among your students.

WHAT TO EXPECT FROM THIS VOLUME

Each of the three parts of this book serves a distinct purpose. Part I, Multiculturalism and Intersectionality in the Psychology Classroom, includes three chapters that provide the foundation that we believe is necessary for all instructors interested in transforming their teaching by providing an intersectional perspective and pedagogical strategies that are applicable across courses. We also present the results of a pilot study that examined racial microaggressions in classrooms, giving instructors an inside view of students' experiences.

Part II, Gender, Ethnic, and Sociocultural Perspectives: Specialized Courses and Content Areas, comprises 12 chapters, each with a focus on a specific culture-sharing or sociodemographic group and includes perspectives critical to teaching about these groups. Although most of these chapters present the perspective as it has been taught in a stand-alone course or discuss key topics and activities recommended by the authors, we suggest that all instructors review these chapters because the content and practical recommendations can easily be incorporated in traditional psychology courses.

Part III, Integrating Diversity Into General Psychology Courses, includes nine chapters that offer instructors suggestions for more inclusive materials, activities, and assignments that can be incorporated into the core psychology curriculum. These chapters assist instructors to extend their courses beyond the usual topics and address cultural diversity, offer useful critiques of traditional approaches, and/or deal with issues of power and oppression in the psychology classroom. We recommend that readers select the chapters in this section that most closely align with their teaching. Chapter contributors have taken special care to consult the burgeoning multicultural psychology literature and to guide instructors on applying the suggested strategies from their experiences.

SUPPLEMENTAL RESOURCES

An exciting new feature is a companion website, which includes additional resources for the classroom and an opportunity to update and add new work (see http://pubs.apa.org/books/supp/mena). In this website, you will learn more about the contributors and find sample syllabi, descriptions of exercises, presentation resources, and more. We hope you will peruse the site and use the resources to augment your teaching. We would like to receive your ideas, as well as your feedback regarding what you value most and ways you think this resource can be improved. To facilitate a "feedback loop," we have created an e-mail account (menaquina@gmail.com), which we encourage you to use freely. Psychology classrooms across the nation represent ideal locations for multicultural transformation. In the tradition of the earlier volumes (Bronstein & Quina, 1988, 2003), we hope to inspire continued commitment to transform psychology by elevating the relevance of multiculturalism and intersectionality.

REFERENCES

American Psychological Association. (2013). *APA guidelines for the undergraduate psychology major: Version 2.0.* Retrieved from https://www.apa.org/ed/precollege/about/undergraduate-major.aspx

American Psychological Association. (2017). *Multicultural guidelines: An ecological approach to context, identity, and intersectionality.* Retrieved from http://www.apa.org/about/policy/multicultural-guidelines.pdf

Anzaldúa, G. (1987). *Borderlands la frontera: The new mestiza.* San Francisco, CA: Aunt Lute Books.

Betancourt, H., & López, S. R. (1993). The study of culture, ethnicity, and race in American psychology. *American Psychologist, 48,* 629–637. http://dx.doi.org/10.1037/0003-066X.48.6.629

Bowleg, L. (2012). The problem with the phrase *women and minorities*: Intersectionality—an important theoretical framework for public health. *American Journal of Public Health, 102,* 1267–1273. http://dx.doi.org/10.2105/AJPH.2012.300750

Bronstein, P., & Quina, K. (Eds.). (1988). *Teaching a psychology of people: Resources for gender and sociocultural awareness.* Washington, DC: American Psychological Association.

Bronstein, P., & Quina, K. (Eds.). (2003). *Teaching gender and multicultural awareness: Resources for the psychology classroom.* Washington, DC: American Psychological Association. http://dx.doi.org/10.1037/10570-000

Cardemil, E. V., Moreno, O., & Sanchez, M. (2011). One size does not fit all: Cultural considerations in evidence-based practice for depression. In D. W. Springer, A. Rubin, & C. Beevers (Eds.), *Treatment of depression in adolescents and adults* (pp. 221–243). Hoboken, NJ: Wiley. http://dx.doi.org/10.1002/9781118094754.ch6

Crenshaw, K. (1989). Demarginalizing the intersection of race and sex: A Black feminist critique of antidiscrimination doctrine, feminist theory, and antiracist politics. *University of Chicago Legal Forum, 1989,* 139–167.

Denmark, F. L., & Paludi, M. A. (2008). *Psychology of women: A handbook of issues and theories* (2nd ed.). Westport, CT: Praeger.

Dunn, D. S., Brewer, C. L., Cautin, R. L., Gurung, R. A., Keith, K. D. McGregor, L. N., . . . Voight, M. J. (2010). The undergraduate psychology curriculum: Call for a core. In D. F. Halpern (Ed.), *Undergraduate education in psychology: A blueprint for the future of the discipline* (pp. 47–61). Washington, DC: American Psychological Association.

Gergen, M. M., & Gergen, K. J. (2000). Qualitative inquiry: Tensions and transforma-tions. In N. K. Denzin & Y. S. Lincoln (Eds.), *The handbook of qualitative research* (2nd ed., pp. 1025–1046). Thousand Oaks, CA: Sage.

Hall, C. C. I. (2014). The evolution of the revolution: The successful establishment of multicultural psychology. In F. T. L. Leong, L. Comas-Díaz, G. C. Nagayama Hall, V. C. McLoyd, & J. E. Trimble (Eds.), *APA handbook of multicultural psychology: Vol. 1. Theory and research* (pp. 3–18). Washington, DC: American Psychological Association. http://dx.doi.org/10.1037/14189-001

Helms, J. E., Jernigan, M., & Mascher, J. (2005). The meaning of race in psychology and how to change it: A methodological perspective. *American Psychologist, 60,* 27–36. http://dx.doi.org/10.1037/0003-066X.60.1.27

Karnieli-Miller, O., Strier, R., & Pessach, L. (2009). Power relations in qualitative research. *Qualitative Health Research, 19,* 279–289. http://dx.doi.org/10.1177/1049732308329306

Krieger, N. (2012). Methods for the scientific study of discrimination and health: An ecosocial approach. *American Journal of Public Health, 102,* 936–944. http://dx.doi.org/10.2105/AJPH.2011.300544

Leong, F. T. L., Comas-Díaz, L., Nagayama Hall, G. C., McLoyd, V. C., & Trimble, J. E. (Eds.). (2014). *APA handbook of multicultural psychology: Vol. 1. Theory and research.* Washington, DC: American Psychological Association. http://dx.doi.org/10.1037/14189-000

Mena, J. A., & Rogers, M. R. (2017). Factors associated with multicultural teaching competence: Social justice orientation and multicultural environment. *Training and Education in Professional Psychology, 11,* 61–68. http://dx.doi.org/10.1037/tep0000143

Parent, M. C., DeBlaere, C., & Moradi, B. (2013). Approaches to research on inter-sectionality: Perspectives on gender, LGBT, and racial/ethnic identities. *Sex Roles, 68,* 639–645. http://dx.doi.org/10.1007/s11199-013-0283-2

Phinney, J. S. (1996). When we talk about American ethnic groups, what do we mean? *American Psychologist, 51,* 918–927. http://dx.doi.org/10.1037/0003-066X.51.9.918

Rogers, M. R., & O'Bryon, E. C. (2014). Multicultural training models and curriculum. In F. T. L. Leong, L. Comas-Díaz, G. C. Nagayama Hall, V. C. McLoyd, & J. E. Trimble (Eds.), *APA handbook of multicultural psychology: Vol. 2. Applications and training* (pp. 659–679). Washington, DC: American Psychological Association. http://dx.doi.org/10.1037/14187-037

Sevelius, J. M. (2013). Gender affirmation: A framework for conceptualizing risk behavior among transgender Women of Color. *Sex Roles, 68,* 675–689. http://dx.doi.org/10.1007/s11199-012-0216-5

Sue, D. W. (2013). Race talk: The psychology of racial dialogues. *American Psychologist, 68,* 663–672. http://dx.doi.org/10.1037/a0033681

Sue, D. W., & Sue, D. (2013). *Counseling the culturally diverse: Theory and practice* (6th ed.). Hoboken, NJ: Wiley.

Trimble, J. E., Stevenson, M. R., & Worell, J. P. (2004). *Toward an inclusive psychology: Infusing the introductory psychology textbook with diversity content.* Retrieved from https://www.apa.org/pi/oema/programs/recruitment/inclusive-textbooks.pdf

MULTICULTURALISM AND INTERSECTIONALITY IN THE PSYCHOLOGY CLASSROOM

1

Teaching From an Intersectional Perspective

An Overview

Brittney Poindexter and Kathryn Quina

Intersectionality is an increasingly popular theoretical concept and framework in psychology and other social sciences. Kimberlé Williams Crenshaw (1989) introduced the term into the discourse of Black feminist scholarship to denote how pervasive power structures and systems of privilege and oppression, particularly racism, sexism, and heterosexism, collectively influence the individual life experience. In this chapter, we suggest ways to incorporate an intersectional approach in psychology classrooms and explore intersectional awareness as a tool for promoting social consciousness and social justice among students.[1]

Sojourner Truth's powerful 1851 "Ain't I a Woman?" speech still rings true: Without the simultaneous consideration of race and gender, the lived experience of Black and other Women of Color cannot be understood (Butler, 1997). Crenshaw (1989) confronted shortcomings of both feminist and antiracist discourses, arguing that analyses of race without gender, or of gender without race, commonly exclude the consideration of Black women. Crenshaw (1991) offered a powerful analysis of violence against Women of Color, linking their intersecting social location to their victimization and showing how intersectionality can be broadly applied to combat societal inequalities.

An intersectional approach has been applied across many disciplines to understand better how multiple social identities interconnect at the individual

---

[1]The companion webpage for this book also features additional materials for instructors, including a sample syllabus and class schedule for a multicultural psychology course, a PowerPoint presentation explaining multiculturalism, and a classroom exercise that encourages students to think about their own intersectional identities (http://pubs.apa.org/books/supp/mena).

http://dx.doi.org/10.1037/0000137-002
Integrating Multiculturalism and Intersectionality Into the Psychology Curriculum: Strategies for Instructors, J. A. Mena and K. Quina (Editors)

level to reveal the impact of systems of oppression and societal inequities at the sociostructural level (Bowleg, 2012; Grzanka, 2014). It has evolved into a theoretical framework that provides a means for analyzing complex identities, their location within social power structures, and the multiple axes of oppression that shape the human experience (Cole, 2009; Guidroz & Berger, 2009). We strongly recommend that instructors (and perhaps students) review the American Psychological Association's (2017) *Multicultural Guidelines*, which provides an excellent description of intersectionality in action with supporting data and a layered ecological model approach that can readily be applied by the instructor.

Rosenthal (2016) asserted that, in psychology, intersectionality presents researchers and educators with an opportunity to use our work to promote social justice and equity at individual and societal levels. In psychological research, theoretical and empirical studies have used an intersectional framework to examine the impact and experience of various phenomena, including health disparities (Hankivsky & Dhamoon, 2011), psychological distress (Bowleg, Brooks, & Ritz, 2008; Settles, 2006), and stigma and discrimination (Choo & Ferree, 2010). Yet, psychology instructors seldom incorporate intersectionality into diversity courses (Dill, 2009). As more psychology courses incorporate the exploration of gender, race, ethnicity, sexual orientation, and social class, intersectionality can help inform the communication and consumption of class material (Case & Lewis, 2012).

WHAT IS INTERSECTIONALITY?

Intersectionality is conceptualized as the awareness that social identities mutually constitute and interdepend on one another, creating a unique individual experience. The value in this approach is not merely that we are complex beings; intertwining social identities can also reveal the impact of interconnected systems of oppression and social inequality in society. Intersectionality helps, not only to deconstruct categories such as gender and race but also to uncover how the very act of categorization has excluded the individuals who purportedly existed in that category, such as "women" versus "Black women" (McCall, 2005).

Even scholars with common goals and approaches differ in their definitions of the term and the data of intersectionality. May (2015) delivered a wide-reaching critique of how scholars have misunderstood, and at times misapplied, an intersectional framework, including privileging one identity over another, relying on familiar categories and labels, and limiting analyses to a single- or even dual-identity focus. Thus, we caution that this is a still-developing field; we encourage instructors and students to embrace its evolutions.

Intersectionality as a Theoretical and Analytic Framework

As noted earlier, Black feminist scholars were instrumental in the conceptualization of intersectionality (Collins, 1991; Crenshaw, 1989; hooks, 1989). Patricia Hill Collins (1991) critiqued feminist scholarship and social theories as lacking in universality because of their exclusion of differing social contexts.

She described the experience of Black women in the United States as being compounded by distinct social practices and shared history that fall within a unique matrix made up of multiple forms of domination and characterized by intersecting oppressions (Collins, 2000). Her definition put forth that no single identity outweighed another and that within this matrix of domination an individual can simultaneously experience both privilege and oppression.

Shields (2008) further asserted that treating social categories as if they are independent fails to appreciate "that one category of identity, such as gender, takes its meaning as a category in relation to another category" (p. 302). Attempting to understand individual experiences via a single facet of identity circumvents the intersecting oppressions they may manifest.

Collins and Bilge (2016) expanded on the heuristic value of intersectionality by examining individuals who are located at the margins of power along multiple dimensions. Focusing on only one single dimension—for example, only women or only a specific minoritized group—can limit our understanding of oppression, diluting or masking the impact of other factors. This complexity can best be illuminated when we make those who fall at the intersections of society—for example, Black, lower socioeconomic status women—the focus of our analyses, rather than just members of only one of those categories.

Core Tenets of Intersectionality

There is no consensus on the exact definition of intersectionality, and there are numerous conceptualizations, contradictions, and critiques of the construct in the literature (Collins, 2015; Warner & Shields, 2013). In particular, applications of intersectionality in the field of psychology vary, depending on how it is used. As a framework or a theory, scholars can build an understanding of oppression and privilege through multiple social locations (Syed, 2010); as an analytic strategy, both qualitative (Bowleg & Bauer, 2016) and quantitative (Else-Quest & Hyde, 2016a, 2016b) research can be reframed to better understand the impact of multiple oppressions. Intersectionality can also become a tool for social activism (Rosenthal, 2016; Warner & Shields, 2013), locating oppressed individuals in the margins of societal privilege regardless of labeling. Despite varying definitions, Lynn Weber (2006) affirmed that intersectionality can be conceptualized in many ways and put forth some common threads present in much of the literature. Three core theoretical tenets are presented: simultaneity, multilevel power differential, and contextual social constructions.

Simultaneity

Individuals are characterized as simultaneously belonging to multiple socially constructed categories, such as gender, race, ethnicity, sexual orientation, and class. The experience of one social category is linked to the other, and the link between these intersecting categories is not additive; that is, the social inequality does not increase with each additional marginalized category. These social categories are mutually constituted, meaning that one facet of identity (e.g., race) cannot explain an individual's disparate or inequitable experiences at the sociocultural level, without intersecting with other identities (e.g., gender). For example, Lisa Bowleg (2012) described the hypothetical negative experiences of a middle-class Latina lesbian at her doctor's office as "linked to multiple and interlocking sexism, heterosexism, and racism" (p. 1269). In sum, social inequality is shaped by the intersections of multiple identities, and the experience of each category may vary depending on the individual and their specific social location.

Multilevel Power Differential

Each socially constructed identity category can be characterized in terms of an aspect of inequality or a power differential. Recognition of these differentials, their persistence, and their impact on individuals and society as a whole is essential to an effective intersectional psychology. Multiple intersecting identities (e.g., race × gender) at the individual level reflect larger, complex social inequalities (e.g., racism × sexism) at the sociostructural level (Bowleg, 2012; Weber, 1998). For individuals belonging to historically marginalized groups, intersectionality offers a unique point of view for exploring their experiences. First, it rejects simple comparisons, which tend to depict their experiences as deviations from the norms of White middle-class society (Weber & Parra-Medina, 2003). Further, because not all social categories are equally disadvantaged in an individual's social location, intersectionality can integrate both high social status (e.g., racial majority, upper or middle class) and low social status (e.g., ethnic minority; lesbian, gay, bisexual, transgender, or queer [LGBTQ]) aspects of the individual. It allows for an examination of how these social identities together act to produce outcomes of both disparity and advantage (Collins, 1991; Nash, 2008). Ultimately, this complex understanding of social inequalities and social justice can counteract ever-present intersecting systems of power and oppression that help maintain social disparities.

Contextual Social Constructions

Social categories, such as race, gender, social class, and sexual orientation, are constructions of social identity, defined by the dominant culture, that are deeply rooted in both historical and geographical context (Weber, 2006). For example, Caiola, Docherty, Relf, and Barroso (2014) stated,

> Social constructions of race are not based on the assumption that discrete, biological races exist; rather, they are concerned with how race is constructed by historical conditions such as slavery and segregation and leads to inequity based on hierarchies and systems of oppression. (p. 289)

The dynamic nature of these social constructions amounts to consistent change as cultural, economic, and political shifts take place. Throughout history and across social groups, constructions of race, gender, and sexuality have evolved, and the social processes that inundate societies with racism, sexism, and heterosexism have done the same. An intersectional perspective requires the consideration of social and historical context when attempting to understand the impact of systems of oppression and the hegemonic ideologies that maintain social inequity.

TEACHING WITH AN INTERSECTIONAL PERSPECTIVE

In this volume, instructors will find a number of strategies and tools for teaching psychology from an intersectional perspective. Scholars who have incorporated intersectionality into their courses describe unique advantages and implications in its application.

Pedagogical Issues

Kim Case and Michelle Lewis (2012) used intersectionality to "support the development of a critical framework for making privilege and power visible, examining social location and complex identities, exploring subjugated knowledge and developing strategies for empowerment" (p. 262). They also contended that the *matrix of domination* "offers a pedagogically useful conceptual structure for unraveling unique social locations that include both disadvantaged and advantaged identities" (p. 260).

Case's (2013) *Deconstructing Privilege: Teaching and Learning as Allies in the Classroom* offers myriad strategies for teaching about this difficult construct. In *Intersectional Pedagogy: Complicating Identity and Social Justice*, Case (2017) created a valuable resource with both scholarly explications and practical examples of using intersectionality to enhance learning, encourage student activism, and promote social justice and equality. Case also maintains a website filled with valuable lessons, syllabi, resources, videos, and an invitation to join a pedagogical community (http://www.drkimcase.com/teaching).

Case and Lewis (2017) developed lessons incorporating intersectionality into their undergraduate and graduate courses that focused on LGBTQ psychology at a historically Black- and Hispanic-serving university. They engaged students in a variety of exercises to increase their understanding of the complex intersections of multiple identities, specifically the diversity of identities in LGBTQ communities. Teaching LGBTQ psychology through this intersectional lens allowed students of varying backgrounds to understand better the systems of oppression they had likely never experienced and social identities that differed from their own. For those students belonging to historically marginalized groups (e.g., students of color, LGBTQ students), the intersectional approach to teaching these courses allowed these students to identify and critically analyze both their privileged and oppressed identities. Alternatively, students with primarily privileged identities also benefited from the intersectional pedagogy through the deconstruction of categorical identities and dismantling of cultural assumptions about specific categories.

Kliman (2005) offered a thoughtful discussion of what it means to be situated in a matrix of intersectional identities, in the context of family therapy. She also provided a reproducible image of such a matrix that students can fill in with their own situation (Kliman, 2010). As one marks their position(s) on the wheel and connects the dots, their intersectionality takes on a graphic image. The more marginalized the person, the larger that image within the matrix. Students can fill out this matrix and then reflect on the simultaneous effects of their identities and roles. More advanced students can also reflect on how they might take a psychotherapy client's location in such a matrix into consideration and how similarities or differences might shape their interventions.

Conducting Intersectional Research

In psychology, we often speak of our "methodological tool kit," which enables us to look at a problem from a variety of analytic approaches and statistical evaluations. A number of researchers have suggested that intersectionality should be a prominent feature of that tool kit.

The early research establishing the importance of an intersectional approach has frequently been based on qualitative data from those who have experienced the impact of multiple oppressions (e.g., Bowleg, 2008). Listening to the voices of those who have been "othered" reveals rich information about their lives and, further, allows the researcher to explore the nuances of living within and negotiating social margins. Qualitative research is particularly valuable for psychology's still-emergent awareness of intersectionality. As argued elsewhere in this volume (Chapter 20), courses in research methods should incorporate a discussion of qualitative methods and their potential for increasing the validity of our scholarship.

Else-Quest and Hyde (2016a, 2016b) challenged quantitative researchers to incorporate intersectional frameworks into quantitative empirical research. The authors proposed a number of ways in which intersectional social locations can also be examined through quantitative methods, particularly more sophisticated multivariate approaches such as meta-analysis and multilevel modeling. Their approach goes beyond merely adding in multiple social locations as independent variables; they offer excellent examples that can be used in a classroom that understands statistical probabilities (Else-Quest & Hyde, 2016b).

Else-Quest and Hyde (2016a, 2016b) stressed that to be intersectional research must be framed with regard to the impacts of inequality and power. Bowleg and Bauer (2016) pushed this assertion further, stressing the need to investigate inequalities at the larger socio-structural level by including group-level variables. For example, neighborhood-level violence rates are likely crucial to understanding mental health in the same way that local air quality matters in relation to health. Incarcerated Black men are often left out of studies, not only distorting the reality of inequalities in the Black community but also missing the social, political, and economic underpinnings of current incarceration practices. Bowleg and Bauer provided additional suggestions for conducting research, including a mixed-methods approach. Taken together, the articles in Issues 2 and 3 of *Psychology of Women Quarterly*, Volume 40, provide a thoughtful exploration of the assumptions of intersectional research, along with engaging examples of effective research.

Intersectionality as a Social Justice Strategy

Collins and Bilge (2016) explored the utility of intersectionality as a tool for promoting social change. As noted, inequity occurs within a larger system of interconnecting structures of power and opportunity. To effect lasting change, we must understand those structures and evaluate strategies in light of that knowledge. The intersectional approach allows one to assess the sources of inequities and reframe strategies for solutions; what started as a theoretical framework becomes a source of empowerment (see Dill, 2009). Dessel and Corvidae (2017) offered practical strategies for integrating social justice and intersectionality in the classroom.

For example, intersectionality has been particularly helpful in shaping public health priorities. The United Nations Department of Economic and Social Affairs (UN-DESA) publishes *Population Facts*, an easy-to-follow series of online reports based on worldwide data (http://www.un.org/en/development/desa/population/publications/factsheets/index.shtml). A class discussion can be developed regarding the data, which themselves are interesting, but in addition, students can break up into small groups to discuss strategies for interventions to solve the problem. Particularly engaging is the issue of childhood mortality, defined as survival rates for the first 5 years of life (UN-DESA, 2015). I (KQ) presented the UN-DESA "main effects" data showing higher survival rates for children from the richest households, whose mothers had more education and who lived in urban areas, as well as the obvious impact of economics, and I invited students to brainstorm solutions. I then presented the full report with its more nuanced interaction effects and the challenges of deciding who to help around the globe, which led to a more thoughtful discussion. For example, in urban areas, wealth was not a significant factor in child mortality, presumably because more services were accessible. In the most underdeveloped continent identified in the study, Africa, mortality rates were consistently high across all wealth groups, again likely due to the lack of services. Mothers' education can also become a topic of discussion: In other parts of the world, girls are prohibited from obtaining any but the most basic education, so any intervention would have to consider cultural and ethnic traditions.

Intersectional Awareness

An awareness of intersectionality can itself have a beneficial impact on student attitudes and beliefs. On the basis of her work with feminist activists, Greenwood (2008) suggested that women who viewed themselves as having multiple intersecting identities would be more effective navigating diverse positions within and across their activist groups. Greenwood and Christian (2008) further suggested that the group consciousness that arises from having complex intersectional experiences could translate into a greater general cognitive capacity, as one learns to consciously evaluate and negotiate multiple identities and perspectives.

Curtin, Stewart, and Cole (2015) proposed a new social–cognitive variable of intersectional awareness, developing a measure to assess "individual differences in recognizing intersections of social identities . . . as well as across different contexts" (p. 513). They discussed three studies that demonstrate relationships between intersectional awareness and personality traits (notably openness to experience and perspective taking), attitudes toward inequality as a complex process (such as challenging the status quo), and intentions to engage in rights-based social justice activity. They also offered helpful suggestions for approaching diversity-related issues in the classroom, applying techniques to increase sensitivity to, and support for, marginalized groups through greater awareness of individual and structural inequalities.

CONCLUSION

Case's (2013, 2017) authors demonstrated that teaching with an intersectional framework offers students the opportunity to understand diversity beyond the usual categorical structure, developing student learning goals, coursework, and student evaluation through an intersectional lens. Regardless of students' social location, intersectional teaching can enhance student learning and understanding of complex diversity concepts (Case & Lewis, 2012). Including this theoretical framework in more courses in psychology opens the possibility for students and faculty to engage in thoughtful and constructive discussions about social identity, promoting a better understanding of social intersections that could decrease stereotyping and cultural generalizations and enhance conversations about power and privilege.

Rosenthal (2016) argued that the inclusion of themes of intersectionality, social justice, and equity should be standard practice in multicultural and diversity curricula. This suggestion is certainly merited given the provided feedback and experience of instructors who have implemented an intersectional framework. Psychology curricula could especially benefit from incorporating intersectionality into diversity courses to decrease the focus on social categorization, improve understanding of the connections between individual social locations and socio-structural manifestations of oppression, and promote social justice and community activism among students.

REFERENCES

American Psychological Association. (2017). *Multicultural guidelines: An ecological approach to context, identity, and intersectionality.* Retrieved from http://www.apa.org/about/policy/multicultural-guidelines.pdf

Bowleg, L. (2008). When Black + lesbian + woman ≠ Black lesbian woman: The methodological challenges of qualitative and quantitative intersectionality research. *Sex Roles, 59,* 312–325. http://dx.doi.org/10.1007/s11199-008-9400-z

Bowleg, L. (2012). The problem with the phrase *women and minorities*: Intersectionality—an important theoretical framework for public health. *American Journal of Public Health, 102,* 1267–1273. http://dx.doi.org/10.2105/AJPH.2012.300750

Bowleg, L., & Bauer, G. (2016). Quantifying intersectionality. *Psychology of Women Quarterly, 40,* 337–341. http://dx.doi.org/10.1177/0361684316654282

Bowleg, L., Brooks, K., & Ritz, S. F. (2008). "Bringing home more than a paycheck": An exploratory analysis of Black lesbians' experiences of stress and coping in the workplace. *Journal of Lesbian Studies, 12,* 69–84. http://dx.doi.org/10.1300/10894160802174342

Butler, M. G. (1997). *The words of Truth.* Retrieved from http://www.sojournertruth.org/Library/Speeches/

Caiola, C., Docherty, S. L., Relf, M., & Barroso, J. (2014). Using an intersectional approach to study the impact of social determinants of health for African American mothers living with HIV. *Advances in Nursing Science, 37,* 287–298. http://dx.doi.org/10.1097/ANS.0000000000000046

Case, K. A. (2013). *Deconstructing privilege: Teaching and learning as allies in the classroom.* New York, NY: Routledge. http://dx.doi.org/10.4324/9780203081877

Case, K. A. (2017). *Intersectional pedagogy: Complicating identity and social justice.* New York, NY: Routledge.

Case, K. A., & Lewis, M. K. (2012). Teaching intersectional LGBT psychology: Reflections from historically Black and Hispanic-serving universities. *Psychology and Sexuality, 3,* 260–276. http://dx.doi.org/10.1080/19419899.2012.700030

Case, K. A., & Lewis, M. K. (2017). Teaching intersectional psychology in racially diverse settings. In K. A. Case (Ed.), *Intersectional pedagogy: Complicating identity and social justice* (pp. 129–149). New York, NY: Routledge.

Choo, H. Y., & Ferree, M. M. (2010). Practicing intersectionality in sociological research: A critical analysis of inclusions, interactions, and institutions in the study of inequalities. *Sociological Theory, 28,* 129–149. http://dx.doi.org/10.1111/j.1467-9558.2010.01370.x

Cole, E. R. (2009). Intersectionality and research in psychology. *American Psychologist, 64,* 170–180. http://dx.doi.org/10.1037/a0014564

Collins, P. H. (1991). *Black feminist thought: Knowledge, consciousness, and the politics of empowerment.* New York, NY: Routledge.

Collins, P. H. (2000). *Black feminist thought: Knowledge, consciousness and the politics of empowerment* (2nd ed.). New York, NY: Routledge.

Collins, P. H. (2015). Intersectionality's definitional dilemmas. *Annual Review of Sociology, 41,* 1–20. http://dx.doi.org/10.1146/annurev-soc-073014-112142

Collins, P. H., & Bilge, S. (2016). *Intersectionality.* Malden, MA: Polity Press.

Crenshaw, K. (1989). Demarginalizing the intersection of race and sex: A Black feminist critique of antidiscrimination doctrine, feminist theory and antiracist politics. *University of Chicago Legal Forum, 140,* 139–167.

Crenshaw, K. (1991). Mapping the margins: Intersectionality, identity politics, and violence against Women of Color. *Stanford Law Review, 43,* 1241–1299. http://dx.doi.org/10.2307/1229039

Curtin, N., Stewart, A. J., & Cole, E. R. (2015). Challenging the status quo: The role of intersectional awareness in activism for social change and pro-social intergroup attitudes. *Psychology of Women Quarterly, 39,* 512–529. http://dx.doi.org/10.1177/0361684315580439

Dessel, A., & Corvidae, T. (2017). Experiential activities for engaging intersectionality in social justice pedagogy. In K. A. Case (Ed.), *Intersectional pedagogy: Complicating identity and social justice* (pp. 214–231). New York, NY: Routledge.

Dill, B. T. (2009). Intersections, identities, and inequalities in higher education. In B. T. Dill & R. E. Zambrana (Eds.), *Emerging intersections: Race, class, and gender in theory, policy, and practice* (pp. 229–252). New Brunswick, NJ: Rutgers.

Else-Quest, N. M., & Hyde, J. S. (2016a). Intersectionality in quantitative psychological research: I. Theoretical and epistemological issues. *Psychology of Women Quarterly, 40*(2), 155–170. http://dx.doi.org/10.1177/0361684316629797

Else-Quest, N. M., & Hyde, J. S. (2016b). Intersectionality in quantitative psychological research: II. Methods and techniques. *Psychology of Women Quarterly, 40*(3), 319–336. http://dx.doi.org/10.1177/0361684316647953

Greenwood, R. (2008). Intersectional political consciousness: Appreciation for intra-group differences and solidarity in diverse groups. *Psychology of Women Quarterly, 32,* 36–47. http://dx.doi.org/10.1111/j.1471-6402.2007.00405.x

Greenwood, R., & Christian, A. (2008). What happens when we unpack the invisible knapsack? Intersectional political consciousness and inter-group appraisals. *Sex Roles, 59,* 404–417. http://dx.doi.org/10.1007/s11199-008-9439-x

Grzanka, P. R. (2014). *Intersectionality: A foundations and frontiers reader*. Boulder, CO: Westview Press.

Guidroz, K., & Berger, M. T. (2009). A conversation with founding scholars of intersectionality: Kimberle Crenshaw, Nira Yuval-Davis, and Michelle Fine. In M. T. Berger & K. Guidroz (Eds.), *The intersectional approach: Transforming the academy through race, class & gender* (pp. 61–78). Chapel Hill: The University of North Carolina Press.

Hankivsky, O., & Dhamoon, L. S. (2011). *Health inequities in Canada: Intersectional frameworks and practices*. Vancouver, Canada: University of British Columbia Press.

hooks, b. (1989). *Talking back: Thinking feminist, thinking Black*. Boston, MA: Sound End Press.

Kliman, J. (2005). Many differences, many voices: Toward social justice in family therapy. In M. P. Mirkin, K. Suyemoto, & B. Okun (Eds.), *Psychotherapy with women: Exploring diverse contexts and identities* (pp. 42–63). New York, NY: Guilford Press.

Kliman, J. (2010, Winter). Intersections of social privilege and marginalization: A visual teaching tool. *American Family Therapy Association Monograph Series*, 39–48.

May, V. M. (2015). *Pursuing intersectionality, unsettling dominant imaginaries*. New York, NY: Routledge.

McCall, L. (2005). The complexity of intersectionality. *Signs: Journal of Women in Culture and Society, 30*, 1771–1800. http://dx.doi.org/10.1086/426800

Nash, J. C. (2008). Rethinking intersectionality. *Feminist Review, 89*, 1–15. http://dx.doi.org/10.1057/fr.2008.4

Rosenthal, L. (2016). Incorporating intersectionality into psychology: An opportunity to promote social justice and equity. *American Psychologist, 71*, 474–485. http://dx.doi.org/10.1037/a0040323

Settles, I. H. (2006). Use of an intersectional framework to understand Black women's racial and gender identities. *Sex Roles, 54*, 589–601. http://dx.doi.org/10.1007/s11199-006-9029-8

Shields, S. A. (2008). Gender: An intersectionality perspective. *Sex Roles, 59*, 301–311. http://dx.doi.org/10.1007/s11199-008-9501-8

Syed, M. (2010). Disciplinarity and methodology in intersectionality theory and research. *American Psychologist, 65*, 61–62. http://dx.doi.org/10.1037/a0017495

Truth, S. (1851). *Ain't I a woman?* Retrieved from https://www.nps.gov/wori/learn/historyculture/sojourner-truth.htm

United Nations Department of Economic and Social Affairs. (2015). Inequality in early childhood survival. *Population Facts*. Retrieved from http://www.un.org/en/development/desa/population/publications/pdf/popfacts/PopFacts_2015-3.pdf

Warner, L. R., & Shields, S. A. (2013). The intersections of sexuality, gender, and race: Identity research at the crossroads. *Sex Roles, 68*, 803–810. http://dx.doi.org/10.1007/s11199-013-0281-4

Weber, L. (1998). A conceptual framework for understanding race, class, gender, and sexuality. *Psychology of Women Quarterly, 22*, 13–32. http://dx.doi.org/10.1111/j.1471-6402.1998.tb00139.x

Weber, L. (2006). Reconstructing the landscape of health disparities research: Promoting dialogue and collaboration between feminist intersectional and biomedical paradigms. In A. J. Schulz & L. Mullings (Eds.), *Gender, race, class and health: Intersectional approaches* (pp. 21–59). San Fransisco, CA: Jossey-Bass.

Weber, L., & Parra-Medina, D. (2003). Intersectionality and women's health: Charting a path to eliminating health disparities. *Advances in Gender Research, 7*, 181–230. http://dx.doi.org/10.1016/S1529-2126(03)07006-1

2

Developing a Culturally Competent and Inclusive Curriculum

A Comprehensive Framework for Teaching Multicultural Psychology

Annemarie Vaccaro

How can instructors create inclusive classroom spaces? What are the best multicultural resources for psychology classes? How should educators respond to intense debate or student resistance to multicultural topics? In this chapter, I offer a brief overview of strategies documented in the empirical and best practice literature. I also draw on my experiences as a multicultural course instructor and facilitator of faculty development workshops on multicultural inclusion.

In *Dynamics of Multicultural Teaching and Learning*, Adams and Love (2009) suggested that focusing narrowly on students, teachers, materials, or pedagogy is myopic. Instead, a more comprehensive approach is necessary for effective multicultural teaching and learning. Their four-quadrant model incorporates what students bring to the classroom, what instructors bring to the classroom, curriculum and resources, and how instructors teach. In this chapter, I build on their useful framework and offer tangible action steps for "doing" multicultural psychology.

http://dx.doi.org/10.1037/0000137-003
Integrating Multiculturalism and Intersectionality Into the Psychology Curriculum:
Strategies for Instructors, J. A. Mena and K. Quina (Editors)
Copyright © 2019 by the American Psychological Association. All rights reserved.

THE "WHO" OF MULTICULTURAL TEACHING: UNDERSTANDING OUR STUDENTS

In any psychology classroom, students can self-identify with a variety of races, ethnicities, genders, sexual orientations, social classes, religions, ages, and abilities. These visible and invisible social identities, and their intersections, shape the way students make meaning of themselves and the world around them. More specifically, differences in social identities, experiences, and perspectives can influence classroom dynamics and climate. Social identity development can play a role in how students make meaning of, and respond to, multicultural topics. In general, social identity development models suggest people progress through a series of stages, statuses, or phases as they come to understand themselves in the context of societal privileges and oppressions. Hallmarks of these models include increasing awareness of, assimilation to, and/or resistance of societal privileges and marginalization. Common emotions associated with social identity development include surprise, shame, anger, and hope. Vast differences in identity development can shape classroom dynamics. Although a discussion of all relevant models is outside the scope of this chapter, a couple of examples can help instructors see the value of recognizing their importance. For instance, a conversation could be explosive when White students in early stages of White identity development (cf. Helms, 1993), who refuse to acknowledge racism or feel guilty about White privilege, dialogue with students of color in later stages of development who are immersing themselves in culture and/or resisting dominant ideologies (cf. Cross, 1971; Phinney, 1989). Or a conversation about the psychology of women could go very differently with the presence or absence of women in Downing and Roush's (1985) feminist identity development stages of passive acceptance versus active commitment.

Beyond identity development, instructors must recognize that students show up to our courses with experiences and perspectives shaped by their visible and invisible social identities. Some of the experiences of students from historically underrepresented social identity groups stem from stereotypes, exclusion, and microaggressions. Decades of higher education research has documented how students from marginalized social identity groups experience campuses in general, and classrooms in particular, as chilly, hostile, unwelcoming, and exclusionary (Hall & Sandler, 1984; Solórzano, Ceja, & Yosso, 2000; Yosso, Smith, Ceja, & Solórzano, 2009). By contrast, students from historically dominant social identity groups enter our classrooms wearing "invisible knapsacks" of privilege (Case & Cole, 2013; McIntosh, 2003), the "automatic unearned benefits bestowed upon perceived members of dominant groups based upon social identity" (Case, 2013, p. 2). Students with privilege are often unaware of the power and access associated with their social locations, which in turn can shape classroom dynamics. It is important to note that although much literature about collegiate student experiences focuses on individuals from privileged or marginalized backgrounds, this dichotomous view oversimplifies the complex nature of intersectionality. To fully understand the complicated lives of students, instructors must recognize "the confluence of one's multiple marginalized and privileged identities is an interaction that creates a unique experience" (Museus & Griffin, 2011, p. 8). For a more comprehensive discussion about intersectionality, see Chapter 1, this volume.

As active agents in the learning process, students make meaning of materials and classroom interactions based on their unique social identities, experiences, and perspectives. As such, students' expectations of and responses to instructors, curriculum, and pedagogical processes will be strikingly different. I have chosen to focus on one response that often creates classroom challenges: *resistance*.

> When people are resistant, they are unable to engage with the material. They refuse to consider alternative perspectives that challenge the dominant ideology that maintains the status quo. They resist information of experiences that may cause them to question their worldview. (Goodman, 2011, p. 51)

Resistance to multicultural psychology can manifest in a variety of ways. Students may choose not to register for multicultural psychology courses or skip a particular multiculturally focused session. They might refuse to acknowledge the role that systemic inequities and privilege play in psychology topics and/or become argumentative when inequalities are raised. Students can also engage in resistance via silence (Jones, 2008) or by denying, minimizing, and focusing on good intentions versus the harsh realities of social inequities (Johnson, 2017) during class discussions.

Scholars have documented a multitude of reasons why students from majority or privileged backgrounds resist learning about multicultural issues, including discomfort and guilt (see Goodman, 2011, for a comprehensive analysis). Fewer scholars have examined why students from historically marginalized backgrounds resist classroom conversations about multiculturalism. Marginalized students may not want to bear the burden of being tokenized or serving as the educator about their particular social identity group. They may also cope with narrow portrayals or stereotypical assumptions about people from their social identity group through silence or avoidance (Case & Cole, 2013; Martínez Alemán, 2000).

An intersectional lens can also shed additional light on student resistance. In a qualitative study of students in a multicultural course, I (Vaccaro, 2017) asked students from a variety of intersecting racial, ethnic, gender, and social class backgrounds to describe why they remained silent in class. Some students resisted active engagement via silence when they felt multicultural conversations were too narrow (e.g., focused on a single social identity) and did not resemble their intersectional realities. In response to learning about the experiences of overt discrimination by working-class Women of Color, one middle-class Woman of Color who did not share those experiences pondered, "Am I not enough of a Woman of Color?" Men of Color remained silent when they felt women classmates focused on male privilege without acknowledging their struggles with racism. In sum, students from intersecting privileged and marginalized social identities can be fearful of, feel left out of, or feel invalidated by multicultural conversations.

Action Steps

Because students come from diverse perspectives and social locations, there is no simple solution to engaging students in difficult multicultural psychology work. However, there are a few recommendations for meeting students where they are.

Know Where to Start

Use a precourse assessment with a series of closed- or open-ended questions to gauge where students stand on multicultural topics before attempting to engage them in difficult dialogues, activities, or assignments. I typically use a precourse assessment with open-ended questions such as, What prior course experiences have included multicultural topics? What are the three to four things you are most interested in learning in this class? In what areas of multiculturalism do you feel most confident? Why? In what areas do you feel least confident? Why? Is there anything else regarding your experiences or perspectives on multiculturalism that you would like to share?[1]

Encourage Student Engagement

Instructors may collect note cards at the end of every class session on which students can write anonymous comments, concerns, struggles, and ideas for discussion. This can also be done electronically through a survey program or an anonymous course management portal. Instructors should respond to comments at the beginning or end of each class session so that students know their comments are valued.

Resist Tokenizing Students

Do not identify students by, or ask them to speak for, their social identity group. Although they might have great insight to share, students can feel targeted and tokenized by such expectations. Instead, educators can create classroom spaces where all students are invited (but not required) to share their lived realities. hooks (1994) described an autobiography assignment that "affirm[s] their presence, their right to speak, in multiple ways on diverse topics" (p. 84). hooks asked students to read and listen to short autobiographies, making the "classroom a space where experience is valued, not negated or deemed meaningless" (p. 84). In this activity, all students are invited to share lived realities and are afforded the opportunity to determine what, and how much, they are comfortable sharing.

Address Intersectionality

Instructors can acknowledge (and critique) psychological studies or theories that narrowly describe differences or behavior patterns for particular social identity groups without recognizing intersectionality and/or within-group differences. Educators can also point out ways individuals from the same

---

[1]A precourse assessment questionnaire is available for download at this book's companion website (http://pubs.apa.org/books/supp/mena).

social identity group have unique lived realities, perspectives, and other social identity differences.

THE OTHER "WHO": BECOMING CULTURALLY COMPETENT INSTRUCTORS

The importance of multicultural competence has long been a focus in psychology (American Psychological Association, 1993, 2017). Although components of multicultural competence models vary, there is substantial agreement that three key components shape the way instructors teach and engage with students in multiculturally infused courses: awareness, knowledge, and skills (Campinha-Bacote, 2002; Sue, 2001).

Awareness

Even if instructors understand that diversity is ever-present, they may be unaware of their hidden biases or unable to recognize microaggressions that emerge in their classrooms. *Microaggressions* are "subtle and commonplace exchanges that somehow convey insulting or demeaning messages" (Constantine, 2007, p. 2) to people from nondominant social identity groups (e.g., people of color, women; lesbian, gay, bisexual, transgender, or queer [LGBTQ] people; people with disabilities; people from lower socioeconomic statuses; Sue, 2010a).

Whether microaggressions come in the form of rude comments, racial jokes, or exclusionary policies, the combined effect of daily microaggressions can make a campus or classroom climate hostile for students from marginalized backgrounds (Solórzano et al., 2000; Yosso et al., 2009). Empirical research has shown that microaggressions can be perpetrated by instructors who harbor low academic expectations, assume deficits, tokenize students, or treat individuals as if they were invisible (Gildersleeve, Croom, & Vasquez, 2011; Solórzano et al., 2000). For instance, students in one study talked about faculty members assuming they would not do well academically; when they excelled, faculty questioned them about cheating (Solórzano et al., 2000). Gildersleeve et al. (2011) shared an instance when a faculty member and classmates looked to the only Black student in a class to provide perspective (i.e., speak for his race) during a conversation about a racial identity theory. An ethnographic study of all types of microaggressions (e.g., race, gender, sexual orientation) perpetrated in 60 college classrooms found that the microaggression perpetrator was often the instructor, as opposed to peers (Suárez-Orozco et al., 2015). See Chapter 3, this volume, for more about microaggressions.

Knowledge

Disciplinary and specialty silos often inhibit instructor knowledge about students' campus and classroom realities. When I conduct instructional development workshops, participants often admit they have little knowledge about the diverse backgrounds of their students. Some lament a lack of knowledge about particular ethnic or religious histories, cultures, and customs. Others are confused by the terminology used by the LGBTQ community (e.g., transgender, queer, gender nonconforming, genderqueer). Some instructors recognize the increase in numbers of students with disabilities on college campuses but admit they have little understanding of diagnoses, manifestations, and the corresponding needs of those students (Kimball, Vaccaro, & Vargas, 2016).

Lack of understanding about students is often paired with a lack of knowledge about campus incidents and resources. At decentralized college campuses, instructors may not know about, or how to respond to, campus hate crimes or student protests that profoundly impact students. Campus centers (e.g., multicultural, women's, LGBTQ, disability services, Hillel) and student clubs (e.g., Asian student alliance, Muslim student groups, transgender organizations) can be incredible resources to educators and students. These entities often provide educational programming and social support for members of underrepresented groups. Yet, activities sponsored by such organizations are rarely publicized in venues frequented by instructors.

Skills

It takes skill to engage students in learning about emotion-provoking topics such as discrimination, privilege, race, religion, or sexual orientation. It also requires skill to ensure students feel challenged to grow and validated for taking risks related to multicultural topics. Unfortunately, most graduate students and early career faculty receive little preparation for the craft of teaching in general or for multicultural teaching in particular.

Sue, Torino, Capodilupo, Rivera, and Lin (2009) found that White faculty worried that they did not have the skill to intervene appropriately when classroom conversations about multicultural topics became emotional. Although this particular study focused on White faculty and dialogues about race, I would argue that many instructors harbor fears regarding their skills (or lack thereof) to effectively teach a host of multicultural topics. Many feel they cannot be experts on all forms of multiculturalism, or they are concerned about dealing with emotion and resistance. Instructors have told me that they feel unprepared to effectively navigate resistance, offensive comments, and subtle forms of peer-to-peer classroom exclusion. None of us is perfect, but we cannot become more multiculturally inclusive unless we are willing to try to build our skills— even if it means making and learning from mistakes. I hope that the action steps in this chapter help instructors move beyond such fears.

Action Steps

Cultural competency is not a destination; it is a lifelong journey. To be most effective, instructors must constantly strive to increase their multicultural awareness, knowledge, and skills. Educators can increase their cultural competency in a variety of ways.

Get Informed

A number of professional societies have developed web-based materials and offer workshops designed to increase awareness and knowledge about contemporary multicultural issues. Consider attending a webinar, conference session, or reading at least one manuscript or book per month about the experiences of diverse college students. Create or join "journal groups" that meet regularly to discuss articles and classroom implications.

Focus on Microaggressions

Increase your competency by narrowing in on harmful, yet often invisible, forms of classroom microaggressions. Begin by reading seminal works on racial microaggressions in the psychology literature (e.g., Sue, 2010a, 2010b; Sue et al., 2007), and then delve into the educational literature about the impact of microaggressions in higher education (e.g., Smith, Allen, & Danley, 2007; Solórzano et al., 2000; Yosso et al., 2009). Engage in deep self-reflection about hidden biases and assumptions, either alone or in small consciousness-raising groups with colleagues on your campus or in professional societies.

Practice Skill Building

Develop a multicultural competence group on campus where instructors can practice multicultural skills. The group can develop short vignettes that have emerged when teaching multiculturalism (e.g., resistance, offensive comments, emotional discussions) or when working individually with diverse students (e.g., advising, research). Participants can "act out" or discuss how they would respond to each scenario, giving and receiving constructive feedback.

Utilize Campus Resources

Inform yourself about what is happening on your campus by reviewing staff newsletters, reading student newspapers, following campus-sponsored social media posts, connecting with colleagues, and attending multicultural events. Invite relevant campus organizations or offices to speak to your class.

THE "WHAT" OF MULTICULTURAL TEACHING: CURRICULUM AND RESOURCES

Often, when instructors attempt to infuse multiculturalism into a course, they begin by "adding in" one or two readings, videos, assignments, or activities about diverse peoples or topics. Or they dedicate a single class session to multicultural topics. Although such attempts are a good place to start, merely adding in a little multiculturalism can send the message to students that multicultural topics are optional (i.e., not important) and not part of the standard curriculum. Effective infusion incorporates multicultural psychology into textbooks, lectures, videos, activities, and assignments throughout the academic term.

Unfortunately, course materials often portray people from marginalized social identity groups in stereotypical or deficit-laden ways. Such portrayals reinforce stereotypes and can cause emotional harm to students who come from those backgrounds. A student of color recently lamented that "the only time I see people who look like me is when we are talking about poverty or disease." She went on to wonder why instructors never acknowledged these deficit images or tried to counterbalance them with more positive, asset-based content.

The discipline of psychology comprises scholars and practitioners from a variety of backgrounds, but this reality is not always conveyed in curricular materials. Furthermore, many curricular materials and visual images of key thinkers focus on White men and their work. It is important to teach students that the discipline of psychology is shaped by a diverse community of scholars— some of whom look like them and some who do not.

Even when course resources include diverse people and perspectives, curricular materials may still not be accessible to all students. For instance, videos without closed-captioning can be inaccessible to students who are deaf, hard of hearing, or visual learners and students whose first language is not English. Another accessibility challenge is the cost of course materials. Low-income students often cannot afford to purchase course books, manuals, lab materials, or other supplies. Without these materials, they are at a serious disadvantage.

Action Steps

To create a more inclusive and accessible curriculum, instructors can do the following.

Audit Curricular Materials

Audit curricular materials for the inclusion of multicultural topics and people from diverse backgrounds. Pay attention to the frequency and type of portrayals (e.g., deficit, stereotypical). Review classroom resources by following a series of prompts to determine the degree to which people from, and issues related to, marginalized social identity groups are included and in what context. For example, are issues of race, class, gender, sexual orientation, age, and religion discussed in every chapter or only a few? Do case studies, test questions, and videos reference mostly middle-class White people? Are people from marginalized backgrounds portrayed through deficit lenses? After your review, offer publishers specific feedback about how their products can be more multiculturally inclusive.

Counter Deficit Messaging

Select textbooks, videos, and other classroom resources that include asset-based multicultural images. Augment less inclusive materials with lecture materials, images, and additional resources that are inclusive of the needs, successes, and contributions of all people—especially those from marginalized backgrounds. Acknowledge deficit notions and invite students to critique, problematize, and discuss pervasive bias in course materials. Explain how models, theories, and concepts are (or can be) applied to diverse communities.

For instance, highlight the many ways in which positive mental health, well-being, resiliency and/or effective coping occur in marginalized communities. Invite expert speakers from multicultural backgrounds to debunk deficit-based assumptions and stereotypes that people from marginalized social identity groups are not successful psychologists.

Ensure Accessibility

Select videos that are closed-captioned, or ask the office of disability services at your institution if they caption videos. Because of the importance of accessibility, video captioning is now required by accreditation agencies. Request or purchase an extra desk copy of expensive course materials that can be placed on reserve in the campus library where low-income students can access them. Instructors should also think carefully about which resources are necessary and consider affordable options and alternatives. Many articles are now available free online rather than including them in a printed course supplement. Post materials and announcements via online portals well in advance, so students who do not have Internet access at home are not digitally excluded from important course information and announcements.

THE "HOW" OF MULTICULTURAL TEACHING: ADOPTING AN INCLUSIVE PEDAGOGY

Effective multicultural instructors are not merely creators of knowledge and agents of dissemination, they are responsible for designing inclusive learning spaces. Strategies that can foster inclusive learning spaces include being approachable, developing trusting relationships with and among students, affirming diverse student experiences, managing classroom dynamics appropriately, acknowledging and reducing power differentials in the classroom, modeling inclusion, and engaging in on-going critical self-reflection (Freire, 1970; hooks, 1994; Sue, Lin, Torino, Capodilupo, & Rivera, 2009; Tuitt, 2006; Vaccaro, August, & Kennedy, 2012).

Scholars who write about critical, inclusive, and transformative pedagogy stress the importance of trusting relationships between instructors and students (hooks, 1994; Tuitt, 2006; Vaccaro et al., 2012). Earning students' trust includes listening to and validating their feelings about multicultural topics (Sue et al., 2009). Students come to college classrooms with a lifetime of experiences with discrimination, privilege, and intersectionality that can, when appropriate, be cultivated in the course of multicultural teaching. Sue, Lin, et al. (2009) also argued that effective multicultural instructors acknowledge the range of emotions students have when learning about multicultural topics.

Creating inclusive learning spaces requires skilled facilitation of classroom dynamics. Instructors have to be able to manage intense dialogue in a manner that encourages engagement while simultaneously discouraging exclusion. Positive interactions can be built into classroom activities, discussions, or interactive lectures. In one study on difficult dialogues, students did not appreciate when instructors ignored exclusion, dismissed the importance of topics to students, or switched topics to avoid heated discussion (Sue, Lin, et al., 2009). For a space to be safe, instructors must address not only offensive comments (e.g., "that's so gay") but also more subtle forms of exclusion (e.g., microaggressions) in a compassionate, firm, and educational manner.

Peer-to-peer exclusion can happen during classroom activities, especially small group projects. One student with a disability told me how he often felt marginalized during small group activities. He felt like they "looked at him differently" and did not entrust him with important group duties. Students of color and women in predominately White classrooms or classrooms consisting mostly of men can also be left out when students are allowed to self-select into working groups. Also, marginalization can manifest in small groups when students from particular social identity groups are ushered into stereotypical roles (e.g., women as note-takers, Asian students as experts). Instructors must find a balance between encouraging group independence with ensuring equitable and safe group environments.

A central tenet in the inclusive pedagogy literature is that educators share the power of knowledge construction with learners (Freire, 1970; hooks, 1994; Tuitt, 2006). By doing so, they co-construct not only knowledge but also an inclusive and affirming learning environment. Such efforts contrast with traditional educational paradigms in which the instructor is believed to hold all the knowledge and power. Sharing power, however, can be daunting for instructors who fear losing classroom control (Sue, Torino, et al., 2009). Decreasing the power differentials between students and educators is one way to create an environment where students feel safe exploring multicultural topics and faculty feel more willing to bring them up (Tuitt, 2006).

Scholars of inclusive pedagogy argue that students are more likely to feel comfortable stretching outside their comfort zone when instructors model inclusion and risk-taking behavior (e.g., acknowledging fears) in regard to multicultural topics (Sue, Torino, et al., 2009; Tuitt, 2006). Tuitt (2006) argued educators should "be willing to demonstrate their humanity by identifying weaknesses and sharing personal accounts" (p. 255). Of course, this is not a traditional approach, and it can engender fears of being exposed as something other than an expert. Research has shown that instructors, especially those from marginalized social identity groups, can find such disclosure and risk taking emotionally taxing (Sue et al., 2011). Instructors have to consider the intersectional identities and cultural competency of students (and themselves) to determine if, when, and how sharing is educationally appropriate.

Action Steps

Instructors can be more multiculturally inclusive by using some of the following pedagogical strategies.

Coconstruct Ground Rules

Share power by beginning a course by coconstructing behavioral expectations with students (i.e., ground rules for safe dialogue). Glean consensus from students and post expectations in the classroom or on a course management system. Revisit and enforce those expectations regularly.

Take Stock of Your Pedagogy

Review writings about "best practices" for multicultural teaching in the psychology and the educational literature. Incorporate key elements of inclusive pedagogy into teaching (e.g., disclosure, risk taking, trust building) and keep a journal about the effectiveness of the strategies. Invite students to offer anonymous feedback about the inclusivity of your pedagogy and take suggestions for improvement seriously. Ask a colleague who is well known for effective multicultural teaching and inclusive pedagogy to observe your teaching and provide suggestions for improvement.

Build Trust

Before beginning dialogues about tough multicultural topics, spend a portion of class time engaging students in trust-building exercises. Instructors can find a variety of basic ice-breaking, "get-to-know-you," and trust-building activities on the Internet. Start with basic introductory activities, move to deeper trust-building exercises, and then engage students in multicultural discussions that require trust.

Address Peer Exclusion

Monitor group activities by listening in on group conversations and inviting students to summarize their group processes. Consider assigning specific or rotating roles and setting group-inclusion ground rules. Instructors can encourage students to provide informal feedback to each other or require students to submit anonymous peer grades on inclusion and other group processes.

CONCLUSION

Offering multiculturally inclusive courses is essential to the preparation of psychology students who will someday become culturally competent practitioners and citizens. A significant barrier to developing such preparation courses is lack of confidence and fear of making mistakes on the part of instructors. Building on Adams and Love's (2009) *Dynamics of Multicultural Teaching and Learning*, I discussed the who, what, and how of "doing" multicultural psychology in hopes of taking the mystery out of this process. I also offered tangible action steps throughout this chapter.

REFERENCES

Adams, M., & Love, B. J. (2009). A social justice education faculty development framework for a post-Grutter era. In K. Skubikowski, C. Wright, & R. Graf (Eds.), *Social justice education: Inviting faculty to transform their institutions* (pp. 2–25). Sterling, VA: Stylus.

American Psychological Association. (1993). Guidelines for providers of psychological services to ethnic, linguistic, and culturally diverse populations. *American Psychologist*, *48*, 45–48. http://dx.doi.org/10.1037/0003-066X.48.1.45

American Psychological Association. (2017). *Multicultural guidelines: An ecological approach to context, identity, and intersectionality.* Retrieved from http://www.apa.org/about/policy/multicultural-guidelines.pdf

Campinha-Bacote, J. (2002). The process of cultural competence in the delivery of healthcare services: A model of care. *Journal of Transcultural Nursing, 13,* 181–184. http://dx.doi.org/10.1177/10459602013003003

Case, K. A. (2013). Beyond diversity and Whiteness: Developing a transformative and intersectional model of privilege studies pedagogy. In K. A. Case (Ed.), *Deconstructing privilege: Teaching and learning as allies in the classroom* (pp. 1–14). New York, NY: Routledge. http://dx.doi.org/10.4324/9780203081877

Case, K. A., & Cole, E. R. (2013). Deconstructing privilege when students resist: The journey back into the community of engaged learners. In K. A. Case (Ed.), *Deconstructing privilege: Teaching and learning as allies in the classroom* (pp. 34–48). New York, NY: Routledge. http://dx.doi.org/10.4324/9780203081877

Constantine, M. G. (2007). Racial microaggressions against African American clients in cross-racial counseling relationships. *Journal of Counseling Psychology, 54,* 1–16. http://dx.doi.org/10.1037/0022-0167.54.1.1

Cross, W. E., Jr. (1971). Toward a psychology of Black liberation: The Negro-to-Black conversion experience. *Black World, 20*(9), 13–27.

Downing, N. E., & Roush, K. L. (1985). From passive acceptance to active commitment: A model of feminist identity development for women. *The Counseling Psychologist, 13,* 695–709. http://dx.doi.org/10.1177/0011000085134013

Freire, P. (1970). *Pedagogy of the oppressed.* New York, NY: Continuum.

Gildersleeve, R. E., Croom, N. N., & Vasquez, P. L. (2011). "Am I going crazy?!": A critical race analysis of doctoral education. *Equity & Excellence in Education, 44,* 93–114. http://dx.doi.org/10.1080/10665684.2011.539472

Goodman, D. J. (2011). *Promoting diversity and social justice: Educating people from privileged groups* (2nd ed.). New York, NY: Routledge. http://dx.doi.org/10.4324/9780203829738

Hall, R. M., & Sandler, B. R. (1984). *Out of the classroom: A chilly climate for women?* Washington, DC: Association of American Colleges, Project on the Status and Education of Women.

Helms, J. E. (1993). *Black and white racial identity: Theory, research and practice.* Westport, CT: Praeger.

hooks, b. (1994). *Teaching to transgress: Education as the practice of freedom.* New York, NY: Routledge.

Johnson, A. G. (2017). *Privilege, power and difference* (3rd ed.). Boston, MA: McGraw Hill.

Jones, S. R. (2008). Student resistance to cross-cultural engagement: Annoying distraction or site for transformative learning. In S. R. Harper (Ed.), *Creating inclusive campus environments for cross-cultural learning and student engagement* (pp. 67–85). Washington, DC: NASPA.

Kimball, E. W., Vaccaro, A., & Vargas, N. (2016). Student affairs professionals supporting students with disabilities: A grounded theory model. *Journal of Student Affairs Research and Practice, 53,* 175–189. http://dx.doi.org/10.1080/19496591.2016.1118697

Martínez Alemán, A. M. (2000). Race talks: Undergraduate Women of Color and female friendships. *The Review of Higher Education, 23,* 133–152. http://dx.doi.org/10.1353/rhe.2000.0006

McIntosh, P. (2003). White privilege and male privilege: A personal account of coming to see correspondences through work in women's studies. In M. S. Kimmel & A. L. Ferber (Eds.), *Privilege: A reader* (pp. 147–160). Boulder, CO: Westview Press.

Museus, S. D., & Griffin, K. A. (2011). Mapping the margins in higher education: On the promise of intersectionality frameworks in research and discourse. In K. A. Griffin & S. D. Museus (Eds.), *Using mixed-methods approaches to study intersectionality in higher education: New directions for institutional research, number 151* (pp. 5–13). San Francisco, CA: Jossey-Bass. http://dx.doi.org/10.1002/ir.395

Phinney, J. S. (1989). Stages of ethnic identity development in minority group adolescents. *The Journal of Early Adolescence, 9,* 34–49. http://dx.doi.org/10.1177/0272431689091004

Smith, W. A., Allen, W. R., & Danley, L. L. (2007). Assume the position . . . you fit the description: Psychological experiences and racial battle fatigue among African American male college students. *American Behavioral Scientist, 51,* 551–578. http://dx.doi.org/10.1177/0002764207307742

Solórzano, D. J., Ceja, M., & Yosso, T. J. (2000). Critical race theory, racial micro-aggressions, and campus racial climate: The experiences of African American college students. *Journal of Negro Education, 69,* 60–73.

Suárez-Orozco, C., Casanova, S., Martin, M., Katsiaficas, D., Cuellar, V., Smith, N., & Dias, S. (2015). Toxic rain in class: Classroom interpersonal microaggressions. *Educational Researcher, 44,* 151–160. http://dx.doi.org/10.3102/0013189X15580314

Sue, D. W. (2001). Multidimensional facets of cultural competence. *The Counseling Psychologist, 29,* 790–821. http://dx.doi.org/10.1177/0011000001296002

Sue, D. W. (2010a). *Microaggressions in everyday life: Race, gender and sexual orientation.* Hoboken, NJ: Wiley.

Sue, D. W. (Ed.). (2010b). *Microaggressions and marginality: Manifestations, dynamics and impact.* Hoboken, NJ: Wiley.

Sue, D. W., Capodilupo, C. M., Torino, G. C., Bucceri, J. M., Holder, A. M., Nadal, K. L., & Esquilin, M. (2007). Racial microaggressions in everyday life: Implications for clinical practice. *American Psychologist, 62,* 271–286. http://dx.doi.org/10.1037/0003-066X.62.4.271

Sue, D. W., Lin, A. I., Torino, G. C., Capodilupo, C. M., & Rivera, D. P. (2009). Racial microaggressions and difficult dialogues on race in the classroom. *Cultural Diversity and Ethnic Minority Psychology, 15,* 183–190. http://dx.doi.org/10.1037/a0014191

Sue, D. W., Rivera, D. P., Watkins, N. L., Kim, R. H., Kim, S., & Williams, C. D. (2011). Racial dialogues: Challenges faculty of color face in the classroom. *Cultural Diversity and Ethnic Minority Psychology, 17,* 331–340. http://dx.doi.org/10.1037/a0024190

Sue, D. W., Torino, G. C., Capodilupo, C. M., Rivera, D. P., & Lin, A. I. (2009). How White faculty perceive and react to difficult dialogues on race: Implications for education and training. *The Counseling Psychologist, 37,* 1090–1115. http://dx.doi.org/10.1177/0011000009340443

Tuitt, F. (2006). Afterword: Realizing a more inclusive pedagogy. In A. Howell & F. Tuitt (Eds.), *Race and higher education: Rethinking pedagogy in diverse college classrooms* (pp. 243–369). Cambridge, MA: Harvard Educational Review.

Vaccaro, A. (2017). Does my story belong? An intersectional critical race feminist analysis of student silence in a diverse classroom. *Journal About Women in Higher Education, 10,* 27–44. http://dx.doi.org/10.1080/19407882.2016.1268538

Vaccaro, A., August, G., & Kennedy, M. S. (2012). *Safe spaces: Making schools and communities welcoming to LGBT youth.* Santa Barbara, CA: Praeger.

Yosso, T., Smith, W., Ceja, M., & Solórzano, D. (2009). Critical race theory, racial micro-aggressions, and campus climate for Latina/o undergraduates. *Harvard Educational Review, 79,* 659–691. http://dx.doi.org/10.17763/haer.79.4.m6867014157m707l

3

Racial Microaggressions and Difficult Dialogues in the Classroom

Tammy Vargas Warner

Much like the rest of the country, college campuses across the United States are confronting the remnants of a self-proclaimed "postracial" society. With the election of our nation's first African American president, there evolved a public perception that equated his election with the end of racism in America. Yet, subsequently, a rise in racial incidents and public protest was observed. College campuses and classrooms have not been immune to these types of incidents but rather, in some cases, have taken a leadership role in increasing public awareness of the racism that still exists in America. Although people of color continue to experience overt instances of racism, today we more commonly engage in a subtle form of racism and oppression known as *racial microaggressions*. *Microaggressions* are typically subtle and often unconscious comments or action made toward people from a marginalized group. Various forms of microaggressions have been discussed in recent literature, involving gender, race, ethnicity, sexuality, religion, and importantly, their intersections (see Nadal et al., 2015). This chapter presents findings from a pilot study designed specifically to capture and categorize the experiences of students of color with racial microaggressions in college classrooms.

RACIAL MICROAGGRESSIONS

Sue and colleagues (2007) defined *racial microaggressions* as "brief and commonplace daily verbal, behavioral, or environmental indignities, whether intentional or unintentional, that communicate hostile, derogatory, or negative

http://dx.doi.org/10.1037/0000137-004
Integrating Multiculturalism and Intersectionality Into the Psychology Curriculum:
Strategies for Instructors, J. A. Mena and K. Quina (Editors)

racial slights and insults toward people of color" (p. 271). Whereas *macroaggressions* involve structural oppression (e.g., policies that systematically disadvantage some groups and privilege others), *microaggressions* usually involve interpersonal incidents (Osanloo, Boske, & Newcomb, 2016). Research specific to student experiences with racial microaggressions in the classroom is limited, although Solórzano, Ceja, and Yosso (2000) and Yosso, Smith, Ceja, and Solórzano (2009) provided a detailed understanding of student experiences with racial microaggressions in the collegiate environment. In general, these acts tend to occur at an unconscious level. Those initiating the aggression are often unaware of the significance of their actions while victims are often left wondering whether they have in fact been victimized. This description resonated deeply with me in my work with students in higher education. In over 13 years as a higher education professional, I have listened to countless stories from students of color describing incidents that I have anecdotally categorized as racial microaggressions. In this chapter, I share student responses from my study as examples of the different ways students of color experience racial microaggressions in college.

The primary contributions to the scholarship on racial microaggressions have emphasized the extensive damaging effects these can have on a person's psychological and emotional well-being (Mercer, Zeigler-Hill, Wallace, & Hayes, 2011; Nadal, 2011; Sue et al., 2007; Sue, Lin, Torino, Capodilupo, & Rivera, 2009; Torres-Harding, Andrade, & Romero Diaz, 2012; Wang, Leu, & Shoda, 2011) and on academic performance and outcomes (Solórzano et al., 2000; Yosso et al., 2009). Sue and colleagues (2007) served as the catalyst for a renewed and widespread interest in exploring issues of racial microaggressions for people of color. Specifically, their taxonomy provided several types of racial microaggressions that range in the level of conscious intent by the perpetrator and consequences for recipients. *Microassaults*, for example, are categorized as more purposeful attacks and are hence more closely related to the traditional forms of racism. They are also easier to recognize by, and are most damaging to, the intended target. The other two forms, *microinsults* and *microinvalidations*, are more covert. These latter two forms of racial microaggressions are more often characterized as rude, insensitive, or exclusionary actions (both verbal and nonverbal) that convey messages meant to "demean a person's racial heritage" or "negate, or nullify the psychological thoughts, feelings or experiential reality of a person of color" (Sue et al., 2007, p. 274).

Racial microaggressions and stereotypes do not have to hold "negative" perceptions to have negative effects (Siy & Cheryan, 2013). Some cultural stereotypes have been categorized as positive and are often said (and believed) with the best of intentions. Have you ever heard, for example, that Asians are good at math or that Africans are fast runners? The harm in stereotypes and assumptions is that they project generalized attributes onto an entire population even in cases in which the particular attribute does not hold true. This is not to say that we should not give credit to (or compliment) those who possess exceptional talents or traits; rather, it should be given according to the person's unique and individual experience.

METHODS

Seventy-four undergraduate students at a large 4-year public institution in the northeast completed an online survey to participate in this study. The student sample was 47% Latinx, 23% Black/African American, 10% Asian/Asian American, 10% multiracial, and 10% identifying as "other." In selecting a gender identity, 31% identified as male and 69% female. The survey included demographic and Likert-type items drawn from themes established in the literature that were relevant to student experiences with racial microaggressions in higher education (McCabe, 2009; Solórzano et al., 2000; Yosso et al., 2009) and the potential impact of these experiences on college outcomes. It also included an open-ended item that allowed respondents to share additional information about their experience.

The data collected in the study were evaluated in several ways. First, survey items were subjected to a confirmatory factor analysis and presented as four distinct ways in which undergraduate students of color experience racial microaggressions in college classrooms. The confirmatory factor analysis indicated that the phenomenon of racial microaggressions in the classroom can best be represented by four underlying factors (or latent variables), described next. An overview of the four factors confirmed through the analysis along with the types of student experiences associated with each factor is displayed in Table 3.1.

Second, frequencies for items related to the potential impact of classroom experiences (i.e., intent to finish, intent to transfer, dropped or failed courses, response to classroom situations) demonstrated how experiences with racial microaggressions might be impacting students of color in college. Last, qualitative data obtained through the open-ended item are shared as examples of how students view their racialized experiences in the classroom.

HOW DO STUDENTS OF COLOR EXPERIENCE RACIAL MICROAGGRESSIONS?

> I'm Asian, and my issue is with professors and classmates making me feel like I should know everything just because of my ethnicity. My classmates want to pair up with me because they think I have all the answers. Professors ask questions about Asian culture and direct them to me, or they look at me when they are being asked. I feel ashamed to ask for help because I am Asian and the stereotype is that I have to be smart.
>
> —(A second-year Asian American student)

There is a sizeable literature about racial microaggressions, particularly pertaining to their definition and potential outcomes. However, measuring the prevalence and experience of racial microaggressions is more complex. Racial microaggressions are phenomena that cannot be represented by a single variable but rather through multiple underlying factors (Nadal, 2011). Sue and colleagues' (2007) work was a breakthrough in the field of racial microaggressions

TABLE 3.1. Experience of Racial Microaggressions in the Classroom: Four Factors

Factor	Associated student experiences
Classroom learning environment	• Stereotypes about people of color heard in the class. • Negative comments about people of color heard in the class. • Racial or ethnic jokes heard in the class. • Students feel singled out or excluded because of their race or ethnicity. • Students feel their views, opinions, or ideas do not matter to others (either peers, course instructor, or both). • Students feel uncomfortable sharing ideas, views, or opinions during class.
Classroom conversations about race and ethnicity	• Instructor feels comfortable talking about issues of race and ethnicity in class. • Students feel comfortable talking about issues of race and ethnicity in class. • Issues of race and ethnicity are discussed in class. • Students learn about views and ideas of other cultures in class.
Instructor expectations	• Students feel instructor thinks they are not smart enough to be in the class. • Students feel their ideas, views, and/or opinion do not matter to instructor. • Students hear stereotypes based on race or ethnicity made by course instructor. • Students feel instructor expects less from them based on their race or ethnicity. • Instructor discusses issues of power, privilege, and oppression in the class. • Instructor encourages students from different backgrounds to work together. • Instructor encourages students to share their opinions, views, and ideas during class. • Instructor understands and respects racial and ethnic diversity. • Instructor cares about student learning.
Peer expectations	• Students feel excluded by peers from study or lab groups. • Students feel peers did not consider them smart enough to be in the course. • Students feel they did not belong in the course based on interactions with their peers. • Students feel their views, ideas, and/or opinions did not matter to their peers. • Students feel peers expected less from them because of their race or ethnicity.

as a conceptual framework for the daily racially motivated interactions that people of color experience at multiple levels. But less is known about how college students of color experience microaggressions and how microaggressions impact these students' educational journey.

This pilot study begins to paint a picture for higher education scholars and practitioners about the ways in which students of color experience racial microaggressions in college classrooms. Confirmatory factor analysis of the pilot data supported four distinct factors related to student experience with classroom-based racial microaggressions that included, in order of strength, the classroom learning environment, classroom conversations about race and ethnicity, instructor (or faculty) expectations, and peer expectations. These findings provide a point of departure for this phenomenon while also providing educators a place to focus attention with regard to initiatives on improving classroom experiences and outcomes for students. Specific examples of ways to improve experiences associated with these factors are provided in the following sections.

HOW DO RACIAL MICROAGGRESSIONS IMPACT STUDENTS OF COLOR?

> As a student of color, I feel very underrepresented here. I come from a Hispanic background, and most of the students at this university are Caucasian. They look at me differently. I have been told to go back to Mexico by other students; however, I am not Mexican. That's not right, and it was hurtful. I really did not know that people my age could be racist.
>
> —(A first-year Latinx student)

Racial microaggressions are associated with negative outcomes; most common are stereotype threat, a diminished sense of belonging, academic self-doubt, and poor academic performance. The term *stereotype threat*, originally conceptualized by Steele and Aronson in 1995 and later expanded by Solórzano and colleagues (2000), describes how repeated exposures to racial microaggressions, and in particular racial stereotypes, can result in the adoption of those preconceived stereotypical behaviors. Negative interactions with peers and faculty have been extensively linked to a diminished sense of belonging. Students of color who experience racial microaggressions inevitably receive confirmation that indeed they do not belong in the environment: a course, an institution, or a college. Students of color can develop a sense of academic self-doubt after being exposed to low expectations from instructors and peers. Repeated experiences with stereotype threat have the cumulative effect of a diminished sense of belonging, and academic self-doubt can ultimately lead to poor academic performance, including poor grades and low persistence and retention rates.

Although this study did not seek to measure how students of color respond to racial microaggressions, some self-reported items were associated with potential responses to classroom experiences. The vast majority of students in this study (93%) reported they had the intention of completing their undergraduate degree at their current institution, yet about 20% admitted they might transfer to another institution before completing their undergraduate degree. More than half (56%) of the students in this study reported having failed or dropped a course. Though this behavior is not directly correlated with the classroom experience, it is categorized by various studies as poor academic performance that may be indirectly related to negative classroom experiences. More interesting, the study findings support prior research that has highlighted the ability of students of color to use *counter-spaces,* safe spaces or outlets where they can talk through their experiences, to persist in the collegiate environment despite the presence of racial microaggressions (see, for example, Solórzano et al., 2000, and Yosso et al., 2009). In this study, a large majority (69%) of students reported discussing their classroom experiences with others. It is possible that having a conversation about the negative classroom experiences provided students of color with a way to make sense of their environment that enabled them to cope well enough to persist. Among students who reported having conversations about the classroom experience, 44% had conversations with either a family member or a student outside of the classroom. These numbers support the idea that although students of color seek an outlet to engage in conversations about their classroom experiences, having these types of conversations in the classroom environment may be challenging.

RACIAL MICROAGGRESSIONS AND DIFFICULT CLASSROOM CONVERSATIONS

> There are far less students of color than Caucasian students here, and I think, because of this, professors shy away from speaking about topics that might involve race or ethnicity. We need more diversity in each classroom.
> —(A fourth-year Middle Eastern student)

A more immediate potential response to racial microaggressions in the classroom is a conversation about racial and ethnic issues, stereotypes, or misconceptions, often categorized as difficult racial dialogues (Sue, Torino, Capodilupo, Rivera, & Lin, 2009). Though students of color continue to be proportionally underrepresented, classrooms are becoming increasingly diverse. Some scholars have argued that increased classroom diversity may increase the potential for racial microaggressions and the occurrence of difficult conversations (Sue, Lin, et al., 2009). This makes sense because, despite increases in structural racial and ethnic diversity on campuses and classrooms, instructors are not any better prepared to facilitate racially charged interactions that may take place in the classroom or the conversations that follow (Young, 2003). Sue, Lin, et al. (2009) found evidence that conversations about race in the classroom often followed incidents of racial microaggression. Therefore, the situation may already be emotionally charged for the student(s) of color positioned at the receiving end of an incident. The way in which the conversation unfolds can also further add tension, frustration, anger, and confusion for all involved. The conversation may also lead to feelings of victimization for the student of color, depending on how well it is facilitated by the instructor (Sue & Constantine, 2007). Effective facilitation is crucial to decrease the negative impact of racial microaggressions on students of color and maintain a positive learning environment for all students. So why are dialogues about race or racial issues so challenging for instructors to engage in and effectively facilitate?

In a qualitative study involving White faculty, Sue, Torino, et al. (2009) examined the ways conversations involving race in the classroom were challenging. Their findings indicated that the "emotionally charged nature" of these conversations along with their "fear of losing control of the classroom" made it difficult for them to engage in these dialogues (p. 1096). Additional findings included faculty's inability to recognize difficult dialogues and lack of training on how to effectively facilitate these conversations. Similarly, Sue and Constantine (2007) examined the damaging, even "disastrous consequences," of ineffective or lack of response to difficult conversations about race in the classroom by faculty members (p. 136). The authors' comments focused on the prevalent under-preparedness of faculty members to respond to and effectively address these classroom conversations along with four basic fears that White faculty must face to effectively facilitate difficult dialogues: (a) fear of appearing racist, (b) fear of realizing their racism, (c) fear of confronting White privilege, and (d) fear of taking personal responsibility to end racism. The lack of preparation and associated fears can have a negative impact on the way faculty approach interactions with students of color and conversations about race in the classroom. The general assumption is that, as educators, our goal is to promote active learning for students. Knowing that our students are most engaged in learning when they feel validated and supported, what do we need to know and do to ensure a positive learning environment for all students?

TRANSCENDING RACIAL MICROAGGRESSIONS AND ENGAGING IN DIFFICULT DIALOGUES

> When it comes to cheating and attendance there is a lot more attention on us [students of color], and I feel like they [instructors] should be paying attention to everyone for those things.
>
> —(A fourth-year Latinx Student)

Presented next are sample strategies that can be enacted in classrooms, as well as at departmental or institutional levels, to avoid racial microaggressions and/or counteract the aftermath of difficult classroom dialogues.

- *Accept and acknowledge that we all have biases.* We are products of our socialization; thus we all hold stereotypes about racial and ethnic backgrounds, sometimes including our own. Even those of us who have spent years actively learning and teaching multicultural competence may still have existing biases and even adopt new biases. The important action step here is to recognize them and continually work to unpack and unmantle these beliefs.

- *Set ground rules for safe and productive learning spaces.* Begin the course with a conversation about civility, respect, and developing a set of ground rules about how participants will engage with one another in the classroom. Include definitions for racial discrimination and microaggressions as part of this conversation. Help students understand that these types of behaviors are hurtful and unproductive and violate the ground rules. Share examples that allow students to understand how racial microaggressions can occur at an unconscious level. Individually or in groups read collections of personal narratives by individuals of color and extract and share examples of microaggressions with their classmates (e.g., Harwood, Choi, Orozco, Browne Huntt, & Mendenhall, 2015). Although the focus of this chapter is on racial microaggressions, instructors can include other forms of discrimination and types of microaggressions in any classroom conversation.

- *Have conversations about race, ethnicity, and cultural differences.* These conversations can be uncomfortable, and our natural inclination is to shy away from having them. We do so because we tend to think of ourselves as not quite knowledgeable enough to engage in these conversations, but would we ever consider ourselves ready? When engaging in these conversations, keep in mind that your racial and ethnic background matters. In these situations, it is useful to be honest about your background and your position as a learner. Positioning yourself as an expert can be challenging for students who do not believe you share their lived experiences. Share information about your efforts to learn along with the ways in which you have gained knowledge about racial and ethnic issues, and show an interest in learning more. By doing so, you are modeling the importance of cultural competence by showing students (all students) that it is important enough to learn even for you as an instructor, and you will earn their respect and trust in the process. During these conversations, provide students of color the opportunity to share their experiences, views, and opinions about racial and ethnic issues. However, be careful not to single them out or position them as "the classroom expert" because doing so carries an assumption and is considered a form of racial microaggression.

- *If you do not yet have sufficient knowledge and skills to lead a conversation with your class, you can bring a guest speaker to the classroom.* Most institutions have a diversity and inclusion leader with access to resources at your institution or in the local area. If not, your institution (or a nearby institution) likely has engaging and talented scholars that specialize in ethnic studies, Africana studies, or related fields. Last, these conversations should preferably be about the course content but could also be introduced in relation to current local or national events or professional development skills. Regardless of the fields your students seek to enter, they will be entering a professional world that is growing more diverse and global and where they will be expected to be aware of these issues.

- *When conversations take a wrong turn, take a time-out.* Even with proper planning and preparation, classroom conversations can take a wrong turn. Ignoring or downplaying an incident of racial microaggression sends the wrong message. Take the time to talk about what just happened. Remain calm and acknowledge that strong feelings will naturally emerge in these types of conversations. Try not to be surprised or angry about the strong emotions that are being displayed. You are setting the tone for your students. Any emotion or energy you are displaying they will also feel permitted to display. Allow individuals to state briefly what is going on for them. Using probing questions and guide students in a discussion about the situation. For example, you may ask questions such as, What did you say? What did those words mean to you? What did you hear? How did that make you feel? A mini-intervention will go a long way in reinforcing the ground rules and modeling appropriate ways to communicate about difficult topics. At the same time, validating the severity of microaggressive behavior can also help to counteract its negative effects on students of color and the classroom dynamic.

- *Learn to incorporate culturally inclusive pedagogy and curriculum.* For many of us, it is easier to teach than to practice. Talking about how we should be more inclusive in our classrooms is easy, but knowing how to do so takes time and willingness to learn (Quaye & Harper, 2007). You can incorporate a multicultural curriculum into virtually any discipline (Clark, 2002). As a start, there are many good resources available throughout this volume. Remember that you do not need to become an expert or expect to master these skills overnight. You can incorporate a few pedagogical approaches into your teaching practice at a time, learn what works for you, and reassess.

- *Address racial microaggressions and dispel myths and stereotypes.* Recognize microaggressions and address them right away. Use facts to help students learn about the misinformation often hidden behind racial microaggressions. Many of us have been socialized to think about different cultures in stereotypical ways. An effective way to break away from these beliefs is to talk openly about stereotypes. Keep in mind that even "good" stereotypes can be harmful. Lead a conversation with your students about helpful resources and/or strategies to replace bias and stereotypes with cultural competence and advocacy.

- *Continually seek professional development opportunities.* Cultural competence is a lifelong process. Continually working on our knowledge and skills will allow us to be better prepared to assist students with their cultural competence. Owning up to our biases, deconstructing our internalized stereotypes, and knowing what we do not know takes work. Each time I teach or attend a cultural competence workshop, I learn something new about myself and those around me. Fortunately, you do not necessarily have to travel a long distance to learn. There may be valuable learning opportunities in your area. Professional organizations often have regional or state subunits that provide local meetings or "drive-in" sessions. There are also a wide variety of organizations that provide online learning opportunities. Online options and local workshops may also be more cost-effective when funding is limited or nonexistent.

CONCLUSION

As educators, we have a responsibility to develop and ensure a positive learning environment for all students. As a more globally diverse population of students becomes the new majority in our classrooms (Krogstad, 2015), this responsibility becomes more pressing. However, instructors, as well as institutions, are insufficiently prepared to meet the educational and cultural needs of students of color, and the pedagogy and curriculum used in the majority of our disciplines do not mirror the diversity of the students whose learning we now facilitate. My research mirrors other studies by demonstrating that racial microaggressions are too often manifested through the learning environment, by both faculty and peers, and that they can negatively impact learning for all students, not just students of color. As highlighted in this chapter, there are simple and more complex strategies we can all implement to provide a safe and positive learning space for students of color. Facilitating the growth and development of our students into culturally competent learners will have a significant impact on their success academically and professionally. To do so, we must first do the same for ourselves.

REFERENCES

Clark, C. (2002). Effective multicultural curriculum transformation across disciplines. *Multicultural Perspectives, 4*(3), 37–46. http://dx.doi.org/10.1207/ S15327892MCP0403_7

Harwood, S. A., Choi, S., Orozco, M., Browne Huntt, M., & Mendenhall, R. (2015). *Racial microaggressions at the University of Illinois at Urbana-Champaign: Voices of students of color in the classroom.* Retrieved from http://www.racialmicroaggressions.illinois.edu/ files/2015/03/RMA-Classroom-Report.pdf.

Krogstad, J. M. (2015). *Reflecting a racial shift, 78 counties turned majority–minority since 2000.* Retrieved from http://www.pewresearch.org/fact-tank/2015/04/08/ reflecting-a-racial-shift-78-counties-turned-majority-minority-since-2000/

McCabe, J. (2009). Racial and gender microaggressions on a predominantly-White campus: Experiences of Black, Latina/o and White undergraduates. *Race, Gender, & Class, 16,* 133–151.

Mercer, S. H., Zeigler-Hill, V., Wallace, M., & Hayes, D. M. (2011). Development and initial validation of the Inventory of Microaggressions Against Black Individuals. *Journal of Counseling Psychology, 58,* 457–469. http://dx.doi.org/10.1037/a0024937

Nadal, K. L. (2011). The Racial and Ethnic Microaggressions Scale (REMS): Construction, reliability, and validity. *Journal of Counseling Psychology, 58,* 470. http://dx.doi.org/ 10.1037/a0025193

Nadal, K. L., Davidoff, K. C., Davis, L. S., Wong, Y., Marshall, D., & McKenzie, V. (2015). A qualitative approach to intersectional microaggressions: Understanding influences of race, ethnicity, gender, sexuality, and religion. *Qualitative Psychology, 2,* 147–163. http://dx.doi.org/10.1037/qup0000026

Osanloo, A. F., Boske, C., & Newcomb, W. S. (2016). Deconstructing macroaggressions, microaggressions, and structural racism in education: Developing a conceptual model for the intersection of social justice practice and intercultural education. *International Journal of Organizational Theory and Development, 4,* 1–18.

Quaye, J. S., & Harper, S. R. (2007). Shifting the onus from racial/ethnic minority students to faculty: Accountability for culturally inclusive pedagogy and curricula. *Liberal Education, 92*(3), 19–24.

Siy, J. O., & Cheryan, S. (2013). When compliments fail to flatter: American individualism and responses to positive stereotypes. *Journal of Personality and Social Psychology, 104,* 87–102. http://dx.doi.org/10.1037/a0030183

Solórzano, D., Ceja, M., & Yosso, T. (2000). Critical race theory, racial microaggressions and campus racial climate: The experiences of African American college students. *Journal of Negro Education, 69,* 60–73.

Steele, C. M., & Aronson, J. (1995). Stereotype threat and the intellectual test performance of African Americans. *Journal of Personality and Social Psychology, 69,* 797–811. http://dx.doi.org/10.1037/0022-3514.69.5.797

Sue, D. W., Capodilupo, C. M., Torino, G. C., Bucceri, J. M., Holder, A. M., Nadal, K. L., & Esquilin, M. (2007). Racial microaggressions in everyday life: Implications for clinical practice. *American Psychologist, 62,* 271–286. http://dx.doi.org/10.1037/0003-066X.62.4.271

Sue, D. W., & Constantine, M. G. (2007). Racial microaggressions as instigators of difficult dialogues on race: Implications for student affairs educators and students. *College Student Affairs Journal, 26,* 136.

Sue, D. W., Lin, A. I., Torino, G. C., Capodilupo, C. M., & Rivera, D. P. (2009). Racial microaggressions and difficult dialogues on race in the classroom. *Cultural Diversity and Ethnic Minority Psychology, 15,* 183–190. http://dx.doi.org/10.1037/a0014191

Sue, D. W., Torino, G. C., Capodilupo, C. M., Rivera, D. P., & Lin, A. I. (2009). How White faculty perceive and react to difficult dialogues on race: Implications for education and training. *The Counseling Psychologist, 37,* 1090–1115. http://dx.doi.org/10.1177/0011000009340443

Torres-Harding, S. R., Andrade, A. L., Jr., & Romero Diaz, C. E. (2012). The Racial Microaggressions Scale (RMAS): A new scale to measure experiences of racial microaggressions in people of color. *Cultural Diversity and Ethnic Minority Psychology, 18,* 153–164. http://dx.doi.org/10.1037/a0027658

Wang, J., Leu, J., & Shoda, Y. (2011). When the seemingly innocuous "stings": Racial microaggressions and their emotional consequences. *Personality and Social Psychology Bulletin, 37,* 1666–1678. http://dx.doi.org/10.1177/0146167211416130

Yosso, T., Smith, W., Ceja, M., & Solórzano, D. (2009). Critical race theory, racial microaggressions, and campus racial climate for Latina/o undergraduates. *Harvard Educational Review, 79,* 659–691. http://dx.doi.org/10.17763/haer.79.4.m6867014157m707l

Young, G. (2003). Dealing with difficult classroom dialogue. In P. Bronstein & K. Quina (Eds.), *Teaching gender and multicultural awareness: Resources for the psychology classroom* (pp. 347–360). Washington, DC: American Psychological Association. http://dx.doi.org/10.1037/10570-025

GENDER, ETHNIC, AND SOCIOCULTURAL PERSPECTIVES: SPECIALIZED COURSES AND CONTENT AREAS

Who Is the Woman in the Psychology of Women?

Addressing Diversity and Intersectionality

Beverly J. Goodwin, Camille J. Interligi, Ashley E. Kasardo,
Maureen C. McHugh, and Andrea D. Poet

The psychology of women (POW) is not a static catalog of research findings regarding how women differ from men, nor is it a series of findings about the lives and experiences of "all women." Rather, it is a dynamic field of theory and research, using classrooms as a form of participatory action research. The goal of POW is to help our students understand their lives, recognize gender as one system of oppression and inequality, and also resist and disrupt gendered marginalization, subordination, and oppression. These goals are most likely to be met when a community of learners together acknowledge multiple aspects of identities and statuses of women in varied contexts, rendering the invisible groups or statuses of women visible and challenging the power and privilege accorded to some people at the expense of other people.

Boylorn (2014) stated, "The stories told about Black [and other marginalized] women are often stories of stereotypes and contradictions disguised as truth" (p. 130). No one classroom exercise, skillfully designed assignment, article, or book will solve these limitations. However, we can become more deliberate in what we teach, how we teach, and the activities we assign.

http://dx.doi.org/10.1037/0000137-005
Integrating Multiculturalism and Intersectionality Into the Psychology Curriculum:
Strategies for Instructors, J. A. Mena and K. Quina (Editors)

DIVERSITY OF WOMEN AND THE INTERSECTIONALITY APPROACH

Over the past half-century, the study of women and gender has become a major focus of psychological science. POW focused on the lives and experiences of Euro American, middle-class, and heterosexual women; other women are examined in relation to White women, and themes of other women's lives are not similarly addressed. This failure to acknowledge or include other groups of women limits our understanding of women's behavior and human behavior (Goodwin, McHugh, & Touster, 2003; hooks, 1994; Hull, Bell-Scott, & Smith, 1982).

Third-wave feminists have criticized psychologists' emphasis on women as a social category because it did not consider the heterogeneity of women within this category. Fine and Gordon (1989) argued that gender intersects with race and ethnicity, social class, age, ability status, sexual orientation, and social context to produce "socially and historically constituted subjectivities" (p. 147). Various social identities combine to place the individual at a unique social location; privileged and marginalized identities (e.g., race, class, age, gender, sexual orientation) interact simultaneously in complicated ways (Crenshaw, 1989; hooks, 1984).

Because they were developed by Black women and other women of color (WOC), intersectional theory and analyses are frequently centered on the experiences of WOC, primarily African American women, illuminating the complexity of race and ethnicity as it intersects with other dimensions of difference (Dill & Zambrana, 2009). Using this perspective, we suggest strategies for teaching that incorporate a variety of privileged and oppressed identities contributing to a woman's lived experience to avoid overgeneralizations and stereotypes, illuminate issues of power and privilege, examine intersections of identity in relation to the matrix of privilege (Case, 2013; Grzanka, 2014), and help all students become cognizant of the importance of diversities in the lives of women, including their own.

REFLECTING ON INTERSECTING IDENTITIES AND PRIVILEGE

The ideas of privilege and oppression experienced in relation to intersecting identities should be introduced early in the class. A good starting point for understanding the importance of intersectionality is to present the TED Talk by Crenshaw (2016). Case (2013) and her contributing authors offered innovative strategies for addressing intersecting dimensions of privilege and oppression. Students can introduce themselves in terms of their intersecting identities, on which they can reflect at multiple points during the course, modeled by the instructor, other students, and guests. Erickson Cornish and colleagues (2010) offered exercises to address intersecting identities and help students recognize the experience of simultaneous oppression and privilege (Banks, Pliner, &

Hopkins, 2013). Students can record a self-interview, guided by questions about privilege and contact with "different" others, and then explore their feelings and perspectives in a reflective essay, in which they are encouraged to recognize how privilege and oppression operate at the intersections of women's lives. Revisiting this essay at the end of the course with another reflection can reinforce what they have learned. Students might use these questions to interview another student or someone in the community who they view as different from themselves.

A "privilege walk" can illustrate how women's lives represent multiple identities, some of which entail privilege and others derogation (http://www.whatsrace.org/pages/games.html; https://people.creighton.edu/~idc24708/Genes/Diversity/Privilege%20Exercise.htm). Students in a line take steps forward (privilege) or back (oppression) in response to questions about experience. Students can also unpack their own "knapsack of privilege," expanding Peggy McIntosh's (2015) essay to include other identities such as religion, social class, ability status, size, and education. Allan Johnson's (2006) Diversity Wheel is a great tool for guiding conversations about systems of privilege and oppression, including gender and social class; for example, readers are asked to imagine how they would be impacted if one of their identities were to change (e.g., sexual orientation or ability status or other identity).

The Global Feminisms Project (https://globalfeminisms.umich.edu/) contains interviews with 53 women activists and scholars, providing "examples of the use of visibility and invisibility to create and maintain privilege, [and] the topics covered provide multiple contexts with which to ground conversations about diverse groups of women" (Rios & Stewart, 2013, p. 118). Each student can present an interview for discussion in class.

We encourage exposure to others from different social categories, privileges, and circumstances throughout this course. Instructors or students can invite campus or community members for a panel discussion, have students conduct interviews with someone unlike themselves, or engage in community activities with a social justice focus. For example, a panel of women who vary in ethnicity, social class, age, sexual orientation, and religion can help dismantle the category WOC. Especially effective are "critical dialogues" with trained facilitators, accompanied by readings and journals to promote critical thinking.

Meeting or learning about groups of women can help students examine their experiences in terms of their diverse nature and intersecting identities. In the video *The Way Home: Women Talk About Race in America* (Butler, 1998), culturally diverse women address differences in perspectives that originate in their intersectionalities. When studying older women, students might spend time learning from women in a nursing home or learn about diversity and sexual orientation by speaking to women-identified individuals at a gay pride event. Although no single text can fully address the complexities of women's lives in terms of intersections of identity, we recommend assigning women's stories and/or adopting an anthology featuring women's narratives, such as Disch (2008); Fiske-Rusciano (2012); Kelly, Parameswaran, and Schniedewind (2011); Kirk and Okazawa-Rey (2012); Roberts (2004); and Shaw and Lee (2014).

Storytelling is a way to break the silence and give women a voice for the expression and analysis of their own experience and can lead to "ideological transformations and to political mobilization" (Romero & Stewart, 1999, p. xii). Telling one's story can result in connection and community and can help resolve shame (Brown, 2004). We encourage students to develop autobiographies, incorporate intersectional identities, and reflect on the power, privilege, or oppression associated with varied identities discussed in class. If comfortable, sharing these autobiographies can contribute to the creation of community in the classroom (hooks, 2003).

WOMEN ACROSS SELECTED INTERSECTIONS OF DIVERSITY

African American Women and Women of Color

Goodwin and Delazar (2000) analyzed over 50 years of POW textbooks to examine the extent to which they included material on African American women. They observed (a) a limited number of rather narrow and stereotypic topics on African American women, (b) considerable variability in the quality and quantity of information, (c) a tendency to represent minorities cross-culturally (Africans), (d) voices of African American and other WOC were often missing or were compared with Whites or other racial groups in empirical studies, and (e) with rare exception, a non-intersectional approach. Hyde and Else-Quest (2013) also found that scant attention has been paid to Asian American, Latina/Hispanic, and Native American women.

Some content areas are especially relevant and unique for African American women and WOC because "the different and complex social forces acting on them may result in different patterns of gender roles and behaviors" (Hyde & Else-Quest, 2013, p. 85). Jackson-Lowman (2014) provided an important historical context of African American women, the values associated with self-identity, and theories of Africana womanism and Black feminist thought while focusing on culture-appropriate perspectives. Similarly, Harris-Perry (2011) included historical and contemporary contexts in her critical analysis to argue against the tired stereotypes of Black women and to identify contemporary Black women's shared struggle to preserve an authentic self and secure recognition of Black women as equal citizens.

Students can discuss how the label WOC is used to (mis)represent women with diverse intersecting identities, including immigration history, cultural heritage, skin color, language, access to education, and relations with the dominant culture (Williams, McCandies, & Dunlap, 2002) and be encouraged to consider the intersectionality of various ethnic and racial identities in their readings and assignments. *Psychological Health of Women of Color: Intersections, Challenges, and Opportunities* (Comas-Díaz & Greene, 2013) and *Womanist and Mujerista Psychologies: Voices of Fire, Acts of Courage* (Bryant-Davis & Comas-Díaz, 2016) have cultivated discourse on WOC, arguing for a more multidimensional and comprehensive understanding of their lives.

Students have provided positive feedback when the lived experiences of WOC are integrated throughout the course and when they have engaged in projects based on autoethnography. On the back cover of their book, Adams, Holman Jones, and Ellis (2015) described *autoethnography* as "a method of research that involves describing and analyzing personal experiences in order to understand cultural experiences. . . . Autoethnography acknowledges and accommodates subjectivity, emotionality, and the researcher's influence on research." Autoethnography can enlighten pedagogy and inspire the design of classroom activities and assignments.

Social Class

Psychology has been criticized for ignoring issues of social class (American Psychological Association, 2007). POW textbooks often stigmatize the poor and fail to address the systems of oppression that influence access to resources, life outcomes, and physical and mental health (see Ming-Liu, 2011). For example, Hyde and Else-Quest (2013) described lower socioeconomic status families as more likely to experience depression and mental health concerns; we supplement this with an analysis of systematic oppressions that influence this reality. Matlin's (2012) explanation that lower socioeconomic status individuals have a lower life expectancy due to inadequate access to health care, exposure to toxins in their environment, and increased stressful life events is an excellent resource for class discussion.

We use a small-group in-class activity to challenge preconceived notions about members of social class groups. Each group receives a card with a target group (poor, working class, middle class, or upper class). Group members are asked to list what comes to mind when they think about people from this background (i.e., stereotypes). They are then prompted to explore where these beliefs originated, including the myth of meritocracy. Discussing their understanding of the "American Dream," including who has access to it and the barriers that limit that access, enhances awareness of inequalities. Resources to accompany this activity include Hochschild (1996) or Kraus, Davidai, and Nussbaum (2015). The exercise Walk in My Shoes (Snyder-Roche, 2011) can help students recognize their social class diversity and privilege. If students are comfortable revealing experiences related to being poor or working class, such exchanges pierce the illusion that everyone in the class comes from a similar background. Sensitivity is crucial because some students may not wish to share this information.

In textbooks, the intersection of social class and race is often limited to poor minorities and middle-class Whites. Hyde and Else-Quest (2013) pointed out that most mental health services are provided to middle- and upper-class White women and offer important factors to consider when working with WOC. The instructor can supplement this point with information about poor White women: Tawni O'Dell's (2000) *Back Roads*, Dorothy Allison's (2005) *Bastard Out of Carolina*, and bell hooks' (2000) excellent examination of White poverty.

Older Women

Though the older adult population is increasing substantially, and women make up a "significant majority" of this cohort (United Nations Department of Economic and Social Affairs, 2010, p. 25), older women are nearly invisible in U.S. culture. Older women are doubly damned by sexism and ageism: marginalized, viewed as dysfunctional, and devalued (McHugh & Interligi, 2014) and not positively presented even in POW texts (McHugh & Interligi, 2013). Current POW texts generally devote less than 10% of their total volume to the lived experiences of older women, and topics such as menopause, widowhood, poverty, and health often receive relatively stereotypic coverage and are discussed in relation to White, middle-class, heterosexual women. Other salient aspects of older women's lives such as sexuality and abuse, deserve attention, along with the lived experiences of non-White; disabled; lesbian, gay, bisexual, transgender, queer, intersex, and asexual (LGBTQIA)–identified; poor; rural; and spiritual older women (McHugh & Interligi, 2014). Students can discuss their experiences with gerontophobia and/or share examples of older women being (mis)represented or discussed in a prejudiced and stereotypical manner in academic as well as mainstream media sources. To highlight the issue of older women's sexuality, we recommend the film *Still Doing It: The Intimate Lives of Women Over 65* (Holtzberg & Fishel, 2004), which includes older women of different ability status, body size, sexual orientation, race, and social class. Students can read narratives about mothers and daughters or about three generations, then interview three generations of a family (often their own) and compose a generational narrative.

Fat Women

Although 27.3% of American women are labeled *overweight* and 34.9% are labeled *obese* (U.S. Department of Health and Human Services, 2011), these women remain mostly invisible in POW texts, including their photos and images (Goodwin et al., 2003; McHugh, Osachy-Touster, Sullivan, & Simone, 2009). It is important that students recognize that fat women represent a subordinated and stigmatized group in our culture.

Weight-based discrimination against women in the United States is well documented (Fikkan & Rothblum, 2012). Matlin (2012) described U.S. culture as "fat hating," questioning the prevailing approach to measuring and labeling "overweight" individuals and offering body acceptance as an alternative perspective. Psychology has a responsibility to appreciate size acceptance and strive to eliminate antifat bias (McHugh & Kasardo, 2012). Discussing the meaning of the terms *overweight, obese,* and *fat* (the preferred term for fat activists) as a description, not a derogation, is important (Baker, 2015). Students can reflect on the terminology they have heard or used and the meaning they associate with weight-related terms and discuss the words, images, or ideas they associate with fatness (Watkins, Farrell, & Hugmeyer, 2012). Material regarding the uncontrollability of weight, the unlikelihood of long-term weight loss, the ineffectiveness of dieting, the stereotypes and myths about fat people, and the consequences of fat oppression for women in the United States should be included (McHugh & Kasardo, 2012).

We can increase students' understanding by acknowledging the pervasiveness of discrimination (Fikkan & Rothblum, 2012; Rothblum & Solovay, 2009), recognizing that comments such as that large women should lose weight or are unhealthy are a hurtful form of prejudice, and teaching students how to refute stereotypes about fat women and the relationship between fat and health (Bacon, 2008; Bacon & Aphramor, 2014). Students can be encouraged to examine their attitude toward size with exercises in Fawcett and Evans (2013) or Sobczak (2014). Abakoui and Simmons (2010) cited an assessment of implicit attitudes and values toward weight. Instructors or students might impact the discussion if they are comfortable sharing size discrimination they have faced or examples of their own size privilege (Watkins et al., 2012). Additional suggestions for classroom presentations and exercises can be found in *The Fat Pedagogy Reader* (Cameron & Russell, 2016). For an activist approach, Cooper's (2016) *Fat Activism: A Radical Social Movement* provides a readable history and examples of fat activism.

Sizism affects education opportunities, employment, relationships, and health care (Fikkan & Rothblum, 2012; Kasardo & McHugh, 2015). Understanding why they are rejected, derogated, and shamed is important for fat women, and recognizing the impact of negative comments about fat women is important for all women. Rothblum and Solovay's (2009) *The Fat Studies Reader* and Schoenfielder and Wieser's (1983) anthology *Shadow on a Tightrope: Writings by Women on Fat Oppression* address the impact of weight stigma and bullying.

Most POW texts recognize appearance concerns and body dissatisfaction as a central concern of women, refer to the cultural "thin ideal," and tie women's weight concerns to the media's focus on women's bodies and the presentation of very thin models. Peer pressure and fat talk among peers contribute to women's weight worries and are often tied to the objectification of women. Less often, racial and ethnic differences in concerns about weight are included. Rubin, Fitts, and Becker (2003) suggested that Black and Latina women may resist dominant White ideologies in regard to weight, styling, health, and spiritual values and that older African American women prefer a larger body size (Hughes, 1997). We incorporate research comparing the body satisfaction of lesbians and heterosexual women (Rothblum, Smith, Ingraham, Eliason, & McHugh, 2015) and the weight concerns of older women (McHugh & Interligi, 2014).

Size intersects with other diversity dimensions (Campos, 2004; Ernsberger, 2009). Theorists argue that fat bias has become a socially acceptable form of expressing racism, classism, and sexism (Oliver, 2006; Saguy, 2013). Anthologies such as Tovar's (2012) *Hot & Heavy: Fierce Fat Girls on Life, Love, & Fashion* offer narratives on the experiences of fat women. Chastain's (2015) *The Politics of Size: Perspectives From the Fat Acceptance Movement* builds consciousness about intersectionality. In *Hunger: A Memoir of My Body*, Roxanne Gay (2015) presents an autobiography of her life as a large Caribbean woman in the United States; her readings lend well to an autobiographical reflection on one's body.

Videos and documentaries can effectively illustrate diversity and intersection-ality within size. Lisa Tillman's (2011) documentary *Off the Menu: Challenging the Politics and Economics of Body and Food* explore cultural body ideals, fears and hatred of fat, weight-based prejudice, and inequalities in the U.S. food system. Popular films such as *Hairspray* (Zadan, Meron, & Shankman, 2007) explore how fat stigma intersects with other types of oppression, and Kulick and Meneley's (2005) *Fat: The Anthropology of an Obsession* offers an international perspective on body size (Watkins et al., 2012). *Embrace* (Body Image Movement, 2017; https://bodyimagemovement.com/embrace-the-documentary) discusses global body image concerns. The movie *Fattitude* is an inspiring new release (http://fattitudethemovie.squarespace.com/home#/awards-and-festivals/). Size accep-tance approaches represent alternatives to the medicalization of size; particularly helpful are Chrisler and Johnston-Robledo (2018), Sobczak (2014), and Bacon's (2008) *Health at Every Size*, which has a program to reinforce its messages in an online community (https://haescommunity.com/haes-connections/). The National Association to Advance Fat Acceptance (http://www.naafaonline.com/dev2/about/index.html), a nonprofit civil rights organization dedicated to ending size discrimination, offers PowerPoints, handouts, and examinations free of charge at http://www.haescurriculum.com (Kasardo, 2015; Matz & Frankel, 2014).

Additional Dimensions of Diversity

We advocate in future POW classes and texts for recognition of additional groups of women that have remained marginalized or invisible, such as single and childless-by-choice women; women with chronic health and mental health issues; atheist, religious, and spiritual women; women with physical disabili-ties; indigenous women; and rural women. Heterosexual, cisgender, and gender-conforming privilege is frequently unacknowledged but is intensely insidious; other nonheterosexual sexual orientations are even less likely to be repre-sented (Blumer, Green, Thomte, & Green, 2013). *Towards Intimacy: Women With Disabilities* (Hubert & McGee, 1993), from the National Film Board of Canada, portrays five women with varied disabilities and diverse backgrounds, focus-ing on their intimate relationships. Critical dialogues can help students rec-ognize the privileges afforded heterosexuals and how various religious perspectives may maintain heterosexual privileges; having women students answer questions about their sexual attractions on an anonymous homo-centric questionnaire can help students recognize heterosexual privilege (Blumer et al., 2013).

Religion is often an important source of identity and can also involve the exercise of power, privilege, and oppression. Introducing a diverse group of Muslim women could counter stereotypes and emphasize the complexity of intersections of religion and other identities. Intergroup dialogues have been recommended as a key pedagogy to learning about heterosexual Jewish and Christian privilege; Dessel, Masse, and Walker (2013) offered practical strategies for classroom activities, such as fishbowl discussions and caucus groups. The

Power Map Out exercise helps students analyze the different types of power and privilege that Jews and Arabs possess and the oppressions they experience in different national contexts.

THE FUTURE OF PSYCHOLOGY OF WOMEN

Understanding oneself and generating knowledge and insight about the world are exciting endeavors. Conversations about intersecting identities expand understanding of the complexity and diversity of women's lives, including our own, and create an engaging classroom for making connections across differences. bell hooks (2003) argued that feminism and women's studies alter the classroom when patriarchal content is challenged, and students can create knowing, build a community of knowers, and liberate themselves. We can continue that process.

REFERENCES

Abakoui, R., & Simmons, R. E. (2010). Sizeism: An unrecognized prejudice. In J. A. Erickson Cornish, B. A. Schreier, L. I. Nadkarni, L. Henderson Metzger, & E. R. Rodolfa (Eds.), *Handbook of multicultural counseling competencies* (pp. 317–349). Hoboken, NJ: Wiley.

Adams, T. E., Holman Jones, S., & Ellis, C. (2015). *Autoethnography*. New York, NY: Oxford University Press.

Allison, D. (2005). *Bastard out of Carolina*. London, England: Penguin.

American Psychological Association. (2007). *Report of the APA Task Force on Socioeconomic Status*. Washington, DC: Author.

Bacon, L. (2008). *Health at every size: The surprising truth about your weight*. Dallas, TX: BenBella Books.

Bacon, L., & Aphramor, L. (2014). *Body respect: What conventional health books get wrong, leave out, and just plain fail to understand about weight*. Dallas, TX: BenBella Books.

Baker, J. (2015). *Things no one will tell fat girls*. Berkeley, CA: Seal Press.

Banks, C. A., Pliner, S. M., & Hopkins, M. B. (2013). Intersectionality and paradigms of privilege: Teaching for social change. In K. A. Case (Ed.), *Deconstructing privilege: Teaching and learning as allies in the classroom* (pp. 102–114). New York, NY: Routledge.

Blumer, M. L. C., Green, M. S., Thomte, N. L., & Green, P. M. (2013). Are we queer yet? Addressing heterosexual and gender-conforming privilege. In K. A. Case (Ed.), *Deconstructing privilege: Teaching and learning as allies in the classroom* (pp. 151–168). New York, NY: Routledge.

Body Image Movement. (2017). *Embrace the documentary*. Retrieved from https://bodyimagemovement.com/embrace-the-documentary/

Boylorn, R. M. (2014). A story and a stereotype: An angry and strong auto/ethnology of race, class, and gender. In R. M. Boylorn & M. P. Orbe (Eds.), *Critical autoethnography: Intersecting cultural identities in everyday life* (pp. 129–143). Walnut Creek, CA: Left Coast Press.

Brown, B. (2004). *Women and shame: Reaching out, speaking truths and building connection*. New York, NY: 3C Press.

Bryant-Davis, T., & Comas-Díaz, L. (Eds.). (2016). *Womanist and* mujerista *psychologies: Voices of fire, acts of courage*. Washington, DC: American Psychological Association.

Butler, S. (Producer). (1998). *The way home: Women talking about race* [Motion picture]. United States: World Trust Educational Services.

Cameron, E., & Russell, C. (2016). (Eds.). *The fat pedagogy reader: Challenging weight-based oppression through critical education.* New York, NY: Peter Lang.

Campos, P. (2004). *Obesity myth: Why America's obsession with weight is hazardous to your health.* New York, NY: Gotham Books.

Case, K. A. (Ed.). (2013). *Deconstructing privilege: Teaching and learning as allies in the classroom.* New York, NY: Routledge. http://dx.doi.org/10.4324/9780203081877

Chastain, E. (2015). *The politics of size: Perspectives from the fat acceptance movement* (Vol. 1–2). Santa Barbara, CA: Praeger.

Chrisler, J., & Johnston-Robledo, I. (2018). *Woman's embodied self: Feminist perspectives on identity and image.* Washington, DC: American Psychological Association. http://dx.doi.org/10.1037/0000047-000

Comas-Díaz, L., & Greene, B. (Eds.). (2013). *Psychological health of women of color: Intersections, challenges, and opportunities.* Santa Barbara, CA: Praeger.

Cooper, C. (2016). *Fat activism: A radical social movement.* Bristol, England: HammerOn Press.

Crenshaw, K. (1989). Demarginalizing the intersection of race and sex: A Black feminist critique of antidiscrimination doctrine, feminist theory, and antiracist politics. *University of Chicago Legal Forum, 14,* 138–167.

Crenshaw, K. (2016, October). The urgency of intersectionality [Video file]. *TEDWomen.* Retrieved from https://www.ted.com/talks/kimberle_crenshaw_the_urgency_of_intersectionality

Dessel, A. B., Masse, J. C., & Walker, L. T. (2013). Intergroup dialogue pedagogy: Teaching about intersectional and unexamined privilege in heterosexual, Christian, and Jewish identities. In K. A. Case (Ed.), *Deconstructing privilege: Teaching and learning as allies in the classroom* (pp. 132–148). New York, NY: Routledge.

Dill, B. T., & Zambrana, R. E. (2009). *Emerging intersections: Race, class, and gender in theory, policy and practice.* New Brunswick, NJ: Rutgers University Press.

Disch, E. (Ed.). (2008). *Reconstructing gender: A multicultural anthology* (5th ed.). Boston, MA: McGraw-Hill Education.

Erickson Cornish, J. A., Schreier, B. A., Nadkarni, L. I., Henderson Metzger, L., & Rodolfa, E. R. (Eds.). (2010). *Handbook of multicultural counseling competencies.* Hoboken, NJ: Wiley.

Ernsberger, P. (2009). Does social class explain the connection between weight and health? In E. Rothblum & S. Solovay (Eds.), *The fat studies reader* (pp. 25–36). New York, NY: New York University Press.

Fawcett, M. L., & Evans, K. M. (2013). *Experiential approach for developing multicultural counseling competence.* Thousand Oaks, CA: Sage.

Fikkan, J. L., & Rothblum, E. (2012). Is fat a feminist issue? Exploring the gendered nature of weight bias. *Sex Roles, 66,* 575–592. http://dx.doi.org/10.1007/s11199-011-0022-5

Fine, M., & Gordon, S. M. (1989). Feminist transformations of/despite psychology. In M. Crawford & M. Gentry (Eds.), *Gender and thought: Psychological perspectives* (pp. 146–174). New York, NY: SpringerVerlag. http://dx.doi.org/10.1007/978-1-4612-3588-0_8

Fiske-Rusciano, R. (Ed.). (2012). *Experiencing race, class, and gender in the United States.* Boston, MA: McGraw-Hill Education.

Gay, R. (2015). *Hunger: A memoir of my body.* New York, NY: Harper.

Goodwin, B. J., & Delazar, M. E. (2000, March). *A review of psychology of women textbooks: Focus on African American women.* Paper presented at the meeting of the Association for Women in Psychology, Salt Lake City, UT.

Goodwin, B. J., McHugh, M. C., & Touster, L. O. (2003). Who is the woman in the psychology of women? In P. Bronstein & K. Quina (Eds.), *Teaching gender and multicultural awareness: Resources for the psychology classroom* (pp. 137–152). Washington, DC: American Psychological Association. http://dx.doi.org/10.1037/10570-010

Grzanka, P. R. (Ed.). (2014). *Intersectionality: A foundations and frontiers reader.* Boulder, CO: Westview Press.

Harris-Perry, M. V. (2011). *Sister citizen: Shame, stereotypes and Black women in America.* New Haven, CT: Yale University Press.

Hochschild, J. L. (1996). *Facing up to the American dream: Race, class, and the soul of the nation.* Princeton, NJ: Princeton University Press. http://dx.doi.org/10.1515/9781400821730

Holtzberg, D. (Producer), & Fishel, D. (Director). (2004). *Still doing it: The intimate lives of women over 60* [Motion picture]. United States: Films Transit International.

hooks, b. (1984). *Feminist theory: From margin to center.* Boston, MA: South End Press.

hooks, b. (1994). *Teaching to transgress: Education as the practice of freedom.* New York, NY: Routledge.

hooks, b. (2000). *Where we stand: Class matters.* New York, NY: Routledge.

hooks, b. (2003). *Teaching community: A pedagogy of hope.* New York, NY: Routledge.

Hubert, N. (Producer), & McGee, D. (Director). (1993). *Toward intimacy* [Motion picture]. Canada: National Film Board of Canada.

Hughes, M. H. (1997). Soul, Black women and food. In C. Counihan & P. Van Esterik (Eds.), *Food and culture: A reader* (pp. 272–280). New York, NY: Routledge.

Hull, G. T., Bell-Scott, P., & Smith, B. (Eds.). (1982). *All the women are White, all the Blacks are men, but some of us are brave: Black women's studies.* Old Westbury, NY: The Feminist Press.

Hyde, J. S., & Else-Quest, N. (2013). *Half the human experience: The psychology of women* (8th ed.). Belmont, CA: Wadsworth.

Jackson-Lowman, H. (Ed.). (2014). *Afrikan American women: Living at the crossroads of race, gender, class, and culture.* San Diego, CA: Cognella Academic Publishing.

Johnson, A. G. (2006). *Privilege, power, and difference* (2nd ed.). New York, NY: McGraw-Hill.

Kasardo, A. E. (2015). *Fat bias in the field of psychology: Examining diversity counseling texts and clinical judgment across college counseling centers* (Doctoral dissertation). Available from ProQuest Dissertations and Theses database. (UMI No. 3700222)

Kasardo, A. E., & McHugh, M. C. (2015). From fat shaming to size acceptance: Challenging the medical management of fat women. In M. C. McHugh & J. C. Chrisler (Eds.), *The wrong prescription for women: How medicine and media create a "need" for treatments, drugs, and surgery* (pp. 179–202). Santa Barbara, CA: Praeger.

Kelly, S., Parameswaran, G., & Schniedewind, N. (Eds.). (2011). *Women: Images and realities, a multicultural anthology* (5th ed.). Boston, MA: McGraw-Hill Education.

Kirk, G., & Okazawa-Rey, M. (Eds.). (2012). *Women's lives: Multicultural perspectives* (6th ed.). Boston, MA: McGraw-Hill Education.

Kraus, M. W., Davidai, S., & Nussbaum, D. (2015, May 1). American dream? Or mirage? *The New York Times.* Retrieved from http://www.nytimes.com/2015/05/03/opinion/sunday/american-dream-or-mirage.html?_r=1

Kulick, D., & Meneley, A. (2005). *Fat: The autobiography of an obsession.* New York, NY: Jeremy P. Tarcher/Penguin.

Matlin, M. W. (2012). *The psychology of women* (7th ed.). Belmont, CA: Wadsworth.

Matz, J., & Frankel, E. (2014). *Beyond a shadow of a diet* (2nd ed.). New York, NY: Routledge. http://dx.doi.org/10.4324/9780203083192

McHugh, M. C., & Interligi, C. (2013, August). *Aging women as represented in Psychology of Women texts.* Paper presented at the meeting of the American Psychological Association, Honolulu, HI.

McHugh, M. C., & Interligi, C. (2014). Sexuality and older women: Desire and desirability. In V. Muhlbauer, J. C. Chrisler, & F. L. Denmark (Eds.), *Women and aging: An international, intersectional power perspective* (pp. 89–116). New York, NY: Springer.

McHugh, M. C., & Kasardo, A. (2012). Anti-fat prejudice: The role of psychology in explication, education and eradication. *Sex Roles, 66,* 617–627. http://dx.doi.org/10.1007/s11199-011-0099-x

McHugh, M. C., Osachy-Touster, L., Sullivan, H., & Simone, E. (2009, March). *Fat yet invisible: Sizism in psychology of women textbooks.* Paper presented at the meeting of the Association for Women in Psychology, Newport, RI.

McIntosh, P. (2015). Extending the knapsack: Using the White privilege analysis to examine conferred advantage and disadvantage. *Women & Therapy, 38,* 232–245. http://dx.doi.org/10.1080/02703149.2015.1059195

Ming-Liu, W. (2011). *Social class and classism in the helping professions: Research, theory, and practice.* Los Angeles, CA: Sage.

O'Dell, T. (2000). *Back roads.* New York, NY: Signet.

Oliver, J. E. (2006). *Fat politics.* New York, NY: Oxford University Press.

Rios, D., & Stewart, A. J. (2013). Recognizing privilege by reducing invisibility: The global feminisms project as a pedagogical tool. In K. A. Case (Ed.), *Deconstructing privilege: Teaching and learning as allies in the classroom* (pp. 115–131). New York, NY: Routledge.

Roberts, T. (Ed.). (2004). *The Lanahan readings in the psychology of women* (2nd ed.). Baltimore, MD: Lanahan.

Romero, M., & Stewart, A. J. (1999). Introduction. In M. Romero & A. J. Stewart (Eds.), *Women's untold stories: Breaking silence, talking back, voicing complexity* (pp. ix–xxi). New York, NY: Routledge.

Rothblum, E., Smith, C., Ingraham, N., Eliason, M., & McHugh, M. C. (2015, March). *Lesbians should take the lead in removing stigma associated with weight.* Paper presented at the meeting of the Association for Women in Psychology, San Francisco, CA.

Rothblum, E., & Solovay, S. (Eds.). (2009). *The fat studies reader.* New York, NY: New York University Press.

Rubin, L. R., Fitts, M. L., & Becker, A. E. (2003). "Whatever feels good in my soul": Body ethics and aesthetics among African American and Latina women. *Culture, Medicine and Psychiatry, 27,* 49–75. http://dx.doi.org/10.1023/A:1023679821086

Saguy, A. C. (2013). *What's wrong with fat?* New York, NY: Oxford University Press. http://dx.doi.org/10.1093/acprof:oso/9780199857081.001.0001

Schoenfielder, L., & Wieser, B. (1983). *Shadow on a tightrope: Writings by women on fat oppression.* Iowa City, IA: Aunt Lute Books.

Shaw, S., & Lee, J. (Eds.). (2014). *Women's voices; feminist visions: Classic and contemporary* (6th ed.). Boston, MA: McGraw-Hill Education.

Snyder-Roche, S. (2011). Take a walk in my shoes. In M. Pope, J. S. Pangelinan, & A. D. Coker (Eds.), *Experiential activities for teaching multicultural competence in counseling* (pp. 185–188). Alexandria, VA: American Counseling Association.

Sobczak, C. (2014). *Embody: Learning to love your unique body.* Carlsbad, CA: Gurze Books.

Tillman, L. (Producer). (2011). *Off the menu: Challenging the politics and economics of body and food* [Motion picture]. United States: Cinema Serves Justice.

Tovar, V. (Ed.). (2012). *Hot & heavy: Fierce fat girls on life, love, & fashion.* Berkeley, CA: Seal Press.

United Nations Department of Economic and Social Affairs, Population Division. (2010). *Demographic profile of the older population.* Retrieved from http://www.un.org/esa/population/publications/worldageing19502050/pdf/90chapteriv.pdf

U.S. Department of Health and Human Services. (2011). *Overweight and obesity.* Retrieved from http://www.mchb.hrsa.gov/whusa11/hstat/hshi/pages/210oo.html

Watkins, P. L., Farrell, A. E., & Hugmeyer, A. D. (2012). Teaching fat studies: From conception to reception. *Fat Studies, 1,* 180–194. http://dx.doi.org/10.1080/21604851.2012.649232

Williams, M. K., McCandies, T., & Dunlap, M. R. (2002). Women of color and feminist psychology: Moving from criticism and critique to integration and application. In L. H. Collins, M. R. Dunlap, & J. C. Chrisler (Eds.), *Charting a new course for feminist psychology* (pp. 65–90). Westport, CT: Praeger.

Zadan, C. (Producer), Meron, N. (Producer), & Shankman, A. (Director). (2007). *Hairspray* [Motion picture]. United States: New Line Cinema.

5

Intersectionality in Teaching the Psychology of Men

Christopher Kilmartin

Men's studies scholars often speak of a hegemonic or dominant form of masculinity that pressures virtually all males to behave and experience the self in culturally defined ways. Yet, depending on how they are socially situated, their strategies for negotiating this pressure can be constrained or expanded, leading scholars to use the plural *masculinities*. Moreover, individual responses to masculine pressure, whether hegemonic or socially situated, are widely variable. A pedagogical strategy for teaching intersectionality first involves describing hegemonic masculinity and helping the student to understand the wide variability in the individual negotiation of gender pressure. Then students can learn how masculinity pressure interacts with other forms of identity (e.g., sexual orientation, gender identity, race, religion, military status, age, physical ability or disability, nationality, socioeconomic status, subculture). Masculinities can be applied to social psychology (e.g., conformity, prejudice, stereotyping, prejudice reduction), clinical psychology (help seeking, gendered expectations for the therapeutic process), neuroscience (sex comparisons in temperament, brain changes resulting from chronic Internet pornography use), personality (psychoanalysis, behaviorism, social learning theory, humanism or existentialism), and other subfields. To understand masculinities in all their complexities, it is also essential to introduce students to other areas of scholarship, such as history, sociology, economics, and biology.

My Psychology of Men course has evolved over 25 years of teaching. My approach is found in a special issue of *Psychology of Men and Masculinity* (Kilmartin, Addis, Mahalik, & O'Neil, 2013; Mahalik, Addis, Kilmartin, & O'Neil, 2013),

http://dx.doi.org/10.1037/0000137-006
*Integrating Multiculturalism and Intersectionality Into the Psychology Curriculum:
Strategies for Instructors*, J. A. Mena and K. Quina (Editors)

along with those of other psychologists with similar levels of experience. The strategies that follow can be incorporated in other psychology courses when addressing topics of gender, sexuality, or stereotyping or issues such as nature–nurture.[1]

PEDAGOGICAL ISSUES

When students enter a course such as Introductory Chemistry, they are well aware that they know little about chemistry. Courses about gender are different—students have grown up in a gendered world, so an ongoing point of intersection is between the scholarly material in the class and their personal experiences. They explore this connection through a simple and yet remarkably effective assignment that I call the "wide open journal." Three times during the semester, they turn in five journal entries (writing an average of about one entry per week) describing gendered incidents they have observed in their everyday lives (e.g., a conversation, movie or television program, something they read, behavior they observed, any other experience in which they notice gender playing out in their worlds). Entries range from relatively insignificant matters such as the fitness center as a gendered space or a moment they observed on television to more profound matters such as catcalling or even sexual assault. As the semester progresses, students see that gender is ubiquitous and become critical of gender arrangements at every turn. I believe, and some of my students' reports bear out, that this lesson changes them forever.

Introducing the Topic

The first lesson is to define *gender*, which I conceptualize as the social pressure to behave and experience the self in ways that the culture deems as appropriate for the body one is perceived as having. It is critical that students locate gender in the culture rather than within every individual. Many believe in the "Mars and Venus" fictions that men are all alike, women are all alike, and all men are different from all women, a set of beliefs not supported by the body of research (Hyde, 2005). I teach this lesson with a frequently used exercise from Paul Kivel (1992). The instructor draws a large box on the board and writes the words "act like a man" on top. The word *act* is critical to underscore that masculinity is largely a performance and so may not reflect the essence of the person displaying the behavior.

Students have no difficulty filling in the box with stereotypical behaviors, preferences, and characteristics associated with men; the descriptions that emerge have themes of aggression, heterosexual promiscuity, dietary and drink

---

[1]The companion website for this book (http://pubs.apa.org/books/supp/mena) features a sample syllabus for a psychology of men course, a PowerPoint presentation that includes topics discussed in this chapter that instructors can use in their lectures, and a list of recommended resources.

preferences, love of sports, the protector role, and an interest in masculine possessions and work. The next question is, "When men and boys step outside the set of descriptors in the box and other people (including women and girls) want them to conform, what names are they called?" Again, the answers are predictable: pussy, bitch, fag, sissy, and so forth—virtually all of which refer to women or gay men. Thus, the social construction of masculinity is as antifemininity and homophobia, both of which are used to police the limits of culturally acceptable masculinity. If a boy or man behaves in a way perceived as feminine, shaming by others pressures him to return to masculine conformity; his behavior is influenced by negative reinforcement (i.e., escape conditioning).

The next question is, "What kinds of things are outside the box?" The answers are again apparent: love of children, crying, displaying vulnerable feelings, doing "women's work," and so forth. Asking "In what situations are these behaviors or characteristics healthy and adaptive?" leads them to understand that one has to break masculine conformity to be a good partner, father, or friend or deal with vulnerable emotions. Men conforming to gendered pressure is incompatible with important life goals or values and gender pressure can cause harm.

Once we have explicit definitions of hegemonic masculinity, we are ready to complicate the issue by looking at similarities and differences across cultures and historic eras. Two classic works still constitute important readings and points for discussion. Gerda Lerner's (1986) history, *The Creation of Patriarchy*, locates male dominance in the shift in division of labor from foraging to agricultural economies. Devlin's (2015) research supports Lerner's theory that foraging societies are more gender egalitarian than is generally believed. It is useful to extend the discussion to modern postindustrial societies where there is increasingly a non-division of labor (Kilmartin & Smiler, 2015). There is ample evidence that gender slowly becomes less of a central feature of public and private life as the basis of the economy transforms. After all, this system evolved over thousands of years, and so it will not devolve overnight.

In David Gilmore's (1990) cross-cultural *Manhood in the Making*, the author notes that there is a kind of family resemblance to masculinity in most parts of the world, with significant variations. For example, Tahiti and Semai cultures draw little distinction between the social roles of men and women and are marked by a lack of competition over scarce resources and no history of warfare; thus, there is no necessity to socialize men into aggression, protectiveness, and acquisitiveness.

In discussions of these two readings, I raise the possibility that, far from being biologically hardwired, masculinity is a product of economics, ideologies, and social needs, all of which can change, and the family resemblance of masculinities may reflect cultural redundancies. If masculinities are "natural" in some sense, Gilmore's two exceptional cultures must be doing something to dissuade men and boys from it. If, however, there is nothing natural about gender, the more stereotypical societies must be socializing males into hegemonic masculinities. Gilmore's title reflects the possibility that boys have to be made into men rather than merely growing into their adult roles.

Once students can understand these historical, cross-cultural, and economic interactions, they can accept that gender roles have processes of both continuity and change and understand how structural inequalities persist—and how they break down. For example, the 114th U.S. Congress, which began its work in 2015, was 80% White, 80% male, and 92% Christian and yet was the most diverse Congress in the history of the country (Bump, 2015). Students can easily retrieve examples of how gender has changed even in their short lifetimes.

Masculinities and Other Identities

Kilmartin and Smiler's (2015) textbook, *The Masculine Self*, attends to issues such as the limitations of the gender binary and essentialist perspectives. Two chapters focus on variations that ensue when gender, particularly hegemonic masculinity, intersects with other statuses, including culture, socioeconomic status, race, age, ethnicity, and sexual orientation. Other useful works are *The Matrix Reader* (Ferber, Jimenez, O'Reilly Herrera, & Samuels, 2009), *Building a Better Man* (Seymour, Smith, & Torres, 2014), *The Psychology of Men and Masculinities* (Levant & Wong, 2017), and *APA Handbook of Men and Masculinities* (Wong & Wester, 2016).

Again, it is critical that students locate these masculinities in the society and subgroup rather than within the individual, lest the instructor unintentionally reinforce the out-group homogeneity effect and stereotyping, especially by majority students. For example, racial minority and poor men may subscribe to hegemonic ideologies, yet they also face strong social-structural barriers to achieving masculine success such as economic power and social status. Aging men are faced with the inevitable decline in their bodies and work roles; those who do not adjust are at risk for a variety of negative outcomes, the most serious of which is an elevated suicide risk (Kilmartin & Smiler, 2015). Men of all minority statuses experience frequent microaggressions that undermine their dignity, comfort, and sense of safety.

Psychology of Men and Mainstream Psychology

After we have described masculinities, summarized the research on sex comparisons, and learned the leading models for conceptualizing gender (gender identity, androgyny, and gender role strain), we look at the dominant personality theories and apply them to men and masculinity.

An obvious jumping-off place is the biologically based theories, beginning with basic explanations of sexual variations in chromosomes and hormones along with abnormalities of sexual development (Kilmartin & Smiler, 2015). I present two theories that are grounded in biologically based assumptions, evolutionary psychology and psychoanalysis, providing the basic tenets as well as scholarly critiques (e.g., evolutionary psychologists often use circular logic, psychoanalytic theory is largely untestable; see Kilmartin & Smiler, 2015).

Next, gender analyses are applied to the major socially based psychological theories: behaviorism (Skinner, 1974), social cognitive theory (Bem, 1993; Thorne, 2009), social role theory (Eagly, 1987), and humanistic–existential theory (Rogers, 1961/2004); again, each is accompanied by scholarly critique. For example, the behaviorist perspective, which emphasizes responsiveness to environments, fails to account for the important dimension of cognitive appraisal of those environments. Social cognitive theories, which are largely focused on social scripts acquired in childhood, fail to explain how children exposed to similar experiences may form very different social scripts. Social role theories do not account for within-sex variability nor explain the roots of the average differences between the sexes. And humanistic–existential theory does not address the various factors in behavior that are well-demonstrated by the other theories, such as reinforcement/punishment, social cognition, and sexual motivations (Kilmartin & Smiler, 2015). In class, students discuss applications of the basic tenets of each theory to the psychology of men.

Privilege and Prejudice

With this solid theoretical grounding, we address intersections between gender and the social justice issues of privilege and prejudice, from systemic rather than individualistic perspectives. Lerner (1986) provided a good start: The author, a social historian, makes it clear that privilege has never applied to all members of a high-status group in equal measure, nor has disadvantage applied to all members of an oppressed group in equal measure. I have found that introducing this idea early in the course can be too challenging for some students because mainstream U.S. culture is highly individualistic. Some students, especially those from privileged backgrounds and those who subscribe to the myth of meritocracy, will disengage when faced with the realities of their unearned advantages and respond with resistance in the form of red herring arguments (e.g., "racism and sexism are over because Oprah is a billionaire"). See Chapter 2, this volume, for strategies for working with student resistance.

Teaching about privilege often brings up resistance and feelings of guilt or shame. Helpful readings include Allan Johnson (2001) and Peggy McIntosh (2009). The Walk of Privilege (Young, 2006) is a powerful exercise. Students come to a large space and are directed to take steps backward or forward in response to statements about their backgrounds, whether disadvantaged (e.g., "if your ancestors came to this country not by choice," "if you did anything in the past week to reduce your risk of sexual violence," "if you ever had to move because your family could not afford to pay the mortgage or rent") or advantaged (e.g., "at least one of your parents has a college degree," "if you attended private school or summer camp," "if you can walk down the street holding hands with your partner without fear," "if people of your race and sex are in the majority of power positions in business and government"). As students begin to separate based on their backgrounds, those in front cannot know how much others are disadvantaged and how much they are privileged unless they turn around and look, demonstrating the important point that privilege tends to remain invisible to those who have it. When the stimulus statements focus on gender, White males are generally in front compared with White females and people of color, demonstrating that although some individual White males may not have high levels of privilege, they do as a group.

It is essential that students understand that being privileged is not the same as feeling privileged and that privilege does not always translate into personal fulfillment. In Brown's (2013) modification of this exercise, participants begin in a large circle and take steps forward for disadvantages and backward for advantages. This variation allows the relatively privileged to view levels of disadvantage and to understand the differences between "frontline" work often done by oppressed groups and "ally" work done by those with greater resources.

These privilege exercises create an outstanding opportunity to explore the intersections of gender, class, sexual orientation, race, ethnicity, cisgendering, and in fact, any divisions among groups. Following the exercise, the instructor engages the class in reflective discussion. For example, calling attention to microaggressions against transgendered people can take the form of statements about discomfort in using public restrooms or being asked intrusive questions by strangers. Kim Case (2013) provided an excellent guide for teaching this difficult topic.

In an individualistic culture, many people from dominant groups think of prejudice as a consciously held attitude. This conceptualization allows people to ignore systemic inequalities and feel like they are doing their part by merely being fair minded. It is critical that students understand that, more than being mere antipathy toward a group, prejudice is a set of practices, some unintentional, that result in an inequality of outcome. Recognizing gender is "in the air" as a social pressure, students can also begin to grasp prejudice as a psychological environment grounded in social practices that result in a lower likelihood that people of certain groups will be able to access the resources necessary to attain similar qualities of life than members of dominant groups. Systemic advantages for some groups are always accompanied by systemic disadvantages for other groups, even though many individuals from privileged groups suffer and many from oppressed groups thrive.

Social Issues

A good examination of the intersections between racism, economic inequality, and gender can be found in the U.S. system of prisons and jails. Although men occupy a large majority of positions of power in government and business, they are also more than 85% of incarcerated persons, comprising a population of more than 2 million prisoners (The Sentencing Project, 2014). Men of color and poor men are a disproportionate majority of this group; they are disadvantaged in every step of the legal process: more likely to be surveilled, stopped, and searched and less likely to be offered alternatives to incarceration or to access competent legal representation. The inequalities are so egregious that Michelle Alexander (2012) described the prison system as "the new Jim Crow."

Much has been made of the so-called boy crisis in schools: Boys as a group get lower grades than girls as a group, are more likely to drop out of school, and are a shrinking minority of the college population. These problems have led some to suggest that schools are prejudiced against boys and that boys would benefit from single-sex education geared toward males' "natural" tendencies (Sax, 2009). This argument assumes that boys are all alike, one that is not borne out by available data (Hyde, 2005), and that we should not ask boys to develop the skills necessary to do well in school. Rather, we should adapt the schools to them, an argument less likely to be advanced in reaction to girls' problems. As Lise Eliot (2009) pointed out, girls and boys can learn from one another; girls can learn activation from boys, boys can learn self-control from girls. Moreover, the more boys and girls are engaging in the same behaviors, the more similar their brains are. Thus, for example, requiring boys to work hard to make up for their average disadvantage in language skills can only be a good thing for them, just as it is for anyone who struggles with any skill compared with their classmates.

The difference in the higher education populations is largely misunderstood as a product of boys not attending college, when in fact boys' college attendance is on the increase for every racial and economic group except for upper income White males, where it is holding steady. The gap between males and females in college attendance is a result of males' increases not being as steep as those of females; and again, the racial divide is significant. Upper income White males are actually a small majority of the college population in their group; poor men and men of color are not as likely to attend college as their female counterparts (Kilmartin & Smiler, 2015).

Sexism against women is a unique form of prejudice. Although it is easy for students to see overt hostility toward women and issues such as unequal pay as social justice issues, it is much more difficult for them to understand benevolent sexism (somewhat synonymous with chivalry) as a form of prejudice. As Peter Glick (2005) pointed out, "if you hate people of a certain race or ethnicity, you don't hang out with them on the weekends." But if you are a heterosexual male sexist, you probably are married to a woman and may have daughters. Benevolent sexism allows sexist men to make cognitive distinctions between the kinds of women who are praiseworthy and those who are deserving of scorn. Glick and Fiske (2001) provided an excellent description of the hostile–benevolent sexism system and supported their assertions with a large international sample. Rudman and Glick (2008) extended this discussion into a variety of social psychology topics including sexual harassment in the workplace, which is disproportionately directed toward women who challenge men's dominance.

Teaching about chivalry is difficult because people are often emotionally attached to it. For example, many men enjoy the feeling of gallantry and helpfulness that boosts their self-esteem, and many women enjoy the feeling that comes with being treated as special, even if many chivalric behaviors are little more than "trivial niceties" like being given a plaque for one's work but not a raise. Glick and Fiske (2001) have done a number of studies on hostile, benevolent, and ambivalent sexism. *Benevolent sexism* encourages people to see women as praiseworthy yet incompetent. In laboratory studies in which participants are led to believe that the person with whom they are interacting online is male or female, men report that they like women more than men but also assign fewer leadership roles and other resources to those perceived as women (see http://faculty.lawrence.edu/glickp/, "Benevolent Sexism").

I have developed several helpful discussion techniques for teaching this difficult topic: One is to ask women whether they are willing to give up chivalry. Some are, but others say, "No, it feels too good"—whereupon I invite them to reflect on other things that, although they may feel good, may not be beneficial to them in the long run. They have no trouble generating a lengthy list. I also ask them to think of a time when they have refused or disapproved of a chivalric act from a man. Generally, they report, he becomes angry, which illustrates that benevolent sexism is bestowed on women who cooperate with men's dominance, and hostile sexism is reserved for those who do not, as shown in Rudman and Glick's (2008) sexual harassment studies. I also invite students to explore the levels of vitriol directed toward feminist bloggers, which include threats of rape and murder (Romano, 2013).

To illustrate the difference between trivial and substantive helpfulness, I use the following example: Suppose you are a woman walking toward a door. A man who is three steps behind you rushes up to three steps ahead of you, gallantly opens the door and smiles. Let us say you do not like this (some would, of course), and you react by giving him a "dirty look." How is he likely to respond? Either he will become angry (you did not cooperate with the benevolence, so you get the hostility), or he will say something like, "I'm only trying to help." My suggestion is that you then say, "I'm glad you're trying to help. Can you help with some pay equity, some child care, and some gender-based violence prevention?"

I also go back to Sandra Bem's (1993) gender schema theory and ask what alternative schema can be taught. We live in a society in which gender is often an organizing principle across many domains of experience; adults teach children gender schema before they are aware that other schemas are possible. As sophisticated pattern-seeking organisms, children learn gender schema when they are repeatedly exposed to gender-polarizing social practices, such as professions that are dominated by one sex or the other, media representations, and divisions of household labor. In the area of benevolence, conceptions of "what men do for women" can be replaced by "what helpful and courteous people do for others in need." I ask traditional-aged, able-bodied college women, "Should I, a middle-aged man, get up on a crowded bus to give my seat to one of you young, fit women?" and "Should you get up on a crowded bus to give your seat to a father with a baby in his arms?" They learn how to separate concepts of helpfulness and civility from the realm of gender.

Psychology of Men Themes

Intersections between gendered social and cultural expectations and areas often described as "men's issues" have a wide-ranging impact and provide ripe areas for discussion. In addition, students can monitor media and raise contemporary gendered social issues as they crop up, such as men's social movements, pornography, prostitution, and the so-called boy crisis in schools. The following are resources for some of these lessons.

Emotions

From birth to around age 40 months, boys show, on average, more signs of emotional responsiveness than girls (Brody & Hall, 2010). That small difference goes the other direction with the rapid language acquisition that takes place at that point in development when adults begin to focus girls on their feelings and boys on their actions. But it is important to return to the point that the lack of emotional expression one may see in some males has a strong element of performance.

Work and Family Roles

Discussions of work and family are essential because gender is largely based on social practices in this area. The U.S. 1950s model of the single male wage earner and single female homemaker was not tenable for many families even in that era and cannot be sustained by most today (Coontz, 2016). Moreover, children are not the economic resource they were in agricultural societies, and many families have access to contraception. Therefore, family practices are changing in the direction of smaller families, dual incomes, and shared domestic work. Still, many heterosexual college men believe that they can negotiate the worlds of work and family using their fathers' and grandfathers' formulas, and it is useful to help them understand that modern economies are unlikely to support them in doing so.

Changing Definitions of the Family

Perhaps the strongest example of this change is the breakneck speed of the acceptance of same-sex marriage in many places in the world. Far from being merely a case of allowing these couples to acknowledge their connection, there are a number of tangible resources (e.g., access to health insurance and inheritance) that ensue from state-sanctioned marriage (Strasser, 2007).

Physical Health

Males' lifespans are significantly shorter than those of females. Although some of this "mortality gap" is rooted in biology, most is attributable to behavioral differences in risk taking and health maintenance (Kilmartin & Smiler, 2015). The gap between the average life expectancy of White (76.3 years) and Black males (71.8 years) in 2015 is a striking example of the intersection of race and gender (National Center for Health Statistics, 2017).

Mental Health

Males commit suicide 4 times more often than females, providing a segue into the intersection of physical and mental health. Males are less likely to ask for help, and there are a number of mental health issues that have a significant gender divide, with more women diagnosed as having depression and anxiety disorders and more men abusing substances (Lynch & Kilmartin, 2013).

One could argue that physical violence is the most important behavioral sex difference, with males committing nearly 90% of it, even though the large majority of males are not violent. In my course, we spend a good deal of time on this topic, unpacking the biological and behavioral research. There are several good films available, including *Tough Guise 2* (Ericsson, Talreja, & Jhally, 2013) about male violence and media and *The Invisible War* (Barklow, Ziering, & Dick, 2012) about sexual assault in the U.S. military.

CONCLUSION

In conclusion, Psychology of Men has the potential to be a rich landscape for exploration into a wide variety of social issues and has a direct bearing on how students deal with the challenges of their lives. I believe that sending students out into a changing world without gender education is like sending them out without computer skills; an understanding of the gendered bases of society will only become more important as students negotiate a changing world.

REFERENCES

Alexander, M. (2012). *The new Jim Crow: Mass incarceration in the age of color blindness.* New York, NY: New Press.

Barklow, T. K. (Producer), Ziering, A. (Producer), & Dick, K. (Director). (2012). *The invisible war* [Motion picture]. United States: Chain Camera Pictures.

Bem, S. L. (1993). *The lenses of gender: Transforming the debate on sexual inequality.* New Haven, CT: Yale University Press.

Brody, L. R., & Hall, J. A. (2010). Gender and emotion in context. In M. Lewis, J. M. Haviland, & L. F. Barrett (Eds.), *Handbook of emotions* (3rd ed., pp. 395–408). New York, NY: Guilford Press.

Brown, A. M. (2013, August 17). Take the privilege walk. *The Indypendent.* Retrieved from https://indypendent.org/2013/08/17/take-privilege-walk

Bump, P. (2015, January 5). The new Congress is 80 percent White, 80 percent male, and 92 percent Christian. *The Washington Post.* Retrieved from http://www.washingtonpost.com/blogs/the-fix/wp/2015/01/05/the-new-congress-is-80-percent-white-80-percent-male-and-92-percent-christian/

Case, K. A. (2013). *Deconstructing privilege: Teaching and learning as allies in the classroom.* New York, NY: Routledge. http://dx.doi.org/10.4324/9780203081877

Coontz, S. (2016). *The way we really are: Coming to terms with America's changing families* (rev. ed.). New York, NY: Basic Books.

Devlin, H. (2015, May 14). Early men and women were equal, say scientists. *The Guardian.* Retrieved from http://www.theguardian.com/science/2015/may/14/early-men-women-equal-scientists?CMP=fb_gu

Eagly, A. H. (1987). *Sex differences in social behavior: A social-role interpretation.* Hillsdale, NJ: Erlbaum.

Eliot, L. (2009). *Pink brain, blue brain: How small differences grow into troublesome gaps—and what we can do about it.* Boston, MA: Houghton Mifflin Harcourt.

Ericsson, S. (Producer), Talreja, S. (Producer), & Jhally, S. (Director). (2013). *Tough guise 2: Violence, manhood, and American culture* [Motion picture]. United States: Media Education Foundation.

Ferber, A., Jimenez, C. M., O'Reilly Herrera, A., & Samuels, D. R. (2009). *The matrix reader: Examining the dynamics of oppression and privilege*. Boston, MA: McGraw-Hill.

Gilmore, D. D. (1990). *Manhood in the making: Cultural concepts of masculinity*. New Haven, CT: Yale University Press.

Glick, P. (2005, August). *Ambivalent gender ideologies and perceptions of the legitimacy and stability of gender hierarchy*. Paper presented at the meeting of the American Psychological Association, Washington, DC.

Glick, P., & Fiske, S. T. (2001). An ambivalent alliance: Hostile and benevolent sexism as complementary justifications for gender inequality. *American Psychologist, 56,* 109–118. http://dx.doi.org/10.1037/0003-066X.56.2.109

Hyde, J. S. (2005). The gender similarities hypothesis. *American Psychologist, 60,* 581–592. http://dx.doi.org/10.1037/0003-066X.60.6.581

Johnson, A. G. (2001). *Privilege, power, and difference*. Mountain View, CA: Mayfield.

Kilmartin, C., Addis, M., Mahalik, J. R., & O'Neil, J. M. (2013). Four experienced professors describe their courses. *Psychology of Men & Masculinity, 14,* 240–247. http://dx.doi.org/10.1037/a0033254

Kilmartin, C. T., & Smiler, A. P. (2015). *The masculine self* (5th ed.). Cornwall-on-Hudson, NY: Sloan.

Kivel, P. (1992). *Men's work: How to stop the violence that tears our lives apart*. Center City, MN: Hazleden.

Lerner, G. (1986). *The creation of patriarchy*. New York, NY: Oxford University Press.

Levant, R. F., & Wong, Y. J. (Eds.). (2017). *The psychology of men and masculinities*. Washington, DC: American Psychological Association. http://dx.doi.org/10.1037/0000023-000

Lynch, J., & Kilmartin, C. T. (2013). *Overcoming masculine depression: The pain behind the mask* (2nd ed.). New York, NY: Routledge/Taylor & Francis.

Mahalik, J. R., Addis, M., Kilmartin, C., & O'Neil, J. M. (2013). Complexities and challenges when teaching the psychology of men: Four experienced professors discuss their pedagogical processes. *Psychology of Men & Masculinity, 14,* 248–255. http://dx.doi.org/10.1037/a0033257

McIntosh, P. (2009). White privilege: Unpacking the invisible knapsack. In V. Taylor, N. Whittier, & L. J. Rupp (Eds.), *Feminist frontiers* (8th ed., pp. 120–126). Boston, MA: McGraw-Hill.

National Center for Health Statistics. (2017). *Health, United States, 2016: With chartbook on long-term trends in health*. Hyattsville, MD: National Center for Health Statistics.

Rogers, C. (2004). *On becoming a person*. London, England: Constable. (Original work published 1961)

Romano, A. (2013, April 17). Feminist blogger in hiding after men's rights death threats. *The Daily Dot*. Retrieved from http://www.dailydot.com/news/feminist-blogger-in-hiding-mra-death-threats/

Rudman, L. A., & Glick, P. (2008). *The social psychology of gender: How power and intimacy shape gender relations*. New York, NY: Guilford Press.

Sax, L. (2009). *Boys adrift: The five factors driving the growing epidemic of unmotivated boys and underachieving young men*. New York, NY: Basic Books.

The Sentencing Project. (2014). *Incarceration*. Retrieved from sentencingproject.org/template/page.cfm?id=107

Seymour, W., Smith, R., & Torres, H. (2014). *Building a better man: A blueprint for decreasing violence and increasing prosocial behavior in men*. New York, NY: Routledge/Taylor & Francis. http://dx.doi.org/10.4324/9781315886152

Skinner, B. F. (1974). *About behaviorism*. New York, NY: Alfred A. Knopf.

Strasser, M. (Ed.). (2007). *Defending same-sex marriage: "Separate but equal" no more: A guide to the legal status of same-sex marriage, civil unions, and other partnerships*. Westport, CT: Praeger.

74   *Christopher Kilmartin*

Thorne, B. (2009). Girls and boys together . . . but mostly apart: Gender arrangements
in elementary schools. In V. Taylor, N. Whittier, & L. J. Rupp (Eds.), *Feminist frontiers*
(8th ed., pp. 176–186). Boston, MA: McGraw-Hill.
Wong, Y. J., & Wester, S. R. (Eds.). (2016). *APA handbook of men and masculinities.*
Washington, DC: American Psychological Association. http://dx.doi.org/10.1037/
14594-000
Young, T. J. (2006). *The privilege walk workshop: Learning about privilege in today's society.*
Retrieved from https://edge.psu.edu/workshops/mc/power/privilegewalk.shtml

6

Integrating Lesbian, Gay, Bisexual, Transgender, and Queer Issues in the Psychology Curriculum

Jacqueline S. Weinstock

In recent years, a subdiscipline of psychology has developed that is

> affirmative of [LGBTQ] people, seeks to challenge prejudice and discrimination against LGBTQ people and the privileging of heterosexuals in psychology and in the broader society. . . . [and provide] a range of psychological perspectives on the lives and experiences of LGBTQ people and on LGBTQ sexualities and genders. (Clarke, Ellis, Peel, & Riggs, 2010, p. 6)

Yet, attention to lesbian, gay, bisexual, transgender, and queer (LGBTQ) psychology in undergraduate programs is still limited. In this chapter, I offer content and strategies for integrating LGBTQ issues into various courses and teaching LGBTQ-focused psychology courses, as well as department-level changes toward an inclusive culture that challenges heterosexism and cisgenderism. I use *transgender* as an umbrella term referring to the diversity of gender identities and expressions that do not fit easily into the prevailing sex/gender binary. *Heterosexism* and *cisgenderism* refer, respectively, to systems of oppression that privilege heterosexual and cisgender identities and expressions and denigrate all other identities and expressions. I intentionally use *they* and similar pronouns to avoid, as well as challenge, the binary gender model.

http://dx.doi.org/10.1037/0000137-007
Integrating Multiculturalism and Intersectionality Into the Psychology Curriculum: Strategies for Instructors, J. A. Mena and K. Quina (Editors)

INCORPORATING LGBTQ ISSUES INTO TRADITIONAL PSYCHOLOGY COURSES

An intersectional perspective provides guidelines for incorporating diverse LGBTQ issues into traditional psychology courses. Two simple strategies are to use inclusive language and LGBTQ-focused studies and examples to illustrate concepts in any course. For example, Evelyn Hooker's (1957) classic "normalization" research study comparing the mental health of White gay and heterosexual men living in a middle-class community setting could teach students much about the scientific method: (a) sampling and appropriate comparison groups (the progress evidenced by the use of a community sample of gay men and the limitation of using a select community sample that ignores intersectional identities); (b) the importance of testing, not just accepting, prevailing beliefs; and (c) the influences of the sociopolitical context on psychological research. Hooker's research demonstrated ways in which LGBTQ people are like heterosexual and cisgender people. At the same time, this emphasis on similarities ignored the impact of oppression on mental health (Clarke et al., 2010; Herek, 1997–2014). The film *Changing Our Minds: The Story of Dr. Evelyn Hooker* (Haugland & Schmiechen, 1992) is a helpful way to enlighten students on these points and the woman behind the work.

The impact of changing views of homosexuality on the mental health of LGBTQ individuals is important for courses in abnormal and clinical psychology and the history of psychology (see Group for the Advancement of Psychiatry: http://www.aglp.org/gap/1_history/; Herek, 1997–2014, 2010). Drescher (2010) and Lev (2005, 2013) critically analyzed the history and politics of homosexuality and gender identity related diagnoses. Teaching this history provides an opportunity for students to explore the interplay between science, religion, and politics and the social construction of disease and health. Students can examine how sexuality, sex, and gender came to be, and continue to be, confounded within psychology, such that gender-variant expressions of self (e.g., interests, dress, personality) are treated as indicative of homosexuality ("inversion theory"; see Bullough, 1979; Meyerowitz, 2002), popularized through the concept of "gaydar" and the related myth that "you can tell who's gay just by looking" (Bronski, Pellegrini, & Amico, 2013). Kite and Deaux's (1987) experimental study of the prevalence of this myth among college students can promote a discussion about whether it remains a common belief and how it may lead individuals, across sexual orientations and gender identities and expressions, to limit their gender expressions.

Murphy (2003) provided an overview of behavioral, psychodynamic, hormonal and drug therapies, and surgical procedures used to try to "redirect sexual orientation" (p. 285). My students have been particularly intrigued by the behavioral prescriptions to exercise, have sex with prostitutes, or marry a good woman or man and by overt and covert sensitization therapies designed to link repulsivity and same-sex sexual desire (Murphy, 2003, p. 286). It is also a great resource for debates regarding reparative and conversion therapies for LGBTQ individuals. Although now recognized by most mental health and medical professional organizations as ineffective as well as harmful and unethical, some continue to argue that a client should be able to develop with a therapist an agreement "to work together to reduce his unwanted attractions and explore his heterosexual potential" (Nicolosi, 2009, para. 5). Throckmorton and Yarhouse (2006) offered an alternative but still problematic "sexual identity therapy." Effective counterarguments are available from the American Psychological Association (APA; 2015), the National Center for Lesbian Rights (2018), and individual state cases banning these therapies with minors (e.g., Bellware, 2015). Biopsychology courses can draw on these resources to examine questions of immutability–flexibility and essentialism–constructionism.

Health psychology should include the impact of anti-LGBTQ treatment in health care and the impact of living in communities where anti-LGBTQ political initiatives succeed. The Institute of Medicine of the National Academies (2011) report identified top priorities for LGBTQ health and research and four perspectives that should guide practice and research: minority stress, life course models, intersectionality, and social ecology. The HIV/AIDS epidemic and the community response may be demonstrated through the documentary *We Were Here* (Weissman & Weber, 2011) and *How to Survive a Plague* (Gertner & France, 2012). Meyer's (2003) work on minority stress, Russell's (2000) *Voted Out: The Psychological Consequences of Anti-Gay Politics*, and McDonald's (1995) documentary, *Ballot 9 Measure*, showcase the consequences of anti-gay amendments. Discussions should be balanced by a focus on strengths and assets in the individual and community responses to these challenges.

In social psychology, LGBTQ issues are relevant to prejudice and bias, microaggressions and hate crimes, the social change process, and interpersonal and intergroup relationships. Herek (1997–2014) summarized the social psychological research on *sexual prejudice*, his term for negative attitudes based on sexual orientation (Herek & McLemore, 2013). Herek and Capitanio's (1995, 1996) research examined heterosexuals' attitudes toward lesbians and gay men and the interpersonal contact theory, and Nadal (2013; see also Nigatu, 2014) and Sue (2010) examined sexual orientation– and gender-related microaggressions. Microaggressions and LGBTQ-focused oppression might be introduced by asking students to respond to questions from Rochlin's (2007) "Heterosexuality Questionnaire" or identify examples of heterosexual and cisgender privilege (see Queers United, 2008; Skolnick & Anonymous, 2009; Taylor, 2010).

In developmental psychology, outcomes for children raised in same-sex parented families can be studied to examine family structure related questions such as whether children need or do best with both a mother and a father. Research by Gartrell, Bos, and Koh (2018), Biblarz and Stacey (2010), and Patterson (2013) is helpful. Students can discuss autobiographies or films of LGBTQ people growing up in different historical and cultural contexts and with various intersectional identities (e.g., *Brother Outsider: The Life and Times of Bayard Rustin*, by Kates & Singer, 2002). Discussions should incorporate both the diversity of LGBTQ identities and experiences and the diversity of developmental trajectories, informed by Bronfenbrenner's (1977) ecological model of development (also see APA, 2017). Also recommended are Rotheram-Borus and Langabeer (2001), Lev (2004), and Fredriksen-Goldsen et al. (2011) and segments from the documentaries *Transgeneration* (Smothers & Simmons, 2005) and *Gen Silent* (Maddux, 2010).

For the psychology of women or gender, Green (2004), Mock (2014), and Serano (2007) explore trans women's and men's experiences, expanding students' thinking about sexism. Discussions of the social construction of heteronormativity and the gender binary may be introduced using Blaise (2005) and the documentary *It's Elementary* (Cohen & Chasnoff, 1997).

TEACHING AN LGBTQ-FOCUSED COURSE

Faculty teaching specific LGBTQ-focused courses[1] face many challenges, especially if they are LGBTQ. For example, Sexual Orientation and Gender Identity (SOGI) majority students with generally accepting attitudes may be concerned they will say something hurtful, whereas those with more negative attitudes may fear being silenced or belittled. Asking LGBTQ students to listen to these attitudes may be experienced as microaggressions. The instructor must teach from a position that is academically rigorous and pedagogically sound, appropriate across the range of student identities and personal needs, and LGBTQ affirmative while respectfully addressing alternative perspectives.

Following the antiracism work of Tatum (1992) and Derman-Sparks and Phillips (1997), I developed the following approach to guide students through three common developmental stages of awareness of the systemic privilege and oppression: (a) limited awareness and belief in a just society, (b) engagement with examinations of internalization of privilege and oppression, and (c) expanding knowledge and skills for social justice work.

Part 1: Constructing an Accountable Learning Community

My main aim for the first few classes is for students to agree to bring only good intentions for their own and each other's development and, as Jos Truitt (2009) explained, to take responsibility for themselves and their words, accept that they will make mistakes, and stay open to being challenged. I have students specify their preferred names and pronouns on name tags and then state these and something else they want to share with the class, thus conveying expectations that we will all use each student's self-identifiers. Next, students gather in small groups to discuss their incoming understanding of key terms. Coming back together, we process the activity in a way that makes it clear

---

[1]Two sample syllabi are available for download from this book's companion website (http://pubs.apa.org/books/supp/mena). One is for an introduction to sexual and gender identities course, and the other is for an advanced seminar on sexual and gender identities.

how wide-ranging students' incoming knowledge and comfort levels are as well as how complicated and in flux terms and definitions are in this field. In other activities, students read and discuss in small groups a brief, yet controversial, article (e.g., free speech vs. hate speech). I instruct groups to either use what Peter Elbow (2008) called the Believing Game (working to understand a given position and why an author holds it) or the Doubting Game (challenging an author's position).[2] When we come together for general discussion, and when students learn the rules for the game they did not play, we discuss the importance of both lenses while acknowledging the intellectual and personal challenges of trying to take the perspective of someone whose ideas are antithetical to one's own. This discussion is typically followed by an examination of the concept and impact of microaggressions, using such readings as Nigatu (2014), Rivera (2010), and Sue (2010, 2011). I also introduce students to common counterproductive behaviors (Charles, 2015). A required private (between student and instructor) weekly reflection journal provides a context for sharing questions and concerns and accessing support when needed. The first journal assignment is the most involved because it asks students to reflect on their background; their personal, professional, and educational goals; their incoming knowledge about sexual and gender minorities; and their sexual and gender identities.[3]

The second aim is to introduce the identities, experiences, and forms of oppression (heterosexism and cisgenderism) most commonly experienced by those who are, or are perceived to be, LGBTQ. Along with academic readings, I incorporate activist reflections and personal stories (e.g., from Bronski et al., 2013, and Ferber, Holcomb, & Wentling, 2016) selected to raise awareness of LGBTQ identities, including how other aspects of LGBTQ people's identities affect their experiences. As students tend to be most interested in and most misinformed about bisexual and trans identities, I recommend selections from, respectively, Diamond (2008), Ochs and Rowley (2009), and Rodriguez Rust (2000); and Bornstein and Bergman (2010), Beemyn and Rankin (2011), Boylan (2003), Green (2004), Mock (2014), and Serano (2007). Erickson-Schroth's (2014) *Trans Bodies, Trans Selves: A Resource for the Transgender Community* may also be assigned.

I explore the diversity of meanings and terms used by individuals to describe same-sex sexuality; sexual identity, orientation, attraction and desire, and behavior; attitudes toward and experiences of sexual fluidity in lesbians and gay men; sexual attraction and its relationship to gender expression among lesbians and gay men; coming out or being out; and historical, developmental, and relationship experiences with oppression. Students may need help understanding some of the diversity of bisexual and transgender identities and experiences,

---

[2]Peter Elbow's paper describing the believing game and the doubting game, as well as separate sets of rules for each game, are available on this book's companion website (http://pubs.apa.org/books/supp/mena).

[3]This journal assignment is available for download from this book's companion website (http://pubs.apa.org/books/supp/mena).

differentiating gender identity and gender expression and how these relate to sexual identities, dispelling myths and misconceptions, and the challenges of coming out. I also address asexuality as a sexual identity (Chasin, 2013).

To further emphasize the diversity of LGBTQ identities, experiences, and sociohistorical contexts, Richen and Welbon's (2013) film, *The New Black: LGBT Rights and African American Communities*, may be used for examining race, religion, and LGBTQ identities and experiences. Panels comprising members of the campus and community may focus on various intersectional identities. Directly searching the media for myths about bisexuality (see Burleson, 2005) is an effective way to both teach about and challenge bisexual oppression. To compare LGBTQ identities and experiences across historical contexts, I show selections from *Before Stonewall: The Making of a Gay and Lesbian Community* (Rosenberg, Scagliotti, & Schiller, 1994) and *After Stonewall* (Basile, Scagliotti, Baus, Hunt, & Scagliotti, 1999).

Part 2: LGBTQ Development in Life Course Perspective

Next, we consider LGBTQ identities and relationships from a developmental life course perspective, looking at the age and the processes by which children first come to understand physical sex categories and gender identities and the implications for families with young children and early childhood education programs. We engage current debates in the field, such as how young children can know and be supported in expressing their gender identities when these differ from their sex assigned at birth and trace children's socialization into heteronormativity and the traditional binary gender system. For middle childhood and adolescence, identity development models for LGBTQ people and cisgender heterosexuals can be examined (Jamil, Harper, & Bruce, 2013; Savin-Williams, 2005). Early, mostly linear, models are problematic, yet they continue to be used by social service and educational professionals, so they should be studied; Jones and Abes's (2013) "queer theory" offers an alternative multi-dimensional model.

Students can examine school curricula to see where and how LGBTQ content is included—for example, in sexuality education and health care, as well as climate issues and LGBTQ student outcomes, particularly with a focus on inequities with cisgender heterosexual students (Robinson & Espelage, 2011). Intersectionality and cultural and historical contextual factors can expand the discussion. GLSEN offers critical resources in this regard (e.g., Diaz & Kosciw, 2009; Kosciw, Greytak, Zongrone, Clark, & Truong, 2018), demonstrating challenges facing LGBTQ subpopulations in U.S. schools and offering resources for change. Students can also read Savin-Williams's (2005) argument and Kuban and Grinnell's (2008) response and conduct a debate on the topic "Coming Out as LGBTQ in Adolescence: No Big Whoop?"

Family of origin responses to having an LGBTQ member are important to explore. Two books, *Nurturing Queer Youth: Family Therapy Transformed* (Fish & Harvey, 2005) and *Ties That Bind: Familial Homophobia and Its Consequences*

(Schulman, 2009), are especially useful for engaging students in thinking critically about tolerance versus acceptance versus transformative nurturance and social justice. Panels of adults sharing their journeys toward understanding and advocacy may also be used. Adult relationships, families of creation, and work settings may be introduced with the film *This Is Family* (Gonzalez, Pilhan, & Erreca, 2009). The U.S. Supreme Court ruling in *Obergefell et al. v. Hodges* (2015) that states must allow same-sex couples to marry can be examined and compared with arguments made for and against interracial marriage. The history of LGBTQs' rejection of marriage as well as of traditional notions of the family can also be examined (e.g., Against Equality, http://www.againstequality.org; Polikoff, 2008).

Aging-related experiences with the health care system allow an exploration of the intersectionality of ageism, heterosexism, cisgenderism, and other experiences of oppression among LGBTQ elders. I show *Gen Silent* (Maddux, 2010) and assign select readings from Orel and Fruhauf (2014). Internalized oppression should also be engaged; Yoshino's (2006) description of the demands of conversion, passing, and covering help to set the stage for personal reflections.

Part 3: An LGBTQ Affirmative Psychology

The discipline of psychology and SOGI advocates can take steps to dismantle inequities and support healthy LGBTQ development. I ask students to develop a list of the top five priorities for LGBTQ-affirmative psychology, applying the four perspectives of the Institute of Medicine of the National Academies (2011) discussed earlier in this chapter (Minority Stress, Life Course Models, Intersectionality, and Social Ecology). Methodologically sound research methods are discussed, along with the dangers of poorly designed psychological research. I illustrate the latter with Regnerus's (2012) research claiming that young adult children of parents who had ever had a same-sex relationship did less well on various outcome variables than young adult children raised by their still-married heterosexual and biological parents, countered by Cheng and Powell's (2015) reanalysis of the data and conclusion that Regnerus's findings were largely an artifact of problematic methodological choices. Students might also be asked to examine the extent to which psychologists adhere to APA's (2015) *Guidelines for Psychological Practice With Transgender and Gender Nonconforming People* (see also Singh & dickey, 2017) in published works and clinical practice and to identify where and how heteronormative and cisgender assumptions remain by reading Morin (1977) followed by Ansara and Hegarty (2012).

I also ask students to explore the challenges and benefits of forming friendships across SOGI, what it means to be an LGBTQ ally or advocate, and SOGI privilege. Recommended readings are Galupo and colleagues (2014), Price (1999), and Tillmann-Healy (2001); useful sources examining advocacy are Ayres and Brown's (2005) *Straightforward* (though some of the case examples are now outdated) and GLAAD's (2015) "Tips for Trans Allies." Debates between civil rights and social justice–focused LGBTQ activism can also be introduced (e.g., Vaid, 2012), along with Mananzala and Spade's (2008) idea that "social justice trickles up, not down" (p. 54).

Wrap-up discussions focus on the resilience and strengths that LGBTQ people demonstrate, leaving students with strengths-based and forward-looking perspectives. Recommended resources include Burnes and Stanley (2017), D'Augelli (1992), Fisher and Komosa-Hawkins (2013), and Riggle and Rostosky (2012).

CONCLUSION

Psychological knowledge has typically reflected and reinforced heterosexism and cisgenderism. A learning environment that affirms all sexual and gender identities will enhance self-esteem, self-understanding, and respect for diverse others, for all students. By making invisible assumptions visible, instructors can help students develop a better understanding of the various ways that psychology is embedded in a context of heterosexism and cisgenderism and thus move the field of psychology forward.

REFERENCES

American Psychological Association. (2015). Guidelines for psychological practice with transgender and gender nonconforming people. *American Psychologist, 70,* 832–864. http://dx.doi.org/10.1037/a0039906

American Psychological Association. (2017). *Multicultural guidelines: An ecological approach to context, identity, and intersectionality.* Retrieved from http://www.apa.org/about/policy/multicultural-guidelines.pdf

Ansara, Y. G., & Hegarty, P. (2012). Cisgenderism in psychology: Pathologizing and misgendering children from 1999 to 2008. *Psychology and Sexuality, 3,* 137–160. http://dx.doi.org/10.1080/19419899.2011.576696

Ayres, I. A., & Brown, J. G. (2005). *Straightforward: How to mobilize heterosexual support for gay rights.* Princeton, NJ: Princeton University Press.

Basile, V. (Producer), Scagliotti, J. (Producer & Director), Baus, J. (Director), & Hunt, D. (Director). (1999). *After Stonewall* [Motion picture]. United States: First Run Features.

Beemyn, G., & Rankin, S. (2011). *The lives of transgender people.* New York, NY: Columbia University Press.

Bellware, K. (2015, August 21). Illinois bans gay conversion therapy for LGBT youths. *Huffington Post.* Retrieved from http://www.huffingtonpost.com/entry/illinois-bans-gay-conversion-therapy_55d668b4e4b020c386de2cc4

Biblarz, T. J., & Stacey, J. (2010). How does the gender of parents matter? *Journal of Marriage and Family, 72,* 3–22. http://dx.doi.org/10.1111/j.1741-3737.2009.00678.x

Blaise, M. (2005). *Playing it straight: Uncovering gender discourses in the early childhood classroom.* New York, NY: Routledge.

Bornstein, K., & Bergman, S. B. (Eds.). (2010). *Gender outlaws: The next generation.* Berkeley, CA: Seal Press.

Boylan, J. F. (2003). *She's not there: A life in two genders.* New York, NY: Broadway Books.

Bronfenbrenner, U. (1977). Toward an experimental ecology of human development. *American Psychologist, 32,* 513–531. http://dx.doi.org/10.1037/0003-066X.32.7.513

Bronski, M., Pellegrini, A., & Amico, M. (2013). *"You can tell just by looking" and 20 other myths about LGBT life and people.* Boston, MA: Beacon Press.

Bullough, V. C. (1979). *Homosexuality: A history.* New York, NY: New American Library.

Burleson, W. E. (2005). *Bi America: Myths, truths, and struggles of an invisible community*. Binghamton, NY: Harrington Park Press.

Burnes, T. R., & Stanley, J. L. (Eds.). (2017). *Teaching LGBTQ psychology: Queering innovative pedagogy and practice*. Washington, DC: American Psychological Association. http://dx.doi.org/10.1037/0000015-000

Charles, C. (2015, November 6). *Ten counterproductive behaviors of social justice educators*. Retrieved from https://www.filmsforaction.org/articles/ten-counterproductive-behaviors-of-social-justice-educators/

Chasin, C. D. (2013). Reconsidering asexuality and its radical potential. *Feminist Studies, 39*, 405–426.

Cheng, S., & Powell, B. (2015). Measurement, methods, and divergent patterns: Reassessing the effects of same-sex parents. *Social Science Research, 52*, 615–626. http://dx.doi.org/10.1016/j.ssresearch.2015.04.005

Clarke, V., Ellis, S. J., Peel, E., & Riggs, D. W. (2010). *Lesbian, gay, bisexual, trans and queer perspectives: An introduction*. New York, NY: Cambridge University Press. http://dx.doi.org/10.1017/CBO9780511810121

Cohen, H. S. (Producer), & Chasnoff, D. (Producer & Director). (1997). *It's elementary: Talking about gay issues in school* [Motion picture]. United States: New Day Films.

D'Augelli, A. R. (1992). Teaching lesbian/gay development: From oppression to exceptionality. In K. M. Harbeck (Ed.), *Coming out of the classroom closet: Gay and lesbian students, teachers, and curricula* (pp. 213–227). New York, NY: Harrington Park Press.

Derman-Sparks, L., & Phillips, C. B. (1997). *Teaching/learning anti-racism: A developmental approach*. New York, NY: Teachers College Press.

Diamond, L. M. (2008). *Sexual fluidity: Understanding women's love and desire*. Cambridge, MA: Harvard University Press.

Diaz, E. M., & Kosciw, J. G. (2009). *Shared differences: The experiences of lesbian, gay, bisexual, and transgender students of color in our nation's schools*. Retrieved from https://www.glsen.org/sites/default/files/Shared%20Differences.pdf

Drescher, J. (2010). Queer diagnoses: Parallels and contrasts in the history of homosexuality, gender variance, and the *Diagnostic and Statistical Manual. Archives of Sexual Behavior, 39*, 427–460. http://dx.doi.org/10.1007/s10508-009-9531-5

Elbow, P. (2008). *The believing game: Methodological believing*. Retrieved from http://works.bepress.com/peter_elbow/20

Erickson-Schroth, L. (Ed.). (2014). *Trans bodies, trans selves: A resource for the transgender community*. New York, NY: Oxford University Press.

Ferber, A. L., Holcomb, K., & Wentling, T. (Eds.). (2016). *Sex, gender and sexuality: The new basics, an anthology*. New York, NY: Oxford University Press.

Fish, L. S., & Harvey, R. G. (2005). *Nurturing queer youth: Family therapy transformed*. New York, NY: Norton.

Fisher, E., & Komosa-Hawkins, K. (Eds.). (2013). *Creating safe and supportive learning environments. A guide for working with lesbian, gay, bisexual, transgender, and questioning youth and families*. New York, NY: Taylor & Francis. http://dx.doi.org/10.4324/9780203807637

Fredriksen-Goldsen, K. I., Kim, H.-J., Emplet, C. A., Muraco, A., Erosheva, E. A., Hoy-Ellis, C. P., . . . Petry, H. (2011). *The aging and health report: Disparities and resilience among lesbian, gay, bisexual, and transgender older adults*. Retrieved from http://caringandaging.org/wordpress/wp-content/uploads/2011/05/Executive-Summary-FINAL.pdf

Galupo, M. P., Bauerband, L. A., Gonzalez, K. A., Hagen, D. B., Hether, S., & Krum, T. (2014). Transgender friendship experiences: Benefits and barriers of friendships across gender identity and sexual orientation. *Feminism & Psychology, 24*, 193–215. http://dx.doi.org/10.1177/0959353514526218

Gartrell, N., Bos, H., & Koh, A. (2018, July 19). National Longitudinal Lesbian Family Study—Mental health of adult offspring. *The New England Journal of Medicine, 379,* 297–299. http://dx.doi.org/10.1056/NEJMc1804810

Gertner, H. (Producer), & France, D. (Producer & Director). (2012). *How to survive a plague* [Motion picture]. United States: Public Square Films.

GLAAD. (2015). *Tips for allies of transgender people.* Retrieved from http://www.glaad.org/transgender/allies

Gonzalez, E. (Producer), Pilhan, M. (Producer), & Erreca, J.-B. (Director). (2009). *This is family* [Motion picture]. United States: Landmark Media.

Green, J. (2004). *Becoming a visible man.* Nashville, TN: Vanderbilt University Press.

Haugland, D. (Producer), & Schmiechen, R. (Director). (1992). *Changing our minds: The story of Dr. Evelyn Hooker* [Motion picture]. United States: Frameline.

Herek, G. M. (1997–2014). *Sexual orientation: Science, education and policy.* Retrieved from http://psychology.ucdavis.edu/rainbow/

Herek, G. M. (2010). Sexual orientation differences as deficits: Science and stigma in the history of American psychology. *Perspectives on Psychological Science, 5,* 693–699. http://dx.doi.org/10.1177/1745691610388770

Herek, G. M., & Capitanio, J. P. (1995). Black heterosexuals' attitudes toward lesbians and gay men in the United States. *Journal of Sex Research, 32,* 95–105. http://dx.doi.org/10.1080/00224499509551780

Herek, G. M., & Capitanio, J. P. (1996). "Some of my best friends": Intergroup contact, concealable stigma, and heterosexuals' attitudes toward gay men and lesbians. *Personality and Social Psychology Bulletin, 22,* 412–424. http://dx.doi.org/10.1177/0146167296224007

Herek, G. M., & McLemore, K. A. (2013). Sexual prejudice. *Annual Review of Psychology, 64,* 309–333. http://dx.doi.org/10.1146/annurev-psych-113011-143826

Hooker, E. (1957). The adjustment of the male overt homosexual. *Journal of Projective Techniques, 21,* 18–31. http://dx.doi.org/10.1080/08853126.1957.10380742

Institute of Medicine of the National Academies. (2011). *The health of lesbian, gay, bisexual, and transgender people: Building a foundation for better understanding: Report brief.* Retrieved from https://www.ncbi.nlm.nih.gov/books/NBK64806/

Jamil, O. B., Harper, G. W., & Bruce, D. (2013). Adolescent development: Identity, intimacy, and exploration. In E. S. Fisher & K. Komosa-Hawkins (Eds.), *Creating safe and supportive learning environments: A guide for working with lesbian, gay, bisexual, transgender, and questioning youth and families* (pp. 29–40). New York, NY: Taylor & Francis.

Jones, S. R., & Abes, E. S. (2013). *Identity development of college students: Advancing multiple frameworks for multiple dimensions of identity.* San Francisco, CA: Jossey-Bass.

Kates, N. (Producer & Director), & Singer, B. (Producer & Director). (2002). *Brother outsider: The life and times of Bayard Rustin* [Motion picture]. United States: Bayard Rustin Film Project.

Kite, M. E., & Deaux, K. (1987). Gender belief systems: Homosexuality and the implicit inversion theory. *Psychology of Women Quarterly, 11,* 83–96. http://dx.doi.org/10.1111/j.1471-6402.1987.tb00776.x

Kosciw, J. G., Greytak, E. A., Zongrone, A. D., Clark, C. M., & Truong, N. L. (2018). *The 2017 National School Climate Survey: The experiences of lesbian, gay, bisexual, transgender, and queer youth in our nation's schools.* Retrieved from https://www.glsen.org/article/2017-national-school-climate-survey-1

Kuban, K., & Grinnell, C. (2008). More Abercrombie than activist? Queer working class rural youth vs. the new gay teenager. In M. B. Sycamore (Ed.), *That's revolting: Queer strategies for resisting assimilation* (pp. 75–86). Brooklyn, NY: Soft Skull Press.

Lev, A. I. (2004). *Transgender emergence: Therapeutic guidelines for working with gender-variant people and their families.* New York, NY: Haworth Press.

Lev, A. I. (2005). Disordering gender identity: Gender identity in the *DSM–IV–TR.* *Journal of Human Sexuality, 17*(3/4), 35–69.

Lev, A. I. (2013). Gender dysphoria: Two steps forward, one step back. *Clinical Social Work Journal, 41,* 288–296. http://dx.doi.org/10.1007/s10615-013-0447-0

Maddux, S. (Producer & Director). (2010). *Gen silent* [Motion picture]. United States: Interrobang Productions.

Mananzala, R., & Spade, D. (2008). The nonprofit industrial complex and trans resistance. *Sexuality Research & Social Policy, 5,* 53–71. http://dx.doi.org/10.1525/srsp.2008.5.1.53

McDonald, H. L. (Producer & Director). (1995). *Ballot 9 measure* [Motion picture]. United States: Sovereign Distribution.

Meyer, I. H. (2003). Prejudice, social stress, and mental health in lesbian, gay, and bisexual populations: Conceptual issues and research evidence. *Psychological Bulletin, 129,* 674–697. http://dx.doi.org/10.1037/0033-2909.129.5.674

Meyerowitz, J. (2002). *How sex changed: A history of transsexuality in the United States.* Cambridge, MA: Harvard University Press.

Mock, J. (2014). *Redefining realness: My path to womanhood, identity, love & so much more.* New York, NY: Atria.

Morin, S. F. (1977). Heterosexual bias in psychological research on lesbianism and male homosexuality. *American Psychologist, 32,* 629–637. http://dx.doi.org/10.1037/0003-066X.32.8.629

Murphy, T. F. (2003). Redirecting sexual orientation techniques and justifications. In S. LaFont (Ed.), *Constructing sexualities: Readings in sexuality, gender, and culture* (pp. 285–299). Upper Saddle River, NJ: Prentice Hall.

Nadal, K. L. (2013). *That's so gay! Microaggressions and the lesbian, gay, bisexual, and transgender community.* Washington, DC: American Psychological Association. http://dx.doi.org/10.1037/14093-000

National Center for Lesbian Rights. (2018). *BornPerfect: Laws & legislation by state.* Retrieved from http://www.nclrights.org/bornperfect-laws-legislation-by-state/

Nicolosi, J. (2009). *What is reparative therapy? Examining the controversy.* Retrieved from http://josephnicolosi.com/what-is-reparative-therapy-exa/

Nigatu, H. (2014, February 19). 19 LGBT microaggressions you hear on a daily basis. *Buzzfeed.* Available from http://www.buzzfeed.com/hnigatu/19-lgbt-microaggressions-you-hear-on-a-daily-basis

Obergefell et al. v. Hodges et al., 135S Ct 2584 (2015).

Ochs, R., & Rowley, S. E. (Eds.). (2009). *Getting bi: Voices of bisexuals around the world* (2nd ed.). Boston, MA: Bisexual Resource Center.

Orel, N. A., & Fruhauf, C. A. (Eds.). (2014). *The lives of LGBT older adults: Understanding challenges and resilience.* Washington, DC: American Psychological Association.

Patterson, C. J. (2013). Sexual orientation and family lives. In G. W. Peterson & K. R. Bush (Eds.), *The handbook of marriage and the family* (pp. 659–681). New York, NY: Springer. http://dx.doi.org/10.1007/978-1-4614-3987-5_27

Polikoff, N. (2008). *Beyond (straight and gay) marriage: Valuing all families under the law.* Boston, MA: Beacon Press.

Price, J. (1999). *Navigating differences: Friendships between gay and straight men.* New York, NY: Haworth Press.

Queers United. (2008). *The heterosexual privilege checklist.* Retrieved from http://queersunited.blogspot.com/2008/10/heterosexual-privilege-checklist.html

Regnerus, M. (2012). How different are the adult children of parents who have same-sex relationships? Findings from the New Family Structures Study. *Social Science Research, 41,* 752–770. http://dx.doi.org/10.1016/j.ssresearch.2012.03.009

Richen, Y. (Producer & Director), & Welbon, Y. (Producer). (2013). *The new black: LGBT rights and African American communities* [Motion picture]. United States: Independent Television Service.

Riggle, E. D. B., & Rostosky, S. S. (2012). *A positive view for LGBTQ: Embracing identity and cultivating well-being*. Lanham, MD: Rowman Littlefield.

Rivera, D. (2010, October 11). The power to define reality. *Psychology Today*. Retrieved from https://www.psychologytoday.com/blog/microaggressions-in-everyday-life/201010/the-power-define-reality

Robinson, J. P., & Espelage, D. L. (2011). Inequities in educational and psychological outcomes between LGBTQ and straight students in middle and high school. *Educational Research, 40*, 315–330. http://dx.doi.org/10.3102/0013189X11422112

Rochlin, M. (2007). The heterosexual questionnaire. In M. S. Kimmel & M. A. Messner (Eds.), *Men's lives* (7th ed., p. 405). Boston, MA: Allyn & Bacon.

Rodriguez Rust, P. C. (2000). *Bisexuality in the United States: A social science reader*. New York, NY: Columbia University Press.

Rosenberg, R. (Producer & Director), Scagliotti, J. (Producer), & Schiller, G. (Producer & Director). (1994). *Before Stonewall: The making of a gay and lesbian community* [Motion picture]. United States: Cinema Guild.

Rotheram-Borus, M. J., & Langabeer, K. A. (2001). Developmental trajectories of gay, lesbian, and bisexual youths. In A. R. D'Augelli & C. J. Patterson (Eds.), *Lesbian, gay, and bisexual identities and youth: Psychological perspectives* (pp. 97–128). New York, NY: Oxford University Press.

Russell, G. M. (2000). *Voted out: The psychological consequences of anti-gay politics*. New York, NY: New York University Press.

Savin-Williams, R. C. (2005). *The new gay teenager*. Cambridge, MA: Harvard University Press. http://dx.doi.org/10.4159/9780674043138

Schulman, S. (2009). *Ties that bind: Familial homophobia and its consequences*. New York, NY: The New Press.

Serano, J. (2007). *Whipping girl: A transsexual woman on sexism and the scapegoating of femininity*. Emeryville, CA: Seal Press.

Singh, A. A., & dickey, l. m. (2017). *Affirmative counseling and psychological practice with transgender and gender nonconforming clients*. Washington, DC: American Psychological Association.

Skolnick, A., & Anonymous. (2009). Privileges held by non-trans people. In A. L. Ferber, K. Holcomb, & T. Wentling (Eds.), *Sex, gender and sexuality: The new basics, an anthology* (pp. 300–301). New York, NY: Oxford University Press.

Smothers, T. (Producer), & Simmons, J. (Director). (2005). *Trans generation* [Motion picture]. United States: New Video.

Sue, D. W. (2010). *Microaggressions in everyday life: Race, gender, and sexual orientation*. Hoboken, NJ: Wiley.

Sue, D. W. (2011, February 27). How does oppression (microaggressions) affect perpetrators. *Psychology Today*. Retrieved from https://www.psychologytoday.com/us/blog/microaggressions-in-everyday-life/201102/how-does-oppression-microaggressions-affect

Tatum, B. D. (1992). Talking about race, learning about racism: The application of racial identity development theory in the classroom. *Harvard Educational Review, 62*, 1–24. http://dx.doi.org/10.17763/haer.62.1.146k5v980r703023

Taylor, E. (2010). Cisgender privilege: On the privileges of performing normative gender. In K. Bornstein & S. B. Bergman (Eds.), *Gender outlaws: The next generation* (pp. 268–272). Berkeley, CA: Seal Press.

Throckmorton, W., & Yarhouse, M. A. (2006). *Sexual identity therapy: Practice framework for managing sexual identity conflicts*. Retrieved from https://sitframework.com/wp-content/uploads/2009/07/sexualidentitytherapyframeworkfinal.pdf

Tillmann-Healy, L. M. (2001). *Between gay & straight: Understanding friendship across sexual orientation*. Walnut Creek, CA: AltaMira Press.

Truitt, J. (2009, August 12). *There are no safe spaces*. Retrieved from http://feministing.com/2009/08/12/there-are-no-safe-spaces/

Vaid, U. (2012). *Irresistible revolution: Confronting race, class and the assumptions of LGBT politics*. New York, NY: Magnus Books.

Weissman, D. (Producer & Director), & Weber, B. (Director). (2011). *We were here: The AIDS years in San Francisco* [Motion picture]. United States: Weissman Projects.

Yoshino, K. (2006). *Covering: The hidden assault on our civil rights*. New York, NY: Random House.

7

Psychology of Asian Americans

Connie S. Chan and Kattalina Berriochoa

The term *Asian American* generally refers to individuals with origins in the Far East, Southeast Asia, or the Indian subcontinent, including Cambodia, China, India, Japan, Korea, Malaysia, Pakistan, the Philippine Islands, Thailand, and Vietnam (U.S. Census Bureau, 2014). Although often categorized together for a number of reasons, including their common ethnic origins, similarities in physical appearance, and a presumption of shared values, Asian Americans are actually a heterogeneous population. Each ethnic group has its own language(s), values, customs, and unique experiences of migration to the United States. In addition, there are many individual and group differences even within ethnic groups. However, many Asian immigrants and Americans of Asian descent have experienced similar group histories of oppression, racial discrimination, and difficulties with acceptance and assimilation in the United States.

IMMIGRATION HISTORY OF ASIAN GROUPS IN THE UNITED STATES

There have been several waves of immigration for Asians coming to the United States (Lee, 1997; Takaki, 1989), each producing cultural and political forces that continue to resonate in the lives of Asian Americans.

http://dx.doi.org/10.1037/0000137-008
Integrating Multiculturalism and Intersectionality Into the Psychology Curriculum: Strategies for Instructors, J. A. Mena and K. Quina (Editors)

The First Immigrations, 1840–1924

Historian Sucheng Chan (1991) pointed out that by the time Chinese men were recruited to immigrate to the United States in the 1840s as laborers and the 1860s as railroad workers, "color prejudice had become . . . a habit of heart and mind" (p. 45) for European Americans, who had already pushed aside, enslaved, and subjugated indigenous peoples, Africans, and Mexicans. Although they were desired for their cheap labor, the Chinese were considered too foreign in their physical appearance, customs, and language to be accepted as Americans. The Chinese Exclusion Act of 1882 made Chinese the first nationality in U.S. history to be explicitly barred from immigration (Espinola, Burns, & Yu, 2018; Lee, 1997; Takaki, 1989). With the Chinese excluded from immigration, Japanese laborers settled in Hawaii and the western U.S. coastal mainland to work on plantations and farms. By 1920, more than 130,000 individuals of Japanese ancestry lived in the United States. These immigration patterns—recruiting Asian ethnic men as laborers while prohibiting women and family members from joining them and excluding them from obtaining legal immigration status—were repeated, in smaller numbers, for Koreans and Filipinos from 1903 to 1920 (S. Chan, 1991).

Immigration and Restrictions, 1924–1965

The 1924 Immigration Act severely limited immigration from all Asian countries until 1965 (S. Chan, 1991). After the Japanese bombing of Pearl Harbor in 1941, strong anti-Asian sentiment affected not only Japanese but also many others from Asian backgrounds. More than 110,000 Americans, including citizens born in the United States, were unjustly and involuntarily confined for up to 3 years in "internment camps," prison-like, barbed wire–enclosed tent cities. After World War II ended, many found their homes had been appropriated and their previous lives destroyed (Nagata, 1993; Takaki, 1989).

There are excellent published personal accounts of the internment camp experience (e.g., Houston & Houston, 1973; Okada, 1976; Weglyn, 1976) and films that offer a moving lesson about institutionalized prejudice on a large scale: the feature movie *Snow Falling on Cedars* (Bass, Baum, & Hicks, 2000) and documentaries *Children of the Camps* (Ina & Holsapple, 1999) and *Unfinished Business: The Japanese Internment Cases* (Okazaki, 1986). Japanese Americans who lived through the internment experience as children can be particularly compelling guest lecturers in the classroom.

In 1965, spurred by the civil rights movement, Congress passed the Immigration and Naturalization Act, abolishing national origins quotas. As a result, between 1965 and 1975 the Asian American population increased dramatically, particularly Koreans, Indians, Chinese, and Filipinos.

New Immigrants and Refugees: 1975–Present

The Vietnam War created a refugee exodus and resulted in over 1,200,000 Southeast Asian refugees arriving in the United States after the end of the

Vietnam war in 1975 (Southeast Asia Research Action Center, 2011). After waging a ground and air war (including dropping well over 2 million tons of bombs in Vietnam, Laos, and Cambodia), the United States withdrew from Vietnam in 1973, leaving many supporters in great danger. Those who managed to escape did so amid terror and horrendous violence and endured arduous stays in refugee camps. First-person Vietnamese accounts of the war and refugee experience are provided in *When Heaven and Earth Changed Places* (Hayslip, 1989) and *South Wind Changing* (Huynh, 1994). Other military conflicts and a genocidal campaign by Pol Pot in Cambodia created another exodus of refugees. *The Killing Fields* (Puttnam, Smith, & Ioffe, 1984) tells the stories of Cambodian refugees who escaped.

Today, the Asian American community is increasing in population through both birth rate and immigration. It is considered the fastest growing immigrant group in the United States; between 2000 and 2010, the Asian population increased by 46%, reaching almost 17.3 million people, about 5.6% of the total population (Hoeffel, Rastogi, Kim, & Hasan, 2012). The five largest Asian ethnic groups are, in order, Chinese, Asian Indian, Filipino, Vietnamese, and Korean (U.S. Census Bureau, 2007).

TEACHING ABOUT ASIAN AMERICAN PSYCHOLOGY

There are many aspects of the Asian immigrant and Asian American experience that can be integrated into a variety of courses. We discuss three important topics: cultural influences, minority group status, and refugee adaptation.

Cultural Influences in Asian American Psychology

Although it is important to make students aware of the great diversity within and among the many Asian American ethnic groups, some generalizations can be made about commonly shared values, beliefs, and customs. These cultural ways may help shape personality, behaviors, communication style, interpersonal relationships, sexuality, and gender role expectations.

Importance of the Family

In the Asian American tradition, the family is still paramount as the basic unit of society (Kwok, 2013). A primary cultural value of collectivism influences all aspects of life, from communication styles to social arrangements. The family unit and relationship are fundamentally based on the notion of respect and authority, and Asian American youth often conform to family rules and demands with these in mind, affecting decisions about career, location of residence, and mate.

Non-Asian faculty and advisors are often surprised when Asian or Asian American college students are willing to choose a major to satisfy their parents even if they are passionate about another discipline. Such cultural conflicts are common among Asian and Asian American students, who must navigate a

difficult journey between their individual needs and desires and often different expectations from their parents and family.

The following scenario can form the basis for a class exercise. A male Korean
American college student seeks counseling because his father expects him to go
to Korea after graduation to choose a bride from three suitable potential wives
the family has selected. He is torn between his desire to fulfill his family's cultural expectations and his desire to keep his relationship with his non-Korean
girlfriend in the United States. He is also expected to live with or near his parents
in the United States once his education is completed and to help support his
extended family. Questions might include, How would you advise and counsel
this student? What resources would you use to understand his cultural and
familial conflicts? Many Asian Americans who have a strong ethnic connection
from early childhood tend to follow traditional values and marry within their
social group (Das, 2006), whereas young, usually highly educated Asian Americans and Asian immigrants to the United States are more likely to marry outside
their social group (Qian & Lichter, 2001).

More assimilated Asian Americans may experience "identity" tension as
they attempt to balance traditional Asian family values (e.g., conformity, self-
sacrifice) and American social values (e.g., individual rights, self-centeredness;
Das, 2006). According to Kwok (2013), family members tend to serve as the
main financial and social support system for most Asian Americans, even as
many young adults are becoming more independent, moving away, and making
their own choices regarding their profession and activities, lifestyle, and choice
of primary relationship. Popular movies such as *The Wedding Banquet* (Hope,
Schamus, & Lee, 1993) and *Saving Face* (Smith, Lassiter, Zee, & Wu, 2004)
address cultural and family conflict for young Asian Americans. Students can
discuss how their family and cultural issues are similar to or different from those
faced by the protagonists in these movies, as well as ways they themselves
might seek an independent life that does not meet parental expectations.

Levels of Acculturation
Acculturation involves the integration of cultural beliefs, values, behaviors,
and language of the host culture (Berry, Trimble, & Olmedo, 1986). Language
challenges, social support issues, difficulty in finding "community," and discrimination all factor into the level of stress experienced by an individual
throughout the process of acculturation (Kwok, 2013). Okazaki and Saw
(2011) stated that Asian immigrant groups often engage in both family- and
community-based cultural maintenance. For many Asian Americans, level of
acculturation is not necessarily correlated with the length of time in the
United States; third- or fourth-generation individuals may hold traditional
Asian cultural values, whereas more recent immigrants may acculturate
quickly into American culture. Thus, Asian American cultural identity can be
conceptualized on a continuum, spanning across primary cultural identifica-
tions, with a mixed Asian and American identity in the middle.

Ask students to make a list of ways in which they identify as "American" and
answer the question "What does it mean to have an American identity?" After

they discuss their answers, ask students to list the ways in which they identify as Asian, Asian American, or the ethnicity with which they do identify. What are the ethnic characteristics they list, and where do they place themselves on the continuum of "ethnic" versus "American" and why? This is a good opportunity to discuss intersectionality and how students understand aspects of their identities as well as what characteristics are identified with Asians and Asian Americans.

Behavior and Communication Style

A keystone of Asian American communication style is *collectivity*, which contrasts with Western *individualism*. Studies have shown that individuals from collective societies are socialized to maintain group harmony through emotional control (Oyserman, Coon, & Kemmelmeier, 2002). Asians and Asian Americans are often perceived as quiet or nonconfrontational, due to their cultural upbringing and desire to avoid conflict in public. The desire to avoid conflict and interpersonal discomfort often results in the constrained expression of emotions and avoidance of potentially controversial topics.

The ability to communicate indirectly without confronting or embarrassing the other person is highly valued, especially if a subject is difficult to discuss openly, such as sexuality. For example, if an Asian American woman wanted to know whether her brother knew that she was a lesbian and in a relationship with another woman, she might not discuss it openly but might tell her brother that she would be spending a weekend with her female partner. Her brother might reply that he had heard where they were staying was a romantic place, communicating his understanding of the relationship without having to address the issue openly.

Research has shown that Asian American families are less likely to report domestic violence. According to Das (2006), fear, privacy, and shame are cultural factors that prevent Asian American women from reporting domestic abuse. These values are so deeply ingrained that Asian American families are more likely to attempt to solve issues in private. Many Asian Americans are reluctant to reveal feelings or personal problems, even to a therapist. This avoidance is especially pronounced in family discussions, where there is often little open and honest communication between generations because of a desire for the appearance of harmony.

Public displays of emotion are particularly discouraged and often associated with shame. Asian Americans generally consider it best to convey emotions through a written message. That way, both the sender and the recipient can experience and express their feelings in private and avoid any risk of public exposure, thus allowing all parties to save face. Asian Americans are often taught to be observant of verbal and nonverbal subtle social cues. A great deal can be communicated through nonverbal means, including a quick look of disapproval from parents to children or a lingering look in which one person might hold the contact of another's eyes for just a second longer. This subtle form of nonverbal communication can often indicate emotional or sexual interest and can be easily missed by the casual observer (C. S. Chan, 1995).

Communication standards in the Asian American community are largely rooted in social boundaries. Disclosing personal information is related to a high degree of proven trust (Park & Kim, 2008). Because interpersonal harmony is considered essential, Asian American individuals often take a conciliatory role in group discussions. They may appear accommodating, conforming, and well-mannered rather than confrontational or attention seeking. Although this behavior usually reflects a desire to avoid conflict, it is often mistaken as unassertiveness or submissiveness. In the classroom, this communication style may be incorrectly interpreted as a sign that a student does not understand the material or is less competent.

Effects of Minority Group Status

The psychology of Asian Americans is influenced by their historical and cultural backgrounds and their marginality because their values, customs, and behaviors differ from those of the majority culture. Asian Americans are likely to be affected by non-Asians' perceptions of them and by the stereotyping and racism in the dominant culture, experiencing racial discrimination both as perpetual foreigners and as a model minority (Ng, Lee, & Pak, 2007).

Perpetual Foreigners

Asian language, customs, religions, foods, family structure, and culture are perceived as distinct from U.S. culture; as such, Asian Americans are often subjected to the stereotype of the "perpetual foreigner" who will never fully assimilate (Ng et al., 2007). Although acknowledging some cultural influences from their Asian background, many identify primarily with mainstream U.S. culture and are shocked when the outside world perceives them as other than American. Non-Asians often ask where they are from and how long they have lived in this country and say that they speak English well—when their families have lived in the United States for decades.

The Model Minority Myth

Perceived success may, ironically, be used as a justification for discrimination against Asian Americans. Often labeled the *model minority*, they are viewed as having "made it" in the United States, because of the purportedly low rates of mental disorders and high levels of achievement among some Asian Americans. This view, however, does not accurately reflect the many stories of the Asian American community.

The model minority myth is best known today for its perpetuation of the stereotype that all Asian Americans excel in academics, employment, and family income (Varma, 2004). Although some Asian American ethnic groups, particularly those who have been in this country for longer periods of time, have a strong record of academic achievement in the United States, many others have far lower levels of achievement than non-Asian peers. Their American experience is oversimplified by aggregating all Asian Americans and ignoring the reality that various ethnic groups continue to struggle with poverty or assimilation issues (Varma, 2004). During the 2010 census, Asian Americans exceeded non-Hispanic Whites in median household income, which would lead one to believe that Asian Americans have reached or surpassed a level of equality with the dominant ethnic group (Hoeffel et al., 2012). However, the poverty rate for Asian Americans was also higher than that of non-Hispanic Whites (U.S. Census Bureau, 2007). These numbers show that in the Asian American community, wide inequality exists: Some groups experience robust social mobility, whereas others struggle with the difficulties inherent in poverty. For example, over 42% of all Asian American adults, but only 5% of Laotian American, Cambodian American, and Khmer Americans, have earned college degrees (Le, 2013).

Stereotypes and Discrimination

Asian Americans also experience unequal consideration for leadership positions, prejudice, and judgment from speaking English with an accent and experience a sense of being an "outsider" in the American workplace (Ely, Padavic, & Thomas, 2012). Upper middle class Asian American professionals may find that although they are viewed as competent technicians or researchers, they are perceived as quiet and lacking leadership qualities and are thus not promoted to managerial positions (Ely et al., 2012; Hyun, 2005). Research on this career "bamboo ceiling" for Asian Americans has shown recurring managerial underrepresentation for Asian Americans, with a lower ratio of managers to professionals relative to Whites (Lai & Babcock, 2013).

In schools and universities, Asian Americans are frequently perceived as quiet but diligent students who "raise the curve" in math and science classes, perpetuating the model minority myth and creating resentment. On average, Asian Americans tend to attain higher educational achievements than the general U.S. population (Varma, 2004); however, this generalization also masks the academic and employment challenges many Asian students face.

A 2010 study by the National Institutes of Health found that for both Asian American men and women, mental and physical health issues are associated with perceived discrimination (Hahm, Ozonoff, Gaumond, & Sue, 2010). Reports of discrimination include being treated with less courtesy and respect, receiving poorer quality services, and perceiving that others think they are not smart, are afraid of them, and think they are dishonest and not as good as others (Hahm et al., 2010). They also frequently report being called derogatory names and slurs and are sometimes threatened by others (Hahm et al., 2010). An accumulation of personal experiences with overt or subtle racial discrimination can, over time, create a sense of frustration that can manifest in physical or mental health issues.

Gender, Sexuality, and Sexual Identity

Patriarchal and conservative values were imported to the Asian American community with the first waves of immigration and continue to influence sexual identity, attitudes, and gender roles (Okazaki, 2002).

Gender-Based Stereotypes

Asian American women have endured several forms of stereotyping on the basis of their race and gender. Students can seek out examples and share these with the class, along with strategies to counter these stereotypes. For example, on the one hand, women are subjected to traditional roles within a patriarchal framework. Collectivism, privacy, and submission are values women are taught from birth in traditional Asian families. Asian women may be more tolerant of male aggression than women from other ethnic groups because they are socialized to be passive and yielding to male family members (Das, 2006).

On the other hand, there is also a perception that Asian women have an exotic sexiness or sexuality. This is based on the Japanese geisha model as well as the similar, but more diabolic, model of the manipulative "dragon lady" (Tajima, 1989). Another stereotype is the "lotus blossom baby"—the fragile, attractive "Suzie Wong" prostitute—who is also a subject of pornography (Tajima, 1989). Such stereotypes of sexuality may lead some men to assume that Asian American women are more available and will not complain or reject them.

Asian American males also experience a form of cultural gender stereotyping as "nerdy" computer and math "geeks"—and consequently not strong leaders—so they are often passed over for promotions, holding only 2.6% of executive jobs at Fortune 500 companies, despite having the highest percentage of college degrees among all groups (Sun, 2014).

Lesbian, Gay, Bisexual, and Transgender Asians and Asian Americans

For Asian American lesbian, gay, bisexual, transgender, and queer (LGBTQ) individuals, issues of sexual orientation are often compounded by minority ethnic statuses. Researchers have found greater vulnerability to adverse mental health consequences for those who identify with both racial and sexual minority status (Cochran, Mays, Alegria, Ortega, & Takeuchi, 2007). Explorations of sexuality, sexual identity, and racial identity offer an opportunity for class discussions of intersexuality and possible conflicts with traditional Asian family values and social norms. Research has shown that Asian Americans are more fearful of social disapproval than their White counterparts, particularly when it concerns social roles and traditional gender roles (Okazaki, 2002), a trait shared with other ethnic LGBTQ individuals, including Hispanic Americans. Although this discussion is especially salient for youth who are also trying to meet family and gender role expectations, others can readily relate to the challenge.

Refugee Experiences: Stress and Adaptation

It is particularly useful for students in clinical and counseling psychology to learn about Asian Americans who have immigrated to the United States in recent decades, many of whom are refugees from political violence or military conflict, forced to flee from extreme violence, torture, rape, or imprisonment. In addition to handling the usual economic, cognitive, and emotional challenges involved in adapting to a new language and culture, as well as experiences of racism, they have had to deal with the psychological effects of the traumas they experienced before leaving their homeland, including posttraumatic stress disorder. Research has shown that one's age during immigration affects mental and physical health (Lam, Yip, & Gee, 2012). Other factors that complicate any immigrant experience include social mobility in the destination country and experiencing unemployment, lack of services, and social stress. These factors, which naturally evolve from immigration, are compounded by a lack of social supports in the country of destination, including mental and physical health services.

Underuse of Mental Health Services

Social stigmas, cognitive barriers, lack of information, and emotional communication are a few reasons why Asian Americans are less likely to seek services and more likely to drop out of mental health treatment than Whites (Leong & Lau, 2001). These barriers are also relevant in accessing medical services, where issues such as stigma and shame are driving factors in the relatively low use of services (Chu & Sue, 2011). Access to health services varies within the Asian American community, with increased physical and mental health vulnerabilities for those living in poverty, women, and elderly people.

Asian cultural values, which emphasize stoicism and discourage the expression of feelings, contribute to this underuse. In some cases, access is deterred by lack of cultural outreach and awareness of services, along with transportation and scheduling difficulties (Leong & Lau, 2001). Traditional values and social stigmas also hinder Asian Americans from seeking health services. For example, Asian Americans are more likely to turn to family and close friends for help before seeking professional treatment (Chu & Sue, 2011). A clinician who works with Asian American individuals can help students understand how diverse and appropriate cultural outreach can increase participation in health services (Abe-Kim et al., 2007).

TEACHING STRATEGIES WITH ASIAN AMERICAN STUDENTS

The cultural values discussed in this chapter have implications for Asian Americans in classroom settings. A few important things to keep in mind are that there is wide variation in the Asian American community, from wide-ranging socioeconomic levels to highly diverse languages spoken; levels of acculturation matter immensely, with individual bicultural identity ranging from strictly separated to a mix; and stereotypes are prevalent and limit our understanding of the complexity of issues that impact the Asian American community.

Instructors can create more effective and culturally sensitive classrooms by acknowledging the personal struggle associated with minority identity statuses. Ideally, they would allow time for Asian American students to become comfortable, make an effort to establish a trusting relationship, avoid exercises that demand public discussion of emotional or personal issues, and provide some structure in discussions, perhaps by being more directive in their questions. Allowing students to express themselves and to participate in class discussions via reading written work, rather than speaking extemporaneously, is often helpful in providing opportunities for class participation.

Given the importance of privacy and saving face, Asian American students may also opt to remain silent about difficulties with class materials or personal problems that are interfering with their performance. For many Asian Americans, there is also a belief that feelings, particularly negative ones such as sadness, anger, guilt, or shame, should be controlled by the individual and that expressing them to others is a sign of character weakness. Problems and concerns may be expressed as psychosomatic difficulties, such as insomnia and stomach pains. In reality, students could be struggling with depression or anxiety (Newton et al., 2014). Mental health supports for students can help to promote more inclusive and supportive classrooms. Structured options that can facilitate effective written communication include journal entries, online discussions, and blogs; the instructor can give feedback that students can review in private. Assignments that give explicit permission or instruction to attend to emotional or personal reactions to course materials and to record these feelings on paper help facilitate communication from students but should not be shared with others without their permission.

Students can interview their parents and other elders to learn their family's story of immigration or personal history while providing a sociohistorical context for understanding their own development. This assignment can be used with all students; if they are from a family that immigrated long ago, they can compare their family's experience with that of an Asian immigrant's family. Students can also interview individuals at an Asian American community organization about their immigration experiences, or they can review some of the many memoirs, novels, and films that address Asian themes, such as *The Woman Warrior: Memoirs of a Childhood Among Ghosts* (Kingston, 1976), *The Joy Luck Club* (novel by Tan, 1989; motion picture produced by Wang, 1994), *The Wedding Banquet* (Hope, Schamus, & Lee, 1993), and *Picture Bride* (Mark, Onodera, & Hatta, 1995). These assignments provide some hands-on experience while making Asian American cultural issues and immigration relevant and alive for all students regardless of cultural background.[1]

CONCLUSION

As the number and diversity of Americans of Asian descent grow, so too does the literature and psychological research on Asian American experiences. This literature focuses on how individuals form identity and struggle or succeed in

---

[1]Additional recommended resources for teaching students about Asian American topics and themes can be found on this book's companion website (http://pubs.apa.org/books/supp/mena).

American society. There is a great need to understand both the diversity and the commonalities among and within the Asian American ethnic groups and to integrate this understanding into the psychology curriculum. It is important to provide an environment in which students from Asian backgrounds feel acknowledged and accepted and in which students from other backgrounds can come to understand and value the diversity of Asian American experiences in their historical and societal contexts.

REFERENCES

Abe-Kim, J., Takeuchi, D. T., Hong, S., Zane, N., Sue, S., Spencer, M. S., . . . Alegría, M. (2007). Use of mental health-related services among immigrant and US-born Asian Americans: Results from the National Latino and Asian American Study. *American Journal of Public Health, 97*, 91–98. http://dx.doi.org/10.2105/AJPH.2006.098541

Bass, R. (Producer), Baum, C. (Producer), & Hicks, S. (Director). (2000). *Snow falling on cedars* [Motion picture]. United States: Universal Pictures.

Berry, J. W., Trimble, J. E., & Olmedo, E. L. (1986). Assessment of acculturation. In J. W. Berry & W. J. Lonner (Eds.), *Field methods in cross cultural research* (pp. 291–324). Thousand Oaks, CA: Sage.

Chan, C. S. (1995). Issues of sexual identity in an ethnic minority: The case of Chinese American lesbians, gay men, and bisexual people. In A. R. D'Angelli & C. R. Patterson (Eds.), *Lesbian, gay and bisexual identities over the lifespan* (pp. 87–101). New York, NY: Oxford University Press.

Chan, S. (1991). *Asian Americans: An interpretive history*. Boston, MA: Twayne.

Chu, J. P., & Sue, S. (2011). Asian American mental health: What we know and what we don't know. *Online Readings in Psychology and Culture, 3*(1), 4. http://dx.doi.org/10.9707/2307-0919.1026

Cochran, S. D., Mays, V. M., Alegria, M., Ortega, A. N., & Takeuchi, D. (2007). Mental health and substance use disorders among Latino and Asian American lesbian, gay, and bisexual adults. *Journal of Consulting and Clinical Psychology, 75*, 785–794. http://dx.doi.org/10.1037/0022-006X.75.5.785

Das, S. (2006). Life in a salad bowl! Marriage, family life, and economic choices in Asian-American communities in the United States. *Race, Gender, & Class, 3*, 248–272.

Ely, R. J., Padavic, I., & Thomas, D. A. (2012). Racial diversity, racial asymmetries, and team learning environment: Effects on performance. *Organization Studies, 33*, 341–362. http://dx.doi.org/10.1177/0170840611435597

Espinola, R. (Producer), Burns, R. (Director), & Yu, L.-S. (Director). (2018). *The Chinese Exclusion Act*. [Motion picture]. United States: Steeplechase Films & Center for Asian American Media.

Hahm, H. C., Ozonoff, A., Gaumond, J., & Sue, S. (2010). Perceived discrimination and health outcomes: A gender comparison among Asian-Americans nationwide. *Women's Health Issues, 20*, 350–358. http://dx.doi.org/10.1016/j.whi.2010.05.002

Hayslip, L. (1989). *When Heaven and Earth changed places*. New York, NY: Doubleday.

Hoeffel, E. M., Rastogi, S., Kim, M. O., & Hasan, S. (2012). *The Asian population: 2010*. Retrieved from https://www.census.gov/prod/cen2010/briefs/c2010br-11.pdf

Hope, T. (Producer), Schamus, J. (Producer), & Lee, A. (Producer & Director). (1993). *The wedding banquet* [Motion picture]. United States: Ang Lee Productions.

Houston, J. W., & Houston, J. D. (1973). *Farewell to Manzanar*. San Francisco, CA: Houghton Mifflin.

Huynh, J. (1994). *South wind changing*. St. Paul, MN: Graywolf Press.

Hyun, J. (2005). *Breaking the bamboo ceiling: Career strategies for Asians*. New York, NY: HarperCollins.

Immigration and Nationality Act of 1965, H.R. 2580; Pub. L. No. 89-236, 79 Stat. 911 (1968).

Ina, S. (Producer & Director), & Holsapple, S. (Director). (1999). *Children of the camps* [Motion picture]. Japan: AsianCrush.

Kingston, M. H. (1976). *The woman warrior: Memoirs of a childhood among ghosts*. New York, NY: Knopf.

Kwok, J. (2013). Factors that influence the diagnoses of Asian Americans in mental health: An exploration. *Perspectives in Psychiatric Care, 49*, 288–292.

Lai, L., & Babcock, L. C. (2013). Asian Americans and workplace discrimination: The interplay between sex of evaluators and the perception of social skills. *Journal of Organizational Behavior, 34*, 310–326. http://dx.doi.org/10.1002/job.1799

Lam, J., Yip, T., & Gee, G. (2012). The physical and mental health effects of age of immigration, age, and perceived difference in social status among first generation Asian Americans. *Asian American Journal of Psychology, 3*, 29–43. http://dx.doi.org/10.1037/a0027428

Le, C. (2013). *A closer look at Asian Americans and education* [Web log]. Retrieved from http://archive.education.jhu.edu/PD/newhorizons/strategies/topics/multicultural-education/A%20closer%20look%20at%20asian%20americans%20and%20education/index.html

Lee, L. C. (1997). An overview. In L. C. Lee & N. Zane (Eds.), *Handbook of Asian American psychology* (pp. 1–19). Thousand Oaks, CA: Sage.

Leong, F. T., & Lau, A. S. (2001). Barriers to providing effective mental health services to Asian Americans. *Mental Health Services Research, 3*, 201–214. http://dx.doi.org/10.1023/A:1013177014788

Mark, D. (Producer), Onodera, L. (Producer), & Hatta, K. (Director). (1995). *Picture bride* [Motion picture]. United States: Miramax Pictures.

Nagata, D. K. (1993). *Legacy of injustice: Exploring the cross-generational impact of the Japanese American internment*. New York, NY: Springer. http://dx.doi.org/10.1007/978-1-4899-1118-6

Newton, V., Nied, D., Rorer, A., Stillwell, D., Wang, E., & Matsuo, H. (2014). Exploring identities and interactions of African American and Asian American college students: Interdisciplinary approach. *Journal of Education and Human Development, 3*, 155–179.

Ng, J. C., Lee, S. S., & Pak, Y. K. (2007). Contesting the model minority and perpetual foreigner stereotypes: A critical review of literature on Asian Americans in education. *Review of Research in Education, 31*, 95–130. http://dx.doi.org/10.3102/0091732X07300046095

Okada, J. (1976). *No-no boy*. Seattle: University of Washington Press.

Okazaki, S. (Producer & Director). (1986). *Unfinished business* [Motion picture]. United States: New Video Group.

Okazaki, S. (2002). Influences of culture on Asian Americans' sexuality. *Journal of Sex Research, 39*, 34–41. http://dx.doi.org/10.1080/00224490209552117

Okazaki, S., & Saw, A. (2011). Culture in Asian American community psychology: Beyond the East–West binary. *American Journal of Community Psychology, 47*, 144–156. http://dx.doi.org/10.1007/s10464-010-9368-z

Oyserman, D., Coon, H. M., & Kemmelmeier, M. (2002). Rethinking individualism and collectivism: Evaluation of theoretical assumptions and meta-analyses. *Psychological Bulletin, 128*, 3–72. http://dx.doi.org/10.1037/0033-2909.128.1.3

Park, Y. S., & Kim, B. S. (2008). Asian and European American cultural values and communication styles among Asian American and European American college students. *Cultural Diversity and Ethnic Minority Psychology, 14*, 47–56. http://dx.doi.org/10.1037/1099-9809.14.1.47

Puttnam, R. (Producer), Smith, I. (Producer), & Ioffe, R. (Director). (1984). *The killing fields* [Motion picture]. United States: Warner Studios.

Qian, Z., & Lichter, D. T. (2001). Measuring marital assimilation: Intermarriage among natives and immigrants. *Social Science Research, 30,* 289–312. http://dx.doi.org/10.1006/ssre.2000.0699

Smith, W. (Producer), Lassiter, J. (Producer), Zee, T. (Producer), & Wu, A. (Director). (2004). *Saving face* [Motion picture]. United States: Sony Pictures.

Southeast Asia Research Action Center. (2011). *Southeast Asian Americans at a glance: Statistics on Southeast Asians adapted from the American Community Survey.* Retrieved from http://www.searac.org/wp-content/uploads/2018/04/STATISTICAL-PROFILE-2010.pdf

Sun, A. (2014, November 20). *4 lies we need to stop telling about Asian-American men.* Retrieved from http://everydayfeminism.com/2014/11/lies-asian-american-men/

Tajima, R. (1989). Lotus blossoms don't bleed. In Asian Women United (Ed.), *Making waves: An anthology of writings by and about Asian American women* (pp. 308–317). Boston, MA: Beacon Press.

Takaki, R. (1989). *Strangers from a different shore.* Boston, MA: Little, Brown.

Tan, A. (1989). *The Joy Luck Club.* New York, NY: Random House.

U.S. Census Bureau. (2007). *The American community—Asians 2004.* Retrieved from https://www.census.gov/library/publications/2007/acs/acs-05.html

U.S. Census Bureau. (2014). *QuickFacts.* Retrieved from https://www.census.gov/quickfacts/fact/table/US/PST045217

Varma, R. (2004). Asian Americans: Achievements mask challenges. *Asian Journal of Social Science, 32,* 290–307. http://dx.doi.org/10.1163/1568531041705103

Wang, W. (Producer & Director). (1994). *The Joy Luck Club* [Motion picture]. United States: Hollywood Pictures.

Weglyn, M. (1976). *Years of infamy.* New York, NY: Morrow.

8

Teaching Africana Psychology

Lisa Whitten, Halford H. Fairchild, and Harriette W. Richard

The number of African American psychologists has doubled since 2005, from 2.7% in 2005 to 5.3% in 2013 (American Psychological Association [APA], 2015). Some metrics have remained stubbornly unchanged in the U.S. professoriate: In 2013, only 6% of full-time faculty and 4% of full professors were African American, up just 1% each from 2005 (U.S. Department of Education, 2018). In 2011, 57% of tenured African American faculty were at Historically Black Colleges and Universities, even though these represent only about 3% of U.S. colleges and universities (Gasman, 2013). To provide talented, culturally grounded faculty and mental health professionals to African descent communities, we must develop more effective strategies to increase the number of African descent psychologists. Teaching Africana psychology[1] is a critical component of this effort.[2]

AFRICANA PSYCHOLOGY DEFINED

Grounded in the notion that African descent peoples' healing must emanate from a foundation in African and African American culture, spirituality, and wisdom, Africana psychology recognizes the powerful impact of institutional

---

[1] We choose the term *Africana* psychology to denote the increasingly international nature of the field (Fairchild, 2017a).
[2] The companion webpage for this book includes materials that instructors can use in their classes, including PowerPoint presentations about important issues in Africana psychology and classroom exercises that help students engage with other crucial topics (http://pubs.apa.org/books/supp/mena).

http://dx.doi.org/10.1037/0000137-009
Integrating Multiculturalism and Intersectionality Into the Psychology Curriculum: Strategies for Instructors, J. A. Mena and K. Quina (Editors)

racism, oppression, and socioeconomic contexts on the life circumstances of African people. Compared with Western epistemology, Africana approaches

- emphasize the collective, with the group and not the individual as the unit of analysis;

- consider current behavior within a historical context (vs. the ahistorical tendency of European American psychology);

- focus on both the material and the immaterial or spiritual (vs. emphasizing only that which can be seen, measured, and manipulated);

- consider introspection ("knowledge from within") as a valid means of data collection (vs. an external orientation characterized by observations, surveys, or experiments);

- see harmony in nature (vs. seeking to control nature);

- counter racism and sexism (vs. ignoring or even promoting those ideologies); and

- remain grounded in a set of values that seeks African liberation on the continent and throughout the African diaspora (vs. the "value-free," "neutral," or "objective" approach of European American psychology; Fairchild, 2000; 2017b).

The goal is to develop theories, research strategies, and therapeutic and community interventions that will result in the psychological, spiritual, and political liberation of African descent people—and all people. We believe it is critical that all students learn about Africana psychology to have a more accurate and complete understanding of psychology as a whole.

TOWARD A LIBERATORY PSYCHOLOGY

Our work has been profoundly influenced by our involvement in the Association of Black Psychologists [ABPsi] since the 70s. ABPsi's mission is the "liberation of the African mind, empowerment of the African character, and enlivenment and illumination of the African spirit" (http://www.abpsi.org/about_mission.html, para. 1). In connection with this mission, we introduce our students to a liberatory pedagogy based on the work of bell hooks (1994) and Paulo Freire (1970), who recognized that the practice of education developed within a context of human exploitation. Freire's *Pedagogy of the Oppressed* described the process of education as one of disempowering students, making them passive receptacles of the teacher's alleged body of knowledge. hooks contemplated the ideologically motivated errors in the storehouse of knowledge and viewed education as a tool of indoctrination. Similarly, the foundations of European and American psychology were laid during eras of imperialism, slavery, colonialism, and wars of conquest against indigenous peoples around the world. Thus, their theories and principles are intertwined with exploitative conquest and tainted by biases that justified that conquest.

Given this historical context, a liberatory pedagogy demands that students see themselves as powerful change agents. A liberatory pedagogy empowers students by making them producers of knowledge and developing in them a set of skills and abilities—writing, speaking, critical thinking—serving them well beyond college. We constantly remind our students and ourselves: Question and challenge everything! We must imagine and articulate visionary strategies focusing on solutions to pressing problems. Solution statements—and the actions they imply—form the end goals of a liberatory pedagogy (Akbar, 1984; Nobles, 2015).

Early connections between African American psychology and liberation theology were made by Akbar (1984). This was a clear call for addressing oppressive and dominant forces at work on people of African descent in America through a different theoretical framework, identifying common oppressive experiences for a specific group and then changing that societal norm, resulting in "justice for all." Todd (2011) offered a concise history and definition of liberation theology while highlighting the challenges, obstacles, and need for this theological framework in psychology. Other researchers have used liberation theology (Cone, 2000) and psychology (Ostrove, Cole, & Oliva, 2009) to examine systematic oppression and target racism, sexism, classism, and intersectionality.

One of us (HHF) used a liberatory psychology by challenging students to write essays for publication focusing on the problems of violence in America (Fairchild, 2016), advancing African American lifespan psychology (Fairchild, 2017a), and using social psychology to reach for world peace (Fairchild & Fairchild, 2018). These books included chapters written by more than 50 undergraduate students. They have been adopted as textbooks at several colleges and universities and have been accessed thousands of times on the Internet.

CURRICULAR CONSIDERATIONS

Students often have limited knowledge of African and African American history, and this course is their first exposure to Africana studies. We assess students' basic knowledge at the start of a course to gauge how much background will be required during the semester and to engaging their learning. Excellent resources are *From Slavery to Freedom* (Franklin & Higgenbotham, 2011), *The Warmth of Other Suns* (Wilkerson, 2010), and *Creating Black Americans: African American History and Its Meanings, 1619 to the Present* (Painter, 2006).

The ABPsi website (http://www.abpsi.org) offers a wealth of resources on African-centered and African American psychology. Students can gain insight into the field, discover issues relevant to the African American community, access publications, and learn about conferences and programs. In addition, the textbook by Belgrave and Allison (2018) provides a comprehensive review of

African American psychology. However, limiting African American psychology to a single unit communicates that the views are limited to those of the professor(s) who taught the unit and, therefore, can be dismissed (Whitten, 2004).

THE POWERFUL ROLE OF TEXTBOOKS

Racism and other forms of oppression still plague our nation and the global community, impacting the mental and physical health of African Americans and all people (Bailey et al., 2017; Bassett & Graves, 2018; Mouzon & McLean, 2017). Yet, most psychology textbooks systematically ignore these critical issues. Teaching African American psychology at predominately White institutions, one of us (HWR) found that her students were amazed that they had not been exposed to ethnic psychologies during their postsecondary careers; they were eager to explore these areas (Richard, 1996, 1997). In 2001, another one of us (LW) was a member of the APA's Commission on Ethnic Minority Recruitment, Retention, and Training Task Force Textbook Initiative Work Group, which recommended that "introductory textbooks . . . make every effort to [include] diverse viewpoints and diversity issues" (Trimble, Stevenson, & Worell, 2003, p. iii), asserting that "incorporating diversity issues into textbooks is not a matter of political correctness. It is a matter of scientific and professional responsibility" (p. iii). Regrettably, recent authors and publishers have not often heeded these words.

We must supplement textbooks and expose students to the terminology and tools they need to understand the effect of racial oppression and, more important, to confront it. We are deeply concerned about apparent efforts to "erase race" from the introduction to psychology curriculum. For example, the index of Wade and Tavris (2011) failed to list the words *race* or *racism*. We recognize that these constructs are socially constructed; yet, they are powerful variables in relation to how people are studied, judged, categorized, and treated and should not be minimized or obscured. Whitten (2004) noted that eliminating the topic of race results in a skewed and inaccurate depiction of psychology. Griggs and Jackson (2013) found that none of the 13 full-length textbooks published since 1997 included a chapter on diversity, and only three included boxed features.

The choice of images for textbooks can be especially problematic. The cover of Wade and Tavris's (2011) *Psychology* is a particularly striking example: The front cover of the text depicts a young African American man playing chess, but turning to the back cover, we discover that his opponent is a dog! For some students and faculty, this is an insulting and deeply disturbing image. One of us (LW) integrated an analysis of this image into her introductory psychology course; students wrote an essay on their interpretation of the image, which provided an important lesson in surfacing and analyzing subtle (and not so subtle) symbolic messages about people of African descent (A. R. Dixon & Telles, 2017).

SOME STIMULATING TOPICS TO CONSIDER

Africana psychology provides an excellent opportunity to dispel myths about welfare, family composition, achievement, and involvement in crime, countering disinformation and distortions perpetuated by the media and by flawed scholarship (A. R. Dixon & Telles, 2017; Piper-Mandy & Rowe, 2010). We suggest three units we have found particularly useful in this regard. Throughout, students are asked to explore intersectionalities in the experiences of African people, answering such questions as, How do race, class, gender, skin color, and sexuality intersect to affect their experiences? How might time and place affect these analyses? What about lesbian, gay, bisexual, transgender, and queer people or those with physical disabilities? To illustrate similarities and differences throughout the African diaspora, students can compare demographic profiles across nations.

African Cultural Retentions (Africanisms)

For many, knowledge of the history of African Americans and other Africans in the new world begins with slavery. This unit provides historical background while placing African descent peoples, throughout the diaspora, in an African cultural context, using an interdisciplinary approach (Cole, 1985). Despite concerted efforts by those who enslaved Africans to separate them from their roots and destroy their heritage, cultural remnants survived and, in some cases, thrived: Holloway (2005) described Africanisms in art, language, folklore, naming practices, and religion, and Mitchell (2004) addressed African cultural retentions in the Black church. Students can study Africanisms in their own lives and communities. One student related the ritual branding practiced by some African American fraternities in which a Greek letter is burned onto an arm or the chest to the scarification practiced by some West African ethnic groups, providing a jumping-off point for interesting qualitative research on cultural connections among African descent students.

   The study of Africanisms should be compared with and connected to psychological theories of racial and cultural identity and African self-consciousness (Hoggard, Jones, & Sellers, 2017; Maxwell, Brevard, Abrams, & Belgrave, 2015). Students find this compelling, and it serves as a solid foundation for a unit on African-centered approaches. The study of African cultural connections can be empowering to African descent students; in addition, it can encourage all students to investigate cultural retentions in their families and communities.

(Re)presenting African American Fathers

Historically, the social sciences have studied African descent peoples using a deficit model, which includes a steady bombardment of negative reports on the status of African American fathers and African Americans in general (T. L. Dixon, 2017). The strengths model counters such negative images, using statistical and other comparisons of African Americans and Whites rarely and only when it is critical to contextualize the condition or status of African Americans. African descent people are studied in relation to each other, in the context of the African diaspora.

To debunk myths and reframe our understanding of African American fathers, Doyle and colleagues (2015) used firsthand accounts to examine the previously "unheard" voices of African American fathers of preadolescent boys to discover four themes: managing emotions, encouragement, discipline, and monitoring. Allen (2016) investigated how African American fathers teach their sons about masculinity. Jayakody and Kalil (2002) highlighted a different type of parental involvement in the life of African American children—*social fathering*—noting that other men, such as relatives or a mother's partner, can play an important role in families characterized by nonresident fathers, thus challenging the widespread notion that children in these families are from "father absent, broken" families that have "no father figure."

Colorism

Some students exclaim, "African Americans are racists, too!" often in reference to prejudice or discrimination based on skin color. Although racism is an intergroup phenomenon, *colorism* is an intragroup phenomenon of power and privilege being accorded to lighter skinned individuals. Although often based in kinship, it has resulted in a connection between power and color; for example, during colonialism, people in power with lighter skin color gave land and wealth to their own. Colorism is not unique to the United States; A. R. Dixon and Telles (2017) provided a comprehensive overview of colorism and how it manifests itself globally. This history has contributed to considerable anger, contention, and pain among people of color in the diaspora. Afro-Latinxs are also addressing colorism in their communities (Adames, Chavez-Dueñas, & Organista, 2016), making this a good illustration of the importance of intersectionality.

Research has found that White people in power discriminate against darker skinned people more often than lighter skinned people (Hochschild & Weaver, 2007; Jones, 2000) and that skin color is related to perceived discrimination and health (Canache, Hayes, Mondak, & Seligson, 2014; Monk, 2015). Students have no shortage of examples: Dark skinned women have reported being told "you're pretty to be so dark"; lighter siblings and cousins are treated preferentially. It should be noted, however, that in some contexts, darker skinned individuals are in the privileged position; for example, a light-skinned student stated that his darker peers label him "weak" and "soft" because of his complexion.

Colorism can diminish the self-worth, self-esteem, and unity of people of African descent (Mucherah & Frazier, 2013; Wilder & Cain, 2011). We encourage our students to conduct research and attend campus programs on this problem to interrupt its pervasive negative impacts. This might include the use of the colorism scale developed by Harvey, Tennial, and Hudson Banks (2017).

HETEROSEXISM IN AFRICAN DESCENT PEOPLES

Heteronormative biases may be more prominent in African and African American communities than many others (Loue, 2014; Miller & Stack, 2014). Identifying the variety of ways that heterosexism is unique in Africana communities (Madson, 2001) can be a great topic for a social justice action project such as launching and evaluating a program or intervention. Dessel, Westmoreland, and Gutiérrez (2016) studied a strategy aimed at reducing heterosexism in Christian African American students. Students can ask, What is the relationship between religion and heterosexism? What strategies might be pursued to ameliorate the problem? How are heteronormative attitudes promulgated in Africana media? What is the relationship between heteronormative values and sexual harassment?

PEDAGOGICAL CONCERNS

A major tenet of liberatory pedagogy is that it is imperative to confront racism in ourselves, our students, and the broader society (Torino & Manese, 2012) and to debunk and deconstruct White psychology and much of White academia (Fairchild, 2000); White students, in particular, may take umbrage at challenges to many of their longstanding beliefs and attitudes. Students may accuse faculty of "playing the race card" when they find it difficult to integrate new ideas about race (Whitten, 2004). Yet, students have to grapple with the meanings of Eurocentrism and White privilege to understand how race contributes to their personal and collective identities (Ambrosio, 2014). Kite (2013), Boatright-Horowitz, Frazier, Harps-Logan, and Crockett (2013), Shine (2011), and Okun (2010) have offered resources to assist faculty with the intense reactions of some students. We advocate the flipped ("in reverse") classroom and avoid the "banking metaphor" of education (Freire, 1970), in which instructors pour informational resources into "empty vessels." We provide many opportunities for students to hone their oral presentation skills, and we facilitate their efforts to present at conferences.

TECHNOLOGY ISSUES

We encourage students to use their smartphones and other devices to fact-check and/or support information presented in readings, lectures, and class discussions. At the start of the semester, students can become coinvestigators in the construction of a statistical profile of African descent peoples. The U.S. Census Bureau (http://www.census.gov) and the Pew Research Center (http://www.pewresearch.org) are good starting points for exploring areas of diversity such as disability, religion, ethnicity, immigration status, Hispanic heritage, and sexual orientation. Instructors can also assign data categories that emphasize

African American productivity, development, health, and strengths, such as home ownership, business ownership, political participation, and academic achievement.

Students can conduct research and develop a "tangible product" (e.g., an app, an educational game) that can benefit African descent communities. For example, after researching African descent fathers, students developed an app that organized resources and information for fathers, including free and low-cost activities they can engage in with their children. Other students used social media to deliver information on HIV prevention and materials aimed at reducing colorism.

INTERNATIONAL ATTENTION TO CULTURE, RACE, AND PSYCHOLOGY

Psychologists around the world are striving to address some of the same issues related to diversity, privilege, and oppression in the curriculum that we confront in the United States. Chiodo, Sonn, and Morda (2014) noted a "relative absence" of Indigenous perspectives and diversity in the Australian psychology curriculum and described the challenges of implementing an intercultural unit. Sonn (2008), a Black man who grew up in South Africa and immigrated to Australia, wrote about using narrative and journaling to encourage students to reflect about the oppression of Aboriginal peoples in teaching "Race, Culture, and Power: Critical Issues in Exploring Intergroup Relations in Australia" to a predominantly White group of students. In Brazil, African descent psychologists sponsored their first conference in 2010 (Silva Bento, 2013). Partly in response to pressure from Black psychologists, the Brazilian Psychology Board has begun what Silva Bento (2013) called "timid efforts" to change and has designed materials to educate Brazilian psychologists about how to manage institutional racism. Javangwe (2013) lamented the Western orientation of psychologists in Zimbabwe and the need to Africanize psychology in their universities. He recommended research on the role of indigenous psychological knowledge systems and urged African American psychologists to partner with Zimbabwean psychologists to promote change.

This small sample of the current efforts to address racial and cultural issues in psychology outside the United States is affirming; it demonstrates that, on a global level, psychologists are confronting these concerns in innovative ways. Ways to apply what students learn in this area include interviewing classmates whose background differs from theirs, connecting remotely with psychology classes in other countries for discussions and joint research or social justice projects, evaluating websites and organizations focusing on psychology in other countries, and investigating approaches to psychology and mental health in their ancestral groups. *Internationalizing the Undergraduate Psychology Curriculum* (Gross, Abrams, & Enns, 2016) is an excellent source for additional ideas.

CONCLUSIONS AND RECOMMENDATIONS

Africana psychology has the potential to powerfully influence students' lives and to enhance their ability to examine and oppose structural oppression. We urge research on the effectiveness of the pedagogical strategies we recommend, as well as on the African descent students who choose to major in psychology. To what degree are they affected by the lack of coverage of race, racism, and other forms of oppression in their textbooks and courses? What insight and wisdom can they offer us on these issues? Consulting students about the curriculum and pedagogical strategies and course evaluations could improve learning outcomes.

We are all profoundly affected by the attitudes, policies, and behaviors associated with structural racism and other forms of oppression. Thus, psychologists and other scholars must continue to investigate race and racism and work to eradicate all forms of oppression. Textbook authors and professors should provide an honest representation of how race (not just culture) was and is applied in theories and research and its role in clinical applications. Eliminating the words *race* and *racism* from textbooks does not absolve psychology of the need to work toward eliminating racism and other forms of oppression, nor does it prevent us from continuing to bring these critical issues to the attention of students, scholars, and policymakers.

Africana psychology was born in racial struggle and has evolved over the past 50 years to empower students to question conventional wisdom and to become the change agents needed to bring about a more globally relevant, inclusive, socially just psychology and a more just world.

REFERENCES

Adames, H. Y., Chavez-Dueñas, N. Y., & Organista, K. C. (2016). Skin color matters in Latino/a communities: Identifying, understanding, and addressing mestizaje racial ideologies in clinical practice. *Professional Psychology: Research and Practice, 47,* 46–55. http://dx.doi.org/10.1037/pro0000062

Akbar, N. (1984). *Chains and images of psychological slavery.* Jersey City, NJ: New Mind Productions.

Allen, Q. (2016). 'Tell your own story': Manhood, masculinity and racial socialization among Black fathers and their sons. *Ethnic and Racial Studies, 39,* 1831–1848. http://dx.doi.org/10.1080/01419870.2015.1110608

Ambrosio, J. (2014). Teaching the psychosocial subject: White students and racial privilege. *International Journal of Qualitative Studies in Education, 27,* 1376–1394. http://dx.doi.org/10.1080/09518398.2013.840402

American Psychological Association. (2015). *Demographics of the U.S. psychology workforce: Findings from the American community survey.* Washington, DC: Author.

Bailey, Z. D., Krieger, N., Agénor, M., Graves, J., Linos, N., & Bassett, M. T. (2017, April 8). Structural racism and health inequities in the USA: Evidence and interventions. *The Lancet, 389*(10077), 1453–1463. http://dx.doi.org/10.1016/S0140-6736(17)30569-X

Bassett, M. T., & Graves, J. D. (2018). Uprooting institutionalized racism as public health practice. *American Journal of Public Health, 108,* 457–458. http://dx.doi.org/10.2105/AJPH.2018.304314

Belgrave, F., & Allison, K. (2018). *African American psychology: From Africa to America* (4th ed.). Thousand Oaks, CA: Sage.

Boatright-Horowitz, S. L., Frazier, S., Harps-Logan, Y., & Crockett, N. (2013). Difficult times for college students of color: Teaching White students about White privilege provides hope for change. *Teaching in Higher Education, 18*, 698–708. http://dx.doi.org/10.1080/13562517.2013.836092

Canache, D., Hayes, M., Mondak, J., & Seligson, M. (2014). Determinants of perceived skin-color discrimination in Latin America. *The Journal of Politics, 76*, 506–520. http://dx.doi.org/10.1017/S0022381613001424

Chiodo, L. N., Sonn, C. C., & Morda, R. (2014). Implementing an intercultural psychology undergraduate unit: Approach, strategies, and outcomes. *Australian Psychologist, 49*, 181–192. http://dx.doi.org/10.1111/ap.12047

Cole, J. (1985). Africanisms in the Americas: A brief history of the concept. *Anthropology and Humanism Quarterly, 10*, 120–126. http://dx.doi.org/10.1525/ahu.1985.10.4.120

Cone, J. H. (2000). Black liberation theology and Black Catholics: A critical conversation. *Theological Studies, 61*, 731–747. http://dx.doi.org/10.1177/004056390006100406

Dessel, A., Westmoreland, A., & Gutiérrez, L. M. (2016). Reducing heterosexism in African American Christian students: Effects of multicultural education courses. *Equity & Excellence in Education, 49*, 241–253. http://dx.doi.org/10.1080/10665684.2016.1194100

Dixon, A. R., & Telles, E. E. (2017). Skin color and colorism: Global research, concepts, and measurement. *Annual Review of Sociology, 43*, 405–424. http://dx.doi.org/10.1146/annurev-soc-060116-053315

Dixon, T. L. (2017, January). *A dangerous distortion of our families: Representations of families, by race, in news and opinion media.* Retrieved from https://colorofchange.org/dangerousdistortion/

Doyle, O., Clark, T. T., Cryer-Coupet, Q., Nebbitt, V. E., Goldston, D. B., Estroff, S. E., & Magan, I. (2015). Unheard voices: African American fathers speak about their parenting practices. *Psychology of Men & Masculinity, 16*, 274–283. http://dx.doi.org/10.1037/a0038730

Fairchild, H. H. (2000). African American psychology. In A. E. Kazdin (Ed.), *Encyclopedia of psychology* (Vol. 1, pp. 92–99). Washington, DC: American Psychological Association.

Fairchild, H. H. (2016). *(Re)solving violence in America.* Delhi, India: IndoAmerican Books.

Fairchild, H. H. (Ed.). (2017a). *Black Lives Matter: Lifespan perspectives.* Delhi, India: IndoAmerican Books.

Fairchild, H. H. (2017b). What is Africana psychology? In H. H. Fairchild (Ed.), *Black Lives Matter: Lifespan perspectives* (pp. 3–17). Delhi, India: IndoAmerican Books.

Fairchild, H. H., & Fairchild, H. F. (Eds.). (2018). *Social psychology and world peace: A primer.* Delhi, India: Indo American Books.

Franklin, J. H., & Higgenbotham, E. B. (2011). *From slavery to freedom* (9th ed.). New York, NY: McGraw-Hill.

Freire, P. (1970). *Pedagogy of the oppressed.* New York, NY: Continuum.

Gasman, M. (2013). *The changing face of historically Black colleges and universities.* Retrieved from http://www.gse.upenn.edu/pdf/cmsi/Changing_Face_HBCUs.pdf

Griggs, R. A., & Jackson, S. L. (2013). Introductory psychology textbooks: An objective analysis update. *Teaching of Psychology, 40*, 163–168. http://dx.doi.org/10.1177/0098628313487455

Gross, D., Abrams, K., & Enns, C. Z. (Eds.). (2016). *Internationalizing the undergraduate psychology curriculum: Practical lessons learned at home and abroad.* Washington, DC: American Psychological Association. http://dx.doi.org/10.1037/14840-000

Harvey, R. D., Tennial, R. E., & Hudson Banks, K. (2017). The development and validation of a colorism scale. *Journal of Black Psychology, 43*, 740–764. http://dx.doi.org/10.1177/0095798417690054

Hochschild, J. L., & Weaver, V. (2007). The skin color paradox and the American racial order. *Social Forces, 86*, 643–670. http://dx.doi.org/10.1093/sf/86.2.643

Hoggard, L. S., Jones, S. T., & Sellers, R. M. (2017). Racial cues and racial identity: Implications for how African Americans experience and respond to racial discrimination. *Journal of Black Psychology, 43*, 409–432. http://dx.doi.org/10.1177/0095798416651033

Holloway, J. B. (2005). *Africanisms in American culture.* Bloomington: Indiana University Press.

hooks, b. (1994). *Teaching to transgress: Education as the practice of freedom.* New York, NY: Routledge.

Javangwe, G. (2013). How to Africanize psychology in Zimbabwean universities: An introductory note. *Journal of Black Psychology, 39*, 336–341. http://dx.doi.org/10.1177/0095798413480681

Jayakody, R., & Kalil, A. (2002). Social fathering in low-income, African American families with preschool children. *Journal of Marriage and Family, 64*, 504–516. http://dx.doi.org/10.1111/j.1741-3737.2002.00504.x

Jones, T. (2000). Shades of brown: The law of skin color. *Duke Law Journal, 49*, 1487–1557. http://dx.doi.org/10.2307/1373052

Kite, M. E. (2013). Teaching about race and ethnicity. In D. S. Dunn, R. R. Gurung, K. Z. Naufel, & J. H. Wilson (Eds.), *Controversy in the psychology classroom: Using hot topics to foster critical thinking* (pp. 169–184). Washington, DC: American Psychological Association. http://dx.doi.org/10.1037/14038-011

Loue, S. (2014). *Understanding theology and homosexuality in African American communities.* New York, NY: Springer Science + Business Media. http://dx.doi.org/10.1007/978-1-4614-9002-9

Madson, L. (2001). A classroom activity exploring the complexity of sexual orientation. *Teaching of Psychology, 28*, 32–35. http://dx.doi.org/10.1207/S15328023TOP2801_08

Maxwell, M., Brevard, J., Abrams, J., & Belgrave, F. (2015). What's color got to do with it? Skin color, skin color satisfaction, racial identity, and internalized racism among African American college students. *Journal of Black Psychology, 41*, 438–461. http://dx.doi.org/10.1177/0095798414542299

Miller, S. J., & Stack, K. (2014). African-American lesbian and queer women respond to Christian-based homophobia. *Journal of GLBT Family Studies, 10*, 243–268. http://dx.doi.org/10.1080/1550428X.2013.825219

Mitchell, H. H. (2004). *Black church beginnings: The long-hidden realities of the first years.* Grand Rapids, MI: Eerdmans.

Monk, E. P., Jr. (2015). The cost of color: Skin color, discrimination, and health among African-Americans. *American Journal of Sociology, 121*, 396–444. http://dx.doi.org/10.1086/682162

Mouzon, D. M., & McLean, J. S. (2017). Internalized racism and mental health among African-Americans, US-born Caribbean Blacks, and foreign-born Caribbean Blacks. *Ethnicity & Health, 22*, 36–48. http://dx.doi.org/10.1080/13557858.2016.1196652

Mucherah, W., & Frazier, A. (2013). How deep is skin-deep? The relationship between skin color satisfaction, estimation of body image, and self-esteem among women of African descent. *Journal of Applied Social Psychology, 43*, 1177–1184. http://dx.doi.org/10.1111/jasp.12081

Nobles, W. W. (2015). From Black psychology to *Sakhu djaer*: Implications for the further development of a Pan African Black psychology. *Journal of Black Psychology, 41*, 399–414. http://dx.doi.org/10.1177/0095798415598038

Okun, T. J. (2010). *The emperor has no clothes: Teaching about race and racism to people who don't want to know.* Charlotte, NC: Information Age.

Ostrove, J. M., Cole, E. R., & Oliva, G. A. (2009). Toward a feminist liberation psychology of alliances. *Feminism & Psychology, 19*, 381–386. http://dx.doi.org/10.1177/0959353509105629

Painter, N. I. (2006). *Creating Black Americans: African American history and its meanings, 1619 to the present.* New York, NY: Oxford University Press.

Piper-Mandy, E., & Rowe, T. D. (2010). Educating African-centered psychologists: Towards a comprehensive paradigm. *The Journal of Pan African Studies, 3*(8), 5–22.

Richard, H. (1996). Filmed in black and white: Teaching the concept of racial identity at a predominantly White university. *Teaching of Psychology, 23,* 159–161.

Richard, H. (1997). The teaching of Afrocentric values by African American parents. *The Western Journal of Black Studies, 21,* 42–50.

Shine, P. (2011). White professors taking responsibility for teaching White students about race, racism, and privilege. *Journal of Progressive Human Services, 22,* 50–67. http://dx.doi.org/10.1080/10428232.2011.564972

Silva Bento, M. A. (2013). Brazilian psychology: A dialog. *Journal of Black Psychology, 39,* 304–306. http://dx.doi.org/10.1177/0095798413480661

Sonn, C. C. (2008). Educating for anti-racism: Producing and reproducing race and power in a university classroom. *Race, Ethnicity and Education, 11,* 155–166. http://dx.doi.org/10.1080/13613320802110266

Todd, N. R. (2011). Community psychology and liberation theologies: Commonalities, collaboration, dilemmas. *Journal of Psychology and Theology, 39,* 200–210. http://dx.doi.org/10.1177/009164711103900303

Torino, G. C., & Manese, J. E. (2012). Creating wiser psychologists: Training to confront racism, sexism, and cultural misunderstanding in clinical practice. In P. K. Lundberg-Love, K. L. Nadal, & M. A. Paludi (Eds.), *Women and mental disorders* (pp. 177–191). Santa Barbara, CA: Praeger/ABC-CLIO.

Trimble, J., Stevenson, M. R., & Worell, J. P. (2003). *Toward an inclusive psychology: Infusing the introductory psychology textbook with diversity content.* Washington, DC: American Psychological Association.

U.S. Department of Education. (2018). *Characteristics of postsecondary faculty.* Retrieved from https://nces.ed.gov/programs/coe/indicator_csc.asp

Wade, C., & Tavris, C. (2011). *Psychology* (10th ed.). New York, NY: Pearson.

Whitten, L. (2004). *Deconstructing playing the race card in psychology courses: An invitation to dialogue and exploration.* Retrieved from https://teachpsych.org/resources/documents/ebooks/eit2004.pdf

Wilder, J., & Cain, C. (2011). Teaching and learning color consciousness in Black families: Exploring family processes and women's experiences with colorism. *Journal of Family Issues, 32,* 577–604. http://dx.doi.org/10.1177/0192513X10390858

Wilkerson, I. (2010). *The warmth of other suns. The epic story of America's great migration.* New York, NY: Random House.

Teaching Latinx Psychology

Jasmine A. Mena and Melba J. T. Vásquez

Latinxs[1] in the United States represent a collection of individuals with diverse experiences stemming from numerous factors, including nationalities, geographic locations, immigration histories, acculturation, and socioeconomic status. Despite this heterogeneity, Latinxs share a history of conquests and colonization and continued discrimination and oppression. The result can be observed even in self-identification labels that are loaded with historical and emotional significance (Taylor, Lopez, Martínez, & Velasco, 2012): Some reject the term *Hispanic* because of its association with Spanish conquest and colonization and its formal use by the U.S. Census Bureau and embrace *Latino/a/x*, a term that acknowledges a shared language and Latin American indigenous populations. In this chapter, we review key content and strategies for a course on Latinx psychology or infusing Latinx psychology content into existing courses.[2]

---

[1]We use *Latinx* to signify non–gender binary and inclusive language.
[2]The companion website for this book (http://pubs.apa.org/books/supp/mena) includes a PowerPoint presentation that addresses topics in this chapter that instructors can use in their own lectures, a list of recommended resources, and instructions for conducting classroom exercises.

http://dx.doi.org/10.1037/0000137-010
Integrating Multiculturalism and Intersectionality Into the Psychology Curriculum: Strategies for Instructors, J. A. Mena and K. Quina (Editors)

DEMOGRAPHIC CHARACTERISTICS OF LATINXS
IN THE UNITED STATES

At 17% of the population, Latinxs represent the largest ethnoracial minority group in the United States (U.S. Census Bureau, 2015). The Latinx population growth is partly attributable to their young median age, fertility rates, and prevalence of interracial relationships (Passel, Livingston, & Cohn, 2012). Instructors can start to dispel stereotypes by informing students that Latinxs hail from 22 countries with diverse customs, histories, and migratory patterns. In the most recent U.S. Census, Latinxs identified as 64% Mexicans, 9.4% Puerto Ricans, 3.8% Salvadorians, 3.7% Cubans, 3.1% Dominicans, and 2.3% Guatemalans. Another 13.7% identified other nations as their countries of origin (U.S. Census Bureau, 2015).

Immigration History and Experiences

Immigration results in significant psychological, cultural, social, economic, and political consequences (American Psychological Association [APA], 2012a). Thus, we must understand the forces for migration and migratory patterns and their impact—including those who did not migrate; indigenous Mexicans were present when the United States expanded into their homelands (Fernández-Armesto, 2014), and Puerto Rico was the first U.S. territory designated as a permanent colony by Spain.

Most Latinxs emigrated after World War II in search of a better life. Many migrants were refugees of war, fleeing political persecution, or seeking economic opportunities; for some, affluence facilitated migration. Key determinants of adjustment following migration include socioeconomic resources, including higher levels of education, occupation, and income (Vega, Gil, & Wagner, 2002). Also important are the context of reception in the host country; governmental policies; school, work, and community resources; and intercultural relations (Haller, Portes, & Lynch, 2011). Instructors can have students create an outline of *Dual Pathways to a Better America: Preventing Discrimination and Promoting Diversity* (APA, 2012b) and discuss the mechanisms and consequences of discrimination, stereotyping, and bias that affect the adjustment of oppressed groups in the United States.

The largest numbers of Latinxs migrate from Mexico. In addition to traditional ethnic enclaves in California, New York, Texas, Florida, New Jersey, and Illinois, since 1990 Latinx immigrants have created new settlement patterns in the Midwest, the Rocky Mountain region, and the Southeast (Suro & Tafoya, 2004). Those with lower levels of education generally migrate within the United States, possibly seeking employment opportunities and family reunification (Frey, 2005). The political shift following the thawing of the relationship between the United States and Cuba in 2015 represents a unique opportunity to examine psychological theories and practices developed in a context characterized by political strife with North America (Rey, 2004).

These diverse historical and demographic patterns can help students view Latinxs in a less stereotypic and more informed way. The documentary film *The State of Arizona* (Sandoval & Tambini, 2014) and news articles can stimulate discussion about the complexities of immigration, immigration policy, and the emotional toll associated with undocumented status. Students may also benefit from a discussion of the June 2018 APA opposition to the White House policy of separating immigrant parents and children who are detained while crossing the border (Henderson Daniel & Evans, 2018).

Educational and Economic Status

Euro-Americans typically equate "education" with formal schooling; however, among traditional Latinxs *educación* has a broader meaning, encompassing not only formal schooling but also moral, social, and personal responsibility (Auerbach, 2007). People with *educación* need not be formally educated, whereas those with esteemed degrees may be considered quite uneducated given their moral character or interpersonal style. Traditional Latinxs view the development of *educación* as the responsibility of the family and education the domain of schools. Students can discuss the advantages and disadvantages of *educación* and education in separate groups. Then, the whole class can discuss how each could influence school-related parental involvement and generate solutions.

Despite high educational aspirations, Latinxs graduate from high school at significantly low rates, which leads to negative economic and social consequences (Aud et al., 2013; Martinez, DeGarmo, & Eddy, 2004). Further, Latinxs' academic achievement declines with increasing length of time in the United States; first generation Latinxs outperform second and third generation Latinx students (Rodríguez, 2002). Latinx students encounter multiple barriers to academic success, including discrimination in schools, academic tracking, a disconnect between teachers and parents, and cultural differences between family and school values (Hill & Torres, 2010). Indicators that contribute to the achievement gap include different (less) access to educational resources, including early childhood education and quality bilingual programs; overrepresentation in lower socioeconomic strata; and differential treatment based on negative gender, racial, and ethnic stereotypes (APA, 2012c).

Although the high school dropout rate for Latinxs decreased from 28% in 2000 to 14% in 2011 (Fry & Taylor, 2014), Latinxs remain the lowest achieving group (Ortiz, Valerio, & Lopez, 2012). Students could review the APA presidential report *Ethnic and Racial Disparities in Education* (APA, 2012c) and discuss the conditions that contribute to academic underachievement and recommendations for advocacy, practice, and research.

The rising cost of higher education prohibits many students from obtaining advanced degrees. Students who are unauthorized to reside in the United States because they were brought as minors (also known as DREAMers as a result of the Development, Relief, and Education for Alien Minors Act) face additional limitations due to the inability to secure financial aid (Migration Policy Institute, 2015). Students can investigate their institution's policies relating to undocumented students and invite leaders of local DREAMers chapters and support groups to discuss their needs and advocacy strategies.

Factors that support the academic perseverance of Latinx youth include parental involvement (Mena, 2011; Ortiz et al., 2012), teacher cultural competence (Alfaro, Umaña-Taylor, Gonzales-Backen, Bámaca, & Zeiders, 2009), and quality classes for English language learners (ELLs; Behnk, Gonzalez, & Cox, 2010). More attention should be brought to the social, personal, and academic assets that Latinx students bring with them to the classroom, including high educational aspirations, strong work ethic, family stability, and high levels of mental health. Pairing strengths with access to quality educational resources (e.g., linguistically appropriate information, quality preschool programs, home-based parental involvement) and cultural values (e.g., sense of obligation to family) can lead to better educational outcomes (APA, 2012c). Student–teacher interactions also matter; students who perceive teachers as uncaring and having low expectations tend to exhibit behavioral problems, yet the same students cooperate with teachers perceived as caring and having high expectations. Thus, it is critical to examine the student–teacher relationship instead of labeling a student as "difficult"; 86% of students referred for disciplinary action are not referred in other classrooms (Gregory & Weinstein, 2008).

Latinx children are exposed to diverse linguistic environments. Some children acquire the Spanish language first, then English on entering the school system; others acquire English early and remain monolingual (García & Scribner, 2009). The growth of the Latinx population has led to increased ELL needs. Students are often divided about the best instruction type for ELLs; they can discuss their views before and after reading the research evidence. For example, teaching children to read in their primary language promotes higher English reading levels (APA, 2012c); in fact, well-executed bilingual programs are 0.2 to 0.3 standard deviations above English-only programs for Latinx ELLs (García & Scribner, 2009).

Economic disparities between Whites and Latinxs can be highlighted with data from the U.S. Census Bureau (2014) reports: Median household income was $40,963 for Latinxs versus $58,270 for Whites, and 23.5% of Latinxs were below the poverty line versus 9.6% of Whites. Students can prepare papers and presentations that examine patterns associated with income and economic disparities and immigration contexts, discrimination experiences, and educational resources, including institutionalized racism and differential access to goods, services, and opportunities based on ethnoracial identity. Students can also design their own programs that address educational barriers and consider unique cultural strengths among Latinx students. This exercise can be conducted in conjunction with three reading assignments: Falicov (2014, Chapter 9), Hill and Torres (2010), and Rosenberg (2013).[3]

---

[3]This exercise is available for download from this book's companion website (http://pubs.apa.org/books/supp/mena)

CULTURAL VALUES

Despite their heterogeneity, Latinxs share a number of cultural values that inform practices and behaviors. The risk of identifying these values is to stereotype, which can be detrimental; rather, these cultural values are descriptions that can be used to assess the degree to which they may be accurate for individual Latinxs.

Familismo and *Personalismo*

Familismo, one of the most influential Latinx cultural values, is a multidimensional construct that includes attitudes about the importance of family and the willingness, or obligation, to place family needs before one's own and behaviors such as financial support, time spent with family, and socializing children to prioritize family needs (Calzada, Tamis-LeMonda, & Yoshikawa, 2013). *Personalismo* refers to positive qualities that facilitate pleasant interactions with friends, family, and the broader community by engaging in interpersonal relationships that are characterized by warmth and friendliness (Santiago-Rivera, Arredondo, & Gallardo-Cooper, 2002). These qualities may contribute to effective professional and leadership abilities and "emotional intelligence" because the ability to interact effectively with others is a generalizable skill and a form of resilience.

Gender Role Socialization

Latinx gender socialization is informed by *marianismo* and *machismo*, which prescribe specific attitudes and behaviors for girls and boys. *Marianismo* adopts characteristics ascribed to the Virgin Mary, including virtue, honor, and maternal style, and instructs Latinas to self-sacrifice and place the needs of the family before their own. It can result in a significant emotional toll; Latinas are expected to *aguantar* (tolerate) pain and suffering, including relational infidelity and disrespect from children (Vásquez & de las Fuentes, 1999), and to suppress sexual desires, reserving sexual behavior for procreation (de las Fuentes, Barón, & Vásquez, 2003). Actual or perceived deviation from *marianismo* could result in a loss of social standing and even accusations that a woman is a "whore" and may lead to parental overprotection of girls compared with boys (González-López, 2004). As with all discussions of traditional cultural values, it is important to avoid stereotyping. Awareness of these gender role prescriptions can allow for awareness of the possible influence of these on individuals and groups.

Machismo grants Latino boys greater freedoms compared with girls, and in many families, males, especially husbands and fathers, are accorded respect and authority. *Machistas* pride themselves on their emotional, physical, and sexual dominance. They may feel entitled to have mistresses and be physically abusive. They may also self-harm through alcohol abuse and dependence (de las Fuentes et al., 2003). In contrast, *caballerismo* captures values associated with being a gentleman, respectable family and community leader, and role model with a sense of responsibility (especially financial) for the well-being of the family.

As married Latinas acculturate to American culture, they may expect independence and autonomy, which may clash with traditional gender norms unless the partner acculturates at a similar rate (Zuniga, 2004). Interestingly, varying socioeconomic conditions may be more accurate predictors of the gender roles than traditional cultural values (e.g., level of education, income; Santiago-Rivera et al., 2002). *Compañeras* (Masse & Buzzell, 2007) is an interesting documentary about women in the first-ever all-female mariachi band as they attempt to balance artistic, professional, and family expectations. Students can watch the film and describe the scenes that reflect more and less traditional gender norms.

Strict traditional Latinx gender roles are a barrier for many sexual minorities and gender nonconforming individuals to be "out" to their families and communities by operating in concert with other cultural values (including *familismo*, *respeto*, and religion and spirituality), creating a pressure not to shame family and community members. Culturally sensitive therapeutic approaches have successfully incorporated traditional Latinx values with sexual and gender identity concerns (Duarté-Vélez, Bernal, & Bonilla, 2010) by highlighting the delicate balance between the needs of the individual (e.g., personal gay identity) and the value for the collective (e.g., conflict due to family values).

Simpatía and *Respeto*

Simpatía is a valued cultural trait and social script of engaging with others in a manner characterized by friendliness, politeness, agreeableness, and interpersonal harmony (Triandis, Marín, Lisansky, & Betancourt, 1984) while managing one's anger and resolving conflict tactfully and indirectly. Passive noncooperation is preferred over confrontation and represents a culturally resonant approach to interpersonal discord among traditional Latinxs.

Respeto (respect) refers to the dutiful and high regard for authority, the family, and the hierarchical family structure (Nazario, 1998). Children are expected to use the formal second-person pronoun *usted* (you) when addressing adults, including their parents. Despite these expectations, children are celebrated and valued as important family members. Among adults, formality is also expected until familiarity and trust are established, after which permission may be granted for the use of first names and informal pronoun *tu* (you). Uninvited familiarity may be perceived as disrespectful and condescending. However, formality should not be equated with coldness; in fact, formality and warmth coexist within Latinx cultural values.

Religion and Spirituality

Catholicism, stemming from Spanish colonization, is the predominant religion practiced by Latinxs. In the New World, Catholicism met spiritual practices stemming from indigenous and Afro-Caribbean traditions and informed by animism and mysticism. These may involve seeking healing from individuals with powers; using herbs, incense, and ceremonies; and making offerings to spirits and saints (Comas-Díaz, 2006). For Latinxs, religious attendance is associated with access to social networks instrumental for adjustment to a new culture, buffering against the negative effects of under-resourced neighborhoods (Alegría, Shrout, et al., 2007). Students can explore the blending of European and native beliefs and practices, augmented by lectures by *curanderos* (healers) and field trips to local herbalists (de las Fuentes et al., 2003).

Students can deepen their understanding of the complexity of cultural values by interviewing two or three individuals of different generations about their cultural values. Sample questions may include, What are some values by which you live? How would you address a disagreement with a child, sibling, parent, and employer?[4] Interviewees can also be presented with a vignette created by the instructor and asked to indicate what the protagonist "should do." In class, instructors can ask students to compare and contrast responses across various features, including, age, generational status, gender, and religiosity.[5] Although responses do not always fit neatly into categories, this occurrence can be used to emphasize Latinx diversity. Likewise, differences between interviewees and students can be used to challenge students' notions of the "right" or "best" way to approach situations and accentuate how students are also products of their cultural contexts.

ACCULTURATION

Acculturation involves the integration of cultural beliefs, values, behaviors, and language of the host culture, whereas *enculturation* involves the integration of the same variables within one's heritage culture (Berry, Trimble, & Olmedo, 1986). Substantial research has examined the role of acculturation in relation to mental illness and well-being (Paniagua, 2013), attitudes toward psychotherapy (Rogers-Sirin, 2013), health outcomes (Lara, Gamboa, Kahramanian, Morales, & Hayes Bautista, 2005), culturally adapted interventions (Griner & Smith, 2006), and acculturative stress (Crockett et al., 2007).

Cultural adaptation may present challenges to Latinxs. Individuals with more collectivistic values and those living in societies like the United States that value assimilation may experience greater acculturative stress (Berry & Kim, 1988). Interestingly, individuals residing in ethnic enclaves, where new migrants can easily engage in daily activities with others from a similar heritage, may remain largely unacculturated to the host culture for much of their lives (Schwartz, Pantin, Sullivan, Prado, & Szapocznik, 2006). Youth are typically enrolled in school soon after migration, which partly explains their rapid acculturation.

Risk and protective factors associated with levels of acculturation highlight the heterogeneity among Latinxs. Among youth, acculturation has been associated with conduct problems (González, Knight, Morgan-Lopez, Saenz, &

---

[4]Visit this book's supplemental website for additional interview questions (http://pubs.apa.org/books/supp/mena).
[5]More details about the classroom component of the cultural values exercise can also be found on this book's companion website (http://pubs.apa.org/books/supp/mena).

Sirolli, 2002), increased substance use (Gfroerer & Tan, 2003), and sexual risk behaviors (Lee & Hahm, 2010). Latinas with low levels of acculturation report fewer sex partners and difficulty negotiating condom use compared with more acculturated Latinas who report the opposite. Latinos (i.e., men) with lower levels of acculturation report more sex partners and lower acceptability of condoms compared with more acculturated Latinos, who report fewer sexual risk behaviors (Sabogal, Perez-Stable, Otero-Sabogal, & Hiatt, 1995). To their advantage, some Latinxs experience the *immigrant paradox*: positive outcomes associated with recent, less acculturated immigrants despite the presence of economic and social risks. For example, Alegría, Mulvaney-Day, and colleagues (2007) reported that Mexican American immigrants had a lower lifetime prevalence of mental illness than comparable U.S.-born samples, whereas Puerto Ricans have a higher lifetime prevalence rate of psychiatric disorders.

Completing an acculturation scale in class and discussing the balance between acculturation and enculturation and associated beliefs, values, and behaviors can help students understand these concepts more fully (Stephenson, 2000; Unger et al., 2002).

ETHNIC AND RACIAL IDENTITY DEVELOPMENT

Ethnic identity development is a dynamic process involving intra- and interpersonal factors. The intrapersonal process involves the development of a self-concept informed by one's social group and associated values and emotional sense of what it means to be part of the group (Cornell & Hartmann, 2006). A strong ethnic identity has been associated with many benefits, including better coping with general and ethnicity-related stress (Kiang, Yip, Gonzales-Backen, Witkow, & Fuligni, 2006). In the United States, Latinx ethnic identity development occurs in a context of marginalization and oppression. Latinxs learn early that they are part of an ethnic group that is, in many ways, devalued by the dominant culture (Quintana & Scull, 2009). In some cases, the media perpetuate damaging gender and racial stereotypes that impact most negatively Latinxs with stronger ethnic identities (Rivadeneyra, Ward, & Gordon, 2007). Students could critically evaluate portrayals of Latinxs in the media to become more informed consumers and less susceptible to internalizing stereotypes.

Approximately 53% of U.S. Latinxs identify as racially White, 37% as some other race, 2.5% as Black, and fewer as indigenous (Ríos, Romero, & Ramírez, 2014). Black Latinxs are likely grossly underrepresented because of the history of race denial in Latin America. The documentary film series *Black in Latin America* (Gates, 2011) can springboard class discussions about Latinx racial identities. These films highlight the racial tensions in five different Caribbean and Latin American nations and help to contextualize the lack of identification with Blackness among Latinxs. There is a dearth of research about the experiences of darker skinned Afro Latinxs, who tend to report greater mental health concerns compared with their lighter skinned and White Latinx counterparts (Ramos, Jaccard, & Guilamo-Ramos, 2003).

Instructors should highlight that discrimination and oppression occur in implicit and explicit ways at both the individual and institutional level, thus requiring intervention at multiple ecological levels. At the beginning and end of a class, students can complete a cultural awareness measure (e.g., Ponterotto, Potere, & Johansen, 2002) devoted to critical self-reflection and an action plan to work toward a nondiscriminatory culturally inclusive identity.

CULTURALLY RESPONSIVE TREATMENTS WITH LATINXS

Instructors who teach abnormal psychology or Latinx psychology courses with students interested in clinical psychology can incorporate the topic of culturally responsive treatments with Latinxs. After introducing the topic, instructors can assign readings including Bernal and Domenech Rodríguez's (2012) meta-analysis of 65 experimental studies and 620 clients, which found that cultural adaptations work better than traditional therapies. These adaptations include incorporating cultural content and values, using the client's preferred language, and matching clients with therapists of similar ethnoracial identities. Instructors are also encouraged to discuss the best uses of cultural adaptations. Whaley and Davis (2007) suggested that cultural adaptations may be most important when engaging the client in treatment, rather than the outcome, whether in content, language, or approach. For example, Miranda et al. (2006) provided child care and transportation to enable low-income minority women to take part and gave participants educational sessions about depression and its treatment before delivering the intervention. Their culturally adapted cognitive behavior therapy, developed by Muñoz and Mendelson (2005), helped validate the values and experiences particular to their ethnoracial group—for example, using the common *dicho* (saying) *la gota de agua labra la piedra* (a drop of water carves a rock) to illustrate how thoughts, although transient, can gradually influence one's view of life and cause depression (Whaley & Davis, 2007). Students can read the APA presidential report, *Crossroads: The Psychology of Immigration in the New Century* (APA, 2012a), which provides a comprehensive overview of evidence-informed mental health treatment considerations. Instructors can ask students to name three treatment considerations included in the report and describe the research basis for them and an application example. Students can also read the report to learn about education, research, and policy recommendations to be inclusive of the gifts and talents of immigrants in the United States.

CONCLUSION

The Latinx population is young, growing, and diverse. We hope the contents of this chapter illuminate the most salient and influential factors impacting the Latinx population, though we do not purport to have exhausted the topics relevant to this population. We urge instructors to expose students to the topics herein and further explore experiences arising from intersectional identities; in doing so, we will help train a more culturally sensitive, knowledgeable, and skilled society.

REFERENCES

Alegría, M., Mulvaney-Day, N., Torres, M., Polo, A., Cao, Z., & Canino, G. (2007). Prevalence of psychiatric disorders across Latino subgroups in the United States. *American Journal of Public Health*, *97*, 68–75. http://dx.doi.org/10.2105/AJPH.2006.087205

Alegría, M., Shrout, P. E., Woo, M., Guarnaccia, P., Sribney, W., Vila, D., . . . Canino, G. (2007). Understanding differences in past year psychiatric disorders for Latinos living in the US. *Social Science & Medicine*, *65*, 214–230. http://dx.doi.org/10.1016/j.socscimed.2007.03.026

Alfaro, E. C., Umaña-Taylor, A. J., Gonzales-Backen, M. A., Bámaca, M. Y., & Zeiders, K. H. (2009). Latino adolescents' academic success: The role of discrimination, academic motivation, and gender. *Journal of Adolescence*, *32*, 941–962. http://dx.doi.org/10.1016/j.adolescence.2008.08.007

American Psychological Association. (2012a). *Crossroads: The psychology of immigration in the new century*. Retrieved from http://www.apa.org/topics/immigration/report.aspx

American Psychological Association. (2012b). *Dual pathways to a better America: Preventing discrimination and promoting diversity*. Retrieved from http://www.apa.org/pubs/info/reports/promoting-diversity.aspx

American Psychological Association. (2012c). *Ethnic and racial disparities in education: Psychology's contributions to understanding and reducing disparities*. Retrieved from http://www.apa.org/ed/resources/racial-disparities.aspx

Aud, S., Wilkinson-Flicker, S., Kristapovich, P., Rathbun, A., Wang, X., & Zhang, J. (2013). *The condition of education 2013* (NCES 2013-037). Retrieved from https://nces.ed.gov/pubs2013/2013037.pdf

Auerbach, S. (2007). From moral supporters to struggling advocates reconceptualizing parent roles in education through the experience of working-class families of color. *Urban Education*, *42*, 250–283. http://dx.doi.org/10.1177/0042085907300433

Behnke, A., Gonzalez, L., & Cox, R. (2010). Latino students in new arrival states: Factors and services to prevent youth from dropping out. *Hispanic Journal of Behavioral Sciences*, *32*, 385–409. http://dx.doi.org/10.1177/0739986310374025

Bernal, G. E., & Domenech Rodríguez, M. M. (Eds.). (2012). *Cultural adaptations: Tools for evidence-based practice with diverse populations*. Washington, DC: American Psychological Association. http://dx.doi.org/10.1037/13752-000

Berry, J. W., & Kim, U. (1988). Acculturation and mental health. In P. R. Dasen, J. W. Berry, & N. Sartorius (Eds.), *Health and cross-cultural psychology* (pp. 207–238). Newbury Park, CA: Sage.

Berry, J. W., Trimble, J. E., & Olmedo, E. L. (1986). Assessment of acculturation. In W. J. Lonner & J. W. Berry (Eds.), *Field methods in cross-cultural research: Cross-cultural research and methodology series* (Vol. 8, pp. 291–324). Thousand Oaks, CA: Sage.

Calzada, E. J., Tamis-LeMonda, C. S., & Yoshikawa, H. (2013). Familismo in Mexican and Dominican families from low-income, urban communities. *Journal of Family Issues*, *34*, 1696–1724. http://dx.doi.org/10.1177/0192513X12460218

Comas-Díaz, L. (2006). Latino healing: The integration of ethnic psychology into psychotherapy. *Psychotherapy: Theory, Research, Practice, Training*, *43*, 436–453. http://dx.doi.org/10.1037/0033-3204.43.4.436

Cornell, S. E., & Hartmann, D. (2006). *Ethnicity and race: Making identities in a changing world*. Newbury Park, CA: Pine Forge Press.

Crockett, L. J., Iturbide, M. I., Torres Stone, R. A., McGinley, M., Raffaelli, M., & Carlo, G. (2007). Acculturative stress, social support, and coping: Relations to psychological adjustment among Mexican American college students. *Cultural Diversity and Ethnic Minority Psychology, 13,* 347–355. http://dx.doi.org/10.1037/1099-9809.13.4.347

de las Fuentes, C., Barón, A., & Vásquez, M. (2003). Teaching Latino psychology. In P. Bronstein & K. Quina (Eds.), *Teaching gender and multicultural awareness: Resources for the psychology classroom* (pp. 207–220). Washington, DC: American Psychological Association. http://dx.doi.org/10.1037/10570-015

Duarté-Vélez, Y., Bernal, G., & Bonilla, K. (2010). Culturally adapted cognitive-behavior therapy: Integrating sexual, spiritual, and family identities in an evidence-based treatment of a depressed Latino adolescent. *Journal of Clinical Psychology, 66,* 895–906. http://dx.doi.org/10.1002/jclp.20710

Falicov, C. J. (2014). *Latino families in therapy* (2nd ed.). New York, NY: Guilford Press.

Fernández-Armesto, F. (2014). *Our America: A Hispanic history of the United States.* New York, NY: Norton.

Frey, W. H. (2005). *Immigration and domestic migration in US metro areas: 2000 and 1990 census findings by education and race* (Population Studies Center Research Report 05-472). Retrieved from http://frey-demographer.org/reports/R-2005-1_ImmDomesticMigrationMetroAreas.pdf

Fry, R., & Taylor, P. (2014). *Hispanic high school graduates pass Whites in rate of college enrollment.* Retrieved from http://www.pewhispanic.org/2013/05/09/hispanic-high-school-graduates-pass-whites-in-rate-of-college-enrollment/

García, E. E., & Scribner, K. P. (2009). Latino pre-k–3 education. In F. A. Villarruel, G. Carlo, J. M. Gau, M. Azmitia, N. J. Cabrera, & T. J. Chahin (Eds.), *Handbook of US Latino psychology: Developmental and community-based perspectives* (pp. 267–289). Thousand Oaks, CA: Sage.

Gates, H. L. (Producer). (2011). *Black in Latin America* [Motion picture]. United States: Public Broadcasting System.

Gfroerer, J. C., & Tan, L. L. (2003). Substance use among foreign-born youths in the United States: Does the length of residence matter? *American Journal of Public Health, 93,* 1892–1895. http://dx.doi.org/10.2105/AJPH.93.11.1892

González, N. A., Knight, G. P., Morgan-Lopez, A. A., Saenz, D., & Sirolli, A. (2002). Acculturation and the mental health of Latino youths: An integration and critique of the literature. In J. M. Contreras, K. A. Kerns, & A. M. Neal-Barnett (Eds.), *Latino children and families in the United States: Current research and future directions* (pp. 45–74). Westport, CT: Praeger.

González-López, G. (2004). Fathering Latina sexualities: Mexican men and the virginity of their daughters. *Journal of Marriage and Family, 66,* 1118–1130. http://dx.doi.org/10.1111/j.0022-2445.2004.00082.x

Gregory, A., & Weinstein, R. S. (2008). The discipline gap and African Americans: Defiance or cooperation in the high school classroom. *Journal of School Psychology, 46,* 455–475. http://dx.doi.org/10.1016/j.jsp.2007.09.001

Griner, D., & Smith, T. B. (2006). Culturally adapted mental health intervention: A meta-analytic review. *Psychotherapy: Theory, Research, Practice, Training, 43,* 531–548. http://dx.doi.org/10.1037/0033-3204.43.4.531

Haller, W., Portes, A., & Lynch, S. M. (2011). Dreams fulfilled and shattered: Determinants of segmented assimilation in the second generation. *Social Forces, 89,* 733–762. http://dx.doi.org/10.1353/sof.2011.0003

Henderson Daniel, J., & Evans, A. C., Jr. (2018, June 14). [Letter to President Donald Trump]. Retrieved from https://www.apa.org/advocacy/immigration/separating-families-letter.pdf

Hill, N. E., & Torres, K. (2010). Negotiating the American dream: The paradox of aspirations and achievement among Latino students and engagement between their families and schools. *Journal of Social Issues, 66,* 95–112. http://dx.doi.org/10.1111/j.1540-4560.2009.01635.x

Kiang, L., Yip, T., Gonzales-Backen, M., Witkow, M., & Fuligni, A. J. (2006). Ethnic identity and the daily psychological well-being of adolescents from Mexican and Chinese backgrounds. *Child Development, 77,* 1338–1350. http://dx.doi.org/10.1111/j.1467-8624.2006.00938.x

Lara, M., Gamboa, C., Kahramanian, M. I., Morales, L. S., & Hayes Bautista, D. E. (2005). Acculturation and Latino health in the United States: A review of the literature and its sociopolitical context. *Annual Review of Public Health, 26,* 367–397. http://dx.doi.org/10.1146/annurev.publhealth.26.021304.144615

Lee, J., & Hahm, H. C. (2010). Acculturation and sexual risk behaviors among Latina adolescents transitioning to young adulthood. *Journal of Youth and Adolescence, 39,* 414–427. http://dx.doi.org/10.1007/s10964-009-9495-8

Martinez, C. R., Jr., DeGarmo, D. S., & Eddy, J. M. (2004). Promoting academic success among Latino youth. *Hispanic Journal of Behavioral Sciences, 26,* 128–151. http://dx.doi.org/10.1177/0739986304264573

Masse, E. (Producer & Director), & Buzzell, M. (Director). (2007). *Compañeras* [Motion picture]. United States: CHC Productions.

Mena, J. A. (2011). Latino parent home-based practices that bolster student academic persistence. *Hispanic Journal of Behavioral Sciences, 33,* 490–506. http://dx.doi.org/10.1177/0739986311422897

Migration Policy Institute. (2015). *Relief from deportation: Demographic profile of the DREAMers potentially eligible under the deferred action policy.* Retrieved from http://observatoriocolef.org/_admin/documentos/FS24_deferredaction.pdf

Miranda, J., Green, B. L., Krupnick, J. L., Chung, J., Siddique, J., Belin, T., & Revicki, D. (2006). One-year outcomes of a randomized clinical trial treating depression in low-income minority women. *Journal of Consulting and Clinical Psychology, 74,* 99–111. http://dx.doi.org/10.1037/0022-006X.74.1.99

Muñoz, R. F., & Mendelson, T. (2005). Toward evidence-based interventions for diverse populations: The San Francisco General Hospital prevention and treatment manuals. *Journal of Consulting and Clinical Psychology, 73,* 790–799. http://dx.doi.org/10.1037/0022-006X.73.5.790

Nazario, A. (1998). Counseling Latinx families. In W. M. Parker (Ed.), *Consciousness-raising: A primer for multicultural counseling* (2nd ed., pp. 205–255). Springfield, IL: Charles C Thomas.

Ortiz, C. J., Valerio, M. A., & Lopez, K. (2012). Trends in Hispanic academic achievement: Where do we go from here? *Journal of Hispanic Higher Education, 11,* 136–148. http://dx.doi.org/10.1177/1538192712437935

Paniagua, F. A. (2013). *Assessing and treating culturally diverse clients: A practical guide.* Thousand Oaks, CA: Sage.

Passel, J. S., Livingston, G., & Cohn, D. (2012). *Explaining why minority births now out-number White births.* Retrieved from http://www.pewsocialtrends.org/2012/05/17/explaining-why-minority-births-now-outnumber-white-births/

Ponterotto, J. G., Potere, J. C., & Johansen, S. A. (2002). The Quick Discrimination Index: Normative data and user guidelines for counseling researchers. *Journal of Multicultural Counseling and Development, 30,* 192–207. http://dx.doi.org/10.1002/j.2161-1912.2002.tb00491.x

Quintana, S. M., & Scull, N. C. (2009). Latino ethnic identity. In F. A. Villarruel, G. Carlo, J. M. Gau, M. Azmitia, N. J. Cabrera, & T. J. Chahin (Eds.), *Handbook of US Latino psychology: Developmental and community-based perspectives* (pp. 81–98). Thousand Oaks, CA: Sage.

Ramos, B., Jaccard, J., & Guilamo-Ramos, V. (2003). Dual ethnicity and depressive symptoms: Implications of being Black and Latino in the United States. *Hispanic Journal of Behavioral Sciences, 25,* 147–173. http://dx.doi.org/10.1177/0739986303025002002

Rey, F. G. (2004). La crítica en la psicología social latinoamericana y su impacto en los diferentes campos de la psicología [The critic of the Latin American social psychology and its impact in the different areas of psychology]. *Revista Interamericana de Psicología, 38,* 351–360.

Ríos, M., Romero, F., & Ramírez, R. (2014). *Race reporting among Hispanics: 2010.* Retrieved from https://www.census.gov/population/www/documentation/twps0102/twps0102.pdf

Rivadeneyra, R., Ward, L. M., & Gordon, M. (2007). Distorted reflections: Media exposure and Latino adolescents' conceptions of self. *Media Psychology, 9,* 261–290. http://dx.doi.org/10.1080/15213260701285926

Rodríguez, J. L. (2002). Family environment and achievement among three generations of Mexican American high school students. *Applied Developmental Science, 6,* 88–94. http://dx.doi.org/10.1207/S1532480XADS0602_4

Rogers-Sirin, L. (2013). Segmented assimilation and attitudes toward psychotherapy: A moderated mediation analysis. *Journal of Counseling Psychology, 60,* 329–339. http://dx.doi.org/10.1037/a0032453

Rosenberg, T. (2013, April 10). The power of talking to your baby. *The New York Times.* Retrieved from https://opinionator.blogs.nytimes.com/2013/04/10/the-power-of-talking-to-your-baby/

Sabogal, F., Perez-Stable, E. J., Otero-Sabogal, R., & Hiatt, R. A. (1995). Gender, ethnic, and acculturation differences in sexual behaviors: Hispanic and non-Hispanic white adults. *Hispanic Journal of Behavioral Sciences, 17,* 139–159. http://dx.doi.org/10.1177/07399863950172001

Sandoval, C. (Producer), & Tambini, C. (Producer). (2014). *The state of Arizona* [Motion picture]. United States: Camino Bluff Productions.

Santiago-Rivera, A. L., Arredondo, P., & Gallardo-Cooper, M. (2002). *Counseling Latinos and la familia: A practical guide.* Thousand Oaks, CA: Sage.

Schwartz, S. J., Pantin, H., Sullivan, S., Prado, G., & Szapocznik, J. (2006). Nativity and years in the receiving culture as markers of acculturation in ethnic enclaves. *Journal of Cross-Cultural Psychology, 37,* 345–353. http://dx.doi.org/10.1177/0022022106286928

Stephenson, M. (2000). Development and validation of the Stephenson Multigroup Acculturation Scale (SMAS). *Psychological Assessment, 12,* 77–88. http://dx.doi.org/10.1037/1040-3590.12.1.77

Suro, R., & Tafoya, S. M. (2004). *Dispersal and concentration: Patterns of Latino residential settlement* (pp. 2–9). Washington, DC: Pew Hispanic Center.

Taylor, P., Lopez, M. H., Martínez, J., & Velasco, G. (2012). *When labels don't fit: Hispanics and their views of identity.* Retrieved from http://www.pewhispanic.org/2012/04/04/when-labels-dont-fit-hispanics-and-their-views-of-identity/

Triandis, H. C., Marín, G., Lisansky, J., & Betancourt, H. (1984). Simpatía as a cultural script of Hispanics. *Journal of Personality and Social Psychology, 47,* 1363–1375. http://dx.doi.org/10.1037/0022-3514.47.6.1363

Unger, J. B., Gallaher, P., Shakib, S., Ritt-Olson, A., Palmer, P. H., & Johnson, C. A. (2002). The AHIMSA acculturation scale: A new measure of acculturation for adolescents in a multicultural society. *The Journal of Early Adolescence, 22,* 225–251. http://dx.doi.org/10.1177/02731602022003001

U.S. Census Bureau. (2014). *Income and poverty in the United States: 2013.* Retrieved from https://www.census.gov/library/publications/2014/demo/p60-249.html

U.S. Census Bureau. (2015). *The Hispanic population: 2010.* Retrieved from https://www.census.gov/prod/cen2010/briefs/c2010br-04.pdf

Vásquez, M. J., & de las Fuentes, C. (1999). American-born Asian, African, Latina, and American Indian adolescent girls: Challenges and strengths. In N. G. Johnson, M. C. Roberts, & J. Worell (Eds.), *Beyond appearance:*

A new look at adolescent girls (pp. 151–173). Washington, DC: American Psychological Association.

Vega, W. A., Gil, A. G., & Wagner, E. (2002). Cultural adjustment and Hispanic adolescent drug use. In W. A. Vega & A. G. Gil (Eds.), *Drug use and ethnicity in early adolescence* (pp. 125–148). New York, NY: Plenum Press. http://dx.doi.org/10.1007/0-306-47147-7_6

Whaley, A. L., & Davis, K. E. (2007). Cultural competence and evidence-based practice in mental health services: A complementary perspective. *American Psychologist, 62,* 563–574. http://dx.doi.org/10.1037/0003-066X.62.6.563

Zuniga, M. (2004). Latino children and families. In R. Fong (Ed.), *Culturally competent practice with immigrant and refugee children and families* (pp. 183–201). New York, NY: Guilford Press.

10

Weaving American Indian and Alaska Native Topics Into the Psychology Curriculum

Joseph E. Trimble and Gayle Skawen:nio Morse

The terms *Native American* and *Native American Indian* often are used inter-changeably with *American Indian* and *Alaska Native* to refer to the indigenous, aboriginal peoples of North America. The National Congress of American Indians, the National Indian Education Association, and the Society of Indian Psychologists consider *Native American* to be too encompassing of ethnic groups in the United States, an "ethnic gloss" (Trimble & Bhadra, 2014). More accurately, with the extraordinary diversity of tribal backgrounds, many American Indians and Alaska Natives (AIANs) prefer to be referred to by their specific tribal names such as Dine (Navajo); Lakota, Dakota, and Nakota (Sioux); and Tohono O'odham (Papago), rather than an imposed category referring to close to 3 million people who represent more than 565 federally recognized tribes, an additional 225 or so nonfederally recognized tribes, and residents of about 220 Alaska Native villages (Snipp, 1996; U.S. Census Bureau, 2010a). We refer to this group as *American Indians*; however, students should be cautioned against generalizing from one tribal group to another or to Indians or Natives in general. Interestingly, the rapid increase in mixed ethnic and intertribal marriages is creating a subpopulation of American Indians who do not identify with any specific tribe, creating a broad pan-Indian ethnocultural category grounded in borrowed and internalized bits and pieces of different tribal traditions. Thornton (1996) suggested this may lead to a time when one will speak of "Native Americans as people of Native American ancestry or heritage" rather than members of specific tribes (p. 110).

---

http://dx.doi.org/10.1037/0000137-011
Integrating Multiculturalism and Intersectionality Into the Psychology Curriculum:
Strategies for Instructors, J. A. Mena and K. Quina (Editors)

Who belongs in the category of American Indians? Tribes, states, and the Bureau of Indian Affairs require that an individual document any tribal membership claim, creating an interesting issue: A tribe may identify membership by a kinship system or group approval (Bureau of Indian Affairs, 2015) rather than blood quantum (the amount of "Indian blood" a person has), whereas the U.S. Census Bureau uses self-identification. In the 2010 census, almost 3 million citizens identified as AIANs (U.S. Census Bureau, 2013)—a staggering 400% increase from 1960 that strains credulity. Because immigration does not generally occur among AIANs, such remarkable increases must be attributed to the growing inclination of Americans to declare their "Indianness." In addition, more than half of the American Indians in the 2010 census resided in urban areas, where they would be less likely to report tribal affiliation, speak or understand their tribal language, participate in tribal cultural activities, or marry Indians (Snipp, 1996; U.S. Census Bureau, 2010a, b).

TEACHING AMERICAN INDIAN PSYCHOLOGY

American Indian psychology covers an ethnic group that is considerably more diverse than groups that immigrated to North America. In the 17th century, a period of accelerated European colonization of North America, at least 150 tribal groups with unique worldviews and approximately 30 different languages resided east of the Mississippi River.

General Resources

A number of valuable resources are available for incorporating American Indian issues into psychology courses. Reviews include Kelso and Attneave (1981) on North American Indian mental health, Trimble and Bagwell (1995) on psychological and behavioral articles, and Lobb and Watts (1989) on alcohol use and abuse among American Indian youth. Dedicated journals include the *Journal of the National Center for American Indian and Alaska Native Mental Health Research* and the *American Indian Culture and Research Journal.* Supplemental material includes Bataille's (1993) bibliographic dictionary of 231 American Indian women born before 1960, Martin and O'Leary's (1990) bibliography of books and articles that describe the traditional culture and lifeways, and Sandefur, Rindfuss, and Cohen's (1996) edited volume on demographic and public health characteristics. Trimble and Clearing-Sky (2009) summarized the history of AIANs in psychology. The Society of Indian Psychologists (http://www.aiansip.org/) publishes the *Journal of Indigenous Research,* which addresses health and education issues.

Historical and Cultural Considerations in the Course Organization

Psychology tends to decontextualize the individual (Cole, 1996). However, in discussions of Indian and Native experiences, it is important to present topics in a social, political, and historical context. We begin with the history of Indian and European relations and the problems that colonialism presented for both populations (see Duran & Duran, 1995). From the moment of European contact with the Western hemisphere's indigenous population, the native people were viewed as an impediment to European immigration and settlement and the source of considerable intergroup conflict.[1] The indigenous people had claims to large tracts of resource-rich territory and the power to maintain and control them; the colonialists wanted those lands for settlement. Initially, many native groups were willing to share their resources, but as waves of Europeans arrived, their demands increased, leading to intense dissension and fighting (Trimble, 1987a).

This history closely follows Park's (1950) model of race relations, with one exception. Park maintained that "the race relations cycle takes the form . . . of contact, competition, accommodation and eventual assimilation (and this is) progressive and irreversible" (p. 150). However, many AIAN groups never reached Park's final stage of full assimilation into the mainstream of American life. Useful historical sources are Berkhofer (1978) and Thornton (1987).

We often provide alternative perspectives to conventional findings. In an introductory psychology unit on psychopathology, we include ethnographic descriptions of different tribes' views on extreme forms of behavioral and affective expressions (Reimer, 1999; Trimble, Manson, Dinges, & Medicine, 1984), including tribal-specific concepts such as "ghost sickness," soul loss and soul gain, spirit intrusion, and taboo breaking (Clements, 1932; Human Relations Area Files, http://hraf.yale.edu). This often provokes lively discussions about the implications and meaning of the concepts across tribal groups, particularly in light of contemporary approaches to diagnoses: What constitutes abnormal behavior in one culture may not be considered deviant in another, or there may be no concept of abnormality. Cultural context is now recognized in the *Diagnostic and Statistical Manual of Mental Disorders* (fifth ed.; American Psychiatric Association, 2013), and although not specifically focused on culture, the *International Statistical Classification of Diseases and Related Health Problems* (10th rev.; World Health Organization, 2010) considered local schemes that took into account language and cultural variations.

Suggested Topics for Inclusion

Students tend to respond most favorably to our material when presented in the context of a more familiar topic, adding related information and encouraging them to apply principles they have already learned.

Research Design and Methodology

Conducting field-based research with Indians and Natives presents special challenges to the scientific method and all that conventional laboratory science represents (Trimble, Scharron-del Rio, & Casillas, 2013). The setting of the

---

[1] A sample lecture for discussing intergroup conflict in the classroom is available from this book's companion webpage (http://pubs.apa.org/books/supp/mena).

community, local lifeways and thoughtways, and the validity of research proto-cols can influence study outcomes in unpredictable ways.

Cross-cultural researchers have developed culturally sensitive approaches for designing studies and protocols. Kim and Berry (1993) described specific research approaches that more effectively capture information with unique ethnocultural groups; see also Manson (1997). For example, the Akwesasne Mohawk Protocol for Reviewing Environmental and Scientific Research Pro-posals (Akwesasne Task Force on the Environment, 1996; Kloos et al., 2012) describes guidelines for conducting culturally sensitive and acceptable com-munity research in the Mohawk community, including a cultural training component undergirded by Mohawk values and belief systems. The com-munity drives the research questions, methods, and even data management (Santiago-Rivera, Morse, Hunt, & Lickers, 1998).

A native-sensitive research project grounded in a community-based partici-patory research model is the Yup'ik Experiences of Stress and Coping project (Rivkin et al., 2010). Designed to fit the local cultural lifeways and thoughtways, community members and tribal entities informed the understanding of the constructs, validation of results, and dissemination of findings. Such cultural understandings are critical for informing interventions that reflect communi-ties' unique histories, realities, and worldviews (Trimble et al., 2013).

Measurement equivalence occurs when constructs under investigation mean the same thing, or measure the same characteristic, across cultural groups (Johnson, 1998; Trimble & Vaughn, 2014). Explaining equivalence to students reinforces the notion that not all cultures conceive of behavior, cognition, and affect in the same ways. We typically provide students with five to 10 survey items and ask them to obtain translations of the items from international stu-dents and then ask other students from the countries represented in the first translation to translate the items back into English. Often the exercise takes place in class, a more powerful lesson. We discuss the universal applicability of the forced-choice response scales used in conventional surveys and other research strategies (Berry, Poortinga, Segall, & Dasen, 1992; Trimble, 1977).

Personality, Identity, and Self-Image

To begin a discussion of personality issues, we ask students to draw a picture of an American Indian. Not surprisingly, they often draw a person wearing a feather or blanket with a sort of blank look on her or his face—a good stimulus for con-sideration of perceived image versus reality. We ask students what influenced their perceptions and attributions and to describe the personality of the image they drew, again probing as to origins of their descriptions. We then discuss the presumed relationship between ethnic identity and self-image and problems such as poverty, alcoholism, and suicide (Trimble, 1987b, 2000). Often, students believe that people from oppressed cultures or impoverished backgrounds cannot possibly have positive self-images or stable personalities. We challenge this perspective with Rosenberg's (1989) research on Black and White adoles-cent self-esteem and recent literature in positive psychology on American Indians' strengths and resilience (G. S. Morse, McIntyre, & King, 2016).

We introduce the emic versus etic approaches and present case studies from classic anthropology, in which distinguished ethnographers portrayed AIAN tribes as collective, single-minded personality types (P. J. Deloria, 1998). For example, Honigmann (1954) described the Kaska Indian of northern British Columbia and the Yukon Territory as "unaccustomed and unwilling to respond to any leader," "flexible rather than rigid in his behavior," and showing a "tendency to suppress in his behavior all strong emotion" (pp. 9–10). We ask students to comment on and debate these statements and their etic approach.

Counseling and Psychotherapy

Mainstream psychology often emphasizes individualism, assertiveness, status, open communication with strangers, and other approaches at odds with the traditional lifeways and thoughtways of nonacculturated Indians and Natives (Gonzalez & Trimble, 2015; King, Trimble, Morse, & Thomas, 2014; Trimble, King, LaFromboise, Bigfoot, & Norman, 2014). We provide tribal-specific conceptualizations of illness, shamanism, and traditional healing (Hawk Wing, 1997; Trimble et al., 1984; Voss, Douville, Little Soldier, & Twiss, 1999), pointing out that complicated procedures involving the community, and often incorporating dancing, have evolved to deal with individual problems (Jilek, 1989). Most Native-oriented approaches and diagnostic categories center on the spiritual domain; for example, Powers (1982) described the Yuwipi man among the Lakota as "particularly suited and trained by the spirits to diagnose and treat 'Indian sickness,' illnesses that generally were common to the people before the white man arrived" (Mohatt & Eagle Elk, 2000, p. 35). We often work with our classes as a simulated community and work as a team as we examine "cases" and learn how to work effectively in native community settings.[2]

Gonzalez and Trimble (2015), Herring (1999), and Reimer (1999) described models for effective culturally sensitive counseling for American Indian clients and communities. Gone and Trimble's (2012) literature review concluded that "community members themselves are increasingly advocating for culturally alternative approaches and opportunities to address their mental health needs on their own terms" (p. 131). Informative films and videos include *White Shamans, Plastic Medicine Men* (Macy & Hart, 1996); *Pomo Shaman* (Heick & Mueller, 1953); *Denial, Healing and Hope: The Nishnawbe-Aski Nation Youth Forum on Suicide* (Sanders, 1994); and *Indian Horse* (Devonshire, Dolman, Haebler, & Campanelli, 2017).

American Indian psychologists, students, and elders community-sourced the question "Does the APA [American Psychological Association] code of ethics work for us?" (Garcia & Teehee, 2013), inspiring indigenous communities worldwide to develop their own sets of ethical guidelines concerning indigenous psychology (G. S. Morse & Blume, 2014). A teaching manual was developed to assist teachers in these important discussions because this is such a novel indigenous approach to ethics (Thomas & Morse, 2017).

---

[2]This book's companion webpage includes a sample lecture about working culturally and competently with American Indians and Alaskan Natives (http://pubs.apa.org/books/supp/mena).

Alcohol and Drug Use

There is a considerable literature from etiology and epidemiology to treatment and aftercare, and it is rife with myth, stereotypic imagery, and inaccuracy. However, it should be included, because alcohol use and misuse are considered by most U.S. indigenous people to be their most serious and significant health problem, especially for youth residing on reservations (Oetting, Edwards, & Beauvais, 1989), affecting almost every facet of their lives (May, 1992). Non-reservation Indian youth have been found to have levels of drug use lower than those living on reservations but higher than their non-Indian counterparts; Indian boarding school students and high school dropouts report even higher drug use (Beauvais, 1992). Although reservation life has many positive aspects, there may be environmental variables (e.g., pervasive poverty and unemployment) that promote higher levels of substance use.

Fetal alcohol syndrome has an unusually high incidence among Indians and Natives; see May's (1992) research and Dorris's (1990) poignant *The Broken Cord.* Students may bring up the relationship of genetics to alcoholism among American Indians, a topic with little empirical research. The conversation tends to be lively; we encourage them to explore all aspects, including methodological issues.

Evidence has suggested that pollutants from mining, industrial plants, and dumping toxins near reservations have serious psychological and public health implications for the residents. Several studies have found that persistent organic pollutants, arsenic, and mercury are related to neuropsychological deficits and decrements in measures of intelligence in American Indian populations (Haase, McCaffrey, Santiago-Rivera, Morse, & Tarbell, 2009; Newman et al., 2009). We tend to weave current events into historical discussions about who owns the earth and how pollution affects us all, which tend to be thought provoking, with much student engagement. Sometimes students can be divided into teams to debate differing points of view concerning current events, which then allows us to deeply consider the issues and make efforts to understand things from all perspectives.

Stereotypes and Prejudice

Social scientists are uncovering the deleterious impact of perceived discrimination on health care seeking behaviors, including cancer and diabetes (Gonzales, Lambert, Fu, Jacob, & Harding, 2014). Discrimination occurs for AIAN communities via covert and some overt ways where systems of power, privilege, and oppression continue to intersect with the needs of AIAN communities. This intersection of conflicting views and needs fuels the difficulties that AIANs experience.

Popular press and historical depictions can guide discussions about stereotypes (V. Deloria, 1997). Furthermore, helping students to understand intersectional identities may help them to dispel stereotypes and embrace the diversity within AIANs (APA, 2017). We review historical facts, illustrating the many distortions by non-Indians (Berkhofer, 1978; Weatherford, 1988). Next, we examine contemporary conditions and issues that fuel prejudice and discrimination, such as Indian "mascots," showing *In Whose Honor? American Indian*

Mascots in Sports (Rosenstein, 1997). When exposed to common images of American Indian mascots, Indian students generated positive associations but reported depressed self-esteem and community worth and fewer achievement-related possible selves, suggesting that they "remind American Indians of the limited ways others see them and, in this way, constrain how they can see themselves" (Fryberg, Markus, Oyserman, & Stone, 2008, p. 208). Students can critique popular movies involving American Indians (Hilger, 1995; Kilpatrick, 1999). Also useful are literature reviews by Berkhofer (1978), Bird (1999), and Trimble (1987a, 1988) and contemporary concerns discussed by Duran and Duran (1995).

Films examining cultural issues in the United States include *House Made of Dawn* (R. Morse & Teets, 1996) and *Without Reservations: Notes on Racism in Montana* (Hyyppa & Monaco, 1995). Several YouTube videos explore portrayals of Indians and Natives in the media and cinema; we value *Native American Mascot Debate* (WGBH News, 2017), *American Indians Are People NOT Mascots* (Tho, 2011), *How Hollywood Stereotyped the Native American* (framesinmotion2007, 2007), and *In Whose Honor?* (Hansen, 2013).

Suggested Assignments and Activities

Literature Review

Guided by the cross-cultural counseling protohypotheses developed by Sue and Sundberg (1996), students select a hypothesis and prepare a literature review to substantiate its validity. They then design a research strategy for testing the hypothesis with a specific tribal group, including a rationale based on that tribe's lifeways and thoughtways. In a related activity, students identify a social psychological principle of conflict resolution and write an essay illustrating how it could be applied to explain an event in the history of Indian–White relations (Trimble, 1987a).

We Are All Connected

The Lakota phrase *aho mitakuye oyasin* (all my relations), often spoken during and following a prayer and a ceremony to acknowledge all relatives in the moment, demonstrates ancient Lakota wisdom about interconnectedness—in essence, one is thanking all of life. It is more than honoring our relatives; because we are connected to all that is in the world around us, we are honoring all that is about us. It also has contemporary applications; for example, in the Netherlands, work on organizational justice used the notion of "all my relations" to show how indigenous thought can enrich organization justice theory (Whiteman, 2009). Students can read John Guare's (1990) *Six Degrees of Separation* or watch the popular movie of the same title and discuss this theme.

We substantiate this belief early in the course in a yarn exercise that demonstrates that interconnectedness exists in networks with overlapping ties. In small groups of six to 15 people, each person is given a ball of colored yarn; the more colors, the better. The first person offers a self-statement such as "I like lox and bagels; does anyone else like them?" and when another person responds, the first person holds the yarn end and tosses the ball to them. That person then makes a self-statement, and so on, until everyone has spoken several times. Soon, everyone should be connected to several others in the group in a quite colorful network. They can reflect on how "connected" they feel with the visible and "felt" presence of holding the yarn. They can observe "homeostasis" by having one or more people pull on their grasped yarn or let it go limp and observe the result or practice cooperative problem solving by placing a ball onto the yarn pattern and trying as a group to move it around the perimeter.

Classroom Values

In advanced seminars, we address value orientations of different cultural groups (Trimble, 1976) such as collective versus individual-oriented cultures. We demonstrate the value of sharing through the potlatch system of the northwest coast tribes in Canada and the United States. Students are asked to bring something of value to the next class meeting, knowing they may have to give it to someone else. At that class, students sit a circle, placing their valued possession in the center. They must pick out their valued possession and give it to another student in the circle, someone whom they respect and wish to honor for their value to the group. When students do not receive recognition or gifts, the discussion can become spirited as they attempt to deal with being overlooked. Discussions invariably gravitate to the difference between the reciprocity norm and sharing one's possessions without expecting to receive anything in return.

Classroom Debate

Toward the end of the term, students participate in a debate about a controversial Indian and Native issue. Students are randomly assigned to a "pro" or "con" group or an evaluation team—for example, should indigenous populations be left alone to govern themselves (isolationism), or should they be brought into the flow of the modern world through assimilation and modernization tactics and pressures? This debate is informed by Cowell's (1970) haunting video *The Tribe That Hides From Man: The Kreen-Akrore* (MindzLiberal, 2013) and excerpts from his book by the same name (Cowell, 1973/1996).

CONCLUSION

Psychological research about AIANs has historically been limited to mental health and substance abuse problems, in part because these are major concerns to their communities. Recently, scholarship has expanded to a number of areas, providing students the opportunity to compare and contrast this information with conventional presentations of psychological topics. Given the breadth of the current literature, instructors should avoid anecdotal and impressionistic material that can lead to inaccurate generalizations. The careful and thoughtful weaving of AIAN topics can expand students' understanding of diverse cultures and enhance their worldview to include alternative perspectives on human behavior.

REFERENCES

Akwesasne Task Force on the Environment & the Research Advisory Committee. (1996). *Protocol for review of environmental and scientific research proposals.* Hogansburg, NY: Author.

American Psychiatric Association. (2013). *The diagnostic and statistical manual of mental disorders* (5th ed.). Arlington, VA: Author.

American Psychological Association. (2017). *Multicultural guidelines: An ecological approach to context, identity, and intersectionality.* Retrieved from http://www.apa.org/about/policy/multicultural-guidelines.pdf

Bataille, G. (1993). *Native American women: A bibliographical dictionary.* New York, NY: Garland.

Beauvais, F. (Ed.). (1992). Indian adolescent drug and alcohol use: Recent patterns and consequences [Special issue]. *American Indian and Alaska Native Mental Health Research, 5*(l).

Berkhofer, R. (1978). *The White man's Indian.* New York, NY: Vintage.

Berry, J. W., Poortinga, Y. H., Segall, M., & Dasen, R. R. (1992). *Cross cultural psychology: Research and applications.* New York, NY: Cambridge University Press.

Bird, E. S. (1999). Gendered construction of the American Indian in popular media. *Journal of Communication, 49*, 61–83. http://dx.doi.org/10.1111/j.1460-2466.1999.tb02805.x

Bureau of Indian Affairs. (2015). *Bureau of Indian Affairs certificate of degree of Indian or Alaska Native blood instructions.* Retrieved from http://www.indianaffairs.gov/cs/groups/xraca/documents/text/idc1-029262.pdf

Clements, F. E. (1932). Primitive concepts of disease. *American Archaeology and Ethnology, 32*, 185–252.

Cole, M. (1996). *Cultural psychology: A once and future discipline.* Cambridge, MA: Harvard University Press.

Cowell, A. (Producer & Director). (1970). *The tribe that hides from man: The Kreen-Akrore* [Motion picture]. United States: Institute for the Study of Human Issues.

Cowell, A. (1996). *The tribe that hides from man.* London, England: Pimlico. (Original work published 1973)

Deloria, P. J. (1998). *Playing Indian.* New Haven, CT: Yale University Press.

Deloria, V. (1997). *Red earth, White Native Americans and the myth of scientific fact.* New York, NY: Fulcrum.

Devonshire, P. (Producer), Dolman, T. (Producer), Haebler, C. (Producer), & Campanelli, S. (Director). (2017). *Indian horse* [Motion picture]. Canada: Elevation Pictures.

Dorris, M. (1990). *The broken cord.* New York, NY: Harper & Row.

Duran, E., & Duran, B. (1995). *Native American postcolonial psychology.* Albany: State University of New York Press.

framesinmotion2007. (2007, October 31). *How Hollywood stereotyped the Native Americans* [Video file]. Retrieved from https://www.youtube.com/watch?v=_hJFi7SRH7Q

Fryberg, S. A., Markus, H. R., Oyserman, D., & Stone, J. M. (2008). Of warrior chiefs and Indian princesses: The psychological consequences of American Indian mascots. *Basic and Applied Social Psychology, 30*, 208–218. http://dx.doi.org/10.1080/01973530802375003

Garcia, M., & Teehee, M. (2013). *Society of Indian Psychologists commentary on the American Psychological Association* Ethical Principles of Psychologists and Code of Conduct. Retrieved from https://www.aiansip.org/commentary.html

Gone, J. P., & Trimble, J. E. (2012). American Indian and Alaska Native mental health: Diverse perspectives on enduring disparities. *Annual Review of Clinical Psychology, 8*, 131–160. http://dx.doi.org/10.1146/annurev-clinpsy-032511-143127

Gonzales, K. L., Lambert, W. E., Fu, R., Jacob, M., & Harding, A. K. (2014). Perceived racial discrimination in health care, completion of standard diabetes services, and diabetes control among a sample of American Indian women. *The Diabetes Educator*, *40*, 747–755. http://dx.doi.org/10.1177/0145721714551422

Gonzalez, J., & Trimble, J. E. (2015). Counseling North American indigenous peoples. In P. Pedersen, J. Draguns, W. Lonner, M. Sharron-del Rio, & J. E. Trimble (Eds.), *Counseling across cultures* (7th ed., pp. 101–120). Thousand Oaks, CA: Sage.

Guare, J. (1990). *Six degrees of separation: A play*. New York, NY: Random House.

Haase, R. F., McCaffrey, R. J., Santiago-Rivera, A. L., Morse, G. S., & Tarbell, A. (2009). Evidence of an age-related threshold effect of polychlorinated biphenyls (PCBs) on neuropsychological functioning in a Native American population. *Environmental Research*, *109*, 73–85. http://dx.doi.org/10.1016/j.envres.2008.10.003

Hansen, K. (2013, May 6). *In whose honor?* [Video file]. Retrieved from https://www.youtube.com/watch?v=8lUF95ThI7s

Hawk Wing, P. (1997). Lakota teachings: Inipi, Humbleciya, and Yuwipi ceremonies. In D. F. Sandner & S. H. Wong (Eds.), *The sacred heritage: The influence of shamanism on analytical psychology* (pp. 193–202). New York, NY: Routledge.

Heick, W. (Director), & Mueller, G. (Director). (1953). *Pomo shaman* [Motion picture]. United States: University of California American Indian Film Project.

Herring, R. D. (1999). *Counseling with Native American Indians and Alaska Natives: Strategies for helping professionals*. Thousand Oaks, CA: Sage.

Hilger, M. (1995). *From savage to nobleman: Images of Native Americans in film*. Lanham, MD: Scarecrow Press.

Honigmann, J. (1954). *Culture and personality*. New York, NY: Harper & Row.

Hyyppa, J. (Producer), & Monaco, P. (Producer). (1995). *Without reservations: Notes on racism in Montana* [Motion picture]. United States: Native Voices Public Television Workshop.

Jilek, W. (1989). Therapeutic use of altered states of consciousness in contemporary North American dance ceremonials. In C. Ward (Ed.), *Altered states of consciousness and mental health* (pp. 167–185). Newbury Park, CA: Sage.

Johnson, T. P. (1998). Approaches to equivalence in cross-cultural and cross-national survey. In J. A. Harkness (Ed.), *Cross-cultural survey equivalence* (Nachrichten Spezial, No. 3, pp. 1–40). Mannheim, Denmark: Zentrum fur Umfragen, Methoden und Analysen.

Kelso, D., & Attneave, C. (Eds.). (1981). *Bibliography of North American Indian mental health*. Westport, CT: Greenwood Press.

Kilpatrick, J. (1999). *Celluloid Indians: Native Americans and film*. Lincoln: University of Nebraska Press.

Kim, U., & Berry, J. W. (Eds.). (1993). *Indigenous psychologies: Research and experience in cultural context*. Newbury Park, CA: Sage.

King, J., Trimble, J. E., Morse, G. S., & Thomas, L. R. (2014). North American Indian and Alaska Native spirituality and psychotherapy. In S. P. Richards & A. E. Bergin (Eds.), *Handbook of psychotherapy and religious diversity* (2nd ed., pp. 451–472). Washington, DC: American Psychological Association. http://dx.doi.org/10.1037/14371-018

Kloos, B., Hill, J., Thomas, E., Wandersman, A., Elias, M. J., & Dalton, J. H. (2012). *Community psychology: Linking individuals and communities* (3rd ed.). Belmont, CA: Wadsworth.

Lobb, M. L., & Watts, T. W. (1989). *Native American youth and alcohol: An annotated bibliography*. Westport, CT: Greenwood Press.

Macy, T. (Director), & Hart, D. (Director). (1996). *White shamans and plastic medicine men* [Motion picture]. United States: Native Voices.

Manson, S. M. (1997). Ethnographic methods, cultural context, and mental illness: Bridging different ways of knowing and experience. *Ethos*, *25*, 249–258.

Martin, M., & O'Leary, L. (1990). *Ethnographic bibliography of North America* (4th ed. suppl., 1973–1987). New Haven, CT: Human Relations Area Files.

May, P. (1992). Fetal alcohol syndrome and American Indians: A positive challenge in public health and prevention. In E. Haller & L. Aitken (Eds.), *Mashkiki: Old medicine nourishing the new* (pp. 61–68). Lanham, MD: University Press of America.

MindzLiberal. (2013, February 25). *The tribe that hides from man (1970)* [Video file]. Retrieved from https://www.youtube.com/watch?v=AYrLo_BUeUk

Mohatt, G., & Eagle Elk, J. (2000). *The price of a gift: A Lakota healer's story*. Lincoln: University of Nebraska Press.

Morse, G. S., & Blume, A. W. (2014). Does the American Psychological Association Ethical Code work for us? *Journal of Indigenous Research*. Retrieved from https:// digitalcommons.usu.edu/kicjir/vol3/iss1/2/

Morse, G. S., McIntyre, J. G., & King, J. (2016). Positive psychology in American Indians. In E. Chang, C. A. Downey, J. K. Hirsch, & N. Lin (Eds.), *Handbook of positive psychology in racial and ethnic minority groups: Theory, research, assessment, and practice* (pp. 109–127). Washington, DC: American Psychological Association. http://dx.doi.org/10.1037/14799-006

Morse, R. (Producer), & Teets, E. (Producer). (1996). *House made of dawn* [Motion picture]. United States: New Line Home Video.

Newman, J., Gallo, M. V., Schell, L. M., DeCaprio, A. P., Denham, M., & Deane, G. D. (2009). Analysis of PCB congeners related to cognitive functioning in adolescents. *Neurotoxicology, 30,* 686–696. http://dx.doi.org/10.1016/j.neuro.2009.05.006

Oetting, E., Edwards, R., & Beauvais, F. (1989). Drugs and Native American youth. *Drugs & Society, 3,* 1–34. http://dx.doi.org/10.1300/J023v03n01_01

Park, R. E. (1950). *Race and culture.* New York, NY: Free Press.

Powers, W. (1982). *Yuwipi: Vision and experience in Oglala ritual.* Lincoln: University of Nebraska Press.

Reimer, C. S. (1999). *Counseling the Inupiat Eskimo.* Westport, CT: Greenwood Press.

Rivkin, I. D., Lopez, E., Quaintance, T. M., Trimble, J., Hopkins, S., Fleming, C., . . . Mohatt, G. V. (2010). Value of community partnership for understanding stress and coping in rural Yup'ik communities: The CANHR study. *Journal of Health Disparities Research and Practice, 4*(3), 2.

Rosenberg, M. (1989). Old myths die hard: The case of Black self esteem. *Revue Internationale de Psychologie Sociale, 2,* 355–365.

Rosenstein, J. (Producer). (1997). *In whose honor? American Indian mascots in sports* [Motion picture]. United States: Jay Rosenstein Productions.

Sandefur, G., Rindfuss, R., & Cohen, B. (Eds.). (1996). *Changing numbers, changing needs: American Indian demography and public health.* Washington, DC: National Academy Press.

Sanders, L. (Producer & Director). (1994). *Denial, healing and hope: The Nishnawbe-Aski Nation Youth Forum on Suicide* [Motion picture]. Canada: Northern Lights.

Santiago-Rivera, A., Morse, G., Hunt, A., & Lickers, H. (1998). Building a community-based research partnership: Lessons from the Mohawk Nation of Akwesasne. *Journal of Community Psychology, 26,* 163–174. http://dx.doi.org/10.1002/(SICI)1520-6629 (199803)26:2<163::AID-JCOP5>3.0.CO;2-Y

Snipp, C. M. (1996). The size and distribution of the American Indian population: Fertility, mortality, residence, and migration. In G. Sandefur, R. Rindfuss, & B. Cohen (Eds.), *Changing numbers, changing needs: American Indian demography and public health* (pp. 17–52). Washington, DC: National Academy Press.

Sue, D., & Sundberg, N. (1996). Research and research hypotheses about effectiveness in intercultural counseling. In P. Pedersen, J. Draguns, W. Lonner, & J. Trimble (Eds.), *Counseling across cultures* (4th ed., pp. 323–352). Thousand Oaks, CA: Sage.

Tho, S. (2011, December 16). *American Indians are people NOT mascots* [Video file]. Retrieved from https://www.youtube.com/watch?v=Pjy5ASZQb_Y

Thomas, J. T., & Morse, G. S. (2017). *Instructor's manual for the SIP commentary on the APA Ethics Code.* Logan, UT: SIP.

Thornton, R. (1987). *American Indian holocaust and survival: A population history since 1492.* Norman: University of Oklahoma Press.

Thornton, R. (1996). Tribal membership requirements and the demography of "old" and "new" Native Americans. In G. Sandefur, R. Rindfuss, & B. Cohen (Eds.), *Changing numbers, changing needs: American Indian demography and public health* (pp. 103–112). Washington, DC: National Academy Press.

Trimble, J. E. (1976). Value differentials and their importance in counseling American Indians. In P. Pedersen, J. Draguns, W. Lonner, & J. Trimble (Eds.), *Counseling across cultures* (rev. ed., pp. 203–226). Honolulu, HI: University Press of Hawaii.

Trimble, J. E. (1977). The sojourner in the American Indian community: Methodological concerns and issues. *Journal of Social Issues, 33,* 159–174. http://dx.doi.org/10.1111/j.1540-4560.1977.tb02529.x

Trimble, J. E. (1987a). American Indians and interethnic conflict: A theoretical and historical overview. In J. Boucher, D. Landis, & K. Arnold (Eds.), *Ethnic conflict: International perspectives* (pp. 208–229). Beverly Hills, CA: Sage.

Trimble, J. E. (1987b). Self-perception and perceived alienation among American Indians. *Journal of Community Psychology, 15,* 316–333. http://dx.doi.org/10.1002/1520-6629(198707)15:3<316::AID-JCOP2290150305>3.0.CO;2-E

Trimble, J. E. (1988). Stereotypic images, American Indians, and prejudice. In P. Katz & D. Taylor (Eds.), *Toward the elimination of racism: Profiles in controversy* (pp. 181–202). New York, NY: Pergamon. http://dx.doi.org/10.1007/978-1-4899-0818-6_9

Trimble, J. E. (2000). Social psychological perspectives on changing self-identification among American Indians and Alaska Natives. In R. H. Dana (Ed.), *Handbook of cross-cultural multicultural personality assessment* (pp. 197–222). Mahwah, NJ: Erlbaum.

Trimble, J., & Bagwell, W. (Eds.). (1995). *North American Indians and Alaska Natives: Abstracts of psychological and behavioral literature, 1967–1995.* Washington, DC: American Psychological Association.

Trimble, J. E., & Bhadra, N. (2014). Ethnic gloss. In K. Keith (Ed.), *Encyclopedia of cross-cultural psychology* (p. 500). New York, NY: Wiley.

Trimble, J. E., & Clearing-Sky, M. (2009). An historical profile of American Indians and Alaska Natives in psychology. *Cultural Diversity and Ethnic Minority Psychology, 15,* 338–351. http://dx.doi.org/10.1037/a0015112

Trimble, J. E., King, J., LaFromboise, T. D., Bigfoot, D. S., & Norman, D. (2014). North American Indian mental health. In R. Parekh & D. Dominguez (Eds.), *The Massachusetts General Hospital textbook on cultural sensitivity and diversity in mental health* (pp. 119–138). New York, NY: Springer. http://dx.doi.org/10.1007/978-1-4614-8918-4_5

Trimble, J. E., Manson, S., Dinges, N., & Medicine, B. (1984). Towards an understanding of American Indian concepts of mental health: Some reflections and directions. In A. Marsella, N. Sartorius, & P. Pedersen (Eds.), *Mental health services: The cross-cultural context* (pp. 199–220). Beverly Hills, CA: Sage.

Trimble, J. E., Scharron-del Rio, M., & Casillas, D. (2013). Ethical matters and contentions in the principled conduct of research with ethnocultural communities. In F. T. L. Leong, L. Comas-Díaz, G. N. Hall, V. McLloyd, & J. E. Trimble (Eds.), *Handbook of multicultural psychology* (Vol. 1, pp. 59–82). Washington, DC: American Psychological Association.

Trimble, J. E., & Vaughn, L. (2014). Cultural measurement equivalence. In K. Keith (Ed.), *Encyclopedia of cross-cultural psychology* (p. 213). New York, NY: Wiley.

U.S. Census Bureau. (2010a). *American Indian and Alaska Native only.* Retrieved from www.census.gov/programs-surveys/decennial-census/decade.2010.html

U.S. Census Bureau. (2010b). *American Indian and Alaska Native with one or more other race.* Retrieved from www.census.gov/programs-surveys/decennial-census/decade.2010.html

U.S. Census Bureau. (2013). *Overview of race and Hispanic origin: 2010.* Washington, DC: Government Printing Office.

Voss, R., Douville, V., Little Soldier, A., & Twiss, G. (1999). Tribal and shamanic-based social work practice: A Lakota perspective. *Social Work, 44,* 228–241. http://dx.doi.org/10.1093/sw/44.3.228

Weatherford, J. (1988). *Indian givers: How the Indians of the Americas transformed the world.* New York, NY: Fawcett-Columbine.

WGBH News. (2017, June 8). *Native American mascot debate* [Video file]. Retrieved from https://www.youtube.com/watch?v=zGnBW23g9Rc

Whiteman, G. (2009). All my relations: Understanding perceptions of justice and conflict between companies and indigenous peoples. *Organization Studies, 30,* 101–120. http://dx.doi.org/10.1177/0170840608100518

World Health Organization. (2010). *International statistical classification of diseases and related health problems* (10th rev., Vol. 2). Retrieved from http://www.who.int/classifications/icd/ICD10Volume2_en_2010.pdf

11

Intersections Among Religion, Culture, Gender, and Mental Health

Kate Miriam Loewenthal

Religion and spirituality are hugely important to most of humanity. About 85% of the world's population claim adherence to a religious group: Christianity (2.2 billion); Hinduism (1 billion); Islam (1.6 billion); and other religions, including Buddhism, Judaism, Sikhism, and traditional ethnic religions (1.1 billion); leaving 1.1 billion secular, including agnostic and atheist. Although the psychology of religion as a specific field has developed well over recent decades, traditional psychology still fails to attend to religious issues in studying developmental, social, occupational, and other areas of psychology. In this chapter, I offer resources[1] and strategies to address these oversights.

INSTRUCTIONAL FRAMEWORKS

It is important to begin by defining and differentiating among religion, spirituality, and culture. *Religion* involves the acceptance of spirituality, a moral system, and a sense of purpose. *Spirituality* has been defined as the search for and experience of the sacred (Pargament & Mahoney, 2018). Religiosity and spirituality usually co-occur. *Culture* comprises the ideas, customs, and social behavior of a particular people or society (see Loewenthal, 2007). Each of these exerts a strong influence on people's ideas, feelings, and behavior, and it is instructive to help students disentangle the roles of each where possible. When introducing

---

[1]A list of recommended resources is also available on this book's companion webpage (http://pubs.apa.org/books/supp/mena).

http://dx.doi.org/10.1037/0000137-012
Integrating Multiculturalism and Intersectionality Into the Psychology Curriculum: Strategies for Instructors, J. A. Mena and K. Quina (Editors)

the topic, instructors can ask students for examples when the religious and cultural influences may be confused. The celebration of Christmas in Western society is sometimes cited as an example, among others.

It is important to establish ground rules for discussions of beliefs—a student's own or others'. The content can be highly personal, and students may have difficulty viewing topics outside their own religion or culture. Nonjudgmental, respectful treatment of others is essential, and the instructor must be prepared to step in to dispel myths or inappropriate comments.

Class discussions can start with straightforward questions, such as, What are the largest religions in the world? Can you order Islam, Christianity, Buddhism, Judaism, and Hinduism with respect to numbers of followers? In what countries or regions of the world is each religion most likely to be found?[2] They can also locate statistics on different religions in their country. Students often cannot name or locate several of these and are surprised at the diversity.

If students are comfortable doing so, they can discuss how important religious beliefs are to their lives and their friends. They can describe (anonymously) people they have met from different religious groups and the similarities and differences between their experiences of religion. Be prepared to step in to dispel myths and help students distinguish the roles of religion and culture. Often, students' only awareness of systems other than their own comes from media and stereotypes, and they have not differentiated the impacts of religion and culture. They can research a society with repressive laws and practices and ask whether religion seems to direct the repression or whether it is being used as a political tool to maintain power over members.

To help students understand the important distinction between religion and spirituality, they can describe the kinds of impacts each has in their lives or friends' lives. They can share (anonymously) examples of people who are spiritual but not religious to help them explore these concepts more deeply, as well as their roles and identity, cultural and religious contexts, and the impact on mental health.

CONCEPTUAL FRAMEWORKS

Gender, race, and other differences may be mistakenly seen as universal when they are culturally and religiously specific. This chapter adopts an intersectional and identity process approach, looking at ways in which the effects of gender, culture, and religion interact in different contexts and regarding identity as complex and fluid. It also raises issues which should be borne in mind, especially in social, developmental, and clinical (abnormal) psychology courses.

Intersectionality focuses on interactions between different social categories or features of identity, contributing to profound forms of disadvantage and

---

[2] A quiz about the size of various world religions, including a follow-up reflection exercise for students to complete, is also available for download from this book's companion website (http://pubs.apa.org/books/supp/mena).

injustice. Crenshaw (1991) studied and highlighted ways in which battering and rape are features of systematic domination of Women of Color. If either gender or ethnicity were considered in isolation, it would not enable the detection of the difficult, sometimes horrendous experiences resulting from their intersection. Consider Aisha, Edith, and Jonathan.

> Aisha immigrated from Pakistan to the North of England. She worked hard in a poorly paid, boring job and looked after her husband, children, and in-laws. Her husband complained a lot about her cooking and housekeeping. She could not pray, feeling that Allah was not with her, and she became depressed and felt she was not a good Muslim. A neighbor advised seeing a doctor, but her mother-in-law said this would bring shame on the family (Loewenthal, 2015; acknowledgments to Cinnirella & Loewenthal, 1999, and Gilbert, Gilbert, & Sanghera, 2004).
>
> Edith, in the United States, had been forcibly separated from her American Indian family and brought up with a White family. In this family, she was made to believe that she was dirty and inferior, that all American Indians were alcoholics, drunks who would never amount to anything. As an adolescent, she returned to her people and began to hear stories of the trauma experienced by her family and her people. She believes that her shame and disappointment at being told she was inferior and her sharing the experience of her people were factors leading to her alcoholism. She joined a culture-specific sobriety program and, like others, felt that learning about American Indian spirituality and culture were important in helping her to lose her shame of herself, stay sober, and develop an identity in which she could take pride and pleasure (based on Myhra, 2011).
>
> Jonathan is a Jewish businessman living in the United Kingdom. His business faltered, and he became tired and irritable and could not talk peaceably with his wife, from whom he is now divorced. He felt he had lost respect in the community, and he slept and ate poorly. He tried to conceal his consumption of spirits, and he did not socialize in pubs and had no close friends (based on Loewenthal, 2007).

Instructors can prompt students to discuss the factors intersecting with gender for Aisha, Edith, and Jonathan; alcohol use in each case; religious beliefs and identity; and impact on economic productivity.

Identity is complex, fluid, and constantly developing, comprising "elements" that constantly interact. Breakwell's (2010) identity process theory proposes that identity is not a static, neatly labeled entity but a complex dynamic process involving elements varying in salience and value as the individual adapts to circumstances, as in Steve's case.

> Steve is a hardworking, ambitious husband and father. He worked long hours and was getting promotions in his managerial position. Suddenly he was made redundant. He searched for a new job, but he was not successful. His highly valued professional identity lost its salience and value, as did his identity as the provider for the family. He began to feel worthless and useless, sleeping badly and eating poorly. He began to spend more time with his children, even going with his family to church—about which he had previously been scornful. His father identity gained in salience and value, and his religious identity, previously feeble, gained a little salience and value as it hitchhiked on the changes in his husband and father identities (based on Coyle, 2011).

Instructors can help students explore the features of Steve's identity. How do they change in salience and value? What might be their impact on Steve's well-being?

Berry's (1997) acculturation theory describes four conceptions of identity, which enable a more elaborate view of the processes involved in intersectionality: (a) *integration*, in which one's culture and host culture are both valued and salient; (b) *assimilation*, devaluing one's own culture and valuing the host culture; (c) *separation* and *segregation*, valuing one's culture and rejecting the host culture; and (d) *marginalization*, low valuing of both one's culture and the host culture. Are students familiar with minority group members in any of these four positions? Which might be more comfortable? Berry, Kim, Power, Young, and Bujaki (1989) reported that among adults in multicultural societies, integration is associated with the highest levels of well-being, whereas marginalization is associated with the lowest levels.

IMPACTS OF RELIGION AND SPIRITUALITY

Mental Health

Although prolific, research on mental health and religion and spirituality, until recently, was largely restricted to U.S. students of Christian and occasionally Jewish background (see Koenig, King, & Carson, 2012; Loewenthal, 2007, 2015; Pargament et al., 2013). Conclusions to date include, first, weak but positive relationships between measures of religiosity and religious activity and measures of mental health (Koenig et al., 2012; Loewenthal, 2007). Specific effects may vary in different religious and cultural groups; for example, among Jews, the more religiously active engage in limited social drinking. This is associated with low levels of alcohol abuse but may lead to raised prevalence of depression among men because social drinking is not used as a means of coping among men as it is in other religious and cultural groups (Loewenthal et al., 1995; Loewenthal, Lee, MacLeod, Cook, & Goldblatt, 2003; Loewenthal, MacLeod, Cook, Lee, & Goldblatt, 2003). Among American Indians, the covariations of levels of alcohol use, gender, prevalence of depression, and revival of spirituality may follow similar patterns but remain to be fully explored (Beals et al., 2005).

Second, negative effects of particular religious beliefs or practices, such as spiritual abuse or a view of G-d as punitive or indifferent, may be underresearched and underreported (Koenig et al., 2012; Loewenthal, 2007). Third, psychologically damaging rules and practices have been justified and sanctified as religious when there is no such sanction or justification in cases such as female genital mutilation (FGM), discussed later in this chapter. Fourth, barriers to seeking professional help related to religious and cultural factors often involve shame and stigma. Some religions explicitly shun professional treatment options, focusing on explanations such as sin and referring the individual to seek guidance or "education" within their religion (Leavey, Loewenthal, & King, 2007). Fifth, religious behavior has been misdiagnosed as psychotic. Describing a Black American lawyer who believed that a candle dripping wax on a Bible while he prayed was sending heavenly messages, Fulford

(1999) observed that many trainee psychiatrists suspected psychosis. Yossifova and Loewenthal (1999) found individuals described as religiously active were more likely to be judged as psychologically disturbed, compared with individuals with identical case vignettes not said to be religiously active. Sixth, for the significant minority defining themselves as "spiritual but not religious," spirituality may be negatively related to mental health. King et al. (2013) suggested, "People who have a spiritual understanding of life in the absence of a religious framework are vulnerable to mental disorder" (p. 68), including anxiety disorders, abnormal eating attitudes, and drug dependency. After reviewing some of the findings in the literature, instructors can ask students whether they find the conclusions plausible and whether they have come across any relevant examples.

Marriage

Most women have the biological capacity to give birth and nurse infants, whereas men are freer to provide material support for their families and play important roles in caring for and socializing older children. In some cultures, this general pattern has been overlaid by cultural and religious sanctions, even when there are no such religious justifications. Sanctification—even though baseless—adds power to a tradition.

In the United States, religion has been associated with better marital functioning and lower divorce rates. However, most studies have used only single-item or global indices of religion, such as affiliation, importance of religion, or frequency of attendance; more in-depth measures are needed to indicate how these effects are achieved (Mahoney, Pargament, Tarakeshwar, & Swank, 2008). Marriage is desired, religiously sanctioned, and encouraged in most societies and generally entails obligations that would normally have positive effects on well-being, such as love, respect, and support. Yet sometimes marriage entails negative practices that are regarded as religious in origin, although there is no such religious authority. Examples of exploitation and oppression of women can be instructive. For example, before the 1880s, British women experienced the loss of all property after marriage because property was automatically transferred to the husband (Combs, 2005; Griffin, 2003). Even today, in many countries, women's property rights are nonexistent or limited (Agarwal, 1994); it is often customary in South Asia to regard married women as the property of their husband and his family, and contact with a woman's family of origin may cease altogether (see Aisha's vignette, presented earlier).

There are enormous variations in rulings across cultures and religions, making it difficult to generalize about women's rights. Economic activity by women has long been shown to protect against depression (e.g., Brown & Harris, 1989). Yet economic dependency on husbands and fathers continues in many countries, with some occupations closed to married women or even to all women. Citing data from the World Bank report "Women, Business, and the Law," Kate Davidson (2015) reported that, globally, 90% of countries have laws that discriminate against women in employment; in 18 nations, women cannot get a job without their husband's permission. Russia bans 456 occupations to women, and in France, women cannot take any jobs where they must lift more than 25 kilos, even though women often carry children of that weight on a daily basis. Mirza and Jenkins's (2004) review of studies in Pakistan found that economic difficulties and poor education, being a housewife, relationship problems with in-laws, and absence of confiding supportive relationships were associated with depression.

Similarly, the agonizing, life-threatening, and potentially permanently disabling practice of FGM is claimed by practitioners to be important in facilitating a girl's future role as a good wife. FGM is particularly likely in Muslim and adjacent countries, though it probably predates Islam. Although popularly regarded as religiously authorized, there is no religious authority for it, and it is not required in Islam (United Nations Children's Fund, 2013). There are serious health and obstetric consequences and likely psychological dangers, including posttraumatic stress disorder (FGM National Group, 2015).

There are some explicit religious justifications for practices that may be detrimental to well-being: For example, in Islam and some forms of Mormonism, polygamy is permitted although not universally practiced. Polygamy (compared with monogamy) has been reported to be associated with higher level of domestic violence against women and women's psychiatric disturbance, including depression, somatization, and psychoticism (Al-Krenawi, 2013; Karamagi, Tumwine, Tylleskar, & Heggenhougen, 2006).

These issues are particularly relevant when teaching about family relationships and the psychology of women. Students can examine these issues with an eye to distinguishing religious from cultural factors and recognizing the power of using religious sanctity as a persuader. Questions can be raised about class members' hopes for marriage and their views on how religious beliefs and non-belief and culture affect these hopes and experiences.

Domestic Violence

Violence in intimate relationships is likely present in all societies. Severe violence by men is more frequent and results in more serious injuries, although regardless of gender, experiencing domestic violence (DV) is associated with raised risk of a range of outcomes, including depressive disorders, substance abuse, and chronic mental and physical illness (Coker et al., 2002). The brief video *13 Heartbreaking Confessions of Domestic Violence Survivors* (As/Is, 2015) offers an idea of how DV and its aftermath are experienced. Widely regarded as a method of asserting masculine superiority (e.g., Crenshaw, 1991), DV also has a cultural and religious intersection. Hayati, Emmelin, and Eriksson (2014) identified three groups of men's attitudes in rural Indonesia: traditionalists accepted violence as a means of upholding the superior position of men within marriage, pragmatists saw violence as undesirable but sometimes necessary to improve women's behavior, and egalitarians saw no reason for violence. The video *ICRW's* [International Center for Research on Women] *Priya Nanda Talks to BBC News About Violence Against Women in India* (ICRW, 2013) offers examples of changing attitudes in India. Instructors can encourage dialogue by asking students questions such as, Have you encountered beliefs about masculine superiority? Are such beliefs likely to be associated with the use or condoning of violence? What are the beliefs about gender socialization differences and their influence on DV?

Nason-Clark (2004) highlighted several ways in which religions affect the likelihood of DV and responses to it; for example, reported rates of DV among Christian families in the United States are similar to rates reported nationally, suggesting that a religious family is not a guaranteed safe place in spite of affirmative marriage vows. Nason-Clark suggested that religious images of domestic contentment may make the discovery and reporting of DV difficult. Students could consider why religion might be seen as promoting harmony. Professionals and volunteers in women's refuges may see religion as causing and/or supporting abuse. Why might they have such beliefs? They may work to persuade abused women to abandon not only their husbands but also their religion (Whipple, 1987), which can prolong and exacerbate victims' distress. How might these effects happen? Interventions must be culturally sensitive; members of one Jewish community told me their only local DV shelter did not provide a strictly kosher diet or meet other requirements, so strictly Orthodox women were reluctant to seek refuge there (Loewenthal & Rogers, 2004). Religious beliefs may often be important in coping with adversity and may not be readily abandoned (Pargament et al., 2013). Students can be asked to generate examples of religious beliefs as a form of coping.

Cultural norms regarding married women as the property of their husbands and husbands' families may also license the use of violence against wives and have been cited as at least partially responsible for the high suicide rate among young Asian Muslim women immigrants (Ineichen, 2012).

> Fatima, a Muslim woman with three children aged 5, 10, and 11, has been married for 13 years and lives in the heart of the (South Asian immigrant) community. Over the last 10 years, she has experienced physical and emotional abuse from her husband and his family, especially her mother-in-law. She feels trapped and unable to get away. It would mean leaving her children and bringing shame on the family (based on Gilbert et al., 2004).

Gilbert et al.'s (2004) work illustrates a powerful sense of entrapment experienced by many wives, bolstered by the importance of maintaining family honor (*izzat*). This leads to a strong conflict with Western values because women and their families may feel strongly that an abused wife must endure for the sake of preserving *izzat*. Some participants endorsed suicide as a possible response to DV so that *izzat* is not compromised. Here again, culturally supported practices are asserted as embodying sacred values, without justification (Loewenthal, 2013). Many Westerners decry these effects of *izzat* but might there be some positive effects, at least as seen by those within the culture?

Some religions and cultures, such as those in Guatemala and Ecuador, are more collectivist than others, creating a reluctance to seek help for problems and psychological distress (Hofstede, 1980). Because psychotherapy is concerned with promoting individual welfare, it may not be valued or sought in these cultures; even speaking out about DV may be futile or even punished. Seeking therapy may also be seen as a betrayal of religion (Weatherhead & Daiches, 2010). For example, Muslim immigrant women may report services to be culturally and religiously inappropriate, preferring religious and family and social support unless the mental health issue is really serious.

Students can discuss the range of religiously related effects that lead to underreporting of DV and reluctance to seek help and as a group suggest ways to improve sensitivity and provide needed help within such intersections of religion, gender, and culture.

Depression

It has often been suggested that women are more vulnerable to depressive illness than are men (e.g., Nolen-Hoeksema, 2001). For example, unipolar depression is often a response to adversity but may be tempered by coping, temperament, and genetic factors; not being sensitized by early adversity; and social support (Brown & Harris, 1989; Kendler et al., 2010; Mirza & Jenkins, 2004). Each of these factors can be affected by culture and religion, and alcohol use can further add to this complexity. The video *Love at First Drink—An Alcoholic Story* (Turning Point of Tampa Inc, 2010) is one of many offering a view of the experiences and feelings that go along with alcohol use and abuse.

In general, those with higher scores on measures of religious activity and belief tend to experience lower levels of depression. However, this relationship may be moderated by the number of adverse life events, which may vary by gender and by religiosity (Loewenthal et al., 1997; Loewenthal, MacLeod, Goldblatt, Lubitsh, & Valentine, 2000; Smith, McCullough, & Poll, 2003). Among (religious) Jews, men and women are equally likely to experience depressive disorder (Levav et al., 1993; Loewenthal et al., 1995; Pirutinsky, Rosmarin, Pargament, & Midlarsky, 2011), although overall prevalence of depression in Jewish communities is similar to that in the United States (about 10%). One possible factor is that moderate alcohol use lowers the prevalence of depression (Loewenthal, 2009), and Jewish culture does not support recreational drinking and drunkenness.

Although there is cultural variation, and although alcohol consumption among women is rising (Scottish Health Action on Alcohol Problems and the Institute of Alcohol Studies, 2017), women generally consume less alcohol than do men. There are cultural and religious attitudes specific to women's alcohol consumption (Scottish Health Action on Alcohol Problems and the Institute of Alcohol Studies, 2017); Loewenthal, Lee, et al. (2003) found that religious Jews and Protestants expressed concern about the loss of control associated with excessive alcohol intake, and women considered it less appropriate to drink and get drunk than did men and reported less drinking. Quotes from the interviews can be discussed in relation to students' personal, cultural, and religious beliefs.

Because of our history (as Jews) we are permanently on guard in a way . . . there's a feeling that drinking will put you off guard and who knows what might happen . . . there is a need to be kind of "in control." (Jewish man, p. 208)

It can lead to abuse or to violence . . . it can cause husbands hitting wives . . . destroying furniture, things like this . . . attacking wives and children. (Jewish woman, p. 209)

I find it demeaning and undignified [for a woman to be drunk and] out of control. (Jewish woman, p. 209)

Alcohol consumption is higher among California Jews pursuing an assimilationist acculturation style, in which Jewish identity is less valued and less salient than less-assimilated East-coast Jews, especially among men (Levav, Kohn, Golding, & Weissman, 1997). Moderate recreational use of alcohol in coping with stress may be effective in reducing rates of depression among men (e.g., Lipton, 1994), though there are risks (see, e.g., *Alcoholism & Depression*; 101alcoholism, 2011).

What about Muslims? Islam bans the use of alcohol, although the prevalence of depression is generally high, and the rates for women are approximately double those among men (Loewenthal, 2009; Mirza & Jenkins, 2004). This effect may result from the social, economic, and political disempowerment of women in Muslim society, rendering women relatively more vulnerable to adversity and further raising their prevalence of depression.

Historically, many North American Indian (NAI) tribes with strong family interconnections led a somewhat-mobile life, using agriculture and hunting for food. European settlers displaced the Native Americans from their territories and often confined them to reservations. Conditions remain adverse on many reservations (see Chapter 10, this volume). Although there was a division of labor by gender, NAI women were generally treated with respect by men (Crow Dog, 1990; Hungry Wolf, 1982), and before the 19th century, religious leadership was undertaken by both men and women. However, once confined to reservations, men were unable to hunt, and unemployment was high; children were often forcibly sent for adoption by White families to ensure assimilation of Western values; poverty and starvation were widespread. Cheap "Injun liquor" was used by the invading Whites to subdue unrest, and alcoholism and DV became widespread. Mary Crow Dog (1990) described this intersection with gender: As men were deprived of the opportunity of providing for their families by hunting, they began to abuse alcohol and other substances, to drive recklessly, and to abuse women physically. Although forms of adversity differed for men and women, the damage to well-being may have been equally great, involving alienation and enforced assimilation imposed by governmental authority.

Each tribe has its own spiritual and cultural traditions, although the late 20th-century revival of NAI spirituality often incorporates practices shared by different tribes (Crow Dog, 1990). Programs and individual efforts to reduce alcoholism among NAIs have intrinsically meshed with the revival of tribal spirituality. This revival often meant protest and, more often for men, incarceration, leaving women unsupported in the care of their children, again a form of adversity delineated by gender. Yet many also report that the rise in the salience and value of NAI identity and spirituality is a key feature in raising self-esteem, eliminating dependence on alcohol and other substances, and the adoption and pursuit of worthwhile life goals. Quotes from participants in Donovan et al. (2015) reflected the impact of using NAI spiritual healing rituals to combat alcohol abuse:

> I think . . . having Healing of the Canoe as a class in high school definitely helped me and also made changes in some of the other kids' lives. It was a good learning opportunity and a great experience. Good way to learn knowledge about drugs and alcohol. The people that I got a chance to learn with, we strengthened our bond over the three workshops. (p. 62)

This material can help students understand that there is no simple, single cause of depression; instead, we see a range of interactions between identity, religion, acculturation, and gender. Furthermore, the frequent claim of women's proneness to depression is by no means universal; for example, culturally and religiously governed patterns of alcohol use affect the depression gender disparity.

CONCLUSION

Our psychology textbooks still offer little information about religion-related factors and their effects. These influences have to be integrated across the curriculum, not confined to a rarely taught "psychology of religion" course. Intersections, particularly with gender, are tremendously important. For instance, students may have varying views on how religion might disempower or support women, questions they can be encouraged to pursue.

Religious beliefs and practices can be a source of both good and bad feelings and behaviors, and further research should uncover the conditions under which these effects occur. Clearly, there are powerful effects of gender, varying in different religious and cultural contexts and often tragically related to the relative powerlessness of women. There is also a need for additional research examining the effects on mental health, including the effects of living secular and religious lifestyles. Finally, more research is needed on the powerful *sanctification effect*: understanding how customs and habits can acquire religious sanctity even when there are no religious sources to justify them.

REFERENCES

Agarwal, B. (1994). Gender and command over property: A critical gap in economic analysis and policy in South Asia. *World Development, 22,* 1455–1478. http://dx.doi.org/10.1016/0305-750X(94)90031-0

Al-Krenawi, A. (2013). Mental health and polygamy: The Syrian case. *World Journal of Psychiatry, 3,* 1–7. http://dx.doi.org/10.5498/wjp.v3.i1.1

As/Is. (2015, November 17). *13 heartbreaking confessions of domestic violence survivors* [Video file]. Retrieved from https://youtu.be/N1K_tx4pJ2A

Beals, J., Manson, S. M., Whitesell, N. R., Mitchell, C. M., Novins, D. K., Simpson, S., & Spicer, P. (2005). Prevalence of major depressive episode in two American Indian reservation populations: Unexpected findings with a structured interview. *The American Journal of Psychiatry, 162,* 1713–1722. http://dx.doi.org/10.1176/appi.ajp.162.9.1713

Berry, J. W. (1997). Immigration, acculturation and adaptation. *Applied Psychology, 46,* 5–68.

Berry, J. W., Kim, U., Power, S., Young, M., & Bujaki, M. (1989). Acculturation attitudes in plural societies. *Applied Psychology, 38,* 185–206. http://dx.doi.org/10.1111/j.1464-0597.1989.tb01208.x

Breakwell, G. M. (2010). Resisting representations and identity processes. *Papers on Social Representations, 19*(6) 1–6,11.

Brown, G. W., & Harris, T. O. (Eds.). (1989). *Life events and illness.* London, England: Unwin Hyman.

Cinnirella, M., & Loewenthal, K. M. (1999). Religious and ethnic group influences on beliefs about mental illness: A qualitative interview study. *British Journal of Medical Psychology, 72,* 505–524. http://dx.doi.org/10.1348/000711299160202

Coker, A. L., Davis, K. E., Arias, I., Desai, S., Sanderson, M., Brandt, H. M., & Smith, P. H. (2002). Physical and mental health effects of intimate partner violence for men and women. *American Journal of Preventive Medicine, 23,* 260–268. http://dx.doi.org/10.1016/S0749-3797(02)00514-7

Combs, M. B. (2005). "A measure of legal independence": The 1870 Married Women's Property Act and the portfolio allocations of British wives. *The Journal of Economic History, 65,* 1028–1057. http://dx.doi.org/10.1017/S0022050705000392

Coyle, A. (2011). Critical responses to faith development theory: A useful agenda for change? *Archiv für Religionspsychologie/Archive for the Psychology of Religions, 33,* 281–298. http://dx.doi.org/10.1163/157361211X608162

Crenshaw, K. (1991). Mapping the margins: Intersectionality, identity politics, and violence against women of colour. *Stanford Law Review, 43,* 1241–1299. http://dx.doi.org/10.2307/1229039

Crow Dog, M. (1990). *Lakota woman.* New York, NY: Grove Wiedenfeld.

Davidson, K. (2015, September 9). In 18 countries, women cannot get a job without their husband's permission. *The Wall Street Journal.* Retrieved from https://blogs.wsj.com/economics/2015/09/09/in-18-nations-women-cannot-get-a-job-without-their-husbands-permission/

Donovan, D. M., Thomas, L. R., Sigo, R. L. W., Price, L., Lonczak, H., Lawrence, N., . . . Bagley, L. (2015). Healing of the canoe: Preliminary results of a culturally tailored intervention to prevent substance abuse and promote tribal identity for Native youth in two Pacific Northwest tribes. *American Indian and Alaska Native Mental Health Research, 22,* 42–76. http://dx.doi.org/10.5820/aian.2201.2015.42

FGM National Group. (2015). *Psychological aspects.* Retrieved from http://www.fgmnationalgroup.org/psychological_aspects.htm

Fulford, K. W. M. (1999). From culturally sensitive to culturally competent. In K. Bhui & D. Olajide (Eds.), *Mental health service provision for a multi-cultural society* (pp. 111–115). London, England: Saunders.

Gilbert, P., Gilbert, J., & Sanghera, J. (2004). A focus group exploration of the impact of izzat, shame, subordination and entrapment on mental health and service use in South Asian women living in Derby. *Mental Health, Religion & Culture, 7,* 109–130. http://dx.doi.org/10.1080/13674670310001602418

Griffin, B. (2003). Class, gender, and liberalism in Parliament, 1868–1882: The case of the Married Women's Property Acts. *Historical Journal, 46,* 59–87. http://dx.doi.org/10.1017/S0018246X02002844

Hayati, E. N., Emmelin, M., & Eriksson, M. (2014). "We no longer live in the old days": A qualitative study on the role of masculinity and religion for men's views on violence within marriage in rural Java, Indonesia. *BMC Women's Health, 14*(58). http://dx.doi.org/10.1186/1472-6874-14-58

Hofstede, G. (1980). *Culture's consequences: Individual differences in work-related values.* Beverly Hills, CA: Sage.

Hungry Wolf, B. (1982). *The ways of my grandmothers.* New York, NY: Quill.

ICRW. (2013, October 22). *ICRW's Priya Nanda talks to BBC News about violence against women in India* [Video file]. Retrieved from https://youtu.be/fJGx7fj7sHM/

Ineichen, B. (2012). Mental illness and suicide in British South Asian adults. *Mental Health, Religion & Culture, 15,* 235–250. http://dx.doi.org/10.1080/13674676.2011.643861

Karamagi, C. A. S., Tumwine, J. K., Tylleskar, T., & Heggenhougen, K. (2006). Intimate partner violence against women in eastern Uganda: Implications for HIV prevention. *BMC Public Health, 6,* 284. http://dx.doi.org/10.1186/1471-2458-6-284

Kendler, K. S., Kessler, R. C., Walters, E. E., MacLean, C., Neale, M. C., Heath, A. C., & Eaves, L. J. (2010). Stressful life events, genetic liability, and onset of an episode of major depression in women. *Focus, 8,* 459–470.

King, M., Marston, L., McManus, S., Brugha, T., Meltzer, H., & Bebbington, P. (2013). Religion, spirituality and mental health: Results from a national study of English households. *The British Journal of Psychiatry, 202,* 68–73. http://dx.doi.org/10.1192/bjp.bp.112.112003

Koenig, H., King, D., & Carson, V. (Eds.). (2012). *Handbook of religion and health.* New York, NY: Oxford University Press.

Leavey, G., Loewenthal, K., & King, M. (2007). Challenges to sanctuary: The clergy as a resource for mental health care in the community. *Social Science & Medicine, 65,* 548–559. http://dx.doi.org/10.1016/j.socscimed.2007.03.050

Levav, I., Kohn, R., Dohrenwend, B. P., Shrout, P. E., Skodol, A. E., Schwartz, S., . . . Naveh, G. (1993). An epidemiological study of mental disorders in a 10-year cohort of young adults in Israel. *Psychological Medicine, 23,* 691–707. http://dx.doi.org/10.1017/S0033291700025472

Levav, I., Kohn, R., Golding, J. M., & Weissman, M. M. (1997). Vulnerability of Jews to affective disorders. *The American Journal of Psychiatry, 154,* 941–947. http://dx.doi.org/10.1176/ajp.154.7.941

Lipton, R. I. (1994). The effect of moderate alcohol use on the relationship between stress and depression. *American Journal of Public Health, 84,* 1913–1917. http://dx.doi.org/10.2105/AJPH.84.12.1913

Loewenthal, K. M. (2007). *Religion, culture and mental health.* Cambridge, England: Cambridge University Press.

Loewenthal, K. M. (2009). The alcohol-depression hypothesis: Gender and the prevalence of depression among Jews. In L. Sher (Ed.), *Comorbidity of depression and alcohol use disorders* (pp. 31–40). New York, NY: Nova Science Publishers.

Loewenthal, K. M. (2013). Religion, spirituality and culture: Clarifying the direction of effects. In K. I. Pargament, J. Exline, J. Jones, A. Mahoney, & E. Shafranske (Eds.), *Handbook of psychology, religion, and spirituality* (Vol. 1, pp. 239–255). Washington, DC: American Psychological Association.

Loewenthal, K. M. (2015). Psychiatry and religion. In J. D. Wright (Ed.), *International encyclopedia of the social and behavioral sciences* (2nd ed., Vol. 19, pp. 307–312). Oxford, England: Elsevier. http://dx.doi.org/10.1016/B978-0-08-097086-8.27061-X

Loewenthal, K., Goldblatt, V., Gorton, T., Lubitsch, G., Bicknell, H., Fellowes, D., & Sowden, A. (1995). Gender and depression in Anglo-Jewry. *Psychological Medicine, 25,* 1051–1063. http://dx.doi.org/10.1017/S0033291700037545

Loewenthal, K. M., Goldblatt, V., Lubitsch, G., Gorton, T., Bicknell, H., Fellowes, D., & Sowden, A. (1997). The costs and benefits of boundary maintenance: Stress, religion and culture among Jews in Britain. *Social Psychiatry and Psychiatric Epidemiology, 32,* 200–207. http://dx.doi.org/10.1007/BF00788239

Loewenthal, K. M., Lee, M., MacLeod, A. K., Cook, S., & Goldblatt, V. (2003). Drowning your sorrows? Attitudes towards alcohol in UK Jews and Protestants: A thematic analysis. *International Journal of Social Psychiatry, 49*, 204–215. http://dx.doi.org/10.1177/00207640030493006

Loewenthal, K. M., MacLeod, A. K., Cook, S., Lee, M., & Goldblatt, V. (2003). Beliefs about alcohol among UK Jews and Protestants: Do they fit the alcohol-depression hypothesis? *Social Psychiatry and Psychiatric Epidemiology, 38*, 122–127. http://dx.doi.org/10.1007/s00127-003-0609-4

Loewenthal, K. M., MacLeod, A. K., Goldblatt, V., IV, Lubitsh, G., & Valentine, J. D. (2000). Comfort and joy: Religion, cognition and mood in Protestants and Jews under stress. *Cognition and Emotion, 14*, 355–374. http://dx.doi.org/10.1080/026999300378879

Loewenthal, K. M., & Rogers, M. B. (2004). Culture-sensitive counselling, psychotherapy and support groups in the Orthodox-Jewish community: How they work and how are they experience. *International Journal of Social Psychiatry, 50*, 227–240. http://dx.doi.org/10.1177/0020764004043137

Mahoney, A., Pargament, K. I., Tarakeshwar, N., & Swank, A. B. (2008). Religion in the home in the 1980s and 1990s: A meta-analytic review and conceptual analysis of links between religion, marriage, and parenting. *Psychology of Religion and Spirituality, S*, 63–101. http://dx.doi.org/10.1037/1941-1022.S.1.63

Mirza, I., & Jenkins, R. (2004). Risk factors, prevalence, and treatment of anxiety and depressive disorders in Pakistan: Systematic review. *BMJ, 328*, 794–799. http://dx.doi.org/10.1136/bmj.328.7443.794

Myhra, L. L. (2011). "It runs in the family": Intergenerational transmission of historical trauma among urban American Indians and Alaska Natives in culturally specific sobriety maintenance programs. *American Indian and Alaska Native Mental Health Research, 18*, 17–40. http://dx.doi.org/10.5820/aian.1802.2011.17

Nason-Clark, N. (2004). When terror strikes at home: The interface between religion and domestic violence. *Journal for the Scientific Study of Religion, 43*, 303–310. http://dx.doi.org/10.1111/j.1468-5906.2004.00236.x

Nolen-Hoeksema, S. (2001). Gender differences in depression. *Current Directions in Psychological Science, 10*, 173–176. http://dx.doi.org/10.1111/1467-8721.00142

101alcoholism. (2011, October 2). *Alcoholism & depression* [Video file]. Retrieved from https://youtu.be/5clhhl8IV1w

Pargament, K. I., Exline, J., Jones, J., Mahoney, A., & Shafranske, E. (Eds.). (2013). *Handbook of psychology, religion, and spirituality.* Washington, DC: American Psychological Association.

Pargament, K. I., & Mahoney, A. (2018). Spirituality: The search for the sacred. In C. R. Snyder, S. J. Lopez, L. M. Edwards, & S. C. Marques (Eds.), *The Oxford handbook of positive psychology* (3rd ed., pp. 611–620). Oxford, England: Oxford University Press. http://dx.doi.org/10.1093/oxfordhb/9780199396511.013.51

Pirutinsky, S., Rosmarin, D. H., Pargament, K. I., & Midlarsky, E. (2011). Does negative religious coping accompany, precede, or follow depression among Orthodox Jews? *Journal of Affective Disorders, 132*, 401–405. http://dx.doi.org/10.1016/j.jad.2011.03.015

Scottish Health Action on Alcohol Problems and the Institute of Alcohol Studies. (2017). *Women and alcohol: Key issues.* Retrieved from http://www.ias.org.uk/uploads/pdf/IAS%20reports/rp29032018.pdf

Smith, T. B., McCullough, M. E., & Poll, J. (2003). Religiousness and depression: Evidence for a main effect and the moderating influence of stressful life events. *Psychological Bulletin, 129*, 614–636. http://dx.doi.org/10.1037/0033-2909.129.4.614

Turning Point of Tampa Inc. (2010, July 7). *Love at first drink—An alcoholic story* [Video file]. Retrieved from https://youtu.be/qmugk9kWcpE

United Nations Children's Fund. (2013). *Female genital mutilation/cutting: A statistical over-view and exploration of the dynamics of change.* Retrieved from https://www.unicef.org/publications/index_69875.html

Weatherhead, S., & Daiches, A. (2010). Muslim views on mental health and psychotherapy. *Psychology and Psychotherapy, 83*, 75–89. http://dx.doi.org/10.1348/147608309X467807

Whipple, V. (1987). Counseling battered women from fundamentalist churches. *Journal of Marital and Family Therapy, 13*, 251–258. http://dx.doi.org/10.1111/j.1752-0606.1987.tb00704.x

Yossifova, M., & Loewenthal, K. M. (1999). Religion and the judgement of obsession-ality. *Mental Health, Religion & Culture, 2*, 145–151. http://dx.doi.org/10.1080/13674679908406343

12

Disability as an Intersectional Diversity Variable in the Psychology Curriculum

Julie L. Williams

Disability is a socially constructed experience that parallels the experiences of oppression and discrimination of other minority groups. Disability-specific sociopolitical forces of oppression and discrimination are referred to as *ableism*, which Goodley (2014) conceptualized as ways by which normative paradigms are used to privilege able-bodiedness. Goodley stated that ableism "promotes smooth forms of personhood and smooth health; creates space fit for normative citizens; encourages an institutional bias towards autonomous, independent bodies; and lends support to economic and material dependence" (p. 21), resulting in gross inequities for the disabled[1] and a denial of their wholeness.

The American Psychological Association (2017) mandated the profession to promote diversity competence and awareness, expecting practicing psychologists to become active change agents. Yet the treatment of disability in the psychology curriculum is largely limited to a categorical understanding of disability as a medical and private problem (M. Johnson, 2003) needing to be fixed or adjusted to, whereas social and environmental determinants of suffering are ignored. Because of this, many of our students are unaware of what it means to be disabled in a society that devalues disability, and practicing psychologists are ineffective in their efforts to promote well-being, much less being positively and proudly disability identified.

---

[1]The terms *disabled people* and *persons with disability* and *Crip* are being used interchangeably and intentionally so as not to promote the need to separate disability from the person and to reflect current disability linguistics.

http://dx.doi.org/10.1037/0000137-013
Integrating Multiculturalism and Intersectionality Into the Psychology Curriculum: Strategies for Instructors, J. A. Mena and K. Quina (Editors)

Psychology instructors are in a prime position to correct ableism and to challenge students to understand disability as a diversity variable with intersectional impacts, informed by social and political forces. Societal attitudes that have viewed the disability experience as something to be pitied, feared, and even avoided can be changed in the classroom.

DISABILITY HISTORY AND CONTEMPORARY DISABILITY JUSTICE MOVEMENTS

To understand ableism's construction and disability as a socially constructed experience informed by stigma and negative attitudes held by society, students need exposure to disability history and disability laws and an orientation to the contemporary disability movements that extend far beyond the intent and spirit of the Americans With Disabilities Act (United States Department of Justice, n.d.). I recommend the works of disability studies scholars such as *The Ugly Laws* (Schweik, 2009), an overview of the earliest treatment of disabled individuals in the United States as criminals who were to be punished for showing themselves in public, illustrated in a quote from the Chicago City Code of 1811:

> Any person who is diseased or maimed, mutilated, or in any way deformed so as to be an unsightly or disgusting object, or an improper person to be allowed in or on the streets, highways, thoroughfares, or public places in this city, shall not therein or thereon expose himself to public view under the penalty of a fine of $1 for each offense. (p. 1)

In the 1900s, social policy was implemented to deal with "defective" and disabled members of society. Laws and policies were implemented that impacted those with disabilities, to the point of endangering their survival and freedoms. A review of such policies as sterilization, eugenics, or the horrific treatment of the disabled in institutions in the United States can become useful exercises. Individually or in small groups, students can bring in articles from scholarly and popular presses of the time. Sterilization is a particularly noteworthy example: In 1907, the government was given the right to sterilize certain individuals, and the first eugenics law, in Indiana, made sterilization mandatory for criminals, idiots, rapists, and imbeciles in state custody (State of Indiana, 1907, pp. 377–378). These policies listed the insane, the "feeble-minded," the "dependent," and the "diseased" as incapable of regulating their own reproductive abilities, therefore justifying government-forced sterilizations (Krase, 2014). Justice Holmes's infamous quote "Three generations of imbeciles are enough" (in *Buck v. Bell*, 1927, p. 585) reflects the sentiments at this time. The specifics of *Buck v. Bell* are particularly important: Carrie Buck, an 18-year-old female with a developmental disability was raped and became pregnant; because she was deemed promiscuous and mentally disabled, it was recommended she be sterilized. The case went to the Supreme Court, where the decision to sterilize was upheld, opening the door for acceptance of forced sterilizations of the disabled. Within 1 year of this case, 30 more states implemented sterilization laws, resulting in the sterilization of 60,000 individuals between 1907 and the mid-1970s (Disability Justice, n.d.). Oregon's "Board of Social Protection" conducted state-ordered sterilizations on at least 100 teenage girls living at the state training school for delinquent girls before 1941 (Sullivan, 2002), and it was not until 1983 that the governor of Oregon repealed these laws and offered a public apology. This historical pattern of sterilization can then be connected to current practices in which a pattern of gender discrimination continues; in violation of their rights, the sterilization of women with disabilities and Women of Color continues to occur at higher rates than White men and women, often under the guise of medical treatment but also by bypassing individual consent (Human Rights Watch, 2011).

Next, I highlight the progress and social change brought by the movement to deinstitutionalize individuals with developmental disabilities (the mid-1980s to early 1990s). One excellent resource is the video *Lest We Forget: Spoken Histories* (Lyons, 2007), which interviews parents, adults with developmental disabilities, and former professionals who were present during the deinstitutionalization movement in the state of Ohio. In *Willowbrook: The Last Great Disgrace*, journalist Geraldo Rivera (1972) exposed filth and abuses within the facility. These resources show social activism while providing a great deal of information; they can be used in diversity-focused as well as developmental psychology, assessment, or adult and child psychopathology courses to demonstrate the power psychology has over people's lives once we place them in medical or psychological diagnostic categories.

DISABILITY HISTORY TIME LINES

Another approach to disability history, particularly when time is limited, is to help students develop a time line of disability laws depicting movements and priorities. Students can be guided to recognize the implicit invisibility of disability, categories of disabilities that were valued more than others, intersectional impacts reflected in policies impacting women with disabilities (e.g., denials of their reproductive rights), the progression to disability as a collective group, and with help from the instructor, the role psychology played at different points. For example, the earliest disability-service actions, such as vocational rehabilitation laws, began with veterans in 1918. It would be 2 years later, in 1920, before civilian vocational rehabilitation services were made available to all with physical disabilities. In the 1940s, once again war brought disability to the forefront, with World War II veteran rehabilitation and vocational training. During the subsequent 2 decades, disability gained visibility as a civil rights movement, beginning with the independent living movement in the 1960s and evolving into a global civil rights matter with the passage of the Americans With Disabilities Act (ADA) in 1990. This time line also illustrates the relative youth of the disability rights movement relative to other civil rights movements in the United States, as well as the struggle to understand the meaning of disability services versus disability civil rights.

THE AMERICANS WITH DISABILITIES ACT AND CONTEMPORARY DISABILITY JUSTICE MOVEMENTS

Although most individuals are familiar with ADA, many continue to treat it as a "special rights" rather than a civil rights law. Many psychologists do not know the specifics of ADA as it pertains to their profession, including accommodations they are expected to provide; others believe ADA has corrected disability-related inequities. Students can learn about ADA as a civil rights law that is intended to protect against discrimination, consistent with other civil rights laws, while understanding that ADA differs from other civil rights laws in that it comes with protections and a mechanism where access to employment, public transportation, public accommodations, communication, and other areas can be denied. There are notable weaknesses in ADA; access can be denied if the request is deemed "unreasonable" by employers, educators, and/or the government or involves a "historic building." *Lives Worth Living* (Gilkey & Neudel, 2011) is a powerful documentary about ADA and disability rights figures.

DISABILITY JUSTICE AND CONTEMPORARY DISABILITY MOVEMENTS

In effort to further contextualize the disability experience, instructors should address contemporary disability movements and even shifts in language from derogatory terms (e.g., *cripple, imbecile, retarded*) to a person-first language (e.g., *person with a disability*), to the newer identify-first terms (e.g., *autistic, disabled*) and self-identifying terms (e.g., *crip*). Since the passage of ADA, the disability movement has evolved and extended beyond access and equal opportunities to global inclusion and intersectionality (Crenshaw, 1991). Mia Mingus (2011), a disability justice activist, woman, queer, Korean, Crip, wrote in her blog,

> We need to think of access with an understanding of disability justice, moving away from an equality-based model of sameness and "we are just like you" to a model of disability that embraces difference, confronts privilege and challenges what is considered "normal" on every front. . . . building an understanding of disability that is more complex, whole and interconnected than what we have previously found. We are disabled people who are people of color; women, genderqueer and transgender; poor and working class; youth; immigrants; lesbian, gay, bisexual and queer; and more. (para. 5, 11)

Resource Generation offers information on disability justice (http://resource generation.org/2011/11/what-disability-justice-has-to-offer-social-justice/). Justin Dart, another disability rights leader, explained what disability justice means in terms of action: "You cannot be responsible for the members of your own family without being responsible for the society in which they live and the air that they breathe" (National Council on Disability, 1996, Appendix E, para. 27). These movements shift the focus to the environment and, more specifically, society, an empowerment-oriented shift that highlights the importance of intersectionality (Crenshaw, 1991), treating the person as a whole with many intersecting parts of equal value (e.g., gender, race, ethnicity, spirituality), and bringing visibility to those who have not been visible in the disability community (e.g., lesbian, gay, bisexual, transgender, and queer [LGBTQ]; Black; ethnically diverse).

Contemporary movements give evidence to added oppressive experiences of ableism with sexism, heterosexism, and racism for members of the disability community who are further marginalized when they are a person of color, queer, and a woman (Crenshaw, 1991). These are the intersections where suffering is most pronounced, and psychology has a role in working toward not only awareness and visibility but also in facilitating students' understanding of community and safe spaces.

CULTURAL PERSPECTIVES: PERSON-FIRST LANGUAGE FROM DEAF TO CRIP

Contemporary disability movements have reclaimed with power and pride terms previously considered derogatory, similar to the LGB community embracing the term *queer*. These contemporary movements fit nicely in diversity-focused courses but could also be relevant to Women in Psychology, Afrocentric Psychology, and Sexuality courses.

For example, the term *Crip* is now considered to be an inclusive term, representing all people with vastly divergent physical and psychological differences. Crip represents the contemporary disability rights wave and is an "insider" term for disability culture reflecting the community's political reclaiming of the historically derogatory term *cripple*, which not only diminished the person to an image of ugliness but also excluded those with nonphysical disabilities from the disability community. However, students should be aware that to refer to or call a disabled person automatically a Crip would be inappropriate; it is a self-identified term and conveys a choice to connect with a political statement, and it is not to be imposed by "outsiders."

To identify as a Crip or with the Crip community means you identify as a member of or an ally to the disability community and that you recognize a distinct disability culture. As a Crip, you are also fighting to challenge and reclaim the negative words and terminology historically used to objectify and pathologize the minds, bodies, and souls of disabled individuals. The term encompasses all disabilities and members of diverse groups historically invisible and ignored, such as disabled persons of color; disabled members with lesbian, gay, bisexual, transgender, queer, and intersex identities; and those who are both disabled and linguistically diverse.

Crip Theory

Crip theory asserts disability as a viable identity variable to be recognized, acknowledged, and celebrated; recognizes the importance of the intersectionality of one's disability identity with other identity variables (Crenshaw, 1991); acknowledges the historical exclusion of diverse groups within the disability community (e.g., persons of color, gay, lesbian, transgender), which has caused the deepest injury of internalized oppression; and rejects disability hierarchies (levels of value placed on different disability groups) that promoted the fragmentation of the disability community, eroded disability culture, and excluded many from full participation in the disability community and society. Students can examine other historical movements, including empowerment theories such as feminism, intersections with heterosexism, queer theory, African American and Latinx cultural theories, and disability studies' depiction of the invisibility of disability as an identity variable, as well as the historical emphasis on medical abnormality.

Crip Justice

The presence of disability need not be viewed as negative, something to be pitied, feared, hated, or devalued; rather, disability should be seen as bringing value to the world. Crip justice is a call for action from within the self and community rather than passivity or acceptance of the oppressive status quo. Crip justice means that the inequities and injustices inflicted on disabled people are violations of human rights that threaten the freedoms and existence of those who live with disabilities. Crip theory emphasizes the importance of challenging images of normativity, beauty, and sexually oppressive paradigms that have excluded disability from the sexual dialogue.

Deaf Culture

Cultural perspectives vary in the disability community, particularly in the Deaf community. Deaf culture views deafness as a difference rather than a medical deficit; a person who identifies as "big-D" Deaf is located within a community in which social beliefs, lifestyles, art, literary traditions, history, and values are shared. The Deaf identity is one that is held with pride, a view that is consistent with other minority groups; Deaf individuals do not identify as disabled, rather they view deafness as simply a difference in the human condition. As a starting point toward understanding Deaf culture, I recommend the National Association for the Deaf (http://www.nad.org), *For Hearing People Only* (Moore & Levitan, 2003), and *The Mask of Benevolence: Disabling the Deaf Community* (Lane, 1992).

STRATEGIES TO BRING DISABILITY INTO THE PSYCHOLOGY CURRICULUM

It is important to give thought to how to bring this paradigm shift effectively. The approach taken by my institution is integrative and intersectional, and yet, the inclusion of disability is still new and evolving. While still forming their own identities, undergraduate students are hearing new ideas about diversity and may have never considered disability as a diversity variable. Our approach is developmental, attempting to meet students where they are and promote their growth gradually, thus allowing students to speak their truths, suspending judgment and punitive responses. We engage students in basic introductory exercises, such as the diversity shield exercise, in which each student identifies their family of origin, ethnicity, valued foods, activities, and abilities. Students are engaged in weekly journaling exercises about topical readings and class discussions in which students locate themselves in their worldviews and life experiences.

Constructs of power and privilege across diversity variables, including disability, are introduced progressively, assisted by Alan Johnson's (2017) *Privilege, Power, and Difference.* For students to digest conflicting paradigms and information effectively, they must first be aware of their beliefs and what is at stake as they reconsider the validity of some of their beliefs. Johnson's text allows students to consider their worldviews while also providing them with a vocabulary to help them conceptualize discrimination and stigma. As students are digesting these constructs, they are also embarking on their personal discoveries of privileges held and oppressions they have experienced. Diversity training is an affective and personal experience, and instructors must provide support and understanding along the way.

When facilitating awareness of personally held beliefs specific to disability, I typically begin with a location exercise in which students are asked to answer specific questions about disability beliefs. The literature says that commonly held beliefs about disability are that of pity, hero, tragedy, burden, and asexuality (Chan, da Silva Cordoso, & Chronister, 2009). This location exercise is accomplished by asking a series of yes or no questions drawing from this literature. The first seven questions ask whether the respondent has ever avoided, felt pity for, felt fear of, felt slowed down or annoyed by, felt uncomfortable with, or felt inspired by a person with disability; four questions ask whether the respondent has a family member, child, friend, or professor, boss, or authority figure with a disability; and the final two questions ask (a) Have you ever dated a person with a disability? and (b) Do you have a lover or partner with a disability? Students are then asked a silent reflection question: Did you experience discomfort, anxiety, and guilt or validation as you answered these questions?

Students participate as a group but are not asked to publicly share unless they wish to do so and after they are reminded of previously established ground rules about seeking to understand and respect each other's experiences, intent versus impact, and suspending the temptation to judge. If a student takes the risk to share an ableist belief, it is critical for the faculty member, particularly one who wears disability, to be open to and supportive of the disclosure.

Following this exercise, students spend time with another set of questions to localize themselves to disability in the form of their exposure and lived disability experiences. The questions are (a) Where did you learn about disability? (b) Who were your informants about disability? (c) Do you have a disability? (d) Are you a member of the disability community? (e) Are you an advocate? (f) Are you an ally or both?

Again, students are asked to initially silently reflect, make notes if they wish, and then share as a group their comfort and readiness. It is important to speak to the question, "Do you have a disability?" Many disabilities are not visible;

therefore, a student with an invisible disability may impulsively disclose for the first time the presence of their disability. Students should be cautioned that if they have "never" disclosed their disability to peers or others, they should take their time and be sure they are ready to "come out." Disclosing disability status has been likened to the coming out process within the LGBTQ community, and it is important to have support and allies to turn to if reactions are negative. In addition, a person may be outed as a person with a disability by the presence of a visible disability, or another may be comfortably located as having a disability; however, neither may be ready to embrace or acknowledge their membership in a disability community. Again, support is needed, and location should not be assumed nor forced by the instructors. Unfortunately, even in psychology, we are guilty of stigmatizing disabilities (Andrews et al., 2013).

RELEVANT MATERIAL AND RESOURCES

In selecting class materials, it is important to include information that deviates from the medical paradigm, informs students of disability history, contextualizes the disability experience, and explains the social construction of disability. Instructors should initiate their own learning by digesting the scholarship of the disability community and talking with disability experts in psychology and Disability Studies. M. Johnson's (2003) *Make Them Go Away* and *Disability—Do It Right! Your All-in-One How-to Guide* (2006) are helpful. *Divided Understanding: The Social Experience of Disability* (Gill, 2001) illuminates the social experience of disability. Olkin's (2001) *What Psychotherapists Should Know About Disability* and "Can Disability Studies and Psychology Join Hands?" (Olkin & Pledger, 2003) are thoughtful and rich with suggestions. More recent publications reflect disabled voices about sexuality, inequities in health and wellness opportunities (Miles-Cohen & Signore, 2016), disability affirmative interventions, and parenting and reproductive rights, including Andrews and Lund's (2015) "Disability in Psychology Training: Where Are We?" Students should learn about historical figures such as Ed Roberts, Marca Bristo, Fred Fay, Diane Coleman, and Judy Huelsman. Ideally, students can connect with the larger disability studies community via the Society on Disability Studies; although connecting with a variety of disability studies scholars may be difficult and time consuming, students can access website information by joining the online listserv (http://www.disstudies.org). Connecting with members of the disability community cannot be understated: Understanding disability justice cannot be accomplished by the mere reading of materials.

A challenge is finding the best amount and level of information on any one diversity variable to allow adequate time to discuss intersecting variables. Disability interacts with other identity variables in many ways, although research has suggested that it often becomes the most prominent to others who render the individual with a disability nothing else but disabled. Rohmer and Louvet (2009) represented the presence of disability in diverse cartoon images but found that participants paid no attention to other aspects of the images such as race or gender: The figures were no longer Black or White or male or female the moment disability was part of the image. Given the attitudinal beliefs associated with disability, this prominence given to disability denies the individual access to their wholeness, no longer perceived as gay or straight, sexual, or located in other important roles in life.

Disability history could easily be its own semester course. Concise yet in-depth overviews and illustrations of disability movements across time are found in *Lives Worth Living* (Gilkey & Neudel, 2011) and *Sins Invalid* (Berne, 2013), a performance-based work that speaks to the exclusion of persons of color from disability justice movements and challenges images of beauty and sexuality defined by ableist beliefs. Both videos quickly take students through history to current movements and out of their comfort zones and invite conversations. Previewing and researching videos in advance, preferably in consultation with disability experts and trainers, can inform decisions about which courses and which time to use them.

EXPERIENTIAL EXERCISES

Historically, a popular approach toward disability awareness was the disability simulation, in which individuals were placed in mobility—or sensory—limited conditions (e.g., sitting in a wheelchair, being blindfolded). Some have questioned whether disability simulations are appropriate and effective as a vehicle to promote diversity competence.

A major criticism of disability simulations is that they locate the lived experience in a specific disability group and do not allow students the opportunity to see the interaction between the disability, the person, their multiple identities, the environment, and society. Further, disability simulations can overwhelm some students, who can experience emotional and cognitive fatigue when abruptly placed in disability simulations, resulting in more strongly held negative beliefs. For example, being placed in a wheelchair and asked to ambulate for 10 to 30 minutes is physically taxing for someone who has not developed that skill over time—as it is for most wheelchair users. Finally, simulations have been criticized as making the disability experience trivial and "fun," thus minimizing the impact of social and environmental and political variables. For a complete discourse on the pros and cons and appropriate strategies to maximize the benefits of simulations if they are used, see Burgstahler and Doe (2004) and M. Johnson (2006).

The approach taken by our diversity faculty is "immersion" experiences, with members of the disability community as facilitators and experts leading the activities. One experience our team uses involves meeting for a meal in the home of a woman who has a significant physical disability and her partner who has invisible disabilities. During the meal preparation and eating, students are engaged in a discussion about the experiences of the disabled facilitators as a differently able couple, their sexuality, and the pervasive social and economic realities confronting the disabled. Students are then asked to write a reflection

paper, integrating their readings and videos with this experience and then identifying their areas of growth and challenge in their reflections. This experience
has consistently been described as eye opening and moving by students who for
the first time are being allowed to name painful beliefs about beauty and nor-
malcy. The community facilitators identify as Crips and are politically active in
the disability movement and are thus skilled at processing and engaging in the
discourse. By sharing an intimate space in the home of two Crip-identifying
individuals, social distance is removed, and students are forced to "lean in" and
consider not only disability but also intersecting identities of gender, sexuality,
economics, race, and religion and, importantly, to sit with their discomforts.

Journaling can provide instructors with needed feedback and opportunities
to continue to promote growth and learning. In our diversity-focused courses,
students are asked to write weekly one-page journal entries reflecting their
understanding of readings and their location with respect to the materials.
Grading is based on coverage of assigned readings, videos, discussions in class,
and ownership of personal reactions, including honesty and willingness to
engage, and not on agreement or evolved consideration. Students are "not
penalized" for owning a personal struggle with ableism. The response from the
diversity faculty is supportive and encouraging of more reading, immersion,
and/or reflective exercises, providing suggestions as to how students may work
through their struggles.

CONCLUSION

Although we have seen progress in the consideration of disability as a
diversity variable in psychology curricula, there is still evidence of courses that
categorize and medicalize the disability experience, particularly adult psychopathology, assessment, and developmental psychology. Although not intended
to oppress the disabled community, by categorizing disability groups and pre-
scribing normative paradigms of functioning, they are implicitly pathologizing
those with disabilities—labeling an individual as abnormal when a set number
of symptoms have been exhibited based on a variety of parameters concerning
speed, growth, intellect, personality, and socially appropriate behaviors. Some
even carry an unspoken suggestion that these nonnormative behaviors somehow impinge on society and must be fixed. Other courses that can also collude
with medical paradigms of disability are health psychology, neuropsychology,
and rehabilitation psychology. These errors can be corrected by including information about the oppressive social, environmental, and political paradigms that
erroneously locate the problem in the disabled individual rather than locating
the problem in systems where it resides.

We cannot ignore the power our courses have over how we interface with
disability as practicing psychologists and what we are teaching our students to
become as our future health care providers. There are courses in which disability
is simply absent, such as sex therapy, the psychology of women and men, and

social psychology. By infusing the intersection of disability within these topics via readings, assignments, and videos, we can remind all that disability is a viable and normal experience.

We must continue to challenge ourselves, our profession and our society to think beyond medical paradigms of disability. I am here today writing as a Crip-identified, Dwarf, bisexual, Hard of Hearing woman because I fought to get, and ultimately was given, the opportunity to join the faculty of my institution in 2005, where I teach disability-related coursework and the diversity integration courses. Although I have navigated many oppressive variables to get here, the journey was made easier by certain privileges I had. I am grateful and humbled by the experience because I am reminded of the progress we are making and yet also reminded that the journey is far from over. We have a long way to go in psychology to further our understanding of the disability experience as an oppressed group, much less in becoming active change agents in psychology. Therefore, in addition to bringing disability into the psychology curriculum, we have to recruit and mentor disabled junior faculty who venture into the work of disability training. The presence of disability in psychology lags behind the emerging diversity seen for other oppressed groups (e.g., African Americans, LGBTQ) in the profession of psychology (Andrews & Lund, 2015). We cannot get professionals with disabilities into psychology if we do not get degreed individuals with disabilities. We need the formation of a pipeline attending to disability, with attention to recruiting, supporting, and retaining undergraduate and graduate students with disabilities.

REFERENCES

American Psychological Association. (2017). *Multicultural guidelines: An ecological approach to context, identity, and intersectionality.* Retrieved from http://www.apa.org/about/policy/multicultural-guidelines.pdf

Andrews, E. E., Kuemmel, A., Williams, J. L., Pilarski, C. R., Dunn, M., & Lund, E. M. (2013). Providing culturally competent supervision to trainees with disabilities in rehabilitation settings. *Rehabilitation Psychology, 58*, 233–244. http://dx.doi.org/10.1037/a0033338

Andrews, E. E., & Lund, E. M. (2015). Disability in psychology training: Where are we? *Training and Education in Professional Psychology, 9*, 210–216. http://dx.doi.org/10.1037/tep0000085

Berne, P. (Director). (2013). *Sins invalid: An unashamed claim to beauty* [Motion picture]. United States: New Day Films.

Buck v. Bell, 47S. Ct. 584; 71 L. Ed. 1000 (1927).

Burgstahler, S., & Doe, T. (2004). Disability-related simulations: If, when, and how to use them. *Review of Disability Studies, 1*(2), 4–17.

Chan, F., da Silva Cordoso, E., & Chronister, J. A. (Eds.). (2009). *Understanding psychosocial adjustment to chronic illness and disability: A handbook for evidence-based practitioners in rehabilitation.* New York, NY: Springer.

Crenshaw, K. (1991). Mapping the margins: Intersectionality, identity politics, and violence against Women of Color. *Stanford Law Review, 43*, 1241–1299. http://dx.doi.org/10.2307/1229039

Disability Justice. (n.d.). *The fight for civil rights for people with disabilities.* Retrieved from http://disabilityjustice.org/right-to-self-determination-freedom-from-involuntary-sterilization

Gilkey, A. (Producer), & Neudel, E. (Director). (2011). *Lives worth living: The great fight for disability rights.* United States: Storyline Motion Pictures & Independent Television Service.

Gill, C. J. (2001). Divided understandings: The social experience of disability. In G. L. Albrecht, K. D. Seelman, & M. Bury (Eds.), *Handbook of disability studies* (pp. 351–372). Thousand Oaks, CA: Sage. http://dx.doi.org/10.4135/9781412976251.n14

Goodley, D. (2014). *Dis/Ability studies: Theorising disablism and ableism.* New York, NY: Routledge. http://dx.doi.org/10.4324/9780203366974

Human Rights Watch. (2011). *Sterilization of women and girls with disabilities.* Retrieved from https://www.hrw.org/news/2011/11/10/sterilization-women-and-girls-disabilities

Independent Living Institute. (1994). *Eugenics and disability discrimination.* Retrieved from http://www.independentliving.org/docs1/pfeiffe1.html

Johnson, A. G. (2006). *Privilege, power, and difference* (2nd ed.). New York, NY: McGraw-Hill.

Johnson, M. (2003). *Make them go away: Clint Eastwood, Christopher Reeve and the case against disability rights.* Louisville, KY: The Advocado Press.

Johnson, M. (2006). *Disability awareness—do it right! Your all-in-one how-to guide: Tips, techniques & handouts for a successful awareness day.* Louisville, KY: The Advocado Press.

Krase, K. (2014, October 1). History of forced sterilization and current U.S. abuses. *Our Bodies Our Selves.* Retrieved from http://www.ourbodiesourselves.org/health-info/forced-sterilization

Lane, H. (1992). *The mask of benevolence: Disabling the deaf community.* San Diego, CA: Dawnsignpress.

Lyons, M. R. (Producer & Director). (2007). *Lest we forget: Spoken histories* [Motion picture]. United States: Partners for Community Living.

Miles-Cohen, S. E., & Signore, C. (Eds.). (2016). *Eliminating inequities for women with disabilities: An agenda for health and wellness.* Washington, DC: American Psychological Association. http://dx.doi.org/10.1037/14943-000

Mingus, M. (2011, February 12). *Changing the framework: Disability justice.* Retrieved from https://leavingevidence.wordpress.com/2011/02/12/changing-the-framework-disability-justice/

Moore, M. D., & Levitan, L. (2003). *For hearing people only: Answers to some of the most commonly asked questions about the deaf community, its culture, and the "deaf reality."* Silver Spring, MD: Deaf Life Press.

National Council on Disability. (1996). *National disability policy: A progress report—July 1996.* Retrieved from https://www.ncd.gov/progress_reports/July1996

Olkin, R. (2001). *What psychotherapists should know about disability.* New York, NY: Guilford Press.

Olkin, R., & Pledger, C. (2003). Can disability studies and psychology join hands? *American Psychologist, 58,* 296–304. http://dx.doi.org/10.1037/0003-066X.58.4.296

Rivera, G. (1972). *Willowbrook: The last great disgrace* [Video file]. Retrieved from http://www.geraldo.com/page/willowbrook

Rohmer, O., & Louvet, E. (2009). Describing persons with disability: Salience of disability, gender, and ethnicity. *Rehabilitation Psychology, 54,* 76–82. http://dx.doi.org/10.1037/a0014445

Schweik, S. (2009). *The ugly laws: Disability in public.* New York, NY: New York Press.

State of Indiana. (1907). *Laws of the Indiana General Assembly.* Retrieved from https://scholarworks.iupui.edu/handle/1805/1053

Sullivan, J. (2002, November 15). State of Oregon will admit sterilization past. *Free Republic.* Retrieved from http://www.freerepublic.com/focus/news/789755/posts

United States Department of Justice. (n.d.). *Introduction to the ADA.* Retrieved from http://www.ada.gov/ada_intro.htm

13

Teaching About Poverty and Social Class

Fostering Class Consciousness

Heather E. Bullock and Bernice Lott

Social class is a fundamental aspect of human diversity, shaping life experiences, well-being, access to resources, and personal identity (Bullock, 2013; Lott, 2010; Lott & Bullock, 2007). Psychology has contributed greatly to our understanding of how social class "gets into the body" to influence health and development and how classism deepens the disadvantage experienced by low-income persons and communities, both independently and via intersections with discrimination based on other social categories (e.g., ethnicity, gender). Despite its far-reaching impact, social class has been largely neglected in psychology curricula, from introductory courses and textbooks to relevant subdiscipline coursework in social psychology and other areas, even those focused on diversity and multiculturalism (e.g., the psychology of women). Indeed, social class was absent from previous editions of this volume.

Record-setting wealth and income inequality, coupled with long-standing, unacceptably high poverty rates, have rendered class disparities difficult to ignore. Psychologists are increasingly attending to social class and poverty in their research and teaching, a welcome development, but significant gaps remain, including limited coverage of social class in most textbooks and instructors uncomfortable or underprepared to explore class issues with students. In this chapter, we suggest strategies for integrating social class as a core dimension of diversity, with a primary focus on the United States.

http://dx.doi.org/10.1037/0000137-014
Integrating Multiculturalism and Intersectionality Into the Psychology Curriculum:
Strategies for Instructors, J. A. Mena and K. Quina (Editors)

CONCEPTUALIZING SOCIAL CLASS AND POVERTY: TEACHING STRUCTURE AND IDEOLOGY

Social class refers to "a group of individuals or families who occupy a similar position in the economic system of production, distribution, and consumption of goods and services in industrial societies" (Rothman, 2005, p. 6). It is multifaceted, encompassing the material conditions of economic position (e.g., income, wealth) and access to resources (e.g., education, safe housing), as well as subjective understandings of class status and privilege communicated and reinforced via interpersonal interactions and institutions (Piff, Kraus, Côté, Cheng, & Keltner, 2010). Piff stated, "As people reconstruct their days, it's clear that in every single decision they make, class is an essential feature" (DeAngelis, 2015, para. 2), from consumer choices to mode of transportation to the kinds of friends they have. To reinforce this point, students can deconstruct a typical day in their lives via a class lens: Those who are more privileged can be encouraged to do without a valued resource (e.g., foregoing their car for public transportation, not using a smartphone). Such exercises can foster privileged students' appreciation for how they benefit daily from material resources (e.g., convenience, time saving); however, make it clear that these transitory experiences are not equivalent to actual hardship.

Approaches to the measurement of social class vary (Diemer, Mistry, Wadsworth, López, & Reimers, 2013), but income, occupation, prestige, and educational attainment are among the most common indicators used for designating status as "poor," "working class," "middle class," or "wealthy/elite." The Class Action site (http://www.classism.org/resources/) and the American Psychological Association's (APA) Office on Socioeconomic Status (2018) resource guide on including social class in psychology curricula provide bibliographies, films, weblinks, and other information about different social classes.

Class position is indicative of political, social, and economic power, with *power* defined as access to essential resources (e.g., food, medical care, shelter, education); other resources, such as art and recreation; and prospects for economic security (e.g., wealth, money, property; Lott, 2012; Lott & Bullock, 2010). Class relations are power relations. Feminist and critical approaches are helpful in foregrounding power and extending our concerns beyond psychology's traditional emphasis on individual attitudes, beliefs, and behaviors (Lott & Bullock, 2010; Williams & Melchiori, 2014). Assigning first-person accounts of class privilege, economic hardship, and class status, such as Tirado (2014) and Case (2017), can help students draw connections between the personal and political to see relationships between institutional and interpersonal classism and reflect on position and experiences for themselves, their families, and their communities. Students can also benefit from writing their own class narrative and connecting their experiences with the broader social class literature.

Teaching about the structural bases of social class and its inequalities—how social class is conceptualized and measured, the role of institutions in creating and maintaining class status, and the systemic nature of economic inequality—is essential. Students can search the U.S. Census Bureau (2017) for information such as how poverty is defined (i.e., living below thresholds that are based on a formula derived from the "economy food plan" and family size), how poverty thresholds are set (i.e., $19,337 for a family of three in 2016), the large numbers of people living below these thresholds (i.e., 40.6 million people in 2016), and how this number would be greater if families hovering just above the thresholds were included in official estimates. The demographics of poverty are grounded in power relations. High poverty rates among people of color (22% of African Americans and 19.4% of Hispanics), children under the age of 18 (18%), women (14%), and single female–headed households (26.6%) are illustrative of the long reach of racism, sexism, and classism. Teaching students to access and interpret the Census Bureau's annual reports on poverty and income can provide valuable experience in handling government reports and also spur meaningful discussions and critical analyses of the structural sources of poverty (e.g., discrimination, the wage gap, women's overrepresentation in low-paid jobs, unpaid caregiving). The University of Wisconsin's Institute for Research on Poverty (http://www.irp.wisc.edu) offers reports and other helpful resources.

In my (HEB's) class, students work in small groups to (a) estimate the annual, pretax income for a family of three (one parent, two children) that they believe is associated with poverty, wealth, and living "comfortably"; (b) determine how they would measure poverty and what variables to use (e.g., income, expenses); and (c) describe in everyday language what it means to be poor, wealthy, and middle class. This challenging activity sensitizes students to the difficulty of operationally defining poverty and class status (e.g., which variables to use and how to weight them) and the politicized nature of its measurement (e.g., some measures yield lower estimates of poverty). Students consistently overestimate poverty thresholds, associating poverty with far higher incomes than are used by the Census Bureau, facilitating a discussion of gaps between the government's definition of poverty and actual living costs and recognition that full-time work may not be sufficient to lift a family out of poverty. Students break down annual earnings into an estimated hourly wage and discuss the minimum wage, poverty thresholds, and local self-sufficiency wages (e.g., http://www.selfsufficiencystandard.org). Bullock (2013) provided an overview of the sources of women's poverty (see also Graf, Brown, & Patten, 2018).

Focusing on poverty while neglecting broader socioeconomic trends can render the dynamics and the beneficiaries of class inequality invisible, resulting in a gross underestimation of wealth and income inequality (Norton & Ariely, 2011). Kiatpongsan and Norton (2014) found that U.S. participants in their study estimated the U.S. ratio of CEO income to unskilled workers to be just 29.6 to 1, far lower than the actual ratio of approximately 354 to 1. Discussing poverty and wealth together, and their relationship to each other, positions inequality (not just poverty) as problematic. United for a Fair Economy's Ten Chairs activity, a take on "musical chairs," vividly illustrates the skewed distribution of wealth and the racial wealth gap and can be modified to illustrate racial and gender inequalities. Materials and instructions, plus charts and links, are available from the Teaching Economics as if People Mattered website (Giecek, 2018).

It is important to reinforce that inequality is not just a problem for the poor. As Reich (2014) aptly pointed out, economic inequality decreases the chances of upward mobility for all. Epidemiological research has shown the damaging effects of income inequality on population health and societal well-being, not just for low-income groups. In their comprehensive cross-national analysis of multiple dimensions of well-being (e.g., physical health, mental health, educational attainment, imprisonment, child well-being, trust, community life), Wilkinson and Pickett (2009) found that unequal rich countries fared significantly worse than their more equitable counterparts, subsequently concluding "The evidence that large income differences have damaging health and social consequences is already far stronger than the evidence supporting policy initiatives in many other areas of social and economic policy" (Pickett & Wilkinson, 2015, p. 324). Low-income groups shoulder the burden of poverty and economic disparity, but such findings help students see the far-reaching societal consequences of inequality and provide an entry point for evaluating the role of research in social policy and political responses to poverty and economic inequality.

Marking "the poor" as "classed" without critically interrogating the experiences of other social classes contributes to the neutralization of privilege and the false assumption that membership in other social classes is problem free (Lott, 2010). In U.S. society, "middle-class" status is regarded as "normative"; likewise, psychology is dominated by theories derived from studies with White, middle-class college student participants (Fox, Prilleltensky, & Austin, 2009). Questioning unstated norms and values that position middle-class expectations and time lines as normative, whether in textbooks or classroom practices, is essential to recognizing and honoring class diversity. For instructors, this may mean challenging assumptions that "early" parenting among poor and working-class families is inherently deficient or that childhood is a time without worry or responsibilities and questioning what we communicate to students when we ask about their "vacation" travel plans.

To illustrate how our individual "clocks" are shaped by dominant cultural and class-based beliefs, I (HEB) ask students to privately sketch out the expected age at which they plan to reach milestones that they identify as personally important to them (e.g., start a family, get married, complete college) and then share some of these milestones. These personal timelines fuel a fruitful discussion of class (and other) assumptions embedded within culturally prescribed "time frames." For example, students may identify the "right" time to start a family as after completing college or spending several years traveling and/or working in the paid labor force, but this may not be the desired timeline for someone who is not attending college. Openly discussing how class and class biases inform "normative" timelines counteracts dominant group invisibility. Revealing the dynamics of oppression and class hierarchy are particularly important given that traditional middle-class markers of adulthood, such as leaving school and establishing a family, are increasingly out of reach for working-class young people and low earners from middle-class families (Silva, 2013).

Deconstructing meanings of "middle-class" status may involve challenging students' class identification. There is a tendency for individuals to identify as middle class in the United States, even if not supported by objective indicators. In a Pew Research Center (2015) poll, 47% of respondents identified as "middle class," 29% "lower-middle class," and 11% as "upper-middle class." "Middle class" was selected by both those earning over $100,000 (approaching the top quintile of earners) and those earning less than $30,000 (below poverty thresholds, depending on the number of dependents). Disjuncture between objective class status, as determined by markers such as income and education and subjective (perceived) class identification is common, as reflected in the complex identities of academics from working-class backgrounds now grappling with membership in a largely middle-class professoriate (Case, 2017; Muzzatti & Samarco, 2006) and middle-class African Americans negotiating the terrains of race, class, and place (Lacy, 2007; Pattillo, 2013). Class holds different meanings across diverse ethnic and racial groups, and the subjective sense of class may vary greatly depending on experiences of upward or downward mobility.

Consequences of this overidentification are numerous, ranging from denial of class privilege by the wealthy, heightened class stigma and distancing from people who are low income and/or working class, and decreased engagement with economic justice initiatives. Teaching about social class in a college environment in the United States presents the special problem of overcoming students' assumption that "campuses are classless" (Tablante & Fiske, 2015, p. 184). A sizable literature suggests otherwise, with evidence that class disparities in academe are real and have significant effects on college success and satisfaction (e.g., Stephens, Brannon, Markus, & Nelson, 2015). An excellent way to demonstrate this is to ask students to identify items as familiar (or not) from Braun's (2015) list of taken-for-granted social class privileges. Scholarship by Piff and his colleagues can be used to illustrate how psychologists operationalize and study class privilege as well as its deleterious effects (see Piff, 2014; Piff et al., 2010; Piff, Stancato, Côté, Mendoza-Denton, & Keltner, 2012).

Teaching about social class means "taking on" the "American dream," the belief that anyone, regardless of family of origin, background, or socioeconomic position, can move up the socioeconomic ladder through hard work and effort. Unlike race, ethnicity, and gender, social class is perceived to be an earned or achieved status rather than an ascribed identity (Weber, 1998). Deeply entrenched cultural beliefs about opportunity, deservingness, and meritocracy legitimize class disparities. The tenacity and often-contradictory nature of these beliefs are revealed in the results of a Pew Research Center (2015) poll: Although 62% of respondents perceived the U.S. economic system as unfairly favoring powerful interests, 64% also believed "most people who want to get ahead can make it if they're willing to work hard" ("On Core Economic Beliefs,

Differences Between—and Within—Parties," para. 1 and 3). Belief in the possibility of upward mobility is so strong that Kraus and Tan (2015) found that
online survey participants and university students overestimated class mobility
by nearly 23 percentage points.

Gilbert (2008) aptly observed, "Students who willingly wrestle with race,
gender, sexual orientation, and religion often balk at exploring class privilege,
which threatens the fundamental myth that all people in the United States
enjoy equal access to opportunity" (p. 7). Instructors must be ready to help
students debunk an interrelated network of legitimizing beliefs (e.g., social
dominance orientation, belief in a just world, meritocratic beliefs, the Protestant work ethic, individualistic attributions for wealth and poverty, classist, racist,
and sexist stereotypes). Having students privately complete scales assessing
beliefs such as attributions for poverty and wealth (Bullock, Williams, &
Limbert, 2003) can encourage personal reflection and help them see connections between beliefs and policy support (e.g., the positive correlation between
individualistic attributions for poverty and restrictive welfare policies). General
activities related to stereotyping, prejudice, and institutional discrimination can
also raise critical consciousness (visit the Society for the Psychological Study of
Social Issues at https://www.spssi.org/index.cfm?fuseaction=Page.ViewPage&
pageId=1974, Resources for Teaching Social Psychology at http://jfmueller.
faculty.noctrl.edu/crow/prejudice.htm, and the Social Psychology Network at
https://www.socialpsychology.org/teaching.htm#webother).

The self-protective functions of these beliefs about the American dream,
particularly among less privileged students, should not be overlooked. Davidai
and Gilovich (2015) investigated the alignment of such beliefs and actual
mobility. Respondents overestimated the likelihood of upward mobility and
underestimated downward mobility; poorer individuals believed there is more
mobility than wealthier individuals. Beliefs can serve different functions for
diverse groups. Mobility beliefs can also be palliative or a source of hope in
the face of economic adversity. Fostering an appreciation for diverse functions
can avoid reifying beliefs as "good" or "bad" and contextualize the ideological
contours and complexities of class status.

Heightened awareness of structural inequality can be distressing; students
across the class spectrum may require time for critical reflection, particularly
those whose worldviews are being challenged:

> What does it mean to a person of class privilege to acknowledge that health care,
> legal protection, and education services are disparately rendered? How is one's
> status challenged if success depends on privilege rather than on hard work? . . .
> These questions can make students exceedingly uncomfortable and invoke anxi-
> ety, fear, confusion, anger, guilt, and resentment. . . . Many students who do not
> have class privilege subscribe to the notion that their class position is of their own
> making. These students react to conversations about class in a variety of ways,
> from caretaking privileged students who feel guilty, showing pride in their own
> accomplishments, expressing anger, embarrassment, or fear of being judged, or
> shock at discovering their social class. (Gilbert, 2008, p. 8)

Greater class-consciousness can also be overwhelming. Seider (2009) found
that high school students' support for humanitarian aid declined following a

unit on world hunger and global poverty. Seider attributed this to students feeling overwhelmed by the scope of poverty and perceiving economic inequality as intractable and unsolvable.

A strong structural foundation is essential to navigating this complex terrain. "Stacking" topics to systematically build toward increasingly macrolevel analysis helps move students toward structural understandings of class status. For instance, deconstructing classist stereotypes in everyday life and the media early in the course can pave the way for examining children's life chances and educational inequalities before moving to more controversial issues such as "welfare reform." Using multiple communication channels (e.g., readings, films) and activities about the diversity of lived experiences can also help students visualize structural inequality and class privilege. Fictional books and films can stimulate discussion of how social class organizes relationships to power, labor, and ownership (Marshall & Rosati, 2014), from those with political overtones such as *The Hunger Games* series to less political but still powerful fiction and nonfiction (see Class Action, n.d.; Truong, Reppond, Chhun, Gainor, & Walker, n.d.). As Craig (2009) observed, "When we render visible the political nature of texts that our students consider 'apolitical' or 'timeless literature,' we begin to encourage them to question assumptions about other so-called natural categories, such as gender, race, and their own personal experience" (p. 30). Among documentaries, *Class Dismissed: How TV Frames the Working Class* (Jhally & Alper, 2007) analyzed class representations in the media; *People Like Us* (Alvarez & Kolker, 2001) addressed class stigma and privilege in action; and *Inequality for All* (Chaiken, Dungan, & Kornbluth, 2013) provided a vivid tutorial on rising inequality. For tips on using media to teach about social class, see Leistyna and Mollen (2008) and Leistyna (2009).

Cho, Convertino, and Khourey-Bowers's (2015) work with preservice teachers underscores the importance of multipronged lessons. They developed multiple curricular modules with the goals of increasing new teachers' knowledge of poverty, improving connections with low-income parents, and optimizing learning environments for low-income students. This type of multidimensional teaching fosters multicultural sensitivity and justice-oriented learning.

EXPERIENTIAL LEARNING: CONTEXTUALIZING CLASS PRIVILEGE AND DISADVANTAGE

Experiential learning refers broadly to pedagogical strategies that facilitate knowledge and academic growth through direct experience and focused reflection on these experiences (Williams & Melchiori, 2014). Targeted writing assignments and journals in which students examine class in their everyday lives, simulations of the difficult choices poor families confront on a daily basis (e.g., pay for rent vs. child care), and other activities such as constructing "resource inventories" of socioeconomically diverse neighborhoods can encourage critical reflection on class status and privilege (for detailed activities, see APA Office on Socioeconomic Status, 2018; Williams & Melchiori, 2014). Immersion courses can be particularly impactful. For example, Shupe's (2013) students spent 3 weeks in Nicaragua visiting nonprofit organizations and learning about the country. Reflective assignments and interactions with low-income Nicaraguans and anti-poverty advocates fostered application of theory, enhanced appreciation of external barriers to upward mobility, and facilitated critique of one-dimensional poverty interventions (e.g., education is the solution). By exposing students to new cultures, such courses can be particularly effective in heightening critical awareness of social and political structures.

Service learning can be an especially powerful tool for fostering class-consciousness, whether semester-long placements with community organizations or brief immersions in community-based projects (Bringle, Reeb, Brown, & Ruiz, 2016). Service learning can bring social class into sharper focus for both more and less socioeconomically privileged students. Reflecting on class in different and/or unfamiliar contexts and interacting with low-income groups, service providers, and/or community stakeholders as an "intern/resource/team member" can help low-income students position their experiences within larger institutional frameworks and gain valuable experience advancing economic justice. Placements must also be beneficial to host organizations, not just to students and universities, to avoid inadvertently replicating exploitive dynamics of broader class relations.

Seider, Gillmor, and Rabinowicz (2011) found that business majors who had completed a community-based service learning program expressed a greater understanding of the complex factors associated with poverty; nevertheless, their belief that the world is a just place increased slightly. Even when recognizing inequality, faith in the U.S. economic system can remain strong; individualistic and structural attributions for poverty, although seemingly contradictory, are often simultaneously endorsed (Hunt & Bullock, 2016). Hughes et al.'s (2012) evaluation of a service learning program targeting low-income high school students revealed an increased awareness of economic and racial disparities in student mentors' journal entries, yet only a small percentage of reflections discussed strategies to mitigate the effects of poverty. The authors speculated that "the dire conditions of mentoring sites overwhelmed students, causing them to focus more on problems than solutions" (p. 781).

These findings are a powerful reminder that awareness of pervasive inequality can be so discomforting and shocking that it can rob us of our imagination and narrow our scope. As instructors, we must embolden students to "think big," to envision an economically just society, and to develop a road map for change. Asking students to operationally define economic justice and design concrete interventions for decreasing inequality can help keep the focus on social change. At the end of my (HEB's) upper-division course on the psychology of poverty and social class, students are asked to bring in three concrete strategies or areas for improving interclass relations and/or reducing economic inequality—their boldest ideas, no matter how seemingly idealistic or unrealistic—and then identify comprehensive steps for achieving this change.

By parsing "big picture" changes into smaller components and strategizing together, what once seemed unattainable enters the realm of feasibility.

Longer, more comprehensive service learning programs may be more effective than briefer, less-developed programs. Seider, Rabinowicz, and Gillmor (2011) found that students who completed an intensive year-long service course in placements related to poverty and social justice expressed a greater understanding of structural sources of poverty and inequality than a wait-list control group. The 10 to 12 hours per week in the field were complemented by in-class meetings, readings, and discussion sections. Being liberal, Protestant, a woman, and majoring in fields other than business were associated with larger shifts toward a structural understanding of poverty, indicating that diverse groups differ in their receptiveness to these messages.

CONCLUSION

To neglect social class in our teaching is to neglect a central facet of human diversity. Our silence in the classroom reinforces dominant class narratives that position middle-class experiences as "normative" and college campuses as "classless." These are not benign misperceptions. Breaking this silence is essential to fostering class consciousness, preparing students to live in a multicultural world, and to advancing social and economic justice. The impact may be particularly powerful for less privileged students, as illustrated by an intervention designed to ease first-generation students' transition to college (Stephens, Hamedani, & Destin, 2014). A 1-hour workshop with a diverse panel of advanced students who discussed their class backgrounds, obstacles they had overcome, and strategies for academic success reduced the social class achievement gap among first-generation and continuing-education college students by 63% at the end of their first year of college and improved first-generation students' psychosocial outcomes (e.g., psychological adjustment, academic engagement). We have much to gain by integrating social class into our teaching and much to lose if we do not.

REFERENCES

Alvarez, L. (Producer & Director), & Kolker, A. (Producer & Director). (2001). *People like us: Social class in America* [Motion picture]. United States: Center for New American Media.

American Psychological Association Office on Socioeconomic Status. (2018). *Inclusion of social class in psychology curricula: Resources for educators*. Retrieved from http://www.apa.org/pi/ses/resources/publications/social-class-curricula.aspx

Braun, N. (2015, Jan. 19). *Taken-for-granted social class privileges*. Retrieved from http://www.classism.org/taken-granted-social-class-privileges/

Bringle, R. G., Reeb, R., Brown, M. A., & Ruiz, A. I. (2016). *Service learning in psychology: Enhancing undergraduate education for the public good*. Washington, DC: American Psychological Association. http://dx.doi.org/10.1037/14803-000

Bullock, H. E. (Ed.). (2013). *Women and poverty: Psychology, public policy, and social justice*. Chichester, England: Wiley-Blackwell. http://dx.doi.org/10.1002/9781118378748

Bullock, H. E., Williams, W. R., & Limbert, W. M. (2003). Predicting support for welfare policies: The impact of attributions and beliefs about inequality. *Journal of Poverty, 7,* 35–56. http://dx.doi.org/10.1300/J134v07n03_03

Case, K. A. (2017). Insider without: Journey across the working-class academic arc. *Journal of Working-Class Studies, 2,* 16–35.

Chaiken, J. (Producer), Dungan, S. (Producer), & Kornbluth, J. (Director). (2013). *Inequality for all* [Motion picture]. United States: 72 Productions.

Cho, M. H., Convertino, C., & Khourey-Bowers, C. (2015). Helping preservice teachers (PSTs) understand the realities of poverty: Innovative curriculum modules. *Educational Technology Research and Development, 63,* 303–324. http://dx.doi.org/10.1007/s11423-015-9366-9

Class Action. (n.d.). *Annotated class and classism bibliography.* Retrieved from https://classism.org/resources/bibliography/

Craig, C. (2009). "Nobody's a bum all of their life": Teaching class through William Kennedy's *Ironweed. Radical Teacher, 86,* 28–38. http://dx.doi.org/10.1353/rdt.0.0062

Davidai, S., & Gilovich, T. (2015). Building a more mobile America—one income quintile at a time. *Perspectives on Psychological Science, 10,* 60–71. http://dx.doi.org/10.1177/1745691614562005

DeAngelis, T. (2015, February). Class differences. *Monitor on Psychology, 46*(2). Retrieved from http://www.apa.org/monitor/2015/02/class-differences.aspx

Diemer, M. A., Mistry, R., Wadsworth, M. E., López, I., & Reimers, F. (2013). Best practices in conceptualizing and measuring social class in psychological research. *Analyses of Social Issues and Public Policy (ASAP), 13,* 77–113. http://dx.doi.org/10.1111/asap.12001

Fox, D. R., Prilleltensky, I., & Austin, S. (2009). *Critical psychology: An introduction* (2nd ed.). London, England: Sage.

Giecek, T. S. (2018). *The ten chairs.* Retrieved from http://www.teachingeconomics.org/content/index.php?topic=tenchairs

Gilbert, R. (2008, Fall). Raising awareness of class privilege among students. *Diversity & Democracy, 11,* 7–9.

Graf, N., Brown, A., & Patten, E. (2018, April 9). *The narrowing, but persistent, gender gap in pay.* Retrieved from the Pew Research Center website: http://www.pewresearch.org/fact-tank/2018/04/09/gender-pay-gap-facts/

Hughes, C., Steinhorn, R., Davis, B., Beckrest, S., Boyd, E., & Cashen, K. (2012). University-based service learning: Relating mentoring experiences to issues of poverty. *Journal of College Student Development, 53,* 767–782. http://dx.doi.org/10.1353/csd.2012.0076

Hunt, M., & Bullock, H. E. (2016). Ideologies and beliefs about poverty. In D. Brady & L. M. Burton (Eds.), *The Oxford handbook of the social science of poverty* (pp. 93–116). New York, NY: Oxford University Press.

Jhally, S. (Producer), & Alper, L. (Director). (2007). *Class dismissed: How TV frames the working class* [Motion picture]. United States: Media Education Foundation.

Kiatpongsan, S., & Norton, M. I. (2014). How much (more) should CEOs make? A universal desire for more equal pay? *Perspectives on Psychological Science, 9,* 587–593.

Kraus, M. W., & Tan, J. J. X. (2015). Americans overestimate social class mobility. *Journal of Experimental Social Psychology, 58,* 101–111. http://dx.doi.org/10.1016/j.jesp.2015.01.005

Lacy, K. (2007). *Blue-chip Black: Race, class, and status in the new Black middle class.* Berkeley: University of California Press.

Leistyna, P. (2009). Exposing the ruling class in the United States using television and documentary film. *Radical Teacher, 85,* 12–15. http://dx.doi.org/10.1353/rdt.0.0041

Leistyna, P., & Mollen, D. (2008). Teaching social class through alternative media and by dialoguing across disciplines and boundaries. *Radical Teacher, 81,* 20–27. http://dx.doi.org/10.1353/rdt.2008.0005

Lott, B. (2010). *Multiculturalism and diversity: A social psychological perspective.* Chichester, England: Wiley.

Lott, B. (2012). The social psychology of class and classism. *American Psychologist, 67,* 650–658. http://dx.doi.org/10.1037/a0029369

Lott, B., & Bullock, H. E. (2007). *Psychology and economic injustice: Personal, professional, and political intersections.* Washington, DC: American Psychological Association. http://dx.doi.org/10.1037/11501-000

Lott, B., & Bullock, H. E. (2010). Social class and women's lives. *Psychology of Women Quarterly, 34,* 421–424. http://dx.doi.org/10.1111/j.1471-6402.2010.01587.x

Marshall, E., & Rosati, M. (2014). May the odds be ever in your favor: Teaching class and collective action with *The Hunger Games. Rethinking Schools.* Retrieved from http://www.rethinkingschools.org/archive/28_04/28_04_marshall_rosati.shtml

Muzzatti, S. L., & Samarco, V. (Eds.). (2006). *Reflections from the wrong side of the tracks: Class identity, and the working class experience in academe.* Lanham, MD: Rowman & Littlefield.

Norton, M. I., & Ariely, D. (2011). Building a better America—one wealth quintile at a time. *Perspectives on Psychological Science, 6,* 9–12. http://dx.doi.org/10.1177/1745691610393524

Pattillo, M. (2013). *Picket fences: Privilege and peril among the Black middle class* (2nd ed.). Chicago, IL: University of Chicago Press.

Pew Research Center. (2015). *Most say government policies since recession have done little to help middle class, poor.* Retrieved from http://www.people-press.org/2015/03/04/most-say-government-policies-since-recession-have-done-little-to-help-middle-class-poor/

Pickett, K. E., & Wilkinson, R. G. (2015). Income inequality and health: A causal review. *Social Science & Medicine, 128,* 316–326. http://dx.doi.org/10.1016/j.socscimed.2014.12.031

Piff, P. K. (2014). Wealth and the inflated self: Class, entitlement, and narcissism. *Personality and Social Psychology Bulletin, 40,* 34–43. http://dx.doi.org/10.1177/0146167213501699

Piff, P. K., Kraus, M. W., Côté, S., Cheng, B. H., & Keltner, D. (2010). Having less, giving more: The influence of social class on prosocial behavior. *Journal of Personality and Social Psychology, 99,* 771–784. http://dx.doi.org/10.1037/a0020092

Piff, P. K., Stancato, D. M., Côté, S., Mendoza-Denton, R., & Keltner, D. (2012). Higher social class predicts increased unethical behavior. *PNAS, 109,* 4086–4091. http://dx.doi.org/10.1073/pnas.1118373109

Reich, R. B. (2014, May 26). How to shrink inequality. *The Nation.* Retrieved from http://www.thenation.com/article/how-shrink-inequality/

Rothman, R. A. (2005). *Inequality and stratification: Race, class, and gender* (5th ed.). Upper Saddle River, NJ: Prentice Hall.

Seider, S. C. (2009). Overwhelmed and immobilized: Raising the consciousness of privileged young adults about world hunger and poverty. *International Studies Perspectives, 10,* 60–76. http://dx.doi.org/10.1111/j.1528-3585.2008.00358.x

Seider, S. C., Gillmor, S. C., & Rabinowicz, S. A. (2011). The impact of community service learning upon the worldview of business majors versus non-business majors at an American university. *Journal of Business Ethics, 98,* 485–503. http://dx.doi.org/10.1007/s10551-010-0589-8

Seider, S. C., Rabinowicz, S. A., & Gillmor, S. C. (2011). Changing American college students' conceptions of poverty through service learning. *Analyses of Social Issues and Public Policy (ASAP), 11,* 105–126. http://dx.doi.org/10.1111/j.1530-2415.2010.01224.x

Shupe, E. I. (2013). The development of an undergraduate study abroad program: Nicaragua and the psychology of social inequality. *Teaching of Psychology, 40*, 124–129. http://dx.doi.org/10.1177/0098628312475032

Silva, J. M. (2013). *Coming up short: Working-class adulthood in an age of uncertainty.* New York, NY: Oxford University Press. http://dx.doi.org/10.1093/acprof:oso/9780199931460.001.0001

Stephens, N. M., Brannon, T. N., Markus, H. R., & Nelson, J. E. (2015). Feeling at home in college: Fortifying school-relevant selves to reduce social class disparities in higher education. *Social Issues and Policy Review, 9*, 1–24. http://dx.doi.org/10.1111/sipr.12008

Stephens, N. M., Hamedani, M. G., & Destin, M. (2014). Closing the social-class achievement gap: A difference-education intervention improves first-generation students' academic performance and all students' college transition. *Psychological Science, 25*, 943–953. http://dx.doi.org/10.1177/0956797613518349

Tablante, C. B., & Fiske, S. T. (2015). Teaching social class. *Teaching of Psychology, 42*, 184–190. http://dx.doi.org/10.1177/0098628315573148

Tirado, L. (2014). *Hand to mouth: Living in bootstrap America.* New York, NY: Putnam.

Truong, S., Reppond, H., Chhun, L., Gainor, L., & Walker, L. (n.d.). *Fiction.* Retrieved from https://www.apa.org/pi/ses/resources/publications/fiction-popular-media.aspx

U.S. Census Bureau. (2017). *Income and poverty in the United States: 2016.* Retrieved from https://www.census.gov/library/publications/2017/demo/p60-259.html

Weber, L. (1998). A conceptual framework for understanding race, class, gender, and sexuality. *Psychology of Women Quarterly, 22*, 13–32. http://dx.doi.org/10.1111/j.1471-6402.1998.tb00139.x

Wilkinson, R. G., & Pickett, K. (2009). *The spirit level: Why more equal societies almost always do better.* London, England: Allen Lane.

Williams, W. R., & Melchiori, K. M. (2014). Class action: How experiential learning can raise awareness of social class privilege. In K. A. Case (Ed.), *Pedagogy of privilege: Teaching and learning as allies in the classroom* (pp. 169–187). New York, NY: Routledge.

14

Teaching Cultural and Transnational Psychology

Taking Intersectionality Across the Globe

Lynn H. Collins

Transnational psychology is a recent development, building on cultural, cross-cultural, multicultural, feminist, liberation, and intersectional approaches to understanding diversity and the psychological impact of globalization, including cross-border economic activity involving the movement of people and ideas and the interaction of technology, institutions, and policy. Transnational psychology examines historical, sociopolitical, economic, and other influences spanning micro (local community) through macro (regional, global) contexts, and it holds that identities impacted by globalization are dynamic, fluid, and synergistic, rather than merely additive (Collins, Machizawa, & Rice, in press). This chapter offers an overview of the terms and tools of transnational psychology and ways to help increase instructors' and students' global awareness.[1]

GLOBALIZATION AND ITS IMPACTS

In the late 1970s, many countries began to lift tariffs and other restrictive practices and open their markets to global commerce (Wolf, 2014). Treaties, organizations such as the World Trade Organization and the International Monetary

---

[1]This book's companion webpage (http://pubs.apa.org/books/supp/mena) features an overview of transnational psychology, a list of recommended resources on this topic, and instructions for conducting a self-decolonization exercise in the classroom that encourages students to think outside their family and cultural traditions.

http://dx.doi.org/10.1037/0000137-015
Integrating Multiculturalism and Intersectionality Into the Psychology Curriculum: Strategies for Instructors, J. A. Mena and K. Quina (Editors)

Fund, private companies, and financial markets created policies such as "special economic zones"; however, transnational labor laws made it more difficult to advocate for better wages, working conditions, and rights. Although the financial status of the wealthiest in high-income countries improved, it worsened for others. The latter's citizens often migrated to less-developed countries where they earned lower wages under worse working conditions. Globalization often undermined local economies, exacerbating oppression; reinforcing hierarchies associated with class, gender, and race; and disrupting families and educational opportunities (Gelfand, Lyons, & Lun, 2011; McHugh, 2007; Mohanty, 2003a). Other consequences include the decline of local farming and secure employment; erosion of wages, benefits, rights, and services; deprivation of food, water, utilities, health care, and housing (Lindio-McGovern, 2007); and in some states, greater repression and militarization. Global forces also interact with and are adapted to local laws, customs, and political, economic, and social contexts, called *glocalization*. (Yuval-Davis, 2009). Glocalization is often characterized by *creolization*, in which traditional and modern cultures mix together.

Indigenous and migrant women are particularly vulnerable. Migrating families often lean heavily on women, increasing their workload at home and work, while increasing dependence on men to mediate between them and their new social, economic, and legal environment (Roopnarine & Chadee, 2016; Yuval-Davis, 2009). As uncertainty increases, and as women gain access to workspaces in which they were previously not permitted, there is often a corresponding rise in fundamentalist traditions that bolster gendered power differentials.

PSYCHOLOGICAL PERSPECTIVES

Psychology has struggled to find an effective way to locate the unique situations and responses of individuals and groups in relation to the new power dynamics of globalization. Bhatia (2007) offered descriptions of various models students will encounter.

Traditional Western psychology, adopted in early American and European approaches, was universal, linear, and essentialist, asserting all humans have a common ancestry and internal structure and thus common psychic characteristics—defined by Western cultural norms and behaviors. Racial and cultural variants are conceptualized as overlying a common structure, like layers of an onion (Bhatia, 2007; Roopnarine & Chadee, 2016).

International psychology, sometimes called *global psychology*, is conducted across borders, rather than from a unique theoretical perspective. It typically focuses on comparisons between nation states as defined by geographical and governmental borders. Patterns within a nation-state or region are viewed as universal, homogeneous, and static.

Cross-cultural psychology is similar to international psychology but focuses on different cultures, rather than nations. Cross-cultural psychologists have expanded our understanding of cognition, language, social behaviors, acculturation, and cultural identity and elevated awareness of immigrant identity and its progression through stages (Bhatia, 2007).

Cultural psychology views human behavior and mental processes as the product of a progressive, dynamic, reciprocal, organic interaction among the human psyche, culture, and experience. Although it has not addressed the specific contexts of migration and diaspora groups, this approach has impacted the evolution of newer models (Bhatia, 2007).

Indigenous psychologies focus on peoples' relatively static, unimported, unique native behavior, thinking, and culture (Kim & Berry, 1993; Roopnarine & Chadee, 2016). Bhatia (2010) said they raise important issues but struggle with universalism and definitions of *indigenous* and downplay globalization.

Liberation psychology examines the psychology of oppressed communities and how they seek emancipation from sociopolitical structural aspects of oppression (Adams, Dobles, Gomez, Kurtis, & Molina, 2015; Kurtiş & Adams, 2015).

Feminist psychologies focus on dynamics among individuals and groups, particularly gendered power differentials and the process of liberation. They recently incorporated intersectionality from Women of Color psychologies: how systems of discrimination and oppression overlap and are often compounded when individuals are members of more than one disadvantaged social category or group, thereby expanding psychology's understanding of global intersectionality. Feminist psychologies are criticized for being universalist, neocolonialistic, and focused on "gender oppression in Western, Educated, Industrialized, Rich, Democratic" (WEIRD) settings (Henrich, Heine, & Norenzayan, 2011; Kurtiş & Adams, 2015, p. 389).

Transnational psychology and *postcolonial feminism* are useful paradigms for understanding the complex interplay among this array of factors. The foundational anthropological studies of Glick-Schiller, Basch, and Szanton-Blanc (1995) demonstrated how immigrants create and recreate their culture and identities as they transverse borders, cultures, and societies, struggling to keep connections with their countries of origin while continuing to view themselves as a community. They concluded that people are fundamentally changed by their contact with different cultures, technology, media, and relationships. Peoples' experiences may continue to influence their descendants' thinking and behavior (Champagne, 2016).

Transnational psychology expands cultural psychology by incorporating intersections of identity (or identities), human rights, nationhood, and economic and political forces. It critiques identity narratives created by migration, colonialization, culture, diasporic communities, political context, individual experiences, and Western perspectives. Identities formed by the migration process are multifaceted, fused, hybridized, fluctuating, and sometimes fragmented (Bhatia, 2007). By bringing forward the silenced perspectives of marginalized people, transnational psychology can liberate people in majority-world settings (Kurtiş & Adams, 2015). It can close gaps in information, creating a more integrated, pluralistic science of psychology that can explain how local and global centers of power and dominance (e.g., capitalism) result in inequality between people of different socially constructed groups, including those based on gender, nationality, class, and ethnicity.

Postcolonial feminism incorporates concepts useful in examining groups' relationships with power structures (Kurtiş & Adams, 2015). Postcolonial feminism critiques Western thought including psychological paradigms (Ralston, 2009). It provides a useful paradigm because it deconstructs and decolonizes Western ideas and critiques the dominance and exploitation of culturally different others without conceptualizing in binary, differently valued entities. It also examines capitalism's impact on daily life, exploitation of labor forces, intersections of identity, gender stereotypes associated with women's bodies, and traditional masculine notions of national identity (Schutte, 1998).

TRANSNATIONAL PSYCHOLOGY IN THE CLASSROOM

Teaching transnational psychology requires a transformation in instructors' and students' appreciation for the range of impacts of globalization on individuals and groups and the extent to which their realities may influence psychological phenomena. It can be a challenge to move away from assumptions of universality and examine reciprocal interactions among multiple intersecting factors. Instructors can help students "disrupt" their belief systems and look at psychological constructs and data from perspectives found in other cultures.

Mohanty (2003b) described three common pedagogical approaches to internationalizing the curriculum and analyzing "the politics of knowledge at work" (p. 518). In the tourist, consumer, or add and stir models, examples from non-Western or Third World/South cultures are added to European American narratives. This approach covers specific issues (e.g., child labor, honor killings), rather than providing comprehensive information about a group's daily lives. As a result, students feel distant and superior instead of connected to groups. Students are not challenged to critique nationalistic assumptions. The explorer model focuses solely on non-European local and global phenomena. Although this approach allows for a deeper understanding, it separates racial and ethnic issues from international issues. Students still feel disconnected and are not challenged to critique issues of power, agency, and justice (Mohanty, 2003b). This is problematic because globalization is a dynamic economic, political, and ideological phenomenon that inherently connects communities across the world and should be studied and critiqued within that context.

Mohanty (2003b) recommended the comparative or solidarity model, which builds a complex relational understanding of experience, location, and history that considers specific contexts, constructing "a real notion of the universal and of democratization" (p. 521). The local and global are not defined by international borders but as coexisting and interconnected, with common interests and responsibilities. Instead of monolithic terms such as *Third World, Global South,* and *Western,* Mohanty suggested using the one-third/two-thirds (global minority/global majority) or First World/North and Third World/South paradigms, which indicate that haves and have-nots live within bounded regions; however, these terms downplay histories of colonization that *Western* and *Third World* symbolize (Mohanty, 2003b).

Instructors have to go beyond psychology to include diverse individual personal accounts of daily life and information about local politics, religions, ethnic groups, military influence, and more to prevent students from homogenizing and essentializing communities. Communities' common, interlaced histories, experiences, and challenges in the context of power relations should also be explored. Individual and collective experiences of oppression, exploitation, and resistance should be presented to personalize the accounts of globalization's impacts and allow students to experience a sense of connection. Courses should include readings and videos depicting the histories, social dynamics, and economic situations of communities, from micro to macro levels. Short educational videos by Khan Academy (http://www.kahnacademy.org) and Crash Course (http://www.thecrashcourse.com) provide a quick review or introduction to the effects of globalization and glocalization and other topics (e.g., world history, imperialism, colonization, decolonization). Students will especially benefit from listening to the narratives of people affected by globalization, guided by scholars such as Marecek and Senadheera (2012), Lee and Pacini-Ketchabaw (2011), and Amer, Howarth, and Sen (2015). Only after this groundwork has been laid should any relevant psychological issues be discussed.

Evaluating Transnational Research

Many measures and observational categories are not validated for use with non-Western populations, posing challenges to construct equivalence (e.g., Spielberger, 2006). Hambleton and Kanjee (1995) identified potential sources of errors, including different cultural and linguistic meanings, technical and methodological problems, and interpretation of test results, which can limit the usefulness of "objective" survey instruments. Qualitative approaches offer an alternative when objective measures prove less than ideal, requiring instruction on transnational qualitative and ethnographic research approaches (Creswell & Poth, 2017).

Three studies provide a springboard for a class discussion of research approaches and assumptions, Western perspectives, and test validity. Marecek and Senadheera (2012) conducted in-depth interviews of Sri Lankan girls hospitalized for deliberate self-harm to better understand the social ecology of suicidal behavior, including its context in relationships, communication, local meanings, practices, and explanatory systems. They also compared suicide rates across age, gender, religious communities, occupations, and urban and rural areas and examined the impact of wars and the globalized economy on the local community. They concluded that the increase in girls' suicide attempts was due to exposure to new, Western expectations regarding advanced education, heterosexual relations, and out-of-home employment and the need to reconcile their wishes with those of their parents who held more traditional expectations regarding appropriate feminine comportment and sexual respectability. The apparent goals of the suicides were self-expression and communication.

Marecek and Senadheera's (2012) qualitative approach can be contrasted with two more traditional studies of suicide patterns in Sri Lanka. Using police and national hospital admission data, Knipe et al. (2014) focused on access to highly toxic pesticides, often used in suicide attempts. They did not interview survivors or their families to confirm their conclusion that their efforts to restrict access to toxic pesticides were effective in reducing suicide rates, nor did they examine the dynamics behind the suicides, and they discounted a compensatory increase in hanging deaths. Samaraweera, Sumathipala, Siribaddana, Sivayogan, and Bhugra (2008) asked psychiatrists to develop psychological autopsies (diagnoses) after suicide, interviewing each individual's closest relatives or friends and reviewing coroners' reports. They concluded that most attempts were not planned and attributed them to depression and availability of pesticides, but what instigated the suicides was not clear. Students can apply a number of critiques, including whether their measures were culture free, concerns about assuming conceptual equivalence of literally translated items without further validation, whether cultural contexts were understood, and the focus on men despite the higher frequency of suicide in young women (see Chapter 20, this volume).

Transnational Case Studies

Students can create in-depth case studies of members of diasporic groups who have left their homes because of war, poverty, persecution, or better opportunities or who have been acutely affected by globalization (e.g., economic or cultural instability in their home region). Individually or as a class, students can collect information about groups' composition (e.g., gender, strengths, resources, religion, socioeconomic status, ethnicity, age, sexuality, place of origin) and contrast locations and migration paths. Students should describe the political, economic, and social issues affecting the regions in which the groups have lived, including power struggles involving corporate and governmental entities. Students should incorporate personal narratives of diverse group members to remind students of within-group differences. Instructors can invite members of the groups likely to present different experiences to class and interview them using preselected questions from students. The questions can help explore cultural ideologies, inequalities, struggles, sources of empowerment and pride, and experiences of migration of multiple individuals within the group, including how they were received in their new country. Although face-to-face interactions may be the most informative, global communications systems offer other ways to connect with people across the world. International organization websites, social media, and blogs also provide opportunities to learn from people in other regions. Google Translate® can be a useful tool for navigating language boundaries, although its translation ability has limitations. Lindio-McGovern (2007) and Polakoff (2007) have collected powerful testimonies, and organizations such as the Peace Corps, Doctors Without Borders, and UNESCO (the United Nations Educational, Scientific, and Cultural Organization) post stories and videos about daily lives of individuals on their websites. After reviewing

Grabe and Else-Quest's (2012) suggestions for culturally sensitive investigative and data-collection techniques, including appropriate personal contact, advanced students can be challenged to reach out to people to better understand their lives and contexts. These activities help remind students that there are within-group differences. Although written from a cultural rather than transnational perspective, *Internationalizing the Undergraduate Psychology Curriculum* (Gross, Abrams, & Enns, 2016) provides guidance regarding contact with communities from other cultures.

To nurture connection with diasporic groups, students can participate in the Genographic Project (https://genographic.nationalgeographic.com/about/), which traces ancestors' migratory paths from Mitochondrial Eve, the most recent common matrilineal ancestor of all living humans. Before doing so, they should be fully informed about the uses and costs of such tests. Alternatively, they can pick one of the DNA types associated with their ancestors' ethnic or national heritage and trace possible migratory paths. Students should read about the economic, military, religious, cultural, governmental, and environmental forces that may have led their ancestors to migrate and then contemplate how their historical and current "locations" (positions and backgrounds) influence how they think about global others. They might discuss why those leaving Western countries are called *expatriates*, whereas those from non-Western countries are labeled *immigrants* or *refugees*, and why the former are viewed more positively (Koutonin, 2015). With this more personal conceptualization, students can discuss ways the West might respond to the needs of these groups and reduce negative responses toward them, such as stereotyping and discrimination.

APPLYING "CRITICAL" VOCABULARY

Several concepts are useful in deconstructing and critiquing the Western influences embodied in globalization, especially when students are provided with reflection questions as they strive to understand people through a transnational lens. These concepts are also helpful in understanding the spectrum of multicultural and intersectional influences in other courses.

Imperialism and Colonialism

Imperialism describes the process of seeking to increase control over regions and resources; in the process, a culture or country forces its values and customs onto another through occupation, diplomacy, military force, financial incentives, discrimination, or other oppressive practices. Using video clips (http://www.history-world.net, http://www.thecrashcourse.com), students can view historical time lines and discuss major trends for topics such as imperialism, migration, and trade. *Colonialism* frequently occurs in conjunction with imperialism. *Colonization*, when people from one region are placed in another to exploit its resources, often results in the domination and oppression of indigenous people (McHugh, 2007;

Roopnarine & Chadee, 2016). The arrival of Europeans in the Americas is a powerful example (Sellers & Arrigo, 2016; see also Chapter 10, this volume).

Instructors can ask students to apply the concepts transnationally as students are introduced to material about other people and cultures. They can be asked to examine more recent examples of imperialism and colonization, such as military occupations, mass immigrations, and gentrification in specific areas of the Global East, including Asia and the Middle East, that are part of the recent wave of globalization, which began in the 1970s. Students could read about a community recently impacted by imperialism and ask, "What was the imperialistic country seeking? How did it impose its values and customs on this community? How did they achieve this, and what are the consequences for the original population?"

Another approach is to have students look at transnational patterns of exploitation for resources, including gas, oil, and human labor. Pyagbara's (2007) United Nations (UN) working paper illustrating the impacts of oil production on the Ogoni People of Nigeria can be used as an example. In addition to oil extraction, American manufacturing companies have set up factories overseas where they can pay workers less than half the U.S. minimum wage (Chen, 2015). Maplecroft's website (https://www.maplecroft.com) is an interesting site for exploring global trends, including labor practices to help corporations protect their reputations by avoiding involvement in practices such as child labor.

As imperialism replaces native traditions, a *monoculture* may arise, which lacks diversity in values, ideas, and knowledge. Students can read Norberg-Hodge's (1999) critique *Consumer Monoculture: The Destruction of Tradition* and then locate images of specific cultures, cities, or regions before and after globalization. Questions might include, What kinds of influence from an outside culture do you see in this community? How is this country different than it was 30 years ago? Are the changes helpful or harmful to its citizens?

Another negative consequence is *hegemony*, when the dominant culture forces its values and norms on citizens, defining preferred behaviors and normalizing sanctions against those violating these norms. Mandating the use of a particular language can contribute to hegemony, determining symbolism, knowledge, what is communicated, and who can communicate (Mayr, 2008). When the United States sets up schools in other countries, classes may be taught in English, creating a demarcation between those with and without education. Although this increases the likelihood that graduates will communicate more effectively with English-speaking countries, it reduces the use of local languages.

An engaging classroom example involves the classic resource *Our Bodies, Ourselves* (Boston Women's Health Book Collective, 2011). Highly popular in the United States, the volume was viewed as hegemonic and insulting in other parts of the world. People influenced by Latin American cultures tend to be collectivistic, emphasizing the importance of family and community goals, outcomes, rights, cohesiveness, and identity, rather than those of individuals. Women exposed to Latin American culture raised concerns that *Our Bodies, Ourselves* endorsed individualistic and androcentric norms of sexuality, such as the woman taking care of herself and orgasm as the goal. In contrast, women exposed to totalitarian rules in Eastern Europe were accepting of the individualistic tone but uncomfortable with collectivist ideas of communal sisterhood and consensus building, which had been abused by their previous government. Ultimately, the book was revised with input from a more diverse population of women (Davis, 2007). Davis (2007) described how the authors had to confront how their WEIRD positions and situations had influenced how they understood and approached women's sexuality, health, relationships, and the topics covered. Now, the *Our Bodies Ourselves* website (http://www. ourbodiesourselves.org/global-projects/) includes a map of the world with links to each region's page, some of which describe the process of adaptation for that region. Google Translate or a similar application can be used to roughly translate versions into students' preferred languages. A transnational approach would examine how communities' views of their bodies and sexuality change as they interact with other cultures and forces.

In the aftermath of colonization, some communities engage in decolonization, reclaiming their chosen culture by freeing themselves from the external traditions forced on them. Extricating from colonization ideally involves a democratic process through which people rethink, reevaluate, and reclaim their self, community, and governance structures (McHugh, 2007; CrashCourse videos). Students can brainstorm ways that people in more recently colonized regions might reverse that colonization. Two good resources are archived reports, on the website of the U.S. Department of State (https://history.state. gov, search for "decolonization" under Milestones or Countries) and the global issues page of the UN website (http://www.un.org/en/sections/issues-depth/ global-issues-overview/index.html). Particularly interesting are the decolonizations of Asia and Africa, India and Pakistan, and Angola from their European rulers. CrashCourse video #40 describes decolonization, and video #228 describes nonviolent movements, including Gandhi's decolonization of India. A longer movie about Gandhi is also available (Attenborough, 2007).

Diaspora

Diasporic communities are displaced people who share a history of being expatriated from a particular place; they often construct narratives about their country of origin to which they may hope to return and are subjected to discrimination in their new environment and maintain loyalty to their displaced community. Examples include Africans who were enslaved to the Americas and Chinese laborers brought to other Eastern regions and the Americas. More recently, the Iraqi War, Syrian Civil War, and Bolivarian Revolution resulted in massive diasporic communities. Students can gather information about displaced groups residing in their region, using census data, and then a world map, to trace their routes from their places of origin. Helpful reports can be found by searching the UN Development Programme website (http://www.undp.org) and http://www.migrationpolicy.org for information about migration, refugees, and displacement. These should be supplemented with individual narratives to emphasize within-group differences.

Strong Reflexivity, Situated Knowledge, Othering, and Standpoint Epistemology

Researchers bring their perspectives to their research and change as they interact with the focus of their research. Such perspectives can promote understanding if made explicit and subjected to examination (Hirsh & Olson, 1995). Several strategies can enable this analysis.

Strong reflexivity critiques one's knowledge, perspective, and location by identifying the cultural values that shape what one considers the "truth." Much of European American psychology has less relevance in other cultures (e.g., self-esteem, posttraumatic stress disorder, depression, homosexuality, sexual harassment, and attachment). Christopher, Wendt, Marecek, and Goodman (2014) described how, when Westerners stepped in to help after the 2004 Asian tsunami, many were unfamiliar with the local cultures, languages, and practices. As a result, the Western "helpers" inadvertently violated families' privacy by entering their temporary homes and urging victims to participate in therapeutic exercises that were inconsistent with local standards of propriety. Unaware of the far greater need for necessities such as clean water, food, and shelter, this wave of misguided outsiders, who further depleted scarce local resources, was referred to by locals as the "second tsunami."

Strong reflexivity starts with awareness of *situated knowledge*, the perspective resulting from experiences in one's location, position, or place in the world. Once acknowledged, situated knowledge should be subjected to examination and critique. For instance, what one "knows" about a group (knowledge) depends on opinions (perspectives) developed by virtue of one's characteristics (race, gender, socioeconomic status, education, ethnicity, etc.) and personal experiences, and it is thus subject to these biases; we must constantly remind ourselves and our students that no perspective is "value free." Reflexivity requires that one ask the questions "What assumptions am I making because of my ethnicity, class, education level, sex, theoretical perspective, life experiences, and so forth? How does my perspective lead me to select and conceptualize my research and scholarship? How can I use my awareness of my situated knowledge to conceptualize the issues in a better way? How has studying this topic changed how I think about it?" Amer et al. (2015) provided an example with their brief description of the lead author's situation and its potential impact on the research.

A panel of differently situated individuals can be invited to the class to describe their perspectives on their worlds, including day-to-day realities, emotions, expectations, opportunities, and stereotyping of self and other. Locating different perspectives from within a region is especially valuable (e.g., within Dubai, a migrant hotel worker, a college student resident, and a wealthy professional American woman living there temporarily). Students can speak to or learn about individuals in such situations and then report on self-descriptions of each, including personal origins, education level, gender, religion, ethnicity, and more.

Too often, dissimilar people are portrayed in negative ways. Such *othering* can range from stereotyping people from different regions based on perceived differences to claiming to speak for those who they have subjugated. Indeed, most academic research on oppressed or marginalized groups is conducted or supervised by WEIRD researchers, rather than members of the group studied. For each of the three studies on suicide described earlier, instructors can ask students, "Whose voices are speaking for the oppressed people in this article?"

In contrast, *standpoint epistemology* decenters WEIRD thinking by making the views of oppressed groups more visible and important than those of dominant groups. The rationale is that members of dominant groups are more likely to be invested in continuing to conform to their dominant culture and therefore are more likely to obscure reality (Miller, 1986), whereas oppressed groups are less invested in the status quo and therefore more likely to reveal its limitations. Marecek and Senadheera (2012) used this approach by asking questions of girls who had engaged in self-harm behavior, allowing them to tell their stories in their own language. This can lead to a better understanding of the subjective meaning of the event, rather than continuing to rely on Western theories to explain suicidal behavior. Students can discuss how studies such as Amer et al. (2015) bring voices of the marginalized to the forefront and the difference it makes in their understanding of the topic, and they can discuss Rasmussen's (2015) interesting commentary on this team's approach. Students can also discuss sources of bias that arise when people are not allowed to describe their experiences. For example, they can compare Hoang and Yeoh (2012), in which adults speak for children, with Lee and Pacini-Ketchabaw (2011), in which girls describe their own experiences, and discuss potential sources of bias. Wu and Wu (2015) provided another example of a firsthand narrative qualitative research approach.

Moon (2008) and Ortlipp (2008) suggested that researchers keep a diary of their thoughts about the interaction of their characteristics and backgrounds with their research. Students can consider how their background affects their objectivity and understanding to aid in increasing their awareness and the like-lihood of achieving strong reflectivity. In describing her position as a researcher, Ortlipp wrote,

> I am a tertiary supervisor researching other tertiary supervisors. I am a woman, and so far all my participants are women. I am not a neutral participant in the research project from the outset. I have issues, concerns and opinions about [this project]. . . . I should be particularly concerned about my role in the research process as the main instrument of data collection. (p. 698)

CONCLUSION

Many transnational psychology topics are controversial because they challenge Western perspectives. Consider human rights, where the balance between communities' rights to exercise their cultural traditions and their citizens' human rights is frequently subjected to strong debate and sometimes dismissed and equated with Westernization and secularization (Yuval-Davis, 2009). Traditions such as female genital mutilation, marital rape, marital controls, abuse, and honor killings often represent a fight between patriarchal leadership and women's rights. Former occupants of Syria and Iraq face an enormous challenge, forced to flee war and starvation and yet unwelcome in the countries that played a role in their displacement, often because their dress and religion are unfamiliar or feared.

If we are to understand the dynamics and psychological implications of globalization and glocalization, people representing a variety of perspectives (e.g., many positions and situations) should be included in education and research efforts. Theoretically, the more perspectives and voices accessed, the more accurate impressions will be, enhancing the quality of knowledge (McHugh, 2007). Diverse workgroups are also more likely to produce more accurate and effective ideas and approaches to solutions. To demonstrate pluralism in the classroom, groups of demographically similar and dissimilar students can be asked ways to solve a problem, such as how to provide food and shelter for the displaced, to demonstrate the range of answers within heterogeneous and homogeneous groups.

Creating international networks of students and scholars allows us to apply this principle to our research and activism across a diversity of national origins to create better understanding and potential solutions to problems. Gross et al. (2016) and Collins et al. (in press) offer additional guidance regarding engaging students in the classroom, applications, research abroad, immersion programs, service learning programs, and helping students apply for Fulbright Grants. As Hill-Collins (1990) declared more than a quarter-century ago, an inclusive, pluralistic approach is imperative if we are to keep pace with the exciting developments in transnational psychology. Exposure to a transnational approach will hopefully inspire students to become well-informed, active global citizens in the service of democracy and justice (Mohanty, 2003b).

REFERENCES

Adams, G., Dobles, I., Gomez, L. H., Kurtis, T., & Molina, L. E. (2015). Decolonizing psychological science: Introduction to the special thematic section. *Journal of Social and Political Psychology, 3*, 213–238. http://dx.doi.org/10.5964/jspp.v3i1.564

Amer, A., Howarth, C., & Sen, R. (2015). Diasporic virginities: Social representations of virginity and identity formation amongst British Arab Muslim women. *Culture & Psychology, 21*, 3–19. http://dx.doi.org/10.1177/1354067X14551297

Attenborough, R. (Producer & Director). (2007). *Gandhi* [Motion picture]. United States: Sony Pictures Home Entertainment.

Bhatia, S. (2007). Rethinking culture and identity: Towards a transnational cultural psychology. *Journal of Theoretical and Philosophical Psychology, 27–28*, 301–321. http://dx.doi.org/10.1037/h0091298

Bhatia, S. (2010). Theorizing indigenous psychology [Review of the book *Indigenous and Cultural Psychology: People in Context*, by U. Kim, K.-S. Yang, & K.-K. Hwang (Eds.)]. *Theory & Psychology, 20*, 137–140. http://dx.doi.org/10.1177/0959354309345640

Boston Women's Health Book Collective. (2011). *Our bodies, ourselves: A book by and for women*. New York, NY: Touchstone.

Champagne, F. A. (2016). Epigenetic legacy of parental experiences: Dynamic and interactive pathways to inheritance. *Development and Psychopathology, 28*, 1219–1228. http://dx.doi.org/10.1017/S0954579416000808

Chen, S. (2015, April 5). U.S. wages will be 58 times Indonesia's by 2019. *Bloomberg*. Retrieved from http://www.bloomberg.com/news/articles/2015-04-06/u-s-wages-will-be-58-times-indonesia-s-by-2019

Christopher, J. C., Wendt, D. C., Marecek, J., & Goodman, D. M. (2014). Critical cultural awareness: Contributions to a globalizing psychology. *American Psychologist, 69*, 645–655. http://dx.doi.org/10.1037/a0036851

Collins, L. H., Machizawa, S., & Rice, J. K. (Eds.). (in press). *Transnational psychology of women: Expanding international and intersectional approaches*. Washington, DC: American Psychological Association.

Creswell, J. W., & Poth, C. N. (2017). *Qualitative inquiry and research design: Choosing among five approaches*. Los Angeles, CA: Sage.

Davis, K. (2007). *The making of* Our Bodies, Ourselves: *How feminism travels across borders*. Durham, NC: Duke University Press.

Gelfand, M. J., Lyons, S. L., & Lun, J. (2011). Toward a psychological science of globalization. *Journal of Social Issues, 67*, 841–853. http://dx.doi.org/10.1111/j.1540-4560.2011.01731.x

Glick-Schiller, N., Basch, L., & Szanton-Blanc, C. (1995). From immigrant to transmigrant: Theorizing transnational migration. *Anthropological Quarterly, 68*, 48–63. http://dx.doi.org/10.2307/3317464. http://dx.doi.org/10.2307/3317464

Grabe, S., & Else-Quest, N. M. (2012). The role of transnational feminism in psychology: Complementary visions. *Psychology of Women Quarterly, 36*, 158–161. http://dx.doi.org/10.1177/0361684312442164

Gross, D., Abrams, K., & Enns, C. Z. (Eds.). (2016). *Internationalizing the undergraduate psychology curriculum: Practical lessons learned at home and abroad*. Washington, DC: American Psychological Association. http://dx.doi.org/10.1037/14840-000

Hambleton, R. K., & Kanjee, A. (1995). Increasing the validity of cross-cultural assessments: Use of improved methods for test adaptations. *European Journal of Psychological Assessment, 11*, 147–157. http://dx.doi.org/10.1027/1015-5759.11.3.147

Henrich, J., Heine, S., & Norenzayan, A. (2011). The WEIRDest people in the world? *Behavioral and Brain Sciences, 33*, 61–135. http://dx.doi.org/10.1017/S0140525X0999152X

Hill-Collins, P. (1990). *Black feminist thought: Consciousness and the politics of empowerment*. London, England: HarperCollins.

Hirsh, E., & Olson, G. A. (1995). Starting from marginalized lives: A conversation with Sandra Harding. *Journal of Advanced Composition, 15*, 193–225.

Hoang, L. A., & Yeoh, B. S. A. (2012). Sustaining families across transnational spaces: Vietnamese migrant parents and their left-behind children. *Asian Studies Review, 36*, 307–325. http://dx.doi.org/10.1080/10357823.2012.711810

Kim, U., & Berry, J. W. (Eds.). (1993). *Indigenous psychologies: Research and experience in cultural context*. Thousand Oaks, CA: Sage.

Knipe, D. W., Metcalfe, C., Fernando, R., Pearson, M., Konradsen, F., Eddleston, M., & Gunnell, D. (2014). Suicide in Sri Lanka 1975–2012: Age, period and cohort analysis of police and hospital data. *BMC Public Health, 14*, 839. http://dx.doi.org/10.1186/1471-2458-14-839

Koutonin, M. R. (2015, March 13). Why are White people expats when the rest of us are immigrants? *The Guardian*. Retrieved from http://www.theguardian.com/global-development-professionals-network/2015/mar/13/white-people-expats-immigrants-migration

Kurtiş, T., & Adams, G. (2015). Decolonizing liberation: Toward a transnational feminist psychology. *Journal of Social and Political Psychology, 3,* 388–413. http://dx.doi.org/10.5964/jspp.v3i1.326

Lee, J., & Pacini-Ketchabaw, V. (2011). Immigrant girls as caregivers to younger siblings: A transnational feminist analysis. *Gender and Education, 23,* 105–119. http://dx.doi.org/10.1080/09540251003674063

Lindio-McGovern, L. (2007). Conclusion: Women and neoliberal globalization inequities and resistance. *Journal of Developing Societies, 23,* 285–297. http://dx.doi.org/10.1177/0169796X0602300216

Marecek, J., & Senadheera, C. (2012). 'I drank it to put an end to me': Narrating girls' suicide and self-harm in Sri Lanka. *Contributions to Indian Sociology, 46,* 53–82. http://dx.doi.org/10.1177/006996671104600204

Mayr, A. (2008). *Language and power: An introduction to institutional discourse.* New York, NY: A & C Black.

McHugh, N. A. (2007). *Feminist philosophies A–Z.* Edinburgh, Scotland: Edinburgh University Press.

Miller, J. B. (1986). *Toward a new psychology of women* (2nd ed.). Boston, MA: Beacon Press.

Mohanty, C. T. (2003a). *Feminism without borders: Decolonizing theory, practicing solidarity.* Durham, NC: Duke University Press. http://dx.doi.org/10.1215/9780822384649

Mohanty, C. T. (2003b). "Under Western Eyes" revisited: Feminist solidarity through anticapitalist struggles. *Signs: Journal of Women in Culture and Society, 28,* 499–535. http://dx.doi.org/10.1086/342914

Moon, T. (2008). Reflexivity and its usefulness when conducting a secondary analysis of existing data. *Psychology & Society, 1,* 77–83.

Norberg-Hodge, H. (1999). Consumer monoculture: The destruction of tradition. *Global Dialogue, 1,* 70–77.

Ortlipp, M. (2008). Keeping and using reflective journals in the qualitative research process. *Qualitative Report, 13,* 695–705.

Polakoff, E. G. (2007). Introduction to 'Women and Globalization.' *Journal of Developing Societies, 23,* 3–14. http://dx.doi.org/10.1177/0169796X0602300201

Pyagbara, L. S. (2007). *The adverse impacts of oil pollution on the environment and wellbeing of a local indigenous community: The experience of the Ogoni People of Nigeria.* Retrieved from http://www.un.org/esa/socdev/unpfii/documents/workshop_IPPE_pyagbara.doc

Ralston, M. (2009). Towards a truly transnational feminism. *European Journal of Women's Studies, 16,* 400–401. http://dx.doi.org/10.1177/13505068090160040805

Rasmussen, S. (2015). Understanding honor in religious, cultural, and moral experience: Commentary on "Diasporic virginities: Social representations of virginity and constructions of identity amongst British Arab Muslim women" by Howarth, Caroline; Amer, Amena; and Sen, Ragini. *Culture & Psychology, 21,* 20–36. http://dx.doi.org/10.1177/1354067X14551301

Roopnarine, J. L., & Chadee, D. (Eds.). (2016). *Caribbean psychology: Indigenous contributions to a global discipline.* Washington, DC: American Psychological Association. http://dx.doi.org/10.1037/14753-000

Samaraweera, S., Sumathipala, A., Siribaddana, S., Sivayogan, S., & Bhugra, D. (2008). Completed suicide among Sinhalese in Sri Lanka: A psychological autopsy study. *Suicide and Life-Threatening Behavior, 38,* 221–228. http://dx.doi.org/10.1521/suli.2008.38.2.221

Schutte, O. (1998). Cultural alternity: Cross-cultural communication and feminist thought in North-South dialogue. *Hypatia, 13,* 53–72. http://dx.doi.org/10.1111/j.1527-2001.1998.tb01225.x

Sellers, B. G., & Arrigo, B. A. (2016). Economic nomads: A theoretical deconstruction of the immigration debacle. *Journal of Philosophical & Theoretical Criminology, 8,* 37–56.

Spielberger, C. D. (2006). Cross-cultural assessment of emotional states and personality traits. *European Psychologist, 11*, 297–303. http://dx.doi.org/10.1027/1016-9040.11.4.297

Wolf, M. (2014). Shaping globalization. *Finance & Development, 51*(3), 22–25.

Wu, Y., & Wu, H. (2015). Higher education learning experiences among Vietnamese immigrant women in Taiwan. *Adult Education Quarterly, 65*, 133–151. http://dx.doi.org/10.1177/0741713614566673

Yuval-Davis, N. (2009). Women, globalization and contemporary politics of belonging. *Gender, Technology and Development, 13*, 1–19. http://dx.doi.org/10.1177/097185240901300101

15

Nontraditional Students

Multigenerational, Multilocational, and Multicultural

Mary Zahm and Kathryn Quina

Paths to academic credentials for college students in the United States have changed dramatically in the past 2 decades: Almost 40% are over the age of 25; 40% attend part time (more so women); nearly 60% work 20 or more hours weekly; over 25% are raising children, especially Blacks (47%) and Hispanics (42%); nearly 60% attend a 2-year institution; and 4% are veterans (Lumina Foundation, n.d.; National Center for Education Statistics, 2013). Thanks to the Post-9/11 GI Bill and other programs (https://www.benefits. va.gov/gibill/post911_gibill.asp), veterans and military personnel often return to school between and after deployment and make use of online educational opportunities. Increasingly, students are seeking their education in alternative formats, including distance (online) and competency-based learning. Even in traditional classrooms, new technologies have led to more interactive, student-centered pedagogies. To prepare workforce-ready graduates, students frequently seek service learning, internships, and other hands-on opportunities. As we transform education, it is essential to incorporate these students and their diverse perspectives into our classrooms and curricula, striving for greater social justice by increasing access, opportunity, and empowerment.[1]

---

[1]A sample syllabus for a course on the psychology of personal adjustment, along with instructions for classroom exercises, are available on this book's companion webpage (http://pubs.apa.org/books/supp/mena).

http://dx.doi.org/10.1037/0000137-016
Integrating Multiculturalism and Intersectionality Into the Psychology Curriculum:
Strategies for Instructors, J. A. Mena and K. Quina (Editors)

NONTRADITIONAL AND ADULT STUDENTS

The reasons older students give for attending college are varied, including retraining for a new career, accommodating an adult-onset disability, preparing for self-sufficiency due to divorce or a partner's death, moving from welfare to work, pursuing a lifelong dream of a college degree, being a positive role model for their children, or simply seeking the stimulation of new ideas and new learning (e.g., Center for Women Policy Studies, 2002; Kimmel, Gaylor, & Hayes, 2014). The college experience can be transformative for adult students (Foote, 2015; Knowles, Holton, & Swanson, 2005; Nguyen, 2014). We have taught legislators, engineers, scientists, teachers, students proficient in myriad languages, and community leaders. Most have achieved quieter greatness, through parenting, caring for others, surviving illness or injury, resisting oppression, and overcoming childhood traumas or addictions.

Although a college degree is often necessary for workforce participation (e.g., Baum, Ma, & Payea, 2013), only about 40% of U.S. citizens earn any credential beyond a high school diploma (Ryan & Bauman, 2016). Degree attainment is substantially lower among low-income, minority (African Americans, Hispanics, and American Indians), English language learning, and first-generation college students (Engle & Tinto, 2008; Lumina Foundation, n.d.).

These diversities and the life experiences they comprise can enrich the classroom experience in many ways, and many instructors relish the opportunity to teach nontraditional students. Yet, too often, for some, the academic experience can be a source of stress and harm. Oppressive elements in society also exist in academia; students of color and women students have reported they regularly were subjected to overt and subtle racist and sexist comments and other forms of discrimination at their universities (Caplan & Ford, 2014). We have heard far too many instructors express doubts about a student's promise based on age, background or preparation, and personal characteristics—doubts that can inform prejudicial actions. More benign is that typical courses treat all students as if they are there to develop an identity, need preparation to enter society, have unrestricted time to complete on-campus assignments, and are naive about life outside the ivory towers—which is not the case for most adult learners. Successful learning environments require our willingness to be guided by all voices.

TEACHING IN A NONTRADITIONAL CLASSROOM

In our experience, when a class is more accessible to one student, it benefits all students, and interactions in a diverse classroom (even online) can lead to mutual growth. The following are strategies we have successfully used in our combined 75+ years of teaching nontraditional and mixed-age classes, in 2- and 4-year colleges, online and in person.

Make Content Relevant to a Range of Experiences

Many psychology courses draw examples from young adult concerns, such as forming an identity, dating, and forming career goals. Supplement textbook materials with practical tips for parents; expand topics to address healthy relationships, challenges after divorce or death of a partner, or changing identities across the life span. In essays, students can bring in personal examples of new concepts or apply concepts to their family and work lives. M. J. Allen (2000) offered an excellent set of tips for teaching a course blending traditional, nontraditional, and international students. Zahm's (2010) *Create Your Ideal Life* provides a personalized interactive approach for assessing interests and planning for a better quality of life, including financial, physical, relational, and personal, at any age, stage of career, or level of personal development.[2]

Lectures and discussions must include and respect diverse views so that different cohorts can learn from one another (Ayers & Narduzzi, 2009). Invite older students to share what they have learned from their experiences, and invite young students who also have had important experiences, such as teenaged parenting, drug abuse, or dating violence. Women, veterans, ethnoracial minorities, and students with disabilities add important voices. In traditional, hybrid, or online courses, small groups of different ages can discuss their experiences and/or perspectives on a particular issue raised in their readings. Students in developmental psychology, psychology of women or gender, or personal adjustment courses might discuss recollections of family roles and structure, parenting practices, access to education or technology, or importance of organized religion. Structured discussion questions for each group to answer keep students on task. We charge one student with making sure every voice is heard and another with taking notes and reporting back to the whole class, and we follow discussions with a written assignment to ensure thoughtful processing. If time permits, students could create a structured questionnaire that includes questions from the discussion and interview someone of a gender, culture, or generation other than their own and then compare answers with their own. Students can also react to an autobiographical work (e.g., *I Am Malala*; Yousafzai, 2013).

Rules for civility and confidentiality should be included on the syllabus and enforced to the extent possible. Group discussions should encourage experiences that enhance the deep learning of course topics while providing a safe learning environment. Roost and Roost (2014) discussed the challenges veterans face returning to a college environment, particularly after combat duty. Describing his experiences as a teacher, Nathan Kreuter (2012) reminded us

---

[2]Instructions for conducting four classroom exercises related to Zahm (2010) and creating one's ideal life are available from this book's companion webpage (http://pubs.apa.org/books/supp/mena). These exercises ask students to think about their core values and central beliefs, create collages representing their ideal lives, examine the resources they need to create these ideal lives, and compare generational differences in sociocultural contexts.

that there is a great deal of diversity among veterans. We caution not to view veterans only through lenses of their challenges, even when they have visible or invisible wounds, but rather enhance and incorporate their strengths into the classroom.

Respect Students' Time and Energy

Time is the most pressing challenge for many students. Classes may be selected according to family and work schedules, and preplanning according to course deadlines is often a must. Even K–12 school vacations and holidays can limit academic participation for students who shoulder responsibility for child care and family functions. In spite of these demands, most adult students manage time for their studies quite effectively and persist in the face of challenges (Ayers & Narduzzi, 2009).

Solutions that do not decrease academic quality include a syllabus with a clear set of expectations and a well-thought-out schedule, learning experiences that provide flexibility (e.g., take-home or online work), and minimization of "busy work." In smaller classes, traditional exams can be replaced with take-home essays; in larger classes, try online exams with a 24-hour window for completion (many quiz delivery systems allow for a random draw of questions from a larger set). Self-managed experiential learning is helpful; for example, in developmental and gender courses, most students found that visiting a toy store and then writing a reaction paper was an instructive activity, but some had transportation and schedule challenges, and a few parents found it too stimulating for their young children. An option to review the store's circular or website solved the problem. Students also enjoy reviewing a popular book in the contexts of both the scholarly literature and personal experiences; particularly well-liked are Dweck (2006), Kindlon and Thompson (2000), and Norcross (2012).

Supplementary readings and assignments are pursued enthusiastically when they increase understanding of the material. However, work not tied to the course goals, ambiguous instructions, and assignments that go ungraded are viewed dimly, as is the instructor who assigns them. When possible, we replace class time with self-paced work. "Flipped" classrooms allow students to prepare more thoroughly outside of class; online discussions and other assignments can provide a stimulating learning environment (see Estes, Ingram, & Liu, 2014, for pointers). Wlodkowski (2008) offered other strategies for motivating adult students' learning.

Teach to Multiple Cognitive Styles

Research on adult learning has focused on various cognitive dimensions, including developmental processes, learning styles, intellectual skills, relevance of life experiences, and the meaning of the educational experience to the individual (e.g., Donaldson & Graham, 1999). Although age or "stage" is not necessarily a determining factor, older students may have different approaches to learning (Honigsfeld & Dunn, 2006).

Some of our students earned equivalency diplomas after dropping out of high school years ago and thus have fewer prior educational experiences. Jameson and Fusco (2014) reported that older students experienced greater math anxiety and lower self-efficacy for math performance than younger students, even though they often perform complex math functions to solve problems in the workplace "without the anxiety, frustration, and difficulty often exhibited in math classes" (p. 313). Their suggestions, such as making course lessons more relevant with real-life examples, can benefit all students.

Study skills, particularly "test-wisdom," decline with time away from formal education (e.g., Marschall & Davis, 2012). Some first-generation immigrant or international students do not fully understand what a U.S. higher education requires (e.g., Karp & Bork, 2012). Performance is better when assignments and exams are clearly based on explicit learning objectives, have varied formats, assess skills students have had an opportunity to practice, and do not rely on rote memorization. Brown, Roediger, and McDaniel (2014) outlined effective study techniques that help students learn and retain new information, such as frequent self-testing.

Life experiences can also affect the way students approach materials. Belenky, Clinchy, Goldberger, and Tarule (1997) posited that adults often take a more relativistic, in-depth approach to learning, rather than learning by rote. Nicolaides (2015) suggested that adult learners tolerate greater ambiguity across viewpoints. Instructors can accommodate different ways of learning by diversifying their teaching and evaluation strategies and making learning more active and interesting. Providing context for new material, taking time to explain the reasons behind a model or construct, and suggesting different ways students can approach the same problem can provide depth and reduce anxiety. Interdisciplinary courses also can help students more readily grasp the connections between theories, content, and their applications and prepare students for collaborative interdisciplinary teamwork in the workplace.

Applying theories and research from educational psychology to adult learners, Smith and Pourchot (1998) offered strategies for enhancing learning potential, ranging from mnemonic devices to incorporating forgiveness by releasing feelings of resentment and fear caused by embarrassing prior classroom experiences and/or hurtful life experiences.

David and Alice Kolb provide a bibliography and a variety of resources on experiential learning and learning styles, including downloadable papers and syllabi (http://learningfromexperience.com/). Honigsfeld and Dunn (2006) offered classroom management and assignment designs best suited for adult learners with varied learning style preferences; also see *Adult Education Quarterly*, *Adult Learning Journal*, *American Journal of Distance Education*, and the *Journal of Continuing Higher Education*.

Empower Students Through Their Education

The educational experience can be significant for individual growth and meaning making in life (see LeBlanc, Brabant, & Forsyth, 1996). Freire (1998),

Mezirow (1996), and Rassool (1999) offered models of transformation through literacy education that look beyond traditional Western models of teaching to incorporate multicultural awareness. Kroth and Boverie (2000) asserted that helping students examine their "life mission" and "associated assumptions" can "increase learner self-direction, helping the learner to make meaningful learning choices and maximizing motivation" (p. 13). In college success or personal adjustment courses, students can identify the beliefs, values, and attitudes on which they have based life choices and develop ways to change in order to pursue their educational and career goals as well as their desired lifestyle (Zahm, 2010). These approaches can also help students become aware of oppression, strengthen their voice in relationships, and increase their public participation, ultimately creating social change.

Support and encouragement are important for nontraditional students (e.g., Stein & Wanstreet, 2006). Home (1998) found that a lack of family support is one of the most serious deterrents to completing a degree, especially for mothers of young children. Zajacova, Lynch, and Espenshade (2005) assessed stress and academic self-efficacy among nontraditional (including immigrant) students and found that although stress was greater when general self-efficacy was lower, self-efficacy for specific aspects of academic work was a strong predictor of grade point average and other variables related to persistence in school. The challenges can be profound, but achieving in a multidimensional world and successfully managing different domains has been linked to greater health in the long run (Baruch & Barnett, 1986).

NONTRADITIONAL AND MULTILOCATED EDUCATIONAL ENVIRONMENTS

Distance Learning

A growing number of students are enrolling in courses using distance technologies. Hybrid (blended) and online courses should be student centered and highly interactive with the instructor, who serves as the learning facilitator (Finley, Brothen, & Froman, 2005). Ragan (2009) provided an excellent guide to best practices for effective online teaching.

Thoughtful design, planning, and quality are key to learning. Asynchronous (nonsimultaneous) technologies accommodate students' time and access constraints but require more self-discipline, both for students (I. E. Allen & Seaman, 2014) and instructors (Neumann & Neumann, 2010). Flexibility is desirable because technology glitches and life challenges happen. We have found that weekly assignments help students stay current and give us enough time to grade work.

Marschall and Davis (2012) pointed out that many adult students lack the critical reading skills required for success in college, which is especially problematic in online courses. They presented a three-stage framework for teaching critical reading to adult college students based on the intersection of prereading, experiential reading, and postreading. Active and experiential learning can be encouraged through assignments that take the individual into their community to observe, write about, and discuss with fellow students. The list provided by the Association for Experiential Education (http://www.aee.org/what-is-ee) can stimulate creative ideas.

Online courses must be accessible for students with physical, psychological, or learning disabilities, an approach labeled *universal design*. We have found these approaches to be helpful to all students. This includes multiple types of learning activities, outcomes, and assessment strategies and increased engagement and interactions with students (see Center on Postsecondary Education and Disability, 2006; Dell, Dell, & Blackwell, 2015; and the online tutorial "Ten Simple Steps Toward Universal Design of Online Courses," University of Arkansas at Little Rock, n.d.).

We have found that, consistent with Clay (2014), thought-provoking class discussions, frequent interactions with the instructor and classmates, and timely feedback on assignments help students feel connected with the instructor, the course material, each other, and the college or university. Online courses are more time intensive for the instructor, but they are rewarding when one gets to know students personally through their thoughtful essays and lively discussions. Several of our students, including some who were shy about speaking in class and some with learning disabilities, have told us that they were able to participate in class discussions as intellectual equals for the first time in their lives because they could take extra time to polish their contributions.

Service Learning

Internships are increasingly important for career preparation. Carnevale, Smith, Melton, and Price (2015) noted that baccalaureate students who completed an internship were more likely to get a job offer at graduation and earned a higher salary. *Service learning* (SL) is an experiential component integrated into a course that offers an opportunity for active, critical reflection on lessons learned in the classroom while meeting a need in the community (Eyler & Giles, 1999). Students can explore potential career paths, gain practical work experience, and network with professionals in the community through SL. Several studies have demonstrated increases in students' interest in and retention of course material and in personal and cognitive development (Astin, Vogelgesang, Ikeda, & Yee, 2000; Prentice & Robinson, 2010), as well as career development (Peterson, Wardwell, Will, & Campana, 2014). Bringle, Reeb, Brown, and Ruiz (2016) offered suggestions for successful psychology-related SL programs.

The quality of the SL placement and connection to the course content are of utmost importance. Many schools offer a central civic engagement or experiential learning center to identify appropriate placements. In a traditional developmental psychology course, the professor might form an ongoing community partnership with an elementary school principal and have groups of students tutor children or assist with after-school enrichment activities. In a hybrid or online course, students could either select a community partner from a preapproved list or find their own placement and ask the professor for approval. Placements should include service options for all times during the week or on the weekend, as well as completely online, to accommodate students' hectic work and family schedules. Students may also benefit from a placement on campus, tutoring English language learners or providing support to students with a disability.

SL provides an opportunity to expand intercultural awareness and sensitivity. Before starting their placement, students should learn about the people with whom they will work and the setting in which they will be placed to increase awareness of others' plights. Demographic data and recent news stories about the community or agency can illuminate the challenges facing the individuals with whom they will work and suggest potential outcomes and impacts of their service. Students can explore the root causes of social disadvantages, being guided to avoid victim blaming, stereotyping, or reinforcing existing negative biases.

Frequent reflection assignments provide an opportunity for students to openly discuss their service with one another and with the professor, including lessons learned as well as any special achievements or challenges. A final reflection paper documenting the service performed and the lessons learned will help deepen each student's learning experience. Resources for designing all aspects of SL courses, including reflection assignments, are provided by Campus Compact (http://www.compact.org/category/resources/service-learning-resources/). *Service Learning in Psychology* (Bringle et al., 2016) provides practical guidance for integrating these topics into the psychology curriculum.

The most effective assignments reinforce conceptual course material while increasing awareness of the related social problems in the community, promoting civic responsibility, and fostering an appreciation for cultural diversity. As students contribute from their different viewpoints, equality and mutual respect can develop. Discussions comparing "hands-on" insights with course concepts can be lively and enlightening.

As with many nontraditional learning approaches, instructors have to take extra steps to ensure success. Some students may form adverse attitudes toward SL as an "add-on" or mandated volunteer work. The syllabus and first class should clearly show how SL meets the learning objectives and what is required (e.g., time commitment, related assignments), as well as the anticipated benefits. Strong warnings about confidentiality, workplace etiquette, and procedures for staying safe in unfamiliar situations are essential, and the instructor must be vigilant to identify and prevent potential harm to others in the student's setting as well.

CONCLUSION

Working with nontraditional students has taught us to take no aspect of what we do for granted, and we are constantly challenged to be systematic, thoughtful, and flexible. In turn, we have been richly rewarded with the growth and learning we and our students have experienced. The awareness and skills we have gained have made us better teachers and learners with students of all ages and learning styles. We have been fortunate to work in institutions that have taken seriously their mission to educate diverse students and hope that higher education becomes available to all for whom it has seemed out of reach.

REFERENCES

Allen, I. E., & Seaman, J. (2014, January). *Grade change: Tracking online education in the United States.* Boston Park, MA: Babson Survey Research Group. Retrieved from http://www.onlinelearningsurvey.com/reports/gradechange.pdf

Allen, M. J. (2000). Teaching non-traditional students. *APS Observer, 13*(7), 16–17, 21, 23.

Astin, A. W., Vogelgesang, L. J., Ikeda, E. K., & Yee, J. A. (2000). *How service learning affects students.* Retrieved from https://heri.ucla.edu/PDFs/HSLAS/HSLAS.PDF

Ayers, E. L., & Narduzzi, J. L. (2009). Intergenerational learning: Beyond the jargon. *Continuing Higher Education Review, 73*, 218–222.

Baruch, G. K., & Barnett, R. (1986). Role quality, multiple role involvement, and psychological well-being in midlife women. *Journal of Personality and Social Psychology, 51*, 578–585. http://dx.doi.org/10.1037/0022-3514.51.3.578

Baum, S., Ma, J., & Payea, K. (2013). *Education pays 2013: The benefits of higher education for individuals and society.* Retrieved from https://www.luminafoundation.org/resources/education-pays-2013

Belenky, M. F., Clinchy, B. M., Goldberger, N. R., & Tarule, J. M. (1997). *Women's ways of knowing: The development of self, voice, and mind.* New York, NY: Basic Books.

Bringle, R. G., Reeb, R. N., Brown, M. A., & Ruiz, A. I. (2016). *Service learning in psychology: Enhancing undergraduate education for the public good.* Washington, DC: American Psychological Association. http://dx.doi.org/10.1037/14803-000

Brown, P. C., Roediger, H. L., III, & McDaniel, M. A. (2014). *Make it stick: The science of successful learning.* Cambridge, MA: Belknap Press of Harvard University Press. http://dx.doi.org/10.4159/9780674419377

Caplan, P. J., & Ford, J. C. (2014). The voices of diversity: What students of diverse races/ethnicities and both sexes tell us about their college experiences and their perceptions about their institutions' progress toward diversity. *Aporia, 6*(3), 30–69.

Carnevale, A. P., Smith, N., Melton, M., & Price, E. W. (2015). *Learning while earning: The new normal.* Retrieved from https://cew.georgetown.edu/wp-content/uploads/Working-Learners-Report.pdf

Center for Women Policy Studies. (2002). *From poverty to self-sufficiency: The role of postsecondary education in welfare reform.* Washington, DC: Author.

Center on Postsecondary Education and Disability. (2006). *Effective college instruction.* Retrieved from http://www.facultyware.uconn.edu/cfm_pages/rr_links.cfm?cat_id=4

Clay, R. A. (2014). *Learning in a digital world.* Retrieved from https://www.apa.org/monitor/2014/12/elc-learning.aspx

Dell, C. A., Dell, T. F., & Blackwell, T. L. (2015). Applying universal design for learning in online courses: Pedagogical and practical considerations. *The Journal of Educators Online, 13*, 166–192.

Donaldson, J. F., & Graham, S. (1999). A model of college outcomes for adults. *Adult Education Quarterly, 50*, 24–40. http://dx.doi.org/10.1177/074171369905000103

Dweck, C. (2006). *Mindset: The new psychology of success.* New York, NY: Random House.

Engle, J., & Tinto, V. (2008). *Moving beyond access: College success for low-income first-generation students.* Retrieved from http://files.eric.ed.gov/fulltext/ED504448.pdf

Estes, M. D., Ingram, R., & Liu, J. C. (2014). *A review of flipped classroom research, practice, and technology.* Retrieved from https://www.hetl.org/feature-articles/a-review-of-flipped-classroom-research-practice-and-technologies

Eyler, J. S., & Giles, D. E. (1999). *Where's the learning in service-learning?* San Francisco, CA: Jossey-Bass.

Finley, D. L., Brothen, T., & Froman, R. (2005, January). *On-line course management.* Retrieved from http://www.academia.edu/933161/On-Line_Course_Management

Foote, L. S. (2015). Transformational learning: Reflections of an adult learning story. *Adult Learning, 26,* 84–86. http://dx.doi.org/10.1177/1045159515573017

Freire, P. (1998). The adult literacy process as cultural action for freedom. *Harvard Educational Review, 68,* 480–498. http://dx.doi.org/10.17763/haer.40.2.q7n227021n148p26

Home, A. M. (1998). Predicting role conflict, overload and contagion in adult women university students with families and jobs. *Adult Education Quarterly, 48,* 85–97. http://dx.doi.org/10.1177/074171369804800204

Honigsfeld, A., & Dunn, R. (2006). Learning-style characteristics of adult learners. *Delta Kappa Gamma Bulletin, 72*(2), 14–31.

Jameson, M. M., & Fusco, B. R. (2014). Math anxiety, math self-concept, and math self-efficacy in adult learners compared to traditional undergraduate students. *Adult Education Quarterly, 64,* 306–322. http://dx.doi.org/10.1177/0741713614541461

Karp, M. M., & Bork, R. H. (2012). *"They never told me what to expect, so I didn't know what to do": Defining and clarifying the role of a community college student.* (CCRC Working Paper No. 47). Retrieved from http://files.eric.ed.gov/fulltext/ED535078.pdf

Kimmel, S. B., Gaylor, K. P., & Hayes, J. B. (2014). Understanding adult learners by gender. *Academy of Educational Leadership Journal, 18,* 73–89.

Kindlon, D., & Thompson, M. (2000). *Raising Cain: Protecting the emotional life of boys.* New York, NY: Ballantine Books.

Knowles, M. S., Holton, E. F., III, & Swanson, R. A. (2005). *The adult learner* (8th ed.). New York, NY: Routledge. http://dx.doi.org/10.4324/9780080481913

Kreuter, N. (2012). Veterans in the classroom. *Inside Higher Ed.* Retrieved from https://www.insidehighered.com/advice/2012/11/12/essay-teaching-veterans

Kroth, M., & Boverie, P. (2000). Life mission and adult learning. *Adult Education Quarterly, 50,* 134–149. http://dx.doi.org/10.1177/07417130022086955

LeBlanc, J. B., Brabant, S., & Forsyth, C. J. (1996). The meaning of college for survivors of sexual abuse: Higher education and the older female college student. *American Journal of Orthopsychiatry, 66,* 468–473. http://dx.doi.org/10.1037/h0080197

Lumina Foundation. (n.d.). *Today's student.* Retrieved from https://www.luminafoundation.org/todays-student-statistics

Marschall, S., & Davis, C. (2012). A conceptual framework for teaching critical reading to adult college students. *Adult Learning, 23,* 63–68. http://dx.doi.org/10.1177/1045159512444265

Mezirow, J. (1996). Contemporary paradigms of learning. *Adult Education Quarterly, 46,* 158–172. http://dx.doi.org/10.1177/074171369604600303

National Center for Education Statistics. (2013). *Digest of education statistics, 2012* (NCES 2014-015). Washington, DC: U.S. Department of Education.

Neumann, Y., & Neumann, E. F. (2010). The Robust Learning Model (RLM): A comprehensive approach to a new online university. *Journal of College Teaching and Learning, 7,* 28–36. http://dx.doi.org/10.19030/tlc.v7i1.76

Nguyen, S. R. (2014). Transformations encouraged by story telling: Middle Eastern adult learners' experiences abroad. *Adult Learning, 25,* 163–165. http://dx.doi.org/10.1177/1045159514546212

Nicolaides, A. (2015). Generative learning: Adults learning within ambiguity. *Adult Education Quarterly, 65,* 179–195. http://dx.doi.org/10.1177/0741713614568887

Norcross, J. C. (2012). *Changeology: 5 steps to realizing your goals and resolutions.* New York, NY: Simon & Schuster.

Peterson, J. J., Wardwell, C., Will, K., & Campana, K. L. (2014). Pursuing a purpose: The role of career exploration courses and service-learning internships in recognizing and developing knowledge, skills, and abilities. *Teaching of Psychology, 41*, 354–359. http://dx.doi.org/10.1177/0098628314549712

Prentice, M., & Robinson, G. (2010). *Improving student learning outcomes with service learning.* Retrieved from https://eric.ed.gov/?id=ED535904

Ragan, L. (2009). 10 principles of effective online teaching: Best practices in distance education. In C. Hill (Ed.), *Faculty focus, special report* (pp. 3–24). Madison, WI: Magna.

Rassool, N. (1999). *Literacy for sustainable development in the age of information.* Philadelphia, PA: Multilingual Matters.

Roost, A., & Roost, N. (2014). *Supporting veterans in the classroom.* Retrieved from http://www.aaup.org/article/supporting-veterans-classroom#.VxyxaWDNCfQ

Ryan, C. L., & Bauman, K. (2016). *Educational attainment in the United States: 2015.* Retrieved from https://www.census.gov/content/dam/Census/library/publications/2016/demo/p20-578.pdf

Smith, M. C., & Pourchot, T. (Eds.). (1998). *Adult learning and development: Perspectives from educational psychology.* Mahwah, NJ: Erlbaum.

Stein, D., & Wanstreet, C. E. (2006). Beyond yes or no: Factors in adults' decisions to enroll in higher education. *The Journal of Continuing Higher Education, 54*(2), 2–12. http://dx.doi.org/10.1080/07377366.2006.10400094

University of Arkansas at Little Rock. (n.d.). *Ten steps toward universal design of online courses.* Retrieved from https://ualr.edu/disability/online-education/

Wlodkowski, R. J. (2008). *Enhancing adult motivation to learn: A comprehensive guide for teaching all adults* (3rd ed.). San Francisco, CA: Jossey-Bass.

Yousafzai, M. (2013). *I am Malala: The girl who stood up for education and was shot by the Taliban.* London, England: Weidenfeld & Nicolson.

Zahm, M. (2010). *Create your ideal life: Applied psychology of personal adjustment and growth.* Bloomington, IN: AuthorHouse.

Zajacova, A., Lynch, S. M., & Espenshade, T. J. (2005). Self-efficacy, stress, and academic success in college. *Research in Higher Education, 46*, 677–706. http://dx.doi.org/10.1007/s11162-004-4139-z

INTEGRATING DIVERSITY INTO GENERAL PSYCHOLOGY COURSES

16

The Introductory Psychology Course From a More Diverse Human Perspective

Su L. Boatright-Horowitz, Savannah McSheffrey,
Marisa E. Marraccini, and Yvette Harps-Logan

The introductory psychology course is usually a student's first, and often only, formal exposure to the field of psychology, and it may be delivered in a classroom of hundreds of students.[1] Content is strikingly similar across introductory psychology textbooks, and chapter titles overlap with many in this volume. Thus, rather than focusing on content, we identify three goals we consider crucial to student learning and describe teaching strategies that can be incorporated across the course content. An intersectional approach provides a framework that can help students achieve the goals identified by the American Psychological Association (APA; 2016) as important for teaching undergraduates ethical and socially responsible behavior in professional and personal settings.

In our view, a successful introductory course should help students clarify the effects of social context and culture on human behavior; prepare for situations in which their customs, beliefs, and social expectations will be challenged; and increase their awareness and sensitivity when interacting with people physically or culturally different from themselves. These goals can be illuminated through the analytic framework of intersectionality. We have chosen six themes: the nature–nurture issue (beyond dualistic thinking), exploring non-Western viewpoints, social roles and identity development,

---

[1]For larger classes, the exercises in this chapter can easily be introduced during recitation sessions; however, the instructor should ensure that teaching assistants receive training in handling difficult dialogues and provide regular supervision and support.

http://dx.doi.org/10.1037/0000137-017
*Integrating Multiculturalism and Intersectionality Into the Psychology Curriculum:
Strategies for Instructors*, J. A. Mena and K. Quina (Editors)

evaluating intelligence versus performance, sociocultural diversity, and conceptualizations of mental health.

THE NATURE–NURTURE ISSUE

Biological reductionism, attributing complex behavioral tendencies to genetic or biochemical causes, has historically been used to foster prejudice and discrimination and to promote social agendas such as eugenics (Porter, 2012). Even in discussing biological psychology, we stress that dualistic explanations of behavior are inadequate because human behavior is inevitably the result of complex interactions between biology and environment throughout development.

Sexual Orientation

We confront dualistic thinking by introducing alternative, sociocultural influences on behavior, challenging stereotypes, and giving students tools to question reductionist explanations. For instance, researchers have implicated neuroendocrine (Mbugua, 2015), genetic (Balter, 2015; Conrad, 2016), and cortical (Abé, Johansson, Allzén, & Savic, 2014; Rahman & Yusuf, 2015) factors in the development of sexual orientations. However, causality can also be bidirectional; for example, environmental influences may produce biochemical or biological effects, particularly through stress responses (Denton, Rostosky, & Danner, 2014; Hatzenbuehler & McLaughlin, 2014). Students can discuss whether there is a causal link for any of these; the facilitator can expand the discussion by introducing, at appropriate points, that sexual minorities experience more bullying than heterosexuals (S. K. Schneider, O'Donnell, & Smith, 2015), that homosexuality and heterosexuality are neither dichotomous nor mutually exclusive categories of behavior (Rubinstein, Makov, & Sarel, 2013), and that sexual behaviors can involve multiple dimensions based on ideation, activities, and sociocultural factors and may evolve or change across the lifespan (Fausto-Sterling, 2000; Katz-Wise & Hyde, 2015; Pfeffer, 2014). A subsequent reaction paper can examine a related topic, such as contemporary psychologists' view that the problem that needs treatment is homophobia, not same-sex attraction (e.g., Burton, 2015).

Intersexuality

Students can also be challenged to consider the categories of "male" and "female." Some experts suggest that about one in about 1,500 births involve babies with physical characteristics of both sexes (M. Schneider et al., 2006), with even more individuals developing dual characteristics later in life. It often shocks students to learn that intersexuals have been subjected to early surgical procedures and hormonal treatments, in some cases resulting in genital scarring and reduced sexual sensitivity (Fausto-Sterling, Coll, & Lamarre, 2012). We encourage students to consider real-life possibilities by reading the website of the Intersex Society of North America (http://isna.org) and contemplating ways they would promote their child's psychological health if they were born intersexual, including societal changes. This discussion often evolves into the binary bathroom issue (Bentley University, 2017).

EXPLORING NON-WESTERN VIEWPOINTS

Parental Practices

Students are typically surprised to learn that practices they have assumed to promote independence and self-reliance are rare outside of Western societies. For example, developmental psychologists have debated whether the relationship between attachment and parenting style is universal (e.g., Rothbaum & Kakinuma, 2004) or the security of attachment is related to caregiver sensitivity regardless of parenting style (Posada, 2013). Jin, Jacobvitz, Hazen, and Jung (2012) pointed out that the majority of babies worldwide appear to be securely attached, including Korean infants who consistently remain in close proximity to their caregivers. Japanese mothers rarely separate from their babies for the first year, cosleeping and cobathing with them, and few Japanese babies are classified as avoidant of their caregivers. They suggest that Western practices encouraging infants to spend time separate from caregivers (e.g., sleeping in cribs in separate rooms, independent exploration) give rise to variations in insecure attachment behaviors but not in the essential characteristics of attachment formation.

Students can write brief exploratory papers on other cultural patterns, such as child cosleeping arrangements prevalent around the world (Jenni & O'Connor, 2005; Mindell, Sadeh, Kwon, & Goh, 2013), the potential effects of multiple or nonparental caregivers (F. Ryan, 2011), and even the potential effects of urbanization in some cultures (Dwairy, 2004). Bornstein, Putnick, and Lansford (2011) offered other cross-cultural perspectives on parenting.

Personality

Although introductory psychology textbooks caution that the methods used to assess personality may not apply to people from other cultures, they nonetheless limit their coverage to traditional perspectives representing a Western, male-centered perspective. Cheung, van de Vijver, and Leong (2011), among others, suggested combining an *etic approach* (focused on comparing personality across cultures) with an *emic approach* (studying personality in a specific cultural context). For example, selfhood seems more interdependent in non-Western cultures, with self-satisfaction based on maintaining harmonious relations with others (Markus & Kitayama, 1991). Students find a discussion of their own cultural dynamics lively and enlightening.

Students' conceptualizations of personality are often expanded by including feminist approaches, which view gender as a process embedded in a patriarchic social system of power and oppression rather than a stable personality trait or a social role (Shields & Dicicco, 2011), as well as Afrocentric (Mazama, 2001) and Muslim (Abu-Raiya, 2014) paradigms.

ROLES AND IDENTITY DEVELOPMENT

Gender Role Socialization

We begin these classes with some cautions: Current research demonstrates greater similarities in gender roles than differences (Hyde, 2014), abilities are different from roles, and many factors influence an individual's acceptance of traditional gender stereotypes (Hackett, 2011; Rew, 2011). Students then examine gender role differences in their lives, identifying factors that support them, such as family dynamics, educational practices, history, socioeconomics, and religious beliefs. Even government policies can be introduced into the conversation; for example, although communist policies have resulted in more comparable labor force participation for women and men (65% and 77%, respectively), the division of labor in the home has remained unequal, with daughters performing more housework than sons even when mothers are employed outside the home (Hu, 2015). Identifying students' household chores is particularly engaging; women often describe their experiences with gender-related tasks as unequal and unfair.

Ethnic Identity Development

Research has suggested that minority and multiethnic individuals in the United States develop more salient ethnic identities than European Americans (Else-Quest & Morse, 2015; Gillen-O'Neel et al., 2015); furthermore, awareness of racism and a strong sense of ethnic identity are associated with higher self-esteem and greater resistance to the negative effects of stereotyping (Murry, Berkel, Brody, Miller, & Chen, 2009). Students can discuss ways in which a strong sense of ethnic identity can serve as a psychological buffer, mitigating the detrimental effects of racism and negative stereotyping (Aldana & Byrd, 2015; Serrano-Villar & Calzada, 2016). Majority-culture students, in particular, can benefit from consideration of their ethnic identities through reflection papers or other exercises (Case, 2017; Johnston-Guerrero, 2016).

Gender role socialization in the United States takes place through multiple channels, including verbal, nonverbal, direct, or implicit forms of communication by family, friends, teachers, and the media and tends to reflect White, middle-class, and often male experiences. Most students play or have friends who play video games, which often portray women as both helpless and over-sexualized, and racial minorities are largely absent except in sports videos (Mou & Peng, 2009). Students can discuss whether repetitive exposure to these gender and racial stereotypes impacts socialization, referring to evidence of damaging effects such as acceptance of rape myths about women (Dill,

Brown, & Collins, 2008; Stermer & Burkley, 2015). Further, although both males and females participate, most are young males aged 11 to 14 years old (Lenhart, 2015; Rideout, Foehr, & Roberts, 2010), when cognitive schemata for gender roles are developing.

The online communities associated with video gaming can also expose players to blatant sexual and racial harassment. Gray (2012) observed that Black and Latina women tended to form their own clans within their gaming to avoid negative experiences with male players who view them as less important players or mascots. In contrast, White women tended not to acknowledge their secondary status and preferred to play with males, rather than joining clans that shared experiences of oppression. Students can discuss their observations of these intersections of nativism, ethnicity, gender, and oppression in the gaming world and compare them with their daily life. A more extended discussion can incorporate suggestions for changing their behavior and responding to others' behaviors.

INTELLIGENCE AND ACADEMIC PERFORMANCE

Defining and Measuring Intelligence

To address this most contentious area, we begin with a brief review of its history (P. J. Ryan, 1997), methodological controversies (Ford, 2004), and political and societal ramifications (Roberts, 2015). Although most are fresh from experiences with standardized testing, students may not understand that intelligence and test performance are separate concepts or that testing is replete with biases (e.g., Nakano & Watkins, 2013; see also http://www.fairtest.org).

Some IQ test items embody assumptions that do not apply to everyone. For example, performance components of the Weschler scales require visual and motor skills that make them inappropriate for children with visual impairments and diseases such as cerebral palsy (Yin Foo, Guppy, & Johnston, 2013). Cross-cultural perspectives are also important (Sternberg, 2004); for example, Matafwali and Serpell (2014) pointed out that Western standardized test use, still prevalent in sub-Saharan Africa, may yield inaccurate representations of African test-takers' abilities. Students can think about their experiences and suggest similar challenges to their previous conceptions of IQ or intelligence and testing.

Stereotype Threat

Performance on IQ and other tests may be impacted by internalized stereotypic views of one's capabilities (Pennington, Heim, Levy, & Larkin, 2016; Spencer, Logel, & Davies, 2016). Steele and Aronson (1995) showed that African Americans performed more poorly on tests of academic ability with even seemingly minor changes in wording (e.g., a test presented as a measure of their "verbal abilities and limitations" or "psychological factors involved in solving verbal problems," p. 799). Such stereotype threat can also affect women (Nguyen & Ryan,

2008), persons of lower socioeconomic status (Désert, Préaux, & Jund, 2009), student athletes (Dee, 2014), and the elderly (Lambert et al., 2016). Students can consider how stereotype threat may impact their performance and then propose an intervention, perhaps modeled on demonstrated increases in grade point averages and retention rates for both African American and European American students in McIntyre, Paulson, Taylor, Morin, and Lord (2011).

FUNCTIONING IN A DIVERSE SOCIETY

Interpersonal Communication

Interpreting others' messages can help students function more effectively in a diverse society (Byron, 2007; Rimondini, Mazzi, Deveugele, & Bensing, 2015). Differential nonverbal cues, such as gaze direction, touching, and nodding, have been identified between genders, ethnicities, age groups, and cultures (e.g., Helweg-Larsen, Cunningham, Carrico, & Pergram, 2004); for example, directing one's gaze into another person's face can be a sign of disrespect or even threat in some cultures, but to not do so may arouse suspicion in others (e.g., Adams et al., 2010). Japanese individuals tend to gaze more toward eyes, whereas Western European and North American individuals gaze more at mouths, which may affect perceptions of emotional expressions (Jack, Caldara, & Schyns, 2012; Senju et al., 2013). An entertaining classroom demonstration of the subtleties of interpreting facial expressions, as well as cues we use to understand others' emotional expressions, is found at https://www.surveymonkey.com/r/SmileRead?sm=IP3TXB16%2bFxZupI1n0j CEScHwUamvmdenuj%2f0kpvxWY%3d.

Research has shown that Black males are perceived as more threatening when their gaze is directed toward White observers, a finding supported by physiological measurements on the observers (e.g., Richeson, Todd, Trawalter, & Baird, 2008). Students can discuss the implications of these data for widely publicized tragedies such as shootings of unarmed Black men and women by police officers and, if they are comfortable, their own experiences. Students can also review and share contemporary news sources for proposed interventions, such as additional training, that could reduce the effects of bias as law enforcement officers interact with the public.

Prejudice and Racism

Discussions of racism and privilege are an essential element of introductory psychology. Exposures to racism and perceptions of events as racist are strong predictors of psychological stress in Black Americans (e.g., Pieterse, Carter, Evans, & Walter, 2010). Also of concern are racial *microaggressions* ("brief, commonplace, and daily verbal, behavioral, and environmental slights and indignities directed toward Black Americans, often automatically and unintentionally," Sue, Capodilupo, & Holder, 2008, p. 329). We directly address the difficulties of speaking up in the presence of racism to encourage students to take more active roles in reducing the societal racism that surrounds them. Tatum's (1999) article "What Do You Do When You're Called a Racist?" increases students' self-awareness about how they may be perceived by others and stimulates lively discussion; reading Tatum (1994) can add examples of White role models resisting the role of oppressor and protesting against racism.

Privilege

Understanding and acknowledging the concept of privilege allows students to be more sensitive to other people's feelings, experiences, and cultural beliefs, which in turn will be beneficial in the professional workforce. We found that introducing McIntosh's (1988) list of White privileges increases students' awareness of the extent of racism and how it is manifested in daily life (Boatright-Horowitz, Frazier, Harps-Logan, & Crockett, 2013). Students can share personal or media examples of White privilege and discuss its prevalence in U.S. society. Throughout, it is important to remind students that privilege can be based on more than ethnicity or skin color and can also include gender, age, sexual orientation, and other intersecting characteristics (Pratto & Stewart, 2012).

Unfortunately, some college students may require convincing that prejudice and racism are prevalent in modern society: Norton and Sommers (2011) found that the majority of Whites more often viewed themselves as victims of reverse racism than they viewed Blacks as victims of racism. Instructors should expect strong student reactions to the topics of racism and White privilege, including anger and resentment (Boatright-Horowitz, Marraccini, & Harps-Logan, 2012) and negative teaching performance evaluations from White students (Boatright-Horowitz & Soeung, 2009). We encourage instructors to educate their school administrators about these potential negative effects to safeguard their own and other instructors' careers.

CONCEPTS OF MENTAL HEALTH AND ILLNESS

Psychiatric diagnoses have changed across the various editions of the *Diagnostic and Statistical Manual of Mental Disorders* (fifth ed.; *DSM–5*; American Psychiatric Association, 2013). A powerful lesson is the history of perspectives on homosexuality, which was coded as a mental disorder until 1973 (Amaral, Ferraz, & Mota, 2016; Drescher, 2010). The video *Changing Our Minds: The Story of Evelyn Hooker* (Harrison & Schmiechen, 1992) described earlier medical treatments of the disorder: electroconvulsive shock therapy, castration, hysterectomies, massive hormone injections, and lobotomies. Notably, it took nearly 20 more years for homosexuality to be removed from the *International Statistical Classification of Diseases and Related Health Problems* (10th rev.; ICD–10; World Health Organization, 2003; Burton, 2015).

Critics argue that sexism, racism, ageism, classism, and homophobia may be inherent in a number of psychiatric diagnoses and judgments of client dangerousness (see Caplan & Cosgrove, 2004; Elbogen, Williams, Kim, Tomkins, & Scalora, 2001). Instructors can raise these controversies and the possible impacts of such bias. For instance, *DSM–5*'s overemphasis on biological theory (and underemphasis of sociocultural factors, such as gender stereotypes and social-contextual realities) may lead a clinician to overlook sexism in the workplace when diagnosing a female client, failing to recognize that mood disturbances can be reasonable responses to systemic stressors. This is particularly concerning with mental disorders that are more frequently diagnosed in women, such as depression, borderline personality disorder, and eating disorders (Enns & Green, 2013).

Patterns of aberrant behavior and troubling experiences common to specific geographic regions are interesting to students. The *DSM–5* refers to these patterns of behavior as cultural concepts of distress but seems to marginalize the role of culture in psychiatry by placing syndromes that are typically North American (e.g., anorexia nervosa) in the main text, whereas syndromes that seem linked to specific cultural minority groups, such as the Latinx *ataque de nervios* (attack of nerves), continue to be included in an appendix (López & Guarnaccia, 2000; see Paniagua, 2018, for a discussion of cultural issues in the ICD–10). Dadlani, Overtree, and Perry-Jenkins (2012) argued that social identity and cultural backgrounds are not comprehensively integrated into diagnostic criteria, which can lead students to discussions of cultural competence, caution in symptom interpretation, and intersecting experiences of privilege and oppression that shape psychiatric presentation.

CLASSROOM DYNAMICS

We urge teachers to use these strategies and materials with sensitivity and caution and enter the classroom well prepared with multiple options for how the class can be conducted. Students differ in their sophistication and comfort levels in discussions of diversity, and a balance must be achieved in which students feel safe enough to contribute comments about their cultural contexts without the expectation that they speak as a representative of any particular group. Knowing that our ability to maintain this balance will vary from semester to semester, or even from day to day, we try to resist the occasional discouragement that accompanies a social activist approach to teaching. Teachers can modify these discussions and class activities to meet student levels of comfort; when students seem uncomfortable or shy, it may be useful to ask students to briefly write down their thoughts or reactions so the instructor can read them anonymously to the class. When training teaching assistants to lead these discussions, multiple options should be provided to help them find fit with their class dynamics and their teaching styles.

We also try to model sensitivity and respect for cultural differences, even as we propose that certain cultural practices should be eliminated or changed. In doing this, we can affect the lives of individual students, influencing how they perceive themselves and their cultural backgrounds, challenging them to critically examine their beliefs about their cultural practices, and encouraging them to be more sensitive while making it clear that we value them as people. In this way, we hope to model what it means to embrace and respect diversity.

REFERENCES

Abé, C., Johansson, E., Allzén, E., & Savic, I. (2014). Sexual orientation related differences in cortical thickness in male individuals. *PLoS One, 9*(12), e114721. http://dx.doi.org/10.1371/journal.pone.0114721

Abu-Raiya, H. (2014). Western psychology and Muslim psychology in dialogue: Comparisons between a Qura'nic theory of personality and Freud's and Jung's ideas. *Journal of Religion and Health, 53*, 326–338. http://dx.doi.org/10.1007/s10943-012-9630-9

Adams, R. B., Jr., Franklin, R. G., Jr., Rule, N. O., Freeman, J. B., Jr., Kveraga, K., Hadjikhani, N., . . . Ambady, N. (2010). Culture, gaze and the neural processing of fear expressions. *Social Cognitive and Affective Neuroscience, 5*, 340–348. http://dx.doi.org/10.1093/scan/nsp047

Aldana, A., & Byrd, C. M. (2015). School ethnic–racial socialization: Learning about race and ethnicity among African American students. *The Urban Review, 47*, 563–576. http://dx.doi.org/10.1007/s11256-014-0319-0

Amaral, A., Ferraz, I., & Mota, M. (2016). A journey across perversions history—from Middle Ages to *DSM*. *European Psychiatry, 33*, S588–S733. http://dx.doi.org/10.1016/j.eurpsy.2016.01.2186

American Psychiatric Association. (2013). *Diagnostic and statistical manual of mental disorders* (5th ed.). Arlington, VA: Author.

American Psychological Association. (2016). Guidelines for the undergraduate psychology major: Version 2.0. *American Psychologist, 71*, 102–111. http://dx.doi.org/10.1037/a0037562

Balter, M. (2015). Can epigenetics explain homosexuality puzzle? *Science, 350*, 148. http://dx.doi.org/10.1126/science.350.6257.148

Bentley University. (2017, July 17). *Three reasons why all-gender bathrooms are more than just an LGBTQ issue*. Retrieved from https://www.bentley.edu/prepared/three-reasons-why-all-gender-bathrooms-are-more-just-lgbtq-issue

Boatright-Horowitz, S. L., Frazier, S., Harps-Logan, Y., & Crockett, N. (2013). Difficult times for college students of color: Teaching White students about white privilege provides hope for change. *Teaching in Higher Education, 18*, 698–708. http://dx.doi.org/10.1080/13562517.2013.836092

Boatright-Horowitz, S. L., Marraccini, M., & Harps-Logan, Y. (2012). Teaching antiracism: College students' emotional and cognitive reactions to learning about White privilege. *Journal of Black Studies, 43*, 893–911. http://dx.doi.org/10.1177/0021934712463235

Boatright-Horowitz, S. L., & Soeung, S. (2009). Teaching White privilege to White students can mean saying good-bye to positive student evaluations. *American Psychologist, 64*, 574–575. http://dx.doi.org/10.1037/a0016593

Bornstein, M. H., Putnick, D. L., & Lansford, J. E. (2011). Parenting attributions and attitudes in cross-cultural perspective. *Parenting, Science and Practice, 11*, 214–237. http://dx.doi.org/10.1080/15295192.2011.585568

Burton, N. (2015, September). When homosexuality stopped being a mental disorder. *Psychology Today*, Retrieved from https://www.psychologytoday.com/us/blog/hide-and-seek/201509/when-homosexuality-stopped-being-mental-disorder

Byron, K. (2007). Male and female managers' ability to 'read' emotions: Relationships with supervisor's performance ratings and subordinates' satisfaction ratings. *Journal of Occupational and Organizational Psychology, 80*, 713–733. http://dx.doi.org/10.1348/096317907X174349

Caplan, P. J., & Cosgrove, L. (Eds.). (2004). *Bias in psychiatric diagnosis*. Lanham, MD: Jason Aronson.

Case, K. A. (2017). *Intersectional pedagogy: Complicating identity and social justice*. New York, NY: Routledge.

Cheung, F. M., van de Vijver, F. J. R., & Leong, F. T. L. (2011). Toward a new approach to the study of personality in culture. *American Psychologist, 66*, 593–603. http://dx.doi.org/10.1037/a0022389

Conrad, R. (2016). The lure of the gay gene. *The Gay & Lesbian Review Worldwide, 23*, 25–28.

Dadlani, M. B., Overtree, C., & Perry-Jenkins, M. (2012). Culture at the center: A reformulation of diagnostic assessment. *Professional Psychology: Research and Practice, 43*, 175–182. http://dx.doi.org/10.1037/a0028152

Dee, T. (2014). Stereotype threat and the student-athlete. *Economic Inquiry, 52*, 173–182. http://dx.doi.org/10.1111/ecin.12006

Denton, F. N., Rostosky, S. S., & Danner, F. (2014). Stigma-related stressors, coping self-efficacy, and physical health in lesbian, gay, and bisexual individuals. *Journal of Counseling Psychology, 61*, 383–391. http://dx.doi.org/10.1037/a0036707

Désert, M., Préaux, M., & Jund, R. (2009). So young and already victims of stereotype threat: Socio-economic status and performance of 6 to 9 years old children on Raven's progressive matrices. *European Journal of Psychology of Education, 24*, 207–218. http://dx.doi.org/10.1007/BF03173012

Dill, K. E., Brown, B. P., & Collins, M. A. (2008). Effects of exposure to sex-stereotyped video game characters on tolerance of sexual harassment. *Journal of Experimental Social Psychology, 44*, 1402–1408. http://dx.doi.org/10.1016/j.jesp.2008.06.002

Drescher, J. (2010). Queer diagnoses: Parallels and contrasts in the history of homosexuality, gender variance, and the *Diagnostic and Statistical Manual*. *Archives of Sexual Behavior, 39*, 427–460. http://dx.doi.org/10.1007/s10508-009-9531-5

Dwairy, M. (2004). Individuation among Bedouin versus urban Arab adolescents: Ethnic and gender differences. *Cultural Diversity and Ethnic Minority Psychology, 10*, 340–350. http://dx.doi.org/10.1037/1099-9809.10.4.340

Elbogen, E. B., Williams, A. L., Kim, D., Tomkins, A. J., & Scalora, M. J. (2001). Gender and perceptions of dangerousness in civil psychiatric patients. *Legal and Criminological Psychology, 6*, 215–228. http://dx.doi.org/10.1348/135532501168299

Else-Quest, N. M., & Morse, E. (2015). Ethnic variations in parental ethnic socialization and adolescent ethnic identity: A longitudinal study. *Cultural Diversity and Ethnic Minority Psychology, 21*, 54–64. http://dx.doi.org/10.1037/a0037820

Enns, C. Z., & Green, M. (2013). Outcomes of oppression: Sociocultural influences on women's mental health. *Sex Roles, 68*, 510–513. http://dx.doi.org/10.1007/s11199-012-0225-4

Fausto-Sterling, A. (2000). The five sexes, revisited. *The Sciences, 40*(4), 18–23. http://dx.doi.org/10.1002/j.2326-1951.2000.tb03504.x

Fausto-Sterling, A., Coll, C. G., & Lamarre, M. (2012). Sexing the baby: Part 1—What do we really know about sex differentiation in the first three years of life? *Social Science & Medicine, 74*, 1684–1692. http://dx.doi.org/10.1016/j.socscimed.2011.05.051

Ford, D. Y. (2004). *Intelligence testing and cultural diversity: Concerns, cautions, and considerations*. Retrieved from http://files.eric.ed.gov/fulltext/ED505479.pdf

Gillen-O'Neel, C., Mistry, R. S., Brown, C. S., Rodriguez, V. C., White, E. S., & Chow, K. A. (2015). Not excluded from analyses: Ethnic and racial meanings and identification among multiethnic/racial early adolescents. *Journal of Adolescent Research, 30*, 143–179. http://dx.doi.org/10.1177/0743558414560626

Gray, K. L. (2012). Intersecting oppressions and online communities. *Information, Communication & Society, 15*, 411–428. http://dx.doi.org/10.1080/1369118X.2011.642401

Hackett, M. (2011). Domestic violence against women: Statistical analysis of crimes across India. *Journal of Comparative Family Studies, 42*, 267–288.

Harrison, J. (Producer), & Schmiechen, R. (Director). (1992). *Changing our minds: The story of Dr. Evelyn Hooker* [Motion picture]. United States: Changing Our Minds.

Hatzenbuehler, M. L., & McLaughlin, K. A. (2014). Structural stigma and hypothalamic-pituitary-adrenocortical axis reactivity in lesbian, gay, and bisexual young adults. *Annals of Behavioral Medicine, 47*, 39–47. http://dx.doi.org/10.1007/s12160-013-9556-9

Helweg-Larsen, M., Cunningham, S. J., Carrico, A., & Pergram, A. M. (2004). To nod or not to nod: An observational study of nonverbal communication and status in female and male college students. *Psychology of Women Quarterly, 28*, 358–361. http://dx.doi.org/10.1111/j.1471-6402.2004.00152.x

Hu, Y. (2015). Gender and children's housework time in China: Examining behavior modeling in context. *Journal of Marriage and Family, 77*, 1126–1143. http://dx.doi.org/10.1111/jomf.12225

Hyde, J. S. (2014). Gender similarities and differences. *Annual Review of Psychology, 65*, 373–398. http://dx.doi.org/10.1146/annurev-psych-010213-115057

Jack, R. E., Caldara, R., & Schyns, P. G. (2012). Internal representations reveal cultural diversity in expectations of facial expressions of emotion. *Journal of Experimental Psychology: General, 141*, 19–25. http://dx.doi.org/10.1037/a0023463

Jenni, O. G., & O'Connor, B. B. (2005). Children's sleep: An interplay between culture and biology. *Pediatrics, 115*, 204–216. http://dx.doi.org/10.1542/peds.2004-0815B

Jin, M. K., Jacobvitz, D., Hazen, N., & Jung, S. H. (2012). Maternal sensitivity and infant attachment security in Korea: Cross-cultural validation of the Strange Situation. *Attachment & Human Development, 14*, 33–44. http://dx.doi.org/10.1080/14616734.2012.636656

Johnston-Guerrero, M. P. (2016). Embracing the messiness: Critical and diverse perspectives on racial and ethnic identity development. *New Directions for Student Services, 2016*, 43–55. http://dx.doi.org/10.1002/ss.20174

Katz-Wise, S. L., & Hyde, J. S. (2015). Sexual fluidity and related attitudes and beliefs among young adults with a same-gender orientation. *Archives of Sexual Behavior, 44*, 1459–1470. http://dx.doi.org/10.1007/s10508-014-0420-1

Lambert, A. E., Watson, J. M., Stefanucci, J. K., Ward, N., Bakdash, J. Z., & Strayer, D. L. (2016). Stereotype threat impairs older adult driving. *Applied Cognitive Psychology, 30*, 22–28. http://dx.doi.org/10.1002/acp.3162

Lenhart, A. (2015). Teens, technology and friendships *Pew Research Center*. Retrieved from http://www.pewinternet.org/2015/08/06/teens-technology-and-friendships/

López, S. R., & Guarnaccia, P. J. (2000). Cultural psychopathology: Uncovering the social world of mental illness. *Annual Review of Psychology, 51*, 571–598. http://dx.doi.org/10.1146/annurev.psych.51.1.571

Markus, H. R., & Kitayama, S. (1991). Culture and the self: Implications for cognition, emotion, and motivation. *Psychological Review, 98*, 224–253. http://dx.doi.org/10.1037/0033-295X.98.2.224

Matafwali, B., & Serpell, R. (2014). Design and validation of assessment tests for young children in Zambia. *New Directions for Child and Adolescent Development, 2014*, 77–96. http://dx.doi.org/10.1002/cad.20074

Mazama, A. (2001). The Afrocentric paradigm: Contours and definitions. *Journal of Black Studies, 31*, 387–405. http://dx.doi.org/10.1177/002193470103100401

Mbugua, K. (2015). Explaining same-sex sexual behavior: The stagnation of the genetic and evolutionary research programs. *Journal for General Philosophy of Science, 46*, 23–43. http://dx.doi.org/10.1007/s10838-014-9273-5

McIntosh, P. (1988). *White privilege and male privilege: A personal account of coming to see correspondences through work in women's studies.* Retrieved from http://www.collegeart.org/pdf/diversity/white-privilege-and-male-privilege.pdf

McIntyre, R., Paulson, R. M., Taylor, C. A., Morin, A. L., & Lord, C. G. (2011). Effects of role model deservingness on overcoming performance deficits induced by stereotype threat. *European Journal of Social Psychology, 41*, 301–311. http://dx.doi.org/10.1002/ejsp.774

222   *Boatright-Horowitz et al.*

Mindell, J. A., Sadeh, A., Kwon, R., & Goh, D. Y. T. (2013). Cross-cultural differences in the sleep of preschool children. *Sleep Medicine, 14*, 1283–1289. http://dx.doi.org/10.1016/j.sleep.2013.09.002

Mou, Y., & Peng, W. (2009). Gender and racial stereotypes in popular video games. In R. Ferdig (Ed.), *Handbook of research on effective electronic gaming in education* (pp. 922–937). Hershey, PA: IGI Global. http://dx.doi.org/10.4018/978-1-59904-808-6.ch053

Murry, V. M., Berkel, C., Brody, G. H., Miller, S. J., & Chen, Y. F. (2009). Linking parental socialization to interpersonal protective processes, academic self-presentation, and expectations among rural African American youth. *Cultural Diversity and Ethnic Minority Psychology, 15*, 1–10. http://dx.doi.org/10.1037/a0013180

Nakano, S., & Watkins, M. W. (2013). Factor structure of the Weschler Intelligence Scales for Children–Fourth Edition among referred Native American students. *Psychology in the Schools, 50*, 957–968. http://dx.doi.org/10.1002/pits.21724

Nguyen, H. H., & Ryan, A. M. (2008). Does stereotype threat affect test performance of minorities and women? A meta-analysis of experimental evidence. *Journal of Applied Psychology, 93*, 1314–1334. http://dx.doi.org/10.1037/a0012702

Norton, M. I., & Sommers, S. R. (2011). Whites see racism as a zero-sum game that they are now losing. *Perspectives on Psychological Science, 6*, 215–218. http://dx.doi.org/10.1177/1745691611406922

Paniagua, F. A. (2018). ICD-10 versus *DSM–5* on cultural issues. *SAGE Open, 8*(1). http://dx.doi.org/10.1177/2158244018756165

Pennington, C. R., Heim, D., Levy, A. R., & Larkin, D. T. (2016). Twenty years of stereotype threat research: A review of psychological mediators. *PLoS One, 11*(1), e0146487. http://dx.doi.org/10.1371/journal.pone.0146487

Pfeffer, C. A. (2014). "I don't like passing as a straight woman": Queer negotiations of identity and social group membership. *American Journal of Sociology, 120*, 1–44. http://dx.doi.org/10.1086/677197

Pieterse, A. L., Carter, R. T., Evans, S. A., & Walter, R. A. (2010). An exploratory examination of the associations among racial and ethnic discrimination, racial climate, and trauma-related symptoms in a college student population. *Journal of Counseling Psychology, 57*, 255–263. http://dx.doi.org/10.1037/a0020040

Porter, D. (2012). Darwinian disease archeology: Genomic variants and the eugenic debate. *History of Science, 50*, 432–452. http://dx.doi.org/10.1177/007327531205000403

Posada, G. (2013). Piecing together the sensitivity construct: Ethology and cross-cultural research. *Attachment & Human Development, 15*, 637–656. http://dx.doi.org/10.1080/14616734.2013.842753

Pratto, F., & Stewart, A. L. (2012). Group dominance and the half-blindness of privilege. *Journal of Social Issues, 68*, 28–45. http://dx.doi.org/10.1111/j.1540-4560.2011.01734.x

Rahman, Q., & Yusuf, S. (2015). Lateralization for processing facial emotions in gay men, heterosexual men, and heterosexual women. *Archives of Sexual Behavior, 44*, 1405–1413. http://dx.doi.org/10.1007/s10508-014-0466-0

Rew, M. (2011). Religion and development I: Anthropology, Islam, transnationalism and emerging analyses of violence against women. *Progress in Development Studies, 11*, 69–76. http://dx.doi.org/10.1177/146499341001100105

Richeson, J. A., Todd, A. R., Trawalter, S., & Baird, A. A. (2008). Eye-gaze direction modulates race-related amygdala activity. *Group Processes & Intergroup Relations, 11*, 233–246. http://dx.doi.org/10.1177/1368430207088040

Rideout, V., Foehr, U., & Roberts, D. (2010). *Generation M2: Media in the lives of 8- to 18-year-olds*. Menlo Park, CA: Henry J. Kaiser Family Foundation.

Rimondini, M., Mazzi, M. A., Deveugele, M., & Bensing, J. M. (2015). How do national cultures influence lay people's preferences toward doctors' style of communication?

A comparison of 35 focus groups from an European cross national research. *BioMed Central Public Health, 15*(1239). http://dx.doi.org/10.1186/s12889-015-2559-7

Roberts, D. (2015). Can research on the genetics of intelligence be "socially neutral"? *The Hastings Center Report, 45,* S50–S53. http://dx.doi.org/10.1002/hast.499

Rothbaum, F., & Kakinuma, M. (2004). Amae and attachment: Security in cultural context. *Human Development, 47,* 34–39. http://dx.doi.org/10.1159/000075368

Rubinstein, T., Makov, S., & Sarel, A. (2013). Don't bi-negative: Reduction of negative attitudes toward bisexuals by blurring the gender dichotomy. *Journal of Bisexuality, 13,* 356–373. http://dx.doi.org/10.1080/15299716.2013.813419

Ryan, F. (2011). Kanyininpa (holding): A way of nurturing children in Aboriginal Australia. *Australian Social Work, 64,* 183–197. http://dx.doi.org/10.1080/03124 07X.2011.581300

Ryan, P. J. (1997). Unnatural selection: Intelligence testing, eugenics, and American political cultures. *Journal of Social History, 30,* 669–685. http://dx.doi.org/10.1353/jsh/30.3.669

Schneider, M., Bockting, W. O., Ehrbar, R. D., Lawrence, A. A., Rachlin, K. L., & Zucker, K. J. (2006). *Answers to your questions about transgender individuals and gender identity* [Brochure]. Washington, DC: American Psychological Association.

Schneider, S. K., O'Donnell, L., & Smith, E. (2015). Trends in cyberbullying and school bullying victimization in a regional census of high school students, 2006–2012. *The Journal of School Health, 85,* 611–620. http://dx.doi.org/10.1111/josh.12290

Senju, A., Vernetti, A., Kikuchi, Y., Akechi, H., Hasegawa, T., & Johnson, M. H. (2013). Cultural background modulates how we look at other persons' gaze. *International Journal of Behavioral Development, 37,* 131–136. http://dx.doi.org/10.1177/0165025412465360

Serrano-Villar, M., & Calzada, E. J. (2016). Ethnic identity: Evidence of protective effects for young, Latino children. *Journal of Applied Developmental Psychology, 42,* 21–30. http://dx.doi.org/10.1016/j.appdev.2015.11.002

Shields, S. A., & Dicicco, E. C. (2011). The social psychology of sex and gender: From gender differences to doing gender. *Psychology of Women Quarterly, 35,* 491–499. http://dx.doi.org/10.1177/0361684311414823

Spencer, S. J., Logel, C., & Davies, P. G. (2016). Stereotype threat. *Annual Review of Psychology, 67,* 415–437. http://dx.doi.org/10.1146/annurev-psych-073115-103235

Steele, C. M., & Aronson, J. (1995). Stereotype threat and the intellectual test performance of African Americans. *Journal of Personality and Social Psychology, 69,* 797–811. http://dx.doi.org/10.1037/0022-3514.69.5.797

Stermer, S. P., & Burkley, M. (2015). SeX-Box: Exposure to sexist video games predicts benevolent sexism. *Psychology of Popular Media Culture, 4,* 47–55. http://dx.doi.org/10.1037/a0028397

Sternberg, R. J. (2004). Culture and intelligence. *American Psychologist, 59,* 325–338. http://dx.doi.org/10.1037/0003-066X.59.5.325

Sue, D. W., Capodilupo, C. M., & Holder, A. M. B. (2008). Racial microaggressions in the life experience of Black Americans. *Professional Psychology: Research and Practice, 39,* 329–336. http://dx.doi.org/10.1037/0735-7028.39.3.329

Tatum, B. D. (1994). Teaching White students about racism: The search for White allies and the restoration of hope. *Teachers College Record, 95,* 462–476.

Tatum, B. D. (1999). When you're called a racist. *Education Digest, 65,* 29–32.

World Health Organization. (2003). *International statistical classification of diseases and related health problems* (10th rev.). Geneva, Switzerland: Author.

Yin Foo, R., Guppy, M., & Johnston, L. M. (2013). Intelligence assessments for children with cerebral palsy: A systematic review. *Developmental Medicine & Child Neurology, 55,* 911–918. http://dx.doi.org/10.1111/dmcn.12157

17

Teaching Personality and Abnormal Psychology With Inclusivity

Alice W. Cheng, Kathy McCloskey, and Mala L. Matacin

Psychology portrays human beings as unique, with different personality characteristics dimensionally categorized, such as introverted or extroverted, loud or quiet, optimistic or pessimistic, and thoughtful or impulsive. "Acceptable" characteristics are considered "optimal," whereas problematic characteristics are labeled "abnormal," demonstrating an etic bias. We challenge these assumptions by addressing societal and cultural influences on individuals (Lee, 2012) and the saliency of language-based descriptors within different groups (Cortina, Curtin, & Stewart, 2012). In this chapter, we each offer our experiences teaching personality and abnormal psychology, as well as pedagogical issues and challenges in doing so.

PERSONALITY, CONSTRUCTED

The traditional personality course remains culture bound, largely reflecting a White male Western canon of personality theorists that includes "hallowed" males (e.g., Freud and Maslow) and an occasional contemporary male researcher (e.g., Bandura or Mischel). Some include women theorists such as Karen Horney and Melanie Klein, but critiques of this canon are usually absent. I (KM) expand on this canon using feminist and multicultural perspectives. I

Since the publication of Bronstein and Quina (2003), authors Phyllis Bronstein and Sondra Solomon have passed away. Portions of this chapter reflect their original contributions.

http://dx.doi.org/10.1037/0000137-018
Integrating Multiculturalism and Intersectionality Into the Psychology Curriculum:
Strategies for Instructors, J. A. Mena and K. Quina (Editors)

work from the *Theories of Personality* (eighth ed.; Feist, Feist, & Roberts, 2013) textbook because it provides a helpful taxonomy in which to place each theory and theorist and is well suited for critiques through a social constructionist lens. I supplement it with readings from Schustack and Friedman's (2008) *The Personality Reader*.

Course Structure

I notify students early and often that my course will examine personality via (a) social constructionist and historical analyses, (b) dialectical and critical thinking when evaluating theories, and (c) critiquing theories as explanations of personality. Theoretical positions are compared along several dimensions: human nature (optimistic vs. pessimistic); culturally defined ideal versus maladaptive development and functioning; concepts of the self; view of culture, society, and social rules; cross-cultural relevance; personality change; gender; ethnicity; and sexual orientation. Several of these dimensions are identified in Feist et al. (2013).

Because students process new information and tolerate openness and self-exploration differently (e.g., Caviness, Giuffre, & Wasley-Valdez, 2016; Rios, Stewart, & Winter, 2010), I offer them a variety of ways to demonstrate individualized strengths: (a) writing a summary (no more than 30 words) capturing each main point in every reading assignment; (b) leading a class discussion individually and in small groups (e.g., Wentling, 2016) on a chosen theorist, using PowerPoint-like materials; (c) participating in an open critique of each theorist during student-led discussions (e.g., Burke & Trumpy, 2016); and (d) writing a final paper that addresses one contemporary controversy in personality research and theory through a social constructivist lens.

Course Content

I incorporate gender and multiculturalism into traditional areas, as well as including these factors as topics in their own right. I find it indispensable to use supplementary materials to enhance students' understanding of minority-based perspectives on personality, particularly from within underrepresented populations. Thus, I assign original source material, present major objections to a theory, and critique theories and assessment tools from a social justice standpoint.

Psychoanalytic Theory: The Mother of All Vienna Inventions

Although many students have already heard of Freud, they may not have been exposed to some of the earlier ideas about how to classify personality "types" and their accompanying language descriptors. Thus, I begin with a broad overview of such things as the Four humors (sanguine/blood, choleric/yellow bile, phlegmatic and melancholy/black bile) with roots in Western Greco-Roman thought (Flaskerud, 2012) and the five Chinese states or conducts (water, wood, fire, metal, earth; Perkins, 2015) that were thought to correspond to particular biological, mental, and characterological traits that could be combined into more complex categorizations. I then bring this initial historical introduction into a discussion of Freud's theories. For example, I compare and contrast the four humors theory (i.e., too much or not enough of a particular body fluid) with Freud's thermodynamic metaphor of emotional disturbance (i.e., too much or not enough emotional energy, along with emotional "blockages").

I then assign some of Freud's translated writings, followed by selections that consider his theories within sociocultural contexts. For example, students read excerpts from *The Origin and Development of Psychoanalysis* (Freud, 1912/2008) and *The Aetiology of Hysteria* (Freud, 1896/1989), in which they encounter Freud's early theory that hysterical symptoms in adolescence and early adulthood were caused by both the presence of infantile sexuality and childhood sexual abuse. They then read an excerpt from Masson (2008) that supports the common history of childhood sexual abuse in clinical populations and posits why Freud later renounced it—this provides a fascinating example of how sociocultural factors shaped Freud's theorizing and led him to refute the realities of childhood sexual abuse. I also assign a reading on the present-day debate about the validity of recovered memories of sexual abuse (e.g., Freyd & Quina, 2000) to demonstrate the contemporary relevance of these controversies.

Students read Henry Murray's (1940/2008) critique of Freud's psychoanalytic approach as well as responses to Freud's theory by Alfred Adler, Carl Jung, Melanie Klein, Margaret Maher, and Karen Horney (see Feist et al., 2013). Early theorists such as Heinz Kohut, John Bowlby, and Mary Ainsworth illustrate the shift from purely psychoanalytic theory to object relations theory to attachment theory, demonstrating the historicity of the ongoing controversies related to analytic (or neo-analytic) theory. Students can evaluate Freud's assertion that he was describing universal human phenomena after reading about his theory's failures to account for gender and cross-cultural differences (e.g., Contratto & Rossier, 2005; Levinsky-Wohl, 2013).

Biological, Sociocultural, or Both? The Nature–Nurture Controversy

An overview of some early personality frameworks leads to questioning biological explanations of personality differences. Students review Eysenck's theories of biologically based personality traits and Buss's evolutionary theory and critiques of gendered (Reiber, 2015) and ethnocultural (Bianchi & Strang, 2013) "blindness" in hormonal and genetic explanations for differences in aggression, dominance, and emotional stability. Helpful are historical analyses: Eagly and Wood (2013) on controversies over biological rationales for traditional gender role behaviors and "reproductive strategies" (i.e., male promiscuity and rape), Hrdy's (1998) analysis of bias in primate research challenging animal "evidence" for human gender differences, Zuckerman's (1998) compelling cross-cultural challenge to connections between race and personality, and Shields (2016) on the strong influence that gendered social values have on the research process.

Students can discuss the controversy surrounding Raymond B. Cattell, the originator of the Sixteen Personality Factors Questionnaire. In 1997, the American Psychological Association (APA) canceled plans to award Cattell their Gold Medal for Lifetime Achievement when it became clear that he had written extensively about using questionnaires to determine which races were genetically fit and eliminate races labeled unfit (a form of eugenics; Tucker, 2009).

To illustrate environmental influences, I assign textbook chapters on B. F. Skinner's theory (which represents the nurture position), as well as the cognitive and social learning theories of Albert Bandura, Julian Rotter, and Walter Mischel, and finally address the more humanistic, existential theorists such as Erich Fromm, George Kelly, Rollo May, Erik Erikson, Abraham Maslow, and Carl Rogers. Thus, students move from purely environmental influences (behavioral) to bidirectional environment–individual influences (cognitive and social learning) to a largely individualistic focus on human meaning making (existential and humanistic).

I highlight the circular, iterative, and interactional features of the nature–nurture debate (i.e., the both/and phenomenon). I usually assign an article on parenting and gender role socialization, such as a review chapter on the different behaviors, across a range of cultures, that mothers and fathers model, as well as their differential treatment of girls and boys (e.g., Bronstein, 2001). Evidence that parental behaviors are significant in the shaping and reinforcing of gender differences can provide an effective counter to claims that differences in girls' and boys' behaviors are dictated primarily by biology. I also include an article by Haritatos and Benet-Martinez (2008) examining the interface between cultural norms, shifting personalities, and sociocognitive processes reported by many bicultural individuals.

Another answer to the nature–nurture question is: It depends. Sometimes inherited characteristics take precedence, sometimes social and cultural demand characteristics take precedence, and sometimes the primary effect is the result of an interaction between the two. A burgeoning literature highlights the importance of sociocultural and ethnic factors; particularly helpful are Shiraev and Levy's (2010) chapters on emotion, motivation and behavior, social perception and cognition, human development and socialization, and value systems and religious beliefs. Gender and sexual identity are addressed through readings that increase awareness of gender-role messages relative to heterosexual gender-identity development (Striepe & Tolman, 2003) and transgender personality development (Tate, Youssef, & Bettergarcia, 2014). I also include historically seminal anthropological readings about gendered personality development in cultures within and outside the United States (e.g., Mead, 1935/1963).

The Measurement of Personality

Students should know of the important, often unrecognized role women played in the development of personality measures. Widely used clinical diagnostic instruments such as the Draw-A-Man (or Draw-A-Person) test and the Bender Visual Motor Gestalt test were developed by women (O'Connell & Russo, 1980; Stevens & Gardner, 1982). Although Henry Murray is generally credited with the development of the Thematic Apperception Test, he stated that his colleague and one-time mistress Christiana Morgan "had the main role" (Murray, 1985, p. 2) and that the original idea, in fact, came from a Radcliffe student participating in an all-female abnormal psychology class (Roazen, 2003).

I also infuse important social and multicultural issues when teaching about personality research methods. I relate the textbook reading about McCrae and Costa's (1996) five-factor personality model back to the four humors and the five Chinese states, asking students to imagine what people will think of the famous five-factor model in 50 years. The NEO-Personality Inventory (Costa & McCrae, 1985), developed from the Big Five dimensions of Neuroticism, Extraversion, Openness to experience, Agreeableness, and Conscientiousness, is followed by a discussion of Wetzel, Bohnke, Carstensen, Ziegler, and Ostendorf's (2013) findings of gender differences in response styles.

To critique methods, I assign Hall, Yip, and Zárate's (2016) well-reasoned approach for conducting any research addressing diversity issues. They suggested that to be multiculturally valid, research must address (a) generalizability, with methods that examine similarities and universalities across diverse groups; (b) group differences, with methods that examine uniqueness across groups (i.e., a lack of generalizability); and (c) mechanisms of cultural and group influences, with methods that examine the influence of sociocultural norms and beliefs on outward expression (i.e., behavior, language, personality, and so on). These approaches must also include multimodal methodologies that elevate qualitative research to equal status to that of quantitative research and require an emphasis on underrepresented gendered or ethnocultural populations.

ABNORMAL PSYCHOLOGY

In recent years, significant efforts have been made toward creating a more inclusive and multicultural approach to abnormality, such as removing homosexuality from the *Diagnostic and Statistical Manual of Mental Disorders* (*DSM*) in 1973 (Rubinstein, 1995) or changing gender identity disorder to gender dysphoria in the *DSM–5* (American Psychiatric Association, 2013; Zucker et al., 2013). The increasing diversity in the United States is reflected in those seeking mental health care, as well as our students who may work with them in the future. APA recently solidified the importance of multiculturalism in teaching, research, practice, and institutional change in psychology (APA, 2017). To help students overcome the pervasive ethnocentrism of the tendency to judge normality by Western, White, middle-class male standards, I (AWC) integrate issues central to the mental health of marginalized populations into my abnormal psychology course.

230 Cheng, McCloskey, and Matacin

Lack of Diversity Within Psychology

I ask my students to name 10 women psychologists and 10 psychologists of color. Students struggle with the first list and find the second even more challenging. Then I ask them to name 10 male psychologists. The contrast is striking; they easily name 10 or 20 White males. Although more women have entered the field of psychology in the last few decades (U.S. National Science Foundation, 2015), the dominant theories in textbooks remain those of White males. We address the implications of this singular voice in the following ways.

Mental health and mental illness are, to a certain extent, culture dependent, which is particularly problematic when the views of one dominant group define the standard for behavior in a multicultural society with a history of immigration such as the United States. Other forms of diversity such as sexual orientation, disability, or low socioeconomic status make any attempt to analyze normative behaviors through a singular lens even more problematic. To help students understand that "normality" (and thus "abnormality") is relative or culturally dependent, I encourage my students to think of behaviors that are considered normal in the United States but may be deemed abnormal elsewhere, and vice versa. For example, what may be seen as family "enmeshment" in an individualist culture like the United States may be regarded as a healthy and supportive family association in collectivistic cultures (Barrera, Blummer, & Soenksen, 2011).

I assign supplemental articles that question the status quo of how the *DSM* defines abnormality and diagnostic biases (e.g., premenstrual dysphoric disorder and gender dysphoria; see Caplan, 1995), as well as research that is inclusive of participants from diverse backgrounds. For example, Ault and Brzuzy (2009) argued that diagnoses such as gender identity disorder are used to impose societal gender norms on individuals who deviate from that norm. Although this and similar analyses facilitated the renaming and reconstruction of gender identity disorder to gender dysphoria, this diagnosis continues such gender norming.

Diagnosis and Symptom Interpretation

There are structural and systemic challenges in applying clinical diagnoses to members of marginalized populations (Sue & Sue, 2012). For example, acculturative stress can be seen either as social anxiety disorder or as the result of perceived discrimination due to individuals' minority status (Fang, Friedlander, & Pieterse, 2016). People of color who are cautious or who withhold information from authority figures (which includes clinicians) can be interpreted either as paranoid or as exhibiting an adaptive response to systemic oppression (Mosley, Owen, Rostosky, & Reese, 2017). Students can discuss examples from their experiences of behaviors that might seem to be "abnormal" in the absence of context (e.g., stress symptoms during finals week) to help them recognize the need to consider the overall lived experience of an individual and not just focus on symptoms when assigning diagnoses. This can then lead to a discussion of the importance of this lesson in a clinical setting, especially with clients of minority status. Hays's (2016) chapter on culturally responsive diagnostic procedures contains useful therapeutic strategies that consider contextual issues.

Stereotypes and Mental Health

Stereotypes and preconceived conceptualizations of others can have a profound effect on the diagnosis of minority clients, leading clinicians to disregard important presenting symptoms, which result in diagnostic biases (Snowden, 2003). For instance, clinicians in training are less inclined to diagnose Asian Americans with alcohol use disorder when they are primed with the "model minority" stereotype generally associated with this group (Cheng, Chang, O'Brien, Budgazad, & Tsai, 2017). When primed with pictures of African American faces, physicians are more inclined to diagnose African Americans with alcohol and substance use disorders (Moskowitz, Stone, & Childs, 2012). The influence of stereotypes in diagnostics can also be extended to other minority statuses; for example, women are more likely to be diagnosed with a borderline personality disorder (Lester, 2013), whereas the elderly are diagnosed more frequently with depression (Ruppel, Jenkins, Griffin, & Kizer, 2010). Caplan and Cosgrove (2004) and Cheng et al. (2017) offered important documentation of diagnostic bias relevant to other diverse populations.

Mental Health Disparities

Differential prevalence rates of mental health disorders among minority communities (e.g., ethnic, gender, sexual orientation, ability status) compared with majority groups are well documented in the literature (Brodie, 2004; Sutter & Perrin, 2016). For a comprehensive understanding on reasons contributing to the disparity, instructors should familiarize themselves with the U.S. Surgeon General's benchmark report, *Mental Health: Culture, Race, and Ethnicity* (U.S. Department of Health and Human Services, 2001), and the updated report by the Substance Abuse and Mental Health Services Administration (2015).

Actual rates of mental illness in minority populations are disputed, creating good critical thinking points for class discussions: Are reported rates due to structural pressures impinging on minority populations, barriers to services for minority groups, diagnostic biases on the part of mental health providers, or a combination of these issues? Examples include the following:

- Higher rates of severe mental illness diagnoses have been found among Blacks than among other ethnic groups; racial stereotypes, healthy paranoia, and worldview differences have been cited as potential reasons for the differential rates (Feisthamel & Schwartz, 2009; Mosley et al., 2017).

- Latinxs and Blacks are diagnosed more frequently with behavioral-related problems, such as oppositional defiant and conduct disorders, whereas White children with similar symptoms tend to be diagnosed with adjustment or mood disorders (Feisthamel & Schwartz, 2009).

- The disparity in mental health diagnoses starts when individuals are young, which contributes to the school-to-prison pipeline (Nelson, 2014).

- Some findings suggest that mental health problems may not be as prevalent among Asian American populations (Miranda, McGuire, Williams, & Wang, 2008), yet suicide is among the top five leading causes of death among Asian American women aged 10 to 54, a phenomenon not observed in women of other ethnicities (Curtin, Warner, & Hedegaard, 2016).

- Lesbian, gay, bisexual, transgender, and queer (LGBTQ) individuals show a higher prevalence of mood, anxiety, and substance use disorders than do heterosexual individuals (Cochran, Sullivan, & Mays, 2003).

- People with different abilities are at increased risk of developing mental health problems due to the adversities they face, including interpersonal and structural discrimination (Kwok & Cheung, 2007; WHO World Mental Health Survey Consortium, 2004).

Culture-Bound Syndromes

Historically, the *DSM* has excluded input from minority groups because its executive committee members were largely White (and male); likewise, symptoms and diagnoses have also been largely drawn from the majority population. Diagnoses specific to certain cultures were first introduced in the *DSM–IV–TR* (American Psychiatric Association, 2000). However, culture-bound diagnoses were placed in the appendix, signifying their lack of importance and helping to "exoticize" these symptoms, even those also observed in the dominant culture. For example, *shenjing shuairuo* (neurasthenia), a disorder characterized by fatigue and weakness, can be viewed as a specific Chinese mental health phenomenon. An alternative perspective is that the more cognitively focused *DSM* failed to capture physiological symptoms more characteristic of Chinese individuals with depression and anxiety disorders (Chang et al., 2005).

Symptom clusters more commonly found in the dominant culture are placed in the main text of the *DSM*, denoting them as universal and culture free, whereas symptoms more commonly found among minority groups are ignored. For example, eating disorders, which could be considered culturally bound because they are significantly more prevalent among Whites (Hughes, 1998), are found in the main text, illustrating this ethnocentrism. The *International Classification of Mental and Behavioural Disorders* (10th rev.; ICD–10; World Health Organization, 2016) included more comprehensive global input (e.g., *shenjing shuairuo*) but still has shortcomings. For example, ego-dystonic sexual orientation is still listed in the ICD–10, although it was removed from versions of the *DSM* in the late 1980s. Students can examine the current *DSM* and ICD critically to see how both Western-centered and dominant nosology perpetuate ethnocentrism.

Approaches to Eliminating Disparities

Epidemiological data on differences in mental health diagnostic prevalence rates by population groups fail to address causes of these observed disparities. The most common systematic barriers that result in higher rates of ethnic minority misdiagnoses are (a) lower standards of care, (b) poor assessment validity, (c) differential language and/or communication styles, (d) failure to consider social and cultural contexts, (e) poor diagnostic validity, and (f) misinterpretation and/or misuse of information (Cook, Trinh, Li, Hou, & Progovac, 2017; Maura & Weisman de Mamani, 2017; U.S. Department of Health and Human Services, 2001). These barriers can also result in more severe symptomology as well as a global functioning decline for individuals facing such barriers.

For example, African Americans use emergency room visits for mental health–related services at higher rates compared with other ethnic groups (Snowden, Catalano, & Shumway, 2009). When African Americans do receive psychological services, they are less frequently referred for psychotherapy treatments and are discharged earlier in therapy than Whites, yet they are also hospitalized at higher rates (Li, Jenkins, & Sundsmo, 2007). Thus, differential prevalence rates might reflect unequal access to mental health care, delay in seeking help, and lack of quality of services received. Such experiences with the mental health care system are compounded by disproportionately greater sociocultural burdens (e.g., low socioeconomic status, discrimination, poverty) experienced by people of color compared with Whites, as well as the associated stress that can lead to more severe mental health problems (Feisthamel & Schwartz, 2009).

At a more general level, students can consider the validity of a discipline on the basis of a narrow, decontextualized Western worldview. For example, clients of minority status may use language and express symptoms of mental health distress that differ from those on which structured diagnoses for the *DSM* are currently based (Fontes, 2008; Okazaki & Sue, 2000), which could lead to inaccuracy in determining distress and possibly over- or underestimating symptom severity. In addition, assessment tools used for diagnostic purposes are seldom normed with adequate minority representation; for example, the *Minnesota Multiphasic Personality Inventory, Second Edition* (Graham, 1993) is normed with only 19 Asian Americans, representing less than 1% of the entire sample (Okazaki & Sue, 2000).

RESOURCES AND EXERCISES

Littleford (2005) and Littleford and Nolan (2013) provided excellent ideas for increasing general cultural competence in teaching. These authors suggested that creating a multicultural classroom is not only about content but also process. They suggested that instructors should (a) address diverse learning styles by using various teaching and assessment methods, (b) have a good understanding of various cultural groups, and (c) be aware of their emotional, cognitive, and behavioral responses to students of diverse backgrounds. Next, I (MLM) address general strategies for creating classes that are more inclusive using diverse pedagogical practices that can be applied to both personality and abnormal psychology classes.

I begin by letting students know that the course will challenge their assumptions and broaden their thinking and deconstruct the dominant White, patriarchal, cisgender discourse and power structure. I introduce them to a practice of asking questions about what they are reading and seeing: (a) Is it true? (b) What are the assumptions? (c) What is the evidence? (d) How was that evidence created? (e) Through whose lens are we seeing? (f) Who chooses that lens? (g) Who benefits from that lens? and (h) What are other points of view? I also tell students what is important to me, including my choice of required readings; for example, understanding violence is vital to my understanding of the social construction of gender and personality and mental health; I could not ethically teach a class without including it.

Having a handout of basic terminology is helpful. For sex, gender, and orientation terms, I use Hill and Mays's (2011) free, downloadable *The Gender Booklet*. Using McIntosh's (1989) essay, *White Privilege: Unpacking the Invisible Knapsack*, I ask students to similarly unpack their own knapsacks by creating lists and reflect on advantages based on multiple identities (e.g., male, White, cisgender, able-bodied, middle class). This activity could be adapted to include invisible disabilities and mental illnesses. I intersperse the conversation with academic terms we will use for the rest of the semester and also point out their real-life intersectionality. This knapsack assignment reminded one student of the song *White Privilege II* by White hip-hop duo Macklemore and Lewis (2016; lyrics at http://genius.com/Macklemore-and-ryan-lewis-white-privilege-ii-lyrics), leading the class to a discussion from which I also learned a new song and a tool for future classes.

Several authors have written about using music, poetry, autobiography, and novels as avenues to teach sex and gender in personality and abnormal psychology courses (Miller, 2016; selections by Carlson, Chrisler, and Mueller in Ware & Johnson, 2000). Harker (2016) described an exercise to deconstruct gender identity using self-created autobiographical "mix tapes" of songs that represent students' gender identity. This exercise works with other identities (e.g., any combination of religion, age, race) and is shared in a group "music festival."

TED Talks (http://www.ted.com/talks) can be a useful tool. I use one by novelist Chimamanda Ngozi Adichie (2009) on *The Danger of a Single Story*, which can be a platform for students to examine how their own stereotypes develop. Haltinner (2016) asked students to examine a "single story" (stereotype) focused on a culturally held belief and then seek out alternative stories. Students are invited to examine their internalized cultural narrative by questioning who benefits and who suffers from these beliefs. Instructors could compare theories of personality as a single story of human nature; for example, what is the story that dispositional, psychodynamic, or humanist theorists tell about individual differences and similarities? Similarly, Adichie's talk can guide students through the story of mental illness as told by a particular disorder in the *DSM*.

Asking students to engage in careful reading (or reading at all) can be challenging. Purposeful or close reading can increase critical thinking skills and allow instructors to ask questions that guide students to think in a broader way about course content. For example, to help guide the class-based critique on personality theories, instructors could create questions to guide close reading, such as the six I use at the beginning of my class. One specific prompt could be, "What is the evidence that this theory applies to those without a disability?"

Close critical reading can also be applied to images, asking students to "read" the images in the popular press, online, or their textbooks. For example, in examining a particular disorder or personality theory, they can consider (a) who is represented, on the basis of age, race, gender, ability status, or any other cultural dimension; (b) who is missing; (c) whether the images and the text are saying different things: and (d) what these images say about those with mental illness or individual differences. Deconstructing images is useful in revealing the construction of our dominant cultural stories and theories.

Haltinner and Pilgeram's (2016) *Teaching Gender and Sex in Contemporary America* provides not only writing assignments but also sample syllabi. Although the assignments primarily deal with gender and sex, they also include assignments regarding intersections with systems of institutional power, as well as creating intentional classrooms. Graff, Birkenstein, and Durst (2012) provided templates that students can use when learning to summarize text ("they say") and create their own arguments ("I say"). In a personality class, instructors could ask students to summarize a theory ("they say") and critique its implications on the basis of race, sexual orientation, religion, and so on ("I say"). Ware and Johnson (2000) offered ideas for writing about case studies in abnormal psychology, although they did not explicitly address marginalized groups.

Wikis, which use a web-based editing system, appear to increase student confidence and perceived value in working on a collaborative project with others cross culturally (Ertmer et al., 2011; Heng & Marimuthu, 2012). Students can brainstorm ideas, create and edit a shared document, and provide feedback about a relevant topic—all online. For example, on the basis of what they have learned about marginalized groups, they can critique a particular diagnosis, theory, or personality test for its cross-diversity applicability.

Instructors can also incorporate the work and narratives of people of color and other marginalized groups, providing explanations embedded in cultural, economic, and political systems (Littleford, 2005). Caplan (1995) argued that women and marginalized groups were being overpathologized and harmed by the *DSM* (e.g., masochistic personality disorder and premenstrual syndrome). Craig (2016) suggested that instructors name the assumptions behind various studies—rather than saying "research on romantic relationships suggests that," they should say "research on monogamous, heterosexual romantic relationships suggests that" and, if available, also offer findings with different kinds of relationships.

I often use educational documentaries created by the Media Education Foundation (http://www.mediaed.org), which are meant to "inspire critical thinking about the social, political, and cultural impact of American mass media" (Media Education Foundation, 2019, para. 1). The films *Tough Guise* (Ericsson, Talreja, & Jhally, 1999) and *Tough Guise 2* (Earp, 2013) analyzed how male dominance functions in language and media using powerful images. These films can be used to show how White and Black men's "normal personality" is socially constructed and reinforced through larger social structures (e.g., media, patriarchy) that make particular behaviors more likely.

Finally, I do not shy away from pop culture or social media platforms such as Instagram, Twitter, Tumblr, Pinterest, or Facebook. Students can be asked to apply course content by analyzing a character on a show with a particular diagnosis or personality type that appears on such social media platforms. Students can also follow organizations or people on Twitter who have alternative ideas about mental illness or individual differences. For group projects, I have even required students to create their own hashtags to use on various social media platforms. Students who do not wish to have their e-mails associated with these platforms for privacy purposes can create an alternate e-mail for these purposes. I also require students to attend at least two campus and community events that have relevance to the course, such as lectures, panels, movies, or art exhibits and turn in a brief reflection paper integrating two readings.

CONCLUSION

The fields of personality and abnormal psychology have suffered from gender and sociocultural bias. Indeed, standard theoretical models and the resultant research only provide information about a small segment of humanity. Although feminist and multicultural scholars have already provided many new perspectives as well as research tools, this information is just beginning to find its way into our textbooks. Nevertheless, personality and abnormal psychology instructors can create courses that reflect the richness of multiple human realities. By focusing intently on a small stand of oaks, we must not miss the enormous variety of the forest.

REFERENCES

Adichie, C. N. (2009, July). The danger of a single story [Video file]. *TEDGlobal*. Retrieved from https://www.ted.com/talks/chimamanda_adichie_the_danger_of_a_single_story

American Psychiatric Association. (2000). *Diagnostic and statistical manual of mental disorders* (4th ed., text rev.). Washington, DC: Author.

American Psychiatric Association. (2013). *Diagnostic and statistical manual of mental disorders* (5th ed.). Arlington, VA: Author.

American Psychological Association. (2017). *Multicultural guidelines: An ecological approach to context, identity, and intersectionality*. Retrieved from https://www.apa.org/about/policy/multicultural-guidelines.pdf

Ault, A., & Brzuzy, S. (2009). Removing gender identity disorder from the *Diagnostic and Statistical Manual of Mental Disorders*: A call for action. *Social Work, 54*, 187–189. http://dx.doi.org/10.1093/sw/54.2.187

Barrera, A. M., Blummer, M. L., & Soenksen, S. H. (2011). Revisiting adolescent separation-individuation in the contexts of enmeshment and allocentrism. *The New School Psychology Bulletin, 8*, 70–82.

Bianchi, J. M., & Strang, E. (2013). Is evolutionary psychology really value-free? A reconsideration. *Journal of Social, Evolutionary, and Cultural Psychology, 7*, 304–310. http://dx.doi.org/10.1037/h0099189

Brodie, R. E. (2004). Race, sex, and class bias in the diagnosis of *DSM–IV* disorders. *Dissertation Abstracts International: B. The Sciences and Engineering, 64*(11-B), 5774.

Bronstein, P. (2001). Parenting. In J. Worell (Ed.), *Encyclopedia of women and gender* (pp. 795–808). San Diego, CA: Academic Press.

Bronstein, P., & Quina, K. (Eds.). (2003). *Teaching gender and multicultural awareness: Resources for the psychology classroom.* Washington, DC: American Psychological Association. http://dx.doi.org/10.1037/10570-000

Burke, K., & Trumpy, A. (2016). Making the invisible visible: Shining a light on gender and sexuality in courses primarily focused on other topics. In K. Haltinner & R. Pilgeram (Eds.), *Teaching gender and sex in contemporary America* (pp. 273–279). Zurich, Switzerland: Springer-Verlag. http://dx.doi.org/10.1007/978-3-319-30364-2_27

Caplan, P. J. (1995). *They say you're crazy: How the world's most powerful psychiatrists decide who's normal.* Reading, MA: Addison Wesley.

Caplan, P. J., & Cosgrove, L. (2004). *Bias in psychiatric diagnosis.* Lanham, MD: Jason Aronson.

Caviness, C., Giuffre, P., & Wasley-Valdez, M. (2016). They don't get it: The promise and problem of using student resistance as a pedagogical tool. In K. Haltinner & R. Pilgeram (Eds.), *Teaching gender and sex in contemporary America* (pp. 175–183). Zurich, Switzerland: Springer-Verlag. http://dx.doi.org/10.1007/978-3-319-30364-2_18

Chang, D. F., Myers, H. F., Yeung, A., Zhang, Y., Zhao, J., & Yu, S. (2005). Shenjing shuairuo and the *DSM–IV*: Diagnosis, distress, and disability in a Chinese primary care setting. *Transcultural Psychiatry, 42,* 204–218. http://dx.doi.org/10.1177/1363461505052660

Cheng, A. W., Chang, J., O'Brien, J., Budgazad, M. S., & Tsai, J. (2017). Model minority stereotype: Influence on perceived mental health needs of Asian Americans. *Journal of Immigrant and Minority Health, 19,* 572–581. http://dx.doi.org/10.1007/s10903-016-0440-0

Cochran, S. D., Sullivan, J. G., & Mays, V. M. (2003). Prevalence of mental disorders, psychological distress, and mental health services use among lesbian, gay, and bisexual adults in the United States. *Journal of Consulting and Clinical Psychology, 71,* 53–61. http://dx.doi.org/10.1037/0022-006X.71.1.53

Contratto, S., & Rossier, J. (2005). Early trends in feminist therapy, theory, and practice. *Women & Therapy, 28*(3-4), 7–26. http://dx.doi.org/10.1300/J015v28n03_02

Cook, B. L., Trinh, N. H., Li, Z., Hou, S. S., & Progovac, A. M. (2017). Trends in racial-ethnic disparities in access to mental health care, 2004–2012. *Psychiatric Services, 68,* 9–16. http://dx.doi.org/10.1176/appi.ps.201500453

Cortina, L. M., Curtin, N., & Stewart, A. J. (2012). Where is social structure in personality research? A feminist analysis of publication trends. *Psychology of Women Quarterly, 36,* 259–273. http://dx.doi.org/10.1177/0361684312448056

Costa, P. T. Jr., & McCrae, R. R. (1985). *The Neo Personality Inventory manual.* Odessa, FL: Psychological Assessment Resources.

Craig, T. (2016). The pedagogical challenge of teaching privilege, loss, and disadvantage in classrooms of invisible social identities. In K. Haltinner & R. Pilgeram (Eds.), *Teaching gender and sex in contemporary America* (pp. 217–228). New York, NY: Springer International. http://dx.doi.org/10.1007/978-3-319-30364-2_22

Curtin, S. C., Warner, M., & Hedegaard, H. (2016). *Suicide rates for females and males by race and ethnicity: United States, 1999 and 2014.* Retrieved from https://www.cdc.gov/nchs/data/hestat/suicide/rates_1999_2014.htm

Eagly, A. H., & Wood, W. (2013). The nature–nurture debates: 25 years of challenges in understanding the psychology of gender. *Perspectives on Psychological Science, 8,* 340–357. http://dx.doi.org/10.1177/1745691613484767

Earp, J. (Producer & Director). (2013). *Tough guise 2: Violence, manhood, and American culture* [Motion picture]. United States: Media Education Foundation.

Ericsson, S. (Producer), Talreja, S. (Producer), & Jhally, S. (Director). (1999). *Tough guise: Violence, media, and the crisis in masculinity* [Motion picture]. United States: Media Education Foundation.

Ertmer, P. A., Newby, T. J., Liu, W., Tomory, A., Yu, J. H., & Lee, Y. M. (2011). Students' confidence and perceived value for participating in cross-cultural Wiki-based collaborations. *Educational Technology Research and Development, 59*, 213–228. http://dx.doi.org/10.1007/s11423-011-9187-4

Fang, K., Friedlander, M., & Pieterse, A. L. (2016). Contributions of acculturation, enculturation, discrimination, and personality traits to social anxiety among Chinese immigrants: A context-specific assessment. *Cultural Diversity and Ethnic Minority Psychology, 22*, 58–68. http://dx.doi.org/10.1037/cdp0000030

Feist, J., Feist, G. J., & Roberts, T. (2013). *Theories of personality* (8th ed.). New York, NY: McGraw-Hill.

Feisthamel, K. P., & Schwartz, R. C. (2009). Differences in mental health counselors' diagnoses based on client race: An investigation of adjustment, childhood, and substance-related disorders. *Journal of Mental Health Counseling, 31*, 47–59. http://dx.doi.org/10.17744/mehc.31.1.u82021637276wv1k

Flaskerud, J. H. (2012). Temperament and personality: From Galen to *DSM–5. Issues in Mental Health Nursing, 33*, 631–634. http://dx.doi.org/10.3109/01612840.2011.647256

Fontes, L. A. (2008). *Interviewing clients across cultures: A practitioner's guide.* New York, NY: Guilford Press.

Freud, S. (1989). The aetiology of hysteria. In P. Gay (Ed.), *The Freud reader* (pp. 96–111). New York, NY: Norton. (Original work published 1896)

Freud, S. (2008). The origin and development of psychoanalysis. In M. W. Schustack & H. S. Friedman (Eds.), *The personality reader* (2nd ed., pp. 1–5). Boston, MA: Pearson. (Original work published 1912)

Freyd, J. J., & Quina, K. (2000). Feminist ethics in the practice of science: The contested memory controversy as example. In M. Brabeck (Ed.), *Practicing ethics in feminist psychology* (pp. 101–123). Washington, DC: American Psychological Association. http://dx.doi.org/10.1037/10343-005

Graff, G., Birkenstein, C., & Durst, R. (2012). *"They say/I say": The moves that matter in academic writing with readings* (2nd ed.). New York, NY: Norton.

Graham, J. R. (1993). *MMPI–2: Assessing personality and psychopathology.* New York, NY: Oxford University Press.

Hall, G. C. G., Yip, T., & Zárate, M. A. (2016). On becoming multicultural in a mono-cultural research world: A conceptual approach to studying ethnocultural diversity. *American Psychologist, 71*, 40–51. http://dx.doi.org/10.1037/a0039734

Haltinner, K. (2016). Gender bending in the classroom: Teaching gender inequity without reifying gender essentialism and heteronormativity. In K. Haltinner & R. Pilgeram (Eds.), *Teaching gender and sex in contemporary America* (pp. 45–51). Zurich, Switzerland: Springer-Verlag. http://dx.doi.org/10.1007/978-3-319-30364-2_5

Haltinner, K., & Pilgeram, R. (Eds.). (2016). *Teaching gender and sex in contemporary America.* Geneva, Switzerland: Springer International. http://dx.doi.org/10.1007/978-3-319-30364-2

Haritatos, J., & Benet-Martinez, V. (2008). Bicultural identities: The interface of cultural, personality, and socio-cognitive processes. In M. W. Schustack & H. S. Friedman (Eds.), *The personality reader* (2nd ed., pp. 366–371). Boston, MA: Pearson.

Harker, K. (2016). An autoethnograpic mix tape: Deconstructing gender identity through music that has meaning to us. In K. Haltinner & R. Pilgeram (Eds.), *Teaching gender and sex in contemporary America* (pp. 117–129). Zurich, Switzerland: Springer-Verlag. http://dx.doi.org/10.1007/978-3-319-30364-2_13

Hays, P. A. (2016). *Addressing cultural complexities in practice: Assessment, diagnosis, and therapy* (3rd ed.). Washington, DC: American Psychological Association. http://dx.doi.org/10.1037/14801-009

Heng, L. T., & Marimuthu, R. (2012). Let's Wiki in class. *Procedia: Social and Behavioral Sciences, 67*, 269–274. http://dx.doi.org/10.1016/j.sbspro.2012.11.329

Hill, M., & Mays, J. (2011). *The gender booklet*. Retrieved from http://www. thegenderbook.com

Hrdy, S. B. (1998). Raising Darwin's consciousness: Females and evolutionary theory. In B. M. Clinchy & J. K. Norem (Eds.), *The gender and psychology reader* (pp. 265–271). New York, NY: New York University Press.

Hughes, C. C. (1998). The glossary of "culture-bound syndromes" in *DSM–IV*: A critique. *Transcultural Psychiatry, 35*, 413–421. http://dx.doi.org/10.1177/136346159803500307

Kwok, H., & Cheung, P. W. (2007). Co-morbidity of psychiatric disorder and medical illness in people with intellectual disabilities. *Current Opinion in Psychiatry, 20*, 443–449. http://dx.doi.org/10.1097/YCO.0b013e3282ab9941

Lee, M. R. (2012). Teaching gender and intersectionality: A dilemma and social justice approach. *Psychology of Women Quarterly, 36*, 110–115. http://dx.doi.org/10.1177/0361684311426129

Lester, R. J. (2013). Lessons from the borderline: Anthropology, psychiatry, and the risks of being human. *Feminism & Psychology, 23*, 70–77. http://dx.doi.org/10.1177/0959353512467969

Levinsky-Wohl, M. (2013). Juliet Mitchell. *Canadian Journal of Psychoanalysis/Revue Canadienne de Psychanalyse, 21*, 202–214.

Li, S. T., Jenkins, S., & Sundsmo, A. (2007). Impact of race and ethnicity. In M. Hersen, S. M. Turner, & D. C. Beidel (Eds.), *Adult psychopathology and diagnosis* (5th ed., pp. 101–121). Hoboken, NJ: Wiley.

Littleford, L. N. (2005). *Understanding and expanding multicultural competence in teaching: A faculty guide*. Retrieved from http://teachpsych.org/resources/Documents/otrp/resources/littleford05.pdf

Littleford, L. N., & Nolan, S. A. (2013). *Your sphere of influence: How to infuse diversity into your psychology courses*. Retrieved from http://www.apa.org/ed/precollege/ptn/2013/05/cultural-diversity.aspx

Macklemore, & Lewis, R. (2016). White privilege II. On *This unruly mess I've made* [CD]. New York, NY: Macklemore LLC.

Masson, J. M. (2008). The assault on truth: Freud's suppression of the seduction theory. In M. W. Schustack & H. S. Friedman (Eds.), *The personality reader* (2nd ed., pp. 26–30). Boston, MA: Pearson.

Maura, J., & Weisman de Mamani, A. (2017). Mental health disparities, treatment engagement, and attrition among racial/ethnic minorities with severe mental illness: A review. *Journal of Clinical Psychology in Medical Settings, 24*, 187–210. http://dx.doi.org/10.1007/s10880-017-9510-2

McCrae, R. R., & Costa, P. T., Jr. (1996). Toward a new generation of personality theories: Theoretical contexts for the five-factor model. In J. S. Wiggins (Ed.), *The five-factor model of personality: Theoretical perspectives* (pp. 51–87). New York, NY: Guilford Press.

McIntosh, P. (1989, July–August). White privilege: Unpacking the invisible knapsack. *Peace and Freedom Magazine*, pp. 10–12.

Mead, M. (1963). *Sex and temperament in three primitive societies*. New York, NY: William Morrow. (Original work published 1935)

Media Education Foundation. (2019). *Mission*. Retrieved from http://www.mediaed.org/about-mef/what-we-believe/

Miller, A. D. (2016). The mis-education of Lady Gaga: Confronting essentialist claims in the sex and gender classroom. In K. Haltinner & R. Pilgeram (Eds.), *Teaching gender and sex in contemporary America* (pp. 15–25). Zurich, Switzerland: Springer-Verlag. http://dx.doi.org/10.1007/978-3-319-30364-2_2

Miranda, J., McGuire, T. G., Williams, D. R., & Wang, P. (2008). Mental health in the context of health disparities. *The American Journal of Psychiatry, 165*, 1102–1108. http://dx.doi.org/10.1176/appi.ajp.2008.08030333

Moskowitz, G. B., Stone, J., & Childs, A. (2012). Implicit stereotyping and medical decisions: Unconscious stereotype activation in practitioners' thoughts about African Americans. *American Journal of Public Health, 102*, 996–1001. http://dx.doi.org/10.2105/AJPH.2011.300591

Mosley, D. V., Owen, K. H., Rostosky, S. S., & Reese, R. J. (2017). Contextualizing behaviors associated with paranoia: Perspectives of Black men. *Psychology of Men & Masculinity, 18*, 165–175. http://dx.doi.org/10.1037/men0000052

Murray, H. A. (1985). Dr. Henry A. Murray replies [Letter to the editor]. *Second Century: Radcliffe News, 6*(1), 2.

Murray, H. A. (2008). What should psychologists do about psychoanalysis? In M. W. Schustack & H. S. Friedman (Eds.), *The personality reader* (2nd ed., pp. 31–35). Boston, MA: Pearson. (Original work published 1940)

Nelson, C. M. (2014). Students with learning and behavioral disabilities and the school-to-prison pipeline: How we got here, and what we might do about it. In B. G. Cook, M. Tankersley, & T. J. Landrum (Eds.), *Special education past, present, and future: Perspectives from the field* (Vol. 27, pp. 89–115). Bingley, England: Emerald Group.

O'Connell, A., & Russo, N. F. (1980). *Models of achievement: Reflections of eminent women in psychology*. New York, NY: Columbia University Press.

Okazaki, S., & Sue, S. (2000). Implications of test revisions for assessment with Asian Americans. *Psychological Assessment, 12*, 272–280. http://dx.doi.org/10.1037/1040-3590.12.3.272

Perkins, F. (2015). Five conducts (Wu Xing) and the grounding of virtue. *Journal of Chinese Philosophy, 41*, 503–520. http://dx.doi.org/10.1111/1540-6253.12122

Reiber, C. (2015). Moving toward gender equity in the evolutionary behavioral and other sciences: The need for open discussion around the everyday challenges faced by women. *Evolutionary Behavioral Sciences, 9*, 81–85. http://dx.doi.org/10.1037/ebs0000042

Rios, D., Stewart, A. J., & Winter, D. G. (2010). "Thinking she could be the next President": Why identifying with the curriculum matters. *Psychology of Women Quarterly, 34*, 328–338. http://dx.doi.org/10.1111/j.1471-6402.2010.01578.x

Roazen, P. (2003). Interviews on Freud and Jung on Freud and Jung with Henry A. Murray in 1965. *The Journal of Analytical Psychology, 48*, 1–27. http://dx.doi.org/10.1111/1465-5922.t01-1-00001

Rubinstein, G. (1995). The decision to remove homosexuality from the *DSM*: Twenty years later. *American Journal of Psychotherapy, 49*, 416–427. http://dx.doi.org/10.1176/appi.psychotherapy.1995.49.3.416

Ruppel, S. E., Jenkins, W. J., Griffin, J. L., & Kizer, J. B. (2010). Are they depressed or just old? A study of perceptions about the elderly suffering from depression. *North American Journal of Psychology, 12*, 31–42.

Schustack, M. W., & Friedman, H. S. (2008). *The personality reader* (2nd ed.). Boston, MA: Pearson/Allyn & Bacon.

Shields, S. A. (2016). Functionalism, Darwinism, and advances in the psychology of women and gender: From the 19th century to the 21st. *Feminism & Psychology, 26*, 397–404. http://dx.doi.org/10.1177/0959353516663567

Shiraev, E. B., & Levy, D. A. (2010). *Cross-cultural psychology: Critical thinking and contemporary applications*. Boston, MA: Pearson/Allyn & Bacon.

Snowden, L. R. (2003). Bias in mental health assessment and intervention: Theory and evidence. *American Journal of Public Health, 93*, 239–243. http://dx.doi.org/10.2105/AJPH.93.2.239

Snowden, L. R., Catalano, R., & Shumway, M. (2009). Disproportionate use of psychiatric emergency services by African Americans. *Psychiatric Services, 60*, 1664–1671. http://dx.doi.org/10.1176/ps.2009.60.12.1664

Stevens, G., & Gardner, S. (1982). *The women of psychology* (Vol. I & II). Cambridge, MA: Shenkman.

Striepe, M. I., & Tolman, D. L. (2003). Mom, dad, I'm straight: The coming out of gender ideologies in adolescent sexual-identity development. *Journal of Clinical Child and Adolescent Psychology, 32*, 523–530. http://dx.doi.org/10.1207/S15374424JCCP3204_4

Substance Abuse and Mental Health Services Administration. (2015). *A new look at racial/ethnic differences in mental health service use among adults.* Rockville, MD: Author.

Sue, D. W., & Sue, D. (2012). *Counseling the culturally diverse: Theory and practice* (6th ed.). Hoboken, NJ: Wiley.

Sutter, M., & Perrin, P. B. (2016). Discrimination, mental health, and suicidal ideation among LGBTQ people of color. *Journal of Counseling Psychology, 63*, 98–105. http://dx.doi.org/10.1037/cou0000126

Tate, C. C., Youssef, C. P., & Bettergarcia, J. N. (2014). Integrating the study of transgender spectrum and cisgender experiences of self-categorization from a personality perspective. *Review of General Psychology, 18*, 302–312. http://dx.doi.org/10.1037/gpr0000019

Tucker, W. H. (2009). The Cattell convention: The controversy over the award. In W. H. Tucker (Ed.), *The Cattell controversy: Race, science, and ideology* (pp. 139–166). Urbana-Champaign: University of Illinois Press.

U.S. Department of Health and Human Services. (2001). *Mental health: Culture, race, and ethnicity.* Retrieved from https://www.ncbi.nlm.nih.gov/books/NBK44243/

U.S. National Science Foundation. (2015). *Women, minorities, and persons with disabilities in science and engineering.* Retrieved from http://www.nsf.gov/statistics/2015/nsf15311/tables/pdf/tab5-1.pdf

Ware, M. E., & Johnson, D. E. (Eds.). (2000). *Handbook of demonstrations and activities in the teaching of psychology. Vol. III: Personality, abnormal, clinical-counseling, and social* (2nd ed.). New York, NY: Psychology Press/Taylor & Francis.

Wentling, T. (2016). Critical pedagogy: Disrupting classroom hegemony. In K. Haltinner & R. Pilgeram (Eds.), *Teaching gender and sex in contemporary America* (pp. 229–238). Zurich, Switzerland: Springer-Verlag. http://dx.doi.org/10.1007/978-3-319-30364-2_23

Wetzel, E., Bohnke, J. R., Carstensen, C. H., Ziegler, M., & Ostendorf, F. (2013). Do individual response styles matter? Assessing differential item functioning for men and women in the NEO-PI-R. *Journal of Individual Differences, 34*, 69–81. http://dx.doi.org/10.1027/1614-0001/a000102

The WHO World Mental Health Survey Consortium. (2004). Prevalence, severity, and unmet need for treatment of mental disorders in the World Health Organization World Mental Health Surveys. *JAMA, 291*, 2581–2590. http://dx.doi.org/10.1001/jama.291.21.2581

World Health Organization. (2016). *International classification of mental and behavioural disorders, Revision 10.* Geneva, Switzerland: Author.

Zucker, K. J., Cohen-Kettenis, P. T., Drescher, J., Meyer-Bahlburg, H. F., Pfäfflin, F., & Womack, W. M. (2013). Memo outlining evidence for change for gender identity disorder in the *DSM–5. Archives of Sexual Behavior, 42*, 901–914. http://dx.doi.org/10.1007/s10508-013-0139-4

Zuckerman, M. (1998). Some dubious premises in research and theory on racial differences: Scientific, social, and ethical issues. In P. B. Organista, K. M. Chun, & G. Marín (Eds.), *Readings in ethnic psychology* (pp. 59–69). New York, NY: Routledge.

18

Teaching Developmental Psychology

Celebrating the Dialectics of Development

Kathleen S. Gorman and Celeste M. Caviness

Developmental psychology is the study of interindividual differences and intraindividual change. The first accounts for the ways in which individuals differ and the factors that account for such variance, the latter for the ways in which individuals change over time (age) and patterns of these changes across groups of individuals. As such, it is the perfect domain within which to present a framework for the inclusion and infusion of multiculturalism. Further, developmental psychology offers a methodology that allows us to study the course of behavior by examining similarities and differences within and between individuals and over time.

Development represents a synergistic process that is ongoing and constantly changing. Bronfenbrenner's (1977) ecological model provides an enduring framework for the study of the individual and his or her behaviors in context. The individual brings his or her internal and individual diversities—physical, social, cultural—that interact across time and space, in a complex and constantly changing context beginning with parents and siblings and extending out to the community that, in turn, is circumscribed within other contexts including media, policy, government, and the environment. Within this framework, the child, through his or her connections with primary caregivers, links to a wide range of diverse people and experiences. Through work, community, and social exchanges, the diversity of individuals and their communities is captured and reflected.

This chapter offers content and methods for teaching developmental psychology to facilitate a more balanced understanding of two complementary

http://dx.doi.org/10.1037/0000137-019
Integrating Multiculturalism and Intersectionality Into the Psychology Curriculum:
Strategies for Instructors, J. A. Mena and K. Quina (Editors)

243

and competing processes of development: intraindividual change and inter-individual difference. We argue that the course content, methodology, definitions, and demographics should all reflect their inherent diversity. We also need greater inclusivity in our language in the classroom, the way we present material, and the materials chosen for inclusion in the curriculum—for example, avoiding "us" versus "them" and acknowledging "some" instead of "all" when speaking of specific developmental behaviors or processes among groups of diverse individuals. This chapter is presented thematically rather than through a traditional lens of ages and stages, although we have taken care to provide examples and activities that are applicable to different ages and domains of development.

CHOOSING COURSE MATERIALS

Despite efforts by professional organizations, funders, departments, and faculty, there is still a dearth of materials and numerous challenges to teaching from a multiculturally infused perspective. Caviness and Gorman (2015) assessed the inclusion of historically marginalized groups in recently published research across several prominent journals. In *Developmental Psychology*, although nearly 40% (n = 53) of the articles focused on women, fewer than 15% focused specifically on either race or ethnicity (n = 15) or socioeconomic status (SES; n = 17). Most researchers limited their exploration of a multicultural perspective to reporting the demographic characteristics of their sample; for example, gender was reported for 92% of samples, SES for 66%, and race and/or ethnicity for 44%.

In addition, developmental psychology textbooks tend to be fairly uniform and theoretically limited in their approach, at most including chapters or sections within chapters that focus on issues of diversity or multiculturalism. However, there is still a "norm" from which all else deviates rather than incorporating diversity as the core from which to start discussions of development. Although a few texts explicitly take a "multicultural" perspective, they are usually presented as an alternative or supplemental option (Arnett & Maynard, 2017, is a promising exception). Thus, faculty is faced with either using "supplementary materials" or designing a course from scratch without the advantages of a standard text. For advanced level classes, the individually designed course holds great promise, but for an introductory course, the options are limited.

COURSE CONTENT, PERSPECTIVES, AND TERMINOLOGY

Incorporating Diverse Experiences

It is important to fully explore the landscape and avoid the common traps of equating one minority with all minorities—for example, assuming that all people living in poverty are similar or that minorities, whether racial, ethnic, gender, or sexual, are a homogenous group. The intersections of gender, identity, and SES within these groups make them decidedly heterogeneous. This can be challenging, and the language we have to explore these realities is limited. It is also important to be wary of terminology such as *norm* and *average* (statistical and otherwise) that can lead the student to believe that variability from the average suggests deviance rather than difference. For example, when discussing the development of emerging adults (aged 18–25), it is important to explore the realities of all individuals in that age range and not to present those enrolled in college as the standard from which all emerging adults should be examined.

There are other important examples. Food insecurity is highly associated with poverty. However, although the majority of individuals who are food insecure are poor, only about 50% of individuals living below the federal poverty line are food insecure (Coleman-Jensen, Gregory, & Singh, 2014), which means that a large number of low-income households are managing to figure out ways to feed their families. By equating hunger and poverty, we are devaluing the unique attributes of different types of households and missing key questions that should be asked. A similar argument might be made for linking poverty and obesity as if they occurred together when, in fact, the rise in obesity rates is a problem that transcends income and education (Ogden, Lamb, Carroll, & Flegal, 2010). Finally, although Black and Hispanic children are overrepresented among the poor, it is often surprising for students when they realize that the largest single group (absolute value or largest number) of poor children is White.

Another problem is equating risk with causal relationships. A population at greater risk for a negative outcome, be it physical health, mental health, or achievement, does not universally experience specific outcomes. Similarly, populations at low risk for negative outcomes are not free of risk or experiencing the negative outcome. We often find that we have to repeat these findings multiple times because unlearning information that is presumed to be true is often challenging. We must be persistent in our attempts to focus on the facts and not fall into easy stereotyping or assumptions based solely on correlations.

Identifying Contextual Factors

In the developmental framework, it is important to focus on contextual factors that account for associations among variables. For example, income may be statistically related to many outcomes, including poor health, lower education, and higher rates of depression. However, it is more likely that poor health is the result of lack of access to health care, or misdiagnosis relating to race or gender, than income alone. Similarly, higher incomes do not equate with higher abilities to learn but rather with greater access to good schools, enrichment opportunities, and a wide variety of resources. Another example is immigration, where acculturation is generally considered to be a desirable goal: Greater adaptation to mainstream culture is associated with more positive outcomes (e.g., adjustment, achievement). However, a growing body of literature indicates that acculturation is not a simple two-dimensional process and that its effects are not unidirectional (Ferguson, Bornstein, & Pottinger, 2012; Schwartz,

246 Gorman and Caviness

Unger, Zamboanga, & Szapocznik, 2010). In fact, a negative association has been observed between acculturation and a wide range of health and behavioral outcomes, commonly referred to as the *immigrant paradox* (Schwartz et al., 2010). For example, lower levels of acculturation, as measured by predominantly Spanish language use, were found to be associated with somewhat better diets among Hispanic youth compared with English-speaking households (Mazur, Marquis, & Jensen, 2003). When interpreting such outcomes, it is important to reconsider existing theory rather than dismiss an unexpected finding as an aberration.

Acknowledging Multiple Perspectives

We must also be careful not to assume that we understand others' experiences or that because someone is Black or Hispanic or transgender, they share a typical (and predictable) belief or social system. For example, it has been noted that the term *Hispanic* is one that was invented by the United States Census to represent individuals from Spanish-speaking countries from Latin America (as cited in Schwartz et al., 2010). As such, on arrival in the United States, immigrants must "learn" about the Hispanic identity, a concept that is foreign to them and may be perceived as negating their national identity—they are no longer Peruvians or Guatemalans, but Hispanics. Furthermore, Hispanic students from the many Latin American countries may share a common language but little else—their unique cultural and historical backgrounds are often significant contributors to their identity, which may be lost when lumped into the *Hispanic* label. These varying backgrounds and worldviews may create tense, but highly productive, discussions in the classroom. Following a video or multimedia presentation illustrating this point (see the website accompanying this volume at http://pubs.apa.org/books/supp/mena), the class can discuss specific aspects of individuals in the presentation and how their lived experiences are similar to or different from what has been taught in the course, identifying areas where these experiences overlap or diverge from the lives of the students. We have also had success in asking students to examine narratives of individuals living in poverty and identify when they have experienced similar hardship or had far greater access to a wide variety of resources. These discussions have led to thoughtful conversations about the intersection of ethnicity, gender, and social class.

It is important to allow all students to participate while ensuring that biased or stereotyped views are challenged in a way that prompts deeper thinking. We have found that after the first few classes in which the instructor models this behavior, students are willing to challenge each other to clarify or explain their thinking. Through years of acculturation and experience, many students of color are as familiar with stereotypes as their peers and are not always in a position to question them, especially in a classroom they perceive as largely accepting of the stereotyped viewpoint. These large discussion groups work equally well to discuss lesbian, gay, bisexual, transgender, and queer (LGBTQ) individuals and their diverse lives. As with racial and ethnic minority students,

LGBTQ students each have different experiences with coming out, acceptance, and identity that help shape their worldview.

Exploring Conflicting Viewpoints

One example frequently found in the research literature and the popular press, including social media, is the so-called achievement gap, which many times is not defined but usually refers to differences between ethnic and racial minority students and White students—the White students being the referent (see, for example, Burchinal et al., 2011). Notably, some have taken issue with the appropriateness of referring to the achievement gap at all (e.g., Royal, 2012), arguing that it represents a legacy of racial discrimination and continues to use Whites as the gold standard. Royal (2012) stated that the so-called gap places historically marginalized students at a disadvantage and ignores the conditions that lead to such disadvantage. She argued for calling it an *opportunity gap* or a *wealth gap* or some other discrepancy, removing the suggestion that the deficit lies within the individual. Similarly, research has noted increased negative outcomes (e.g., health, substance use, mental health, obesity) among gay women (Institute of Medicine Committee on Lesbian, Gay, Bisexual, and Transgender Health Issues and Research Gaps and Opportunities, 2011). Without considering the context of these women's lives (e.g., social stigma, discrimination), the findings only convey a deviation from the norm (heterosexual women). The terminology associated with both examples suggests an ideal and a failure to live up to standards, standards set by one group and applied inappropriately to others.

Another common notion is that parents are responsible for promoting learning among young children. Much of the research focuses on parenting styles and what parents do or do not do (see, for example, Brooks-Gunn & Markman, 2005). The conclusions of much of this research, often documenting differences between racial and ethnic groups, tend to include recommendations that focus on how to teach minority parents to behave more like White parents. This deficit approach recognizes that certain cultures and behaviors are privileged but argues that this is necessary if we want children to achieve success (Brooks-Gunn & Markman, 2005). Alternatively, others might argue that challenging a set of standards that consistently privileges one group of people over others may be a more effective approach (Callanan & Waxman, 2013; Cole, 2013). Similarly, research has shown that low-income parents, regardless of race and ethnicity or gender, engage in a different style of parenting than middle- and upper-income parents. Although there are significant benefits and downsides to each style, the parenting style favored by middle- and upper-income parents is seen as "better" and the best way to set children up for success in employment, social interactions, and networking, all of which are important in a middle class, White culture (Lareau, 2011).

We have found students are easily engaged in discussing parenting, a topic ripe for exploring multiple issues, particularly when there are conflicting viewpoints such as those mentioned earlier. Students can be divided into small groups to research a specific parenting behavior or style (e.g., discipline style—authoritarian, authoritative, permissive; language preference—standard English, African American English, Spanish; communication style—directive, conversational). Their research could include the tenets of the style, its defining characteristics, advantages and disadvantages, and most critically, whether it is used by and/or advantages one group of people more than another. Group members can present their research findings and debate with other groups the merits or downsides of their parenting style and whether certain types of parents (and therefore children) are being regarded negatively in academia, research, and the popular press. It is important to manage the tone of discussions about parenting; we have found that students are willing to criticize parents if they sense that is the direction the discussion is leaning, but they are equally willing to look for positive aspects of parenting if nudged in that direction. Veering too far in either direction can be counterproductive.

Frequent discussions about language-minority children provide another interesting example. Language-minority children are frequently reported to perform less well in school and to be at risk for poor achievement and behavior problems in school (Hoff, 2013). Rarely does that conversation include reference to the fact that bilingual children have distinct advantages on a wide range of cognitive domains and that research on bilingualism extends beyond classroom achievement and cognition in childhood to the health of elderly people (Alladi et al., 2013; Yoshida, 2008). Why are children's learning disadvantages discussed separately from their advantages? Why are we not examining monolingual children as the disadvantaged population?

Finally, most developmental psychology texts and courses include a cross-cultural component. Although certainly of interest and important for understanding how research from non-Western societies contributes to our theoretical understanding of developmental processes in significant ways (see, for example, Matsumoto & Yoo, 2006; Super, Harkness, Barry, & Zeitlin, 2011), it is equally important to avoid falling into the false dichotomy of "us" (the United States) versus "them" (non-U.S. societies), where "we" is presented as the norm and "they" are explored in the context of how they deviate from that standard. Cross-cultural data on attachment (Van IJzendoorn & Kroonenberg, 1988), for example, can provide an excellent opportunity for exploring the definitions and meaning of attachment but also call into question the cultural assumptions underlying presumed associations between optimal (secure-attachment) styles and outcomes that vary by country.

CLASSROOM-BASED STRATEGIES

Interpreting Data

Although students are often intimidated by charts, tables, and lots of numbers, providing real data to illustrate points being made in class can be extremely effective. For example, as noted earlier, students often have trouble grasping the concept that although Blacks and Hispanics are more likely to live in poverty, Whites constitute the largest single demographic group living in poverty. Poverty statistics, bar graphs, and pie charts can often be used to help illustrate this difficult concept. Graphics can be useful, particularly when trying to illustrate what may be unexpected findings. For example, statistics comparing infant mortality rates in the United States with other industrialized countries can lead to interesting discussions about the contribution of health care and economics to health outcomes (MacDorman & Mathews, 2009), whereas data comparing parental gender, number, and sexual orientation can help students identify parenting factors that significantly contribute to child outcomes (Biblarz & Stacey, 2010).

Undergraduate students, including U.S. students of diverse backgrounds, often have experienced education from a White privilege perspective. Starting a course with a reading about the culturally rich, diverse people of the United States can be illuminating. We often assign students an article such as Hernandez, Denton, and Macartney (2008) to read before the first class and then think about why we asked them to read it and what it has to do with developmental psychology. We challenge them to move from seeing the data—an increase in immigrant populations, a diversity of languages and backgrounds—as problems to be fixed (deficit perspective) to embracing the reality of our culturally diverse society (exploring and celebrating differences).

Other sources of data include narratives, stories, or even analyses of other work. In each of these examples, the methodology is as important as the results; data gathered through different methodologies can help illustrate different answers to similar questions. Engaging with multiple data collection methods also allows an examination of who contributes to and participates in research. Understanding research results on this deeper level can also help students discover examples of "deviant" versus "different" or a homogeneous referent group. Answering questions about barriers to research participation, the impact of funding agencies' priorities, and how journals make decisions about the worthiness for publication can reinforce these concepts.

Classroom Teaching Techniques

Some techniques that instructors of a multiculturally infused course may implement include small group discussions, interviews, anonymous student surveys, quizzes, self-reflection journals, assumed identity journals, stereotype exploration, videos, multimedia learning resources, service learning, debates, "what-if" pilot research, and applied exercises. New advances in technology and media provide additional ways to gather and use information (e.g., clicker technology, TED talks, and student-built educational websites). A few of these are next highlighted as examples.[1]

---

[1]The companion webpage for this book (http://pubs.apa.org/books/supp/mena) features additional items that instructors can use, including a PowerPoint presentation that covers topics addressed in this chapter, classroom exercises, and a list of recommended videos on the Internet.

Small Group Discussions

Allowing students the time and lower-stakes space (i.e., fewer individuals and no instructor listening consistently to every moment of each group discussion) to grapple with new ideas with their peers is important to the learning process (Morey, 2000; Umbach & Wawrzynski, 2005). These small group discussions also encourage student engagement with diverse peers, which in and of itself is beneficial (Bowman & Brandenberger, 2012; Lee, Williams, & Kilaberia, 2012; Mayhew, Wolniak, & Pascarella, 2008; Zúñiga, Williams, & Berger, 2005). For example, at the beginning of a class period, before the week's readings are discussed as a full class, students can explore the key concepts with their peers and come up with main talking points to share with the larger group. Alternatively, instructors may provide students with a set of questions to respond to, either in groups or individually, and to later share in small groups. In both cases, this activity encourages a deeper understanding of one's perspective while allowing each student an accessible starting point to join a larger discussion.

Self-Reflection

To encourage self-reflection, students can keep a journal and reflect on privilege, social class, parenting style during their childhood, or the impact of the week's lesson on different groups by age, gender, ethnicity, and so forth. These journal entries can be entirely self-driven or can be guided by questions posed by instructors or other students about particular readings. Self-exploration has been noted as a "critical incident" for learning about diverse populations and perspectives across a number of types of courses and instructor styles (Anderson, MacPhee, & Govan, 2000). Journaling is also useful as a way for students to process thoughts and feelings stirred up during class and allows the instructor to keep a close watch on the tenor and pulse of the class.

Assumed Identity Journal

As one way to encourage perspective taking, students can be presented with an assumed identity at the beginning of the course. Throughout the semester, students write from the perspective of the assumed identity to foster critical thinking, understanding, and engagement with course material on a deeper level. In contrast to the semester approach, which may be too ambitious for introductory courses, this type of activity can be used for groups, small projects, or even for one-time assignments in which students are challenged to present ideas from a perspective other than their own. For example, during a unit on parenting, students can write from the perspective of a Latina single mother, a gay couple raising children, or a two-parent African American family. Whether they are semester-long or one-time assignments, these identities are highly adaptable. Indeed, the wider the range of ages, genders, races and ethnicities, and SES represented, the richer the discussions when students report as their assumed identity.[2]

---

[2]A full list of identity profiles and writing instructions are available for download from this book's companion webpage (http://pubs.apa.org/books/supp/mena).

Stereotype Exploration

This exercise is effective in one of the first few course meetings. Stereotypes can be generated by class members and written on the board. It is important that instructors let students know they are being asked for stereotypes they have heard or perhaps hold themselves but that it is not assumed that they believe or subscribe to that stereotype. Once a list is created, it is illustrative to ask where the stereotypes come from (e.g., the media, family and friends, or popular opinion). By examining where stereotypes originate, it becomes easier as a class to challenge them and be aware of them. Listing, discussing, and acknowledging common stereotypes is helpful in two ways: First, students have a forum to voice their thoughts or feelings about topics presented later in class that they may be ashamed of or uncomfortable with sharing later; second, as a group, students can agree to think beyond what is easy or "common knowledge." Heading off stereotypes and assumptions through direct acknowledgment and discussion is one recommended strategy in teaching an ethnic- and culture-based course (Gloria, Rieckmann, & Rush, 2000).

Another exercise that can help students understand and buy into the impact of stereotypes and assumptions related to diverse groups is the Implicit Association Test (IAT; https://implicit.harvard.edu/implicit/), an online test assessing implicit or hidden biases that we all hold. The test can be taken on a number of topics, including gender, race and ethnicity, sexual orientation, weight, and so forth. The results from IAT tests can be upsetting to some individuals, so it is important to talk to students beforehand about the test and inform them that everyone holds implicit biases. Students should not be required to share their results if they are not comfortable doing so. Instead, instructors can ask questions such as "Who was surprised by the results they got on the test?" "Do you think it is possible to be a conscientious person, actively fight and acknowledge bias and privilege, and still get results showing bias on this test?" and "What do you think a result showing bias would mean about the messages we receive every day in society?"

Debates

Asking students to argue a position forces them to think critically (e.g., identify key concepts, seek supporting information, argue a position while referencing to facts presented or known) as opposed to falling back on "common beliefs" or stereotypes. Instructors can assign students to two different articles and then ask them to use information from previous classes to identify strengths or weaknesses in the authors' articles or debate with class members about why an author's perspective is limited or representative. A recent published special section of the journal *Developmental Psychology*, "Deficit or Difference: Integrating Diverse Developmental Paths" (Akhtar & Jaswal, 2013), lends itself to interesting discussions. Authors were asked to discuss their research in terms of deficit versus difference and offer their reasoning, providing students with a framework for debate.

Applied Exercises

Having students apply key concepts learned in class to their lives or put course material into practice is a wonderful way to foster learning. For example, during a unit with an emphasis on low-income families, students can identify monthly budget needs, search for actual prices, and try to fit their "needs" into a prede- termined monthly budget.[3] This exercise can help illustrate the daily monetary struggle for the working poor. Alternatively, asking students to prepare and eat all their meals using only the amount of money a family receiving benefits from the Supplemental Nutrition Assistance Program would have available to them for a week has resulted in incredible insights for students. In addition, using current news items or asking students to identify themes from the news that connect to their coursework can be challenging but worthwhile because it forces students to see that the ideas and concepts discussed in class are not isolated but represented in the real, everyday experiences of people in their communities. We have found that at the beginning of the semester, students are uncertain what they are looking for and often bring in articles that con- tain words that have been discussed in class but without particular links to themes of the class. By the end of the semester, they have developed an understanding that their pursuit is not so much a specific article to fulfill the assignment but that much of the "news" offers insights into the theories of development presented in class. Toward the end of the semester, students are also able to identify problems with the articles, whether it is bias in report- ing, authors relying on common stereotypes, or problems with us-versus- them thinking in examples and conclusions drawn in the news items. These kinds of activities lead to rich discussions that allow students to share their ideas and develop connections between their readings and the world in which they live.

CONCLUSION

Teaching developmental psychology is an exciting opportunity to explore the great diversity of development and the rich complexities of human nature across the lifespan. Development is, in some ways, an easy topic to teach because all students have a developmental trajectory that is unique and var- ied that they can use as a reference point. Nonetheless, it poses great chal- lenges to the instructor who wishes to ensure that students are exposed to the vast diversities surrounding them in an unbiased and theoretically sound way. Developmental psychology instructors have to find appropriate texts and resources that meet the needs of their students and elicit engagement and

---

[3]Instructions for two applied exercises—one about creating a budget for a family of three and another focusing on the challenges of being a low-income single parent— are available from the companion webpage for this book (http://pubs.apa.org/books/supp/mena).

critical thinking from them. Instructors must also be sensitive and constantly checking their own biases to allow students the space for individual exploration and learning.

The need for inclusion and acceptance is more critical than ever. The university, the United States, and the world are rife with divisiveness, racism, prejudice, bigotry, sexism, and homophobia. Psychology students will benefit from exposure to points of view that are inclusive and forward thinking. By acknowledging and embracing the diversity of our culture and development, we will best serve our students and set them up to enter the next phase of their development as more open-minded citizens.

REFERENCES

Akhtar, N., & Jaswal, V. K. (2013). Deficit or difference? Interpreting diverse developmental paths: An introduction to the special section. *Developmental Psychology, 49,* 1–3. http://dx.doi.org/10.1037/a0029851

Alladi, S., Bak, T. H., Duggirala, V., Surampudi, B., Shailaja, M., Shukla, A. K., . . . Kaul, S. (2013). Bilingualism delays age at onset of dementia, independent of education and immigration status. *Neurology, 81,* 1938–1944. http://dx.doi.org/10.1212/01.wnl.0000436620.33155.a4

Anderson, S. K., MacPhee, D., & Govan, D. (2000). Infusion of multicultural issues in curricula: A student perspective. *Innovative Higher Education, 25,* 37–57. http://dx.doi.org/10.1023/A:1007584318881

Arnett, J. J., & Maynard, A. (2017). *Human development: A cultural approach* (2nd ed.). New York, NY: Pearson Education.

Biblarz, T. J., & Stacey, J. (2010). How does the gender of parents matter? *Journal of Marriage and Family, 72,* 3–22. http://dx.doi.org/10.1111/j.1741-3737.2009.00678.x

Bowman, N. A., & Brandenberger, J. W. (2012). Experiencing the unexpected: Toward a model of college diversity experiences and attitude change. *The Review of Higher Education, 35,* 179–205. http://dx.doi.org/10.1353/rhe.2012.0016

Bronfenbrenner, U. (1977). Toward an experimental ecology of human development. *American Psychologist, 32,* 513–531. http://dx.doi.org/10.1037/0003-066X.32.7.513

Brooks-Gunn, J., & Markman, L. B. (2005). The contribution of parenting to ethnic and racial gaps in school readiness. *The Future of Children, 15,* 139–168. http://dx.doi.org/10.1353/foc.2005.0001

Burchinal, M., McCartney, K., Steinberg, L., Crosnoe, R., Friedman, S. L., McLoyd, V., & Pianta, R. (2011). Examining the Black–White achievement gap among low-income children using the NICHD study of early child care and youth development. *Child Development, 82,* 1404–1420. http://dx.doi.org/10.1111/j.1467-8624.2011.01620.x

Callanan, M., & Waxman, S. (2013). Commentary on special section: Deficit or difference? Interpreting diverse developmental paths. *Developmental Psychology, 49,* 80–83. http://dx.doi.org/10.1037/a0029741

Caviness, C. M., & Gorman, K. (2015). *Historically marginalized groups in psychological science.* Unpublished manuscript.

Cole, M. (2013). Differences and deficits in psychological research in historical perspective: A commentary on the special section. *Developmental Psychology, 49,* 84–91. http://dx.doi.org/10.1037/a0029623

Coleman-Jensen, A., Gregory, C., & Singh, A. (2014). *Household food security in the United States in 2013* (ERR-173). Washington, DC: U.S. Department of Agriculture, Economic Research Service.

Ferguson, G. M., Bornstein, M. H., & Pottinger, A. M. (2012). Tridimensional acculturation and adaptation among Jamaican adolescent-mother dyads in the United States. *Child Development, 83*, 1486–1493. http://dx.doi.org/10.1111/j.1467-8624.2012.01787.x

Gloria, A. M., Rieckmann, T. R., & Rush, J. D. (2000). Issues and recommendations for teaching and ethnic/culture-based course. *Teaching of Psychology, 27*, 102–107. http://dx.doi.org/10.1207/S15328023TOP2702_05

Hernandez, D., Denton, N., & Macartney, S. (2008). Children in immigrant families: Looking to America's future. *Social Policy Report, 22*, 3–23.

Hoff, E. (2013). Interpreting the early language trajectories of children from low-SES and language minority homes: Implications for closing achievement gaps. *Developmental Psychology, 49*, 4–14. http://dx.doi.org/10.1037/a0027238

Institute of Medicine Committee on Lesbian, Gay, Bisexual, and Transgender Health Issues and Research Gaps and Opportunities. (2011). *The health of lesbian, gay, bisexual, and transgender people: Building a foundation for better understanding.* Washington, DC: National Academies Press.

Lareau, A. (2011). *Unequal childhoods: Class, race, and family life* (2nd ed.). Berkeley: University of California Press.

Lee, A., Williams, R., & Kilaberia, R. (2012). Engaging diversity in first-year college classrooms. *Innovative Higher Education, 37*, 199–213. http://dx.doi.org/10.1007/s10755-011-9195-7

MacDorman, M. F., & Mathews, T. J. (2009). *Behind international rankings of infant mortality: How the United States compares with Europe* (NCHS Data Brief, No. 23). Hyattsville, MD: National Center for Health Statistics

Matsumoto, D., & Yoo, S. H. (2006). Toward a new generation of cross-cultural research. *Perspectives on Psychological Science, 1*, 234–250. http://dx.doi.org/10.1111/j.1745-6916.2006.00014.x

Mayhew, M. J., Wolniak, G. C., & Pascarella, E. T. (2008). How educational practices affect the development of life-long learning orientations in traditionally-aged undergraduate students. *Research in Higher Education, 49*, 337–356. http://dx.doi.org/10.1007/s11162-007-9081-4

Mazur, R. E., Marquis, G. S., & Jensen, H. H. (2003). Diet and food insufficiency among Hispanic youths: Acculturation and socioeconomic factors in the third National Health and Nutrition Examination Survey. *The American Journal of Clinical Nutrition, 78*, 1120–1127. http://dx.doi.org/10.1093/ajcn/78.6.1120

Morey, A. I. (2000). Changing higher education curricula for a global and multicultural world. *Higher Education in Europe, 25*, 25–39. http://dx.doi.org/10.1080/03797720050002170

Ogden, C. L., Lamb, M. M., Carroll, M. D., & Flegal, K. M. (2010, December). *Obesity and socioeconomic status in adults: United States, 2005–2008* (National Center for Health Statistics, No. 50). Washington, DC: U.S. Department of Health & Human Services, Center for Disease Control and Prevention.

Royal, C. (2012, November 8). *Please stop using the phrase 'achievement gap'* [web log post]. Retrieved from http://m.good.is/posts/please-stop-using-the-phrase-achievement-gap?goback=.gde_148853_member_186259636

Schwartz, S. J., Unger, J. B., Zamboanga, B. L., & Szapocznik, J. (2010). Rethinking the concept of acculturation: Implications for theory and research. *American Psychologist, 65*, 237–251. http://dx.doi.org/10.1037/a0019330

Super, C., Harkness, S., Barry, O., & Zeitlin, M. (2011). Think locally, act globally: Contributions of African research to child development. *Child Development Perspectives, 5*, 119–125. http://dx.doi.org/10.1111/j.1750-8606.2011.00166.x

Umbach, P. D., & Wawrzynski, M. R. (2005). Faculty do matter: The role of college faculty in student learning and engagement. *Research in Higher Education, 46,* 153–184. http://dx.doi.org/10.1007/s11162-004-1598-1

Van IJzendoorn, M. H., & Kroonenberg, P. M. (1988). Cross-cultural patterns of attachment: A meta-analysis of the strange situation. *Child Development, 59,* 147–156. http://dx.doi.org/10.2307/1130396

Yoshida, H. (2008, November). The cognitive consequences of early bilingualism. *Zero to Three.* Retrieved from https://www.uh.edu/class/psychology/dcbn/_docs/Zero_Yoshida.pdf

Zúñiga, X., Williams, E. A., & Berger, J. B. (2005). Action-oriented democratic outcomes: The impact of student involvement with campus diversity. *Journal of College Student Development, 46,* 660–678. http://dx.doi.org/10.1353/csd.2005.0069

19

Overcoming Student Defensiveness in Social Psychology Courses

A Collaborative Workshop for Discussing Privilege and Prejudice

Andrea L. Dottolo

Many social psychology courses contain a great deal of information forged from and focusing on a wide diversity of groups and relationships between and within them. Rather than providing an overview of content, this chapter focuses on a specific process for discussing multicultural content, especially addressing negative student reactions. The exercise described here illuminates social psychology constructs as a way to incorporate and understand defensiveness in the classroom.[1]

Fairchild (1970) defined *culture* as "all behavior patterns socially acquired and socially transmitted by means of symbols" (p. 80). This definition is useful, but, like others, it does not mention institutional and social structures that confer dominance of some cultures over others (Williams, 2015). This conceptual gap can be addressed from a feminist perspective, which interrogates systems of institutional power structures by posing such questions such as: Who has power? What is the dominant narrative that values certain groups, ideologies, and cultures over others? Whose voices are missing? Centralizing feminist,

[1]A PowerPoint presentation featuring topics discussed in this chapter and a defensiveness workshop worksheet which instructors can use in their classrooms are available for download from this book's companion webpage (http://pubs.apa.org/books/supp/mena).

The author thanks Rhoda K. Unger, Oliva M. Espin, Sandra M. McEvoy, Sarah M. Tillery, and Champika K. Soysa for helpful feedback and suggestions.

http://dx.doi.org/10.1037/0000137-020
Integrating Multiculturalism and Intersectionality Into the Psychology Curriculum: Strategies for Instructors, J. A. Mena and K. Quina (Editors)

multicultural perspectives throughout the course is one way of achieving this transformation.

A common concern for faculty teaching social psychology, or any course that incorporates multiculturalism, is student defensiveness. Many students have had little exposure to cultures outside their own. Preparing students for a course that addresses "difference" (from them) requires providing them with the conceptual tools and language to understand and identify reactions to challenging material, especially in discussions, and providing a guide for the work of the semester. I also rely on feminist pedagogy, which focuses on naming and addressing the power relationships inherent in education, in a variety of ways (see Freire, 1970; hooks, 1994).

I have created an exercise I call the "defensiveness workshop" to mark the ways it is a collaborative effort, offering a transformative space in which both students and instructors can be reflective and transparent about our triggers, defenses, and prejudices about a range of social, political, and economic issues. In traditional psychology "fight or flight" describes opposing defensive reactions to threat. I use "flight and fight" to explore how humans are much more complicated in our responses, sometimes using multiple defense mechanisms simultaneously. I typically take a full class session at the beginning of the semester to cover the material of the workshop, but instructors can also break it into small parts, covering a few defense mechanisms at a time. My students and I engage in the workshop before any formal reading, but I have also used it as a way to cover material in a particular chapter, such as a discussion of psychodynamic approaches.

Instructors can prepare for multicultural instruction by questioning their own privilege, defensiveness, bias, and cultural assumptions by self-administering the exercises (if they have not done so already) before tackling the topic of defensiveness with students. The workshop requires a level of honest, critical self-awareness on the part of the instructor first to model for the students. Self-awareness is an ever-evolving process, so I encourage instructors to share their challenges, as they feel comfortable, and to be open to the ways in which our students become our teachers. This approach requires students and instructors to examine themselves as active participants in culture as well as observers of "other" cultures.

On the first day of class, I introduce myself by describing my academic and personal history, and I explain how they inform my approach to teaching and learning. As a feminist psychologist, I place social context and power at the center of my teaching and research, not only bringing feminist questions and concerns into my courses but also using principles of feminist pedagogy to guide the process, including challenging traditional pedagogy (and power relationships) and empowerment and building community (see Brown, 1992; Hoffmann & Stake, 1998). Making this explicit at the outset provides students with the cultural context of the classroom that we will collaboratively shape for the remainder of the semester. This might be a place where students can share and reflect on their interests, backgrounds, and cultural experiences to acknowledge and explore ways in which their identities and perspectives are culturally constructed.

Instructors can ask students to list their identities, including race, class, gender, sexuality, age, nation, and religion, followed by questions for writing and/or discussion, such as: Which identities are privileged, and which are marginalized? Is it possible to separate race from gender? Why or why not? See Gay (2018), Hidalgo (1993), and Locke (2014) for more self-awareness exercises and McIntosh (2015) for an activity to explore conferred advantage.

This exercise also introduces the key terms we use throughout the course, and we review definitions of sex, gender, gender identity, sexuality, racism, classism, and multiculturalism, to name a few. Another key term to contextualize and explicate this common vocabulary is *intersectionality*, which can be understood as the idea that our "identities and varied relationships to systems of power and privilege are simultaneous and mutually constitutive" (Dottolo & Stewart, 2008, p. 350). This requires the incorporation and consideration of identities, cultures, and axes of social power, including race and ethnicity alongside class, sexuality, age, nationality, disability, and more. Without an appreciation of intersectionality as a core concept, I believe that classroom work on multiculturalism is incomplete, and we shirk our responsibility to students' knowledge of social psychology as well as their lived experiences.

I use a *flipped classroom*, a relatively recent trend in education that focuses on applied learning and student engagement. The structure reverses the sequence of learning so "that which is traditionally done in class is now done at home, and that which is traditionally done as homework is now completed in class" (Bergmann & Sams, 2012, p. 13). My flipped classroom is devoted to activities, exercises, and demonstrations with little or no lecture, which requires students to complete the assigned reading before class to participate. The flipped classroom does not privilege those who learn best with a lecture format, and the dialogue can build cross-cultural communication skills.

Because class sessions are devoted to exercises, demonstrations, activities, small and large group work, critical reflection, and social engagement, preparing the class to identify and manage difficult and defensive reactions is a necessary step. I have used or adapted materials from the journals *Teaching of Psychology* and *Psychology of Women Quarterly* (teaching briefs), the useful website Breaking the Prejudice Habit (http://breakingprejudice.org), and films and other resources from the Media Education Foundation (http://www.mediaed.org). I encourage instructors to explore supplemental textbook materials not only for social psychology but also other courses on gender and diversity, as well as those in related fields. Finding appropriate exercises requires a great deal of preparation and research, and each instructor should adapt them to their style and comfort.

The flipped classroom may not be an option for some instructors. I have used the defensiveness workshop in my lecture-only classes, partial lecture classes, and in the flipped version. In the lecture version, I created visual slides with the content that follows and presented it in a more traditional manner. My ongoing goal is to find new and different ways for students to engage directly with their assumptions, biases, and perspectives on culture and social structures.

THE DEFENSIVENESS WORKSHOP

Classroom Guidelines

Early in the course, I explain that we will be discussing issues of multicultural-ism, a term already loaded for many students, and that we will together develop classroom guidelines for participation and discussion. I divide students into pairs or triads and ask them to think about their favorite classroom experience and to visualize and informally record the traits and characteristics of the teacher, the students, and themselves in that classroom space. I ask, What was it like to be in that class? How did the students treat each other? How did the instructor behave? After sharing some of those memories, each group writes a minimum of two guidelines for classroom engagement, especially now know-ing the course will center on issues of culture. Students typically construct sim-ilar guidelines, such as trying not to judge or react defensively; keeping an open mind; communicating effectively; making the classroom a safe, confidential place; and creating a sense of community. Each group shares their guidelines and, as a class, we write and revise the collective ground rules.

I am always pleasantly surprised by how well they engage in this activity and how excited they are to share their memories and participate in devel-oping a new class climate. I often suggest a few guidelines or gently caution about wording; for example, students often try to convey the idea that "everyone is entitled to their own opinion." We deconstruct this by discuss-ing the idea that some opinions are grounded in evidence, whereas others are not, and that some "opinions" overtly and intentionally harm other stu-dents or groups of people.

I then add our finalized list to the syllabus and distribute it, thereby making it part of the official class policies. Students find this process refreshing because they took part in creating and defining the classroom space, often a new expe-rience. They feel a sense of ownership and are invested in both the physical and intellectual space of the classroom.

Defense Mechanisms

I start by distributing a list of key terms, encouraging students to ask questions, provide examples, and take notes. We begin with a basic review of *defense mech-anisms*, often described as "methods used by the ego to prevent unconscious anxiety or threatening thoughts from entering consciousness" (Wade & Tavris, 2012, p. 43). We discuss that defensive reactions can be understood as reason-able, understandable psychological responses to anything that is construed as a "threat" (David & Lyons-Ruth, 2005). Exploring the language of defensiveness can help us identify a threat and ask questions about why it is threatening. This is especially important in a classroom context, where we explore issues considered "controversial" (e.g., sexuality, rape, reproductive freedom) or top-ics that cultural assumptions deem "normal" and "natural" (e.g., gender, race, class) and that questioning them might feel like a threat. It is that moment when discomfort, fear, anxiety, anger, or some other negative emotion arises that can sometimes be a clue that we feel threatened. The exercise is intended to provide language to identify those times as critical to the learning process.

Why Do We Sometimes Feel Defensive?

I emphasize that the forms of defensiveness we discuss are not exhaustive and that many overlap.

Ingroup bias involves favoring one's own group on the basis of identification (Tajfel & Turner, 1979). We tend to defend our group, even one that is temporary or arbitrary, and to oppose and demonize the other group (e.g., team sports in gym class, or group projects in academic classes). Simply assigning people to different groups can elicit this defensive strategy. When discussing issues we feel strongly about, in-group bias can be especially apparent. Introducing controversial topics allows students to understand that we can be attached to a position, which we deem the "right" way to do things, according to our cultural norms and practices. For example, when learning about parenting, there is cultural variation about parent–child co-sleeping (Keller et al., 2005). North American parents tend to expect their babies to sleep alone, whereas Mayan Indian, African villager, and rural Italian infants typically sleep with their mother for their first few years of life. Students sometimes respond to this information with in-group bias, suggesting that the North American way is "normal" or universal and the others are "weird," as they might say, and perhaps even detrimental.

Belief in a just world is the faith, trust, and confidence that the world is fair, where *just* is derived from the word *justice*. Students may have encountered this idea in other contexts and classrooms, where it is also known as the "myth of meritocracy," the "just world hypothesis," or the "American dream" (Frank, 2016). I invite students to derive a definition of the term *meritocracy*, and they usually come up with the idea of a system in which people succeed on the basis of merit or accomplishment. This is especially challenging because North Americans collectively desperately want to believe in this idea. I provide the example that if I apply for a job, and I do not receive the job offer, I want to believe that it was because I did not deserve it or that there was another candidate better qualified than me. I do not want to believe that I was rejected for any other reason, such as my gender, ethnicity, culture, sexuality, or social class.

The American dream (another way to describe a belief in a just world) is especially familiar to students, and we discuss that encountering information that does not seem "fair" can evoke defensiveness. There is a painful duality to this conviction: If I believe that if I work hard, I will succeed, I must also believe that those who fail must not have worked hard or deserved the mistreatment, injustice, or marginalized conditions in which they live. Students learn that terms such as *belief*, *hypothesis*, *myth*, and *dream* refer to socially constructed systems, which can feel like absolutes.

Investment in the status quo is the idea that we have a vested interest in the way things are now, in a system that rewards certain characteristics and behaviors.

I share a somewhat trivial personal example to elicit other examples from students: I like lipstick. I have many of them, and I am invested in a culture that rewards me for wearing lipstick. So, if a law were passed tomorrow that made it illegal to wear lipstick, I might invoke claims about culture in a defensive way. At first, some students react with confusion or a chuckle at this example, but it is useful for several reasons. First, it begins with the seemingly mundane as a way to make practical those ways in which we are "invested" in ideas and behaviors and therefore may be potentially threatened. This can model ways for students to think about their attachments and investments. It also opens the possibility for discussing cultural expectations and variations about gender performances—although lipstick might seem small or inconsequential, cultural norms of gender, gender identity, and sexuality (and the consequences when they are transgressed) are not. Yet tabloid covers often have some version of a headline that reads "Who's gay? Who's not?" with photos of suspected gay and lesbian celebrities. We might counter with, "Who cares?" but we have a vested interest in a system that thinks that those differences matter, with material consequences for those sexual identities. I then elicit examples from students about how they might experience an investment in the status quo.

Fear of change, being afraid when emotional and material conditions become different than they were, is closely associated with investment in the status quo (Thornton, 2016). I ask students to consider the following: If the system changes, what will that mean about how I am seen, evaluated, and ranked in society? How will I understand myself? If I cannot wear lipstick, what will that mean? This fear might develop not only if a law was passed prohibiting lipstick but also, for example, if professional standards would not allow lipstick in the workplace or my lesbian feminist community might not respect me for particular performances of femininity.

These examples can be processed with students in a class discussion, or students can be paired to create and share their examples. Alternatively, students might be assigned to find an article, essay, or even a form of popular culture that demonstrates one or more of the defense mechanisms. Instructors might assign a short in-class reading (e.g., an op-ed or blog) after which students identify forms of defensiveness in the text.

Recognizing Defensiveness in the Classroom
The second part of the workshop examines how we recognize defensiveness, so we might be able to identify its manifestations. As in the first part, I discuss each term and elicit discussion.

Denial "occurs when people refuse to admit that something unpleasant is happening" (Wade & Tavris, 2012, p. 43). For example, when learning about the history of bias in intelligence testing, students sometimes respond, "But that can't be true!" Another form of denial is to claim that racial injustice is a thing of the past, that "it's all over now," sometimes accompanied with relief that because African Americans now occupy some top positions in business, government, and more, we no longer have to consider the institutional, cultural, and social impacts of racism. Denial protects us from what we do not want to see, simultaneously absolving us from the responsibility of any wrongdoing (Dorpat, 1985; Matias, 2018). When denial arises in the classroom, instructors must assess the emotional climate and intention of the assertion to maintain a positive, affirming learning environment for all students. Instructors may redirect (e.g., "What does the rest of the class think?") to create space for other students to respond. Another strategy is to ask students to return to the list of defense mechanisms to assess which form is present in the room, reminding the group that this perspective may be shared by many others in the class (to normalize the defense). If a student claims, "But that's not true!" an instructor might ask the class, "Okay, but what might it mean for us if it is true? What is at stake for us if it is?"

Avoidance, like denial, involves evading unpleasant or threatening information (Cramer, 2000). Students who find the content threatening may engage in avoidance by not coming to class, not doing the reading, or not participating. I tell the students how I feel when I encounter commercials for a charity for starving children in an impoverished village of an "underdeveloped" nation. I explain how I feel guilty, angry, scared, and powerless all at the same time. To avoid feeling this way, I change the channel and evade the negative emotions by avoiding the program entirely. Students tend to appreciate my willingness to reveal my vulnerability, relieved to see that I am not immune from defensiveness. I encourage instructors to offer personal examples of defensive strategies throughout this exercise, not only to illuminate the concepts but also to foster identification with the students.

In articulating my defensiveness, as in the previous example, I illustrate how giving voice to our fears is a courageous act of learning. When we are afraid, another way to defend against it is to minimize. *Minimization* occurs when we respond to a threat by reducing it, thus making it more manageable. For example, when encountering reports of the murders of Michael Brown or Eric Garner, two unarmed African American men fatally shot by police officers, a typical minimizing response might be to say, "Not all cops are bad," or worse, "All lives matter." It is important to note that we minimize not only to reduce the problem but also our responsibility for finding solutions (Thomas, Ditzfeld, & Showers, 2013). Cultural norms also prescribe gendered expressions of emotion. Women often experience minimization as a response to their anger, being told to "calm down" or "relax," that their emotions are "too big" or "too much," and that they should be emotionally and physically smaller. Men tend to experience minimization in response to their fear, sadness, or any expression that is deemed by the culture to show vulnerability.

Another way to excuse or downsize our discomfort is through *rationalization*, which involves inventing a "plausible" explanation for acts or opinions that are based on other causes that an individual finds difficult to accept (Buunk & Dijkstra, 2001). An incorrect rationalization as a response to the police shootings is to "justify" them by "explaining" that "African Americans steal" (Michael Brown was accused of stealing cigars), and because the police have to reduce crime, their responses are "understandable." Some students may be surprised to learn that White women, especially teenagers, form the demographic that is most likely to shoplift. "In fact, . . . more than two thirds of the shoplifters apprehended in this nation are White females" (Asquith & Bristow, 2000, p. 273). Yet most retailers do not racially profile White teenage girls.

Blaming the victim occurs when we hold responsible or at fault the person who has been harmed or mistreated (Ryan, 2010). It involves redirecting or displacing anger onto the target of injustice. Students are so familiar with this form of defensiveness in their daily lives that immediately after providing a definition I ask for the first example that comes to their minds. They always instantly mention rape—that a woman who was raped must have been "asking for it." This is a particularly poignant moment to pause and reflect on the ubiquity of violence against women in our lives. Another example involves attitudes about mental illness. Forty-three percent of Americans think that people who have a mental illness "bring it on themselves," 35% think it is a "punishment for sinful behavior," and 19% point to "lack of willpower or self-discipline" (Comer, 2010). I point out that blaming the victim is not only harmful when "we" blame "them," but also, as a culture, we internalize these narratives, blaming ourselves when we inevitably suffer. Women blame other women and themselves for rape, and we blame ourselves for emotional and psychological suffering and illness.

Counterattack involves expressing anger as a form of defense, an attack in response to a perceived threat or attack (Miller & Josephs, 2009). It is a quick response that does not take into consideration the other side and is often reflective of dichotomous thinking. For example, when learning that convicted sex offenders are more likely to be White, middle class, and married (Corrigan, 2006), a student might respond, "Not my husband!" In this instance, the student perceived this information as threatening, as an attack on all White, middle-class, married men, and defended against this with a counterattack.

Protectiveness is guarding someone else from a perceived attack. When encountering the previously mentioned fact about convicted sex offenders, a woman-identified student might turn to one of the men in the class and assure him, "She doesn't mean you!" Again, the information was perceived as a threat (perhaps to all men), and as women are especially socialized as caretakers, they sometimes want to come to the rescue, feeling defensive when they believe someone else and their culture is being attacked.

Anger is an obvious "fight" form of defensiveness (Rodriguez Mosquera, Fischer, Manstead, & Zaalberg, 2008). The anger may be directed toward a specific issue, such as child sexual abuse, or one may experience generalized anger at learning about systems and structures of injustice. Students sometimes feel resentful that information about inequalities might have been "withheld" from them in their academic curricula. We discuss how knowledge is culturally constructed and how the myth of meritocracy is supported. We also discuss that anger is necessary as a part of social change and together brainstorm ways to direct anger into helpful and productive outlets. For example, other cultures have created social systems that look different from those of the United States, but our own ethnocentric culture often makes it challenging for us to learn about how education, medicine, and social welfare are structured in other cultural contexts. I might provide examples of Scandinavian countries, such as Sweden, Norway, and Denmark, to explain that there are alternatives, possibilities, and different ways to imagine social institutions (Eitzen, 2010).

Distancing involves separating or creating space between the self and the injustices of society (Spivey, 2005). This is most evident when students discuss how "society" is unjust or that "society" is "going to hell in a handbasket." We are reminded that the classroom is a microcosm and representation of "society." Psychology instructors might be most familiar with this reaction when students learn about Milgram's (1963) study of obedience. When students discover that a majority of participants administered shock as punishment, some exclaim, "I would never do that!" I remind them that this is precisely what the experts that Milgram consulted had predicted, that Americans "would never do that" (or only at small rates, consistent with the frequency of sadism in the population). Distancing provides protection from those uncomfortable or painful realizations and also increases our hostility toward others. In the Milgram study, the more distance the teacher had from the learner, the bigger the shock they were willing to administer.

Finally, some use *religious* or *biological law* to justify structural inequalities—for example, using the Bible, Torah, and/or Koran to explain why a group of people should be marginalized or oppressed. Another example is when religious scholars "discover" biological differences between groups to legitimate a cultural script, as when in the 19th-century scholars spent a great deal of energy "proving" that women were less intelligent than men on the basis of brain size and shape (Shields, 1975). These claims were used to justify excluding women from education, entering the workforce, voting, and participating in a variety of other social domains. Sometimes students are quick to remark that such "nonsense" happened "a long time ago"; this can allow a transition to the ways in which our current cultural climate is obsessed with biology: The field of evolutionary psychology is growing (Chrisler, 2007), and scholars are still searching for brain-based differences (Brizendine, 2006), hormonal influences (Berenbaum & Beltz, 2016), and the "gay gene" (Hamer, 2011).

CONCLUSION

This exercise is intended to serve as a tool for understanding defensiveness and is often revisited throughout the semester. It provides a useful strategy to address classroom dynamics in the moment, or even in subsequent class periods, when everyone has had a chance to reflect. For example, in the midst of a discussion that is particularly heated or charged, I often interrupt the conversation and instruct students to retrieve their defensiveness workshop handout and consider what is happening at a reactive level. Facilitating the workshop early in the semester also prepares students to discuss the course material, serving as a guide and foundation for the coming weeks. Sometimes students registered for the course with anxieties and concerns about the topics they anticipate will be addressed, and the workshop helps them understand their reactions. Furthermore, the language of defensiveness helps them understand the reactions of individuals in their personal lives.

Most social psychology textbooks include material that either explicitly mentions defensiveness or at least might invoke defensive responses. Other readings to consider include those in interdisciplinary anthologies intended for gender studies, cultural studies, or American studies. Instructors might also consult the references at the end of this chapter to assign as readings to students, depending on the level and context of the course.

Students can apply one or more forms of defensiveness and multiculturalism to their daily lives by finding and writing reactions to cultural examples of defensiveness in the media, especially ways in which news reporters or pundits cover events or issues that are especially racist, classist, sexist, homophobic, ageist, and more, as symptoms of a cultural context.

Students have commented that they appreciated feeling safe, being engaged by the activities, and being comfortable in the learning environment. By cocreating language that helps us better understand our reactions and communicate more effectively and responsibly, we can participate in and facilitate a safe learning environment in which both students and instructors can teach and learn from each other.

REFERENCES

Asquith, J. L., & Bristow, D. N. (2000). To catch a thief: A pedagogical study of retail shoplifting. *Journal of Education for Business, 75*, 271–276. http://dx.doi.org/10.1080/08832320009599027

Berenbaum, S. A., & Beltz, A. M. (2016). How early hormones shape gender development. *Current Opinion in Behavioral Sciences, 7*, 53–60. http://dx.doi.org/10.1016/j.cobeha.2015.11.011

Bergmann, J., & Sams, A. (2012). *Flip your classroom: Reach every student in every class every day.* Eugene, OR: Iste.

Brizendine, L. (2006). *The female brain.* New York, NY: Morgan Road Books.

Brown, J. (1992). Theory or practice—What exactly is feminist pedagogy? *The Journal of General Education, 41*, 51–63.

Buunk, B. P., & Dijkstra, P. (2001). Rationalizations and defensive attributions for high-risk sex among heterosexuals. *Patient Education and Counseling, 45*, 127–132. http://dx.doi.org/10.1016/S0738-3991(01)00114-8

Chrisler, J. C. (2007). The subtleties of meaning: Still arguing after all these years. *Feminism & Psychology, 17*, 442–446. http://dx.doi.org/10.1177/0959353507084323

Comer, R. J. (2010). *Abnormal psychology* (7th ed.). New York, NY: Worth.

Corrigan, R. (2006). Making meaning of Megan's law. *Law & Social Inquiry, 31*, 267–312. http://dx.doi.org/10.1111/j.1747-4469.2006.00012.x

Cramer, P. (2000). Defense mechanisms in psychology today. Further processes for adaptation. *American Psychologist, 55*, 637–646. http://dx.doi.org/10.1037/0003-066X.55.6.637

David, D. H., & Lyons-Ruth, K. (2005). Differential attachment responses of male and female infants to frightening maternal behavior: Tend or befriend versus fight or flight? *Infant Mental Health Journal, 26*, 1–18. http://dx.doi.org/10.1002/imhj.20033

Dorpat, T. (1985). *Denial and defense in the therapeutic situation*. New York, NY: Jason Aronson.

Dottolo, A. L., & Stewart, A. J. (2008). "Don't ever forget now, you're a Black man in America": Intersections of race, class and gender in encounters with the police. *Sex Roles, 59*, 350–364. http://dx.doi.org/10.1007/s11199-007-9387-x

Eitzen, S. (2010). *Solutions to social problems: Lessons from other societies* (5th ed.). Boston, MA: Pearson.

Fairchild, H. P. (1970). *Dictionary of sociology and related sciences*. Totowa, NJ: Rowan & Allanheld.

Frank, R. H. (2016). *Success and luck: Good fortune and the myth of the meritocracy*. Princeton, NJ: Princeton University Press. http://dx.doi.org/10.1515/9781400880270

Freire, P. (1970). *Pedagogy of the oppressed*. New York, NY: Continuum.

Gay, G. (2018). *Culturally responsive teaching: Theory, research, and practice* (3rd ed.). New York, NY: Teachers College Press.

Hamer, D. (2011). *The science of desire: The search for the gay gene and the biology of behavior*. New York, NY: Simon & Schuster.

Hidalgo, N. (1993). Multicultural teacher introspection. In T. Perry & J. Fraser (Eds.), *Freedom's plow: Teaching in the multicultural classroom* (pp. 99–108). New York, NY: Routledge.

Hoffmann, F., & Stake, J. (1998). Feminist pedagogy in theory and practice: An empirical investigation. *NWSA Journal, 10*, 79–97. http://dx.doi.org/10.2979/NWS.1998.10.1.79

hooks, b. (1994). *Teaching to transgress: Education as the practice of freedom*. New York, NY: Routledge.

Keller, H., Abels, M., Lamm, B., Yovsi, R. D., Voelker, S., & Lakhani, A. (2005). Ecocultural effects on early infant care: A study in Cameroon, India and Germany. *Ethos, 33*, 512–541. http://dx.doi.org/10.1525/eth.2005.33.4.512

Locke, D. C. (2014). A model of multicultural understanding. In D. C. Locke & D. F. Bailey (Eds.), *Increasing multicultural understanding: A comprehensive model* (3rd ed., pp. 1–30). London, England: Sage. http://dx.doi.org/10.4135/9781483319582.n1

Matias, C. E. (2018). Before cultural competence: A therapy session on exploring the latent and overt emotionalities of whiteness. In S. S. Poulsen & B. Allan (Eds.), *Cross-cultural responsiveness & systemic therapy* (pp. 21–39). New York, NY: Springer. http://dx.doi.org/10.1007/978-3-319-71395-3_2

McIntosh, P. (2015). Extending the knapsack: Using the White privilege analysis to examine conferred advantage and disadvantage. *Women & Therapy, 38*, 232–245. http://dx.doi.org/10.1080/02703149.2015.1059195

Milgram, S. (1963). Behavioral study of obedience. *The Journal of Abnormal and Social Psychology, 67*, 371–378. http://dx.doi.org/10.1037/h0040525

Miller, A. E., & Josephs, L. (2009). Whiteness as pathological narcissism. *Contemporary Psychoanalysis, 45*, 93–119. http://dx.doi.org/10.1080/00107530.2009.10745989

Rodriguez Mosquera, P. M. R., Fischer, A. H., Manstead, A. S. R., & Zaalberg, R. (2008). Attack, disapproval, or withdrawal? The role of honour in anger and shame responses to being insulted. *Cognition and Emotion, 22*, 1471–1498. http://dx.doi.org/10.1080/02699930701822272

Ryan, W. (2010). Blaming the victim. In P. S. Rothenberg (Ed.), *Race, class, and gender in the United States* (8th ed., pp. 648–658). New York, NY: Worth.

Shields, S. A. (1975). Functionalism, Darwinism, and the psychology of women: A study in social myth. *American Psychologist, 30*, 739–754. http://dx.doi.org/10.1037/h0076948

Spivey, S. E. (2005). Distancing and solidarity as resistance to sexual objectification in a nude dancing bar. *Deviant Behavior, 26*, 417–437. http://dx.doi.org/10.1080/016396290931731

Tajfel, H., & Turner, J. C. (1979). An integrative theory of intergroup conflict. In W. G. Austin & S. Worchel (Eds.), *The social psychology of intergroup relations* (pp. 33–47). Monterey, CA: Brooks-Cole.

Thomas, J. S., Ditzfeld, C. P., & Showers, C. J. (2013). Compartmentalization: A window on the defensive self. *Social and Personality Psychology Compass, 7,* 719–731. http://dx.doi.org/10.1111/spc3.12061

Thornton, S. (2016). Fear of change: Helping children and young people cope. *British Journal of School of Nursing, 11,* 299–301. Advance online publication. http://dx.doi.org/10.12968/bjsn.2016.11.6.299

Wade, C., & Tavris, C. (2012). *Invitation to psychology* (5th ed.). Upper Saddle River, NJ: Prentice Hall.

Williams, R. (2015). *Keywords: A vocabulary of culture and society.* New York, NY: Oxford University Press.

20

Multicultural Considerations in the Psychology Research Methods Course

Jasmine A. Mena, Nathan E. Cook, and Kathryn Quina

Multiculturally informed research methods courses can have a lasting impact on how students evaluate psychological research and on the expansion of psychological science. Psychological research is based on a series of successive decisions that are influenced by values often hidden from researchers' awareness. As a result, the available research may be beneficial for some or even harmful to others. In our research methods courses, we work toward the following goals: (a) developing critical consciousness and reflexive practice, (b) evaluating research designs for challenges to internal validity and reliability and suggestions for reducing them, (c) ensuring the relevance of research to diverse populations, and (d) for courses involving conduct of research, designing and conducting research incorporating multiculturally sensitive approaches. In this chapter, we suggest ways to address ethical, conceptual, and methodological issues in a research methods course sensitive to multiculturalism and diversity.[1]

---

[1]Additional resources that instructors can use in their classes are available on this book's companion webpage (http://pubs.apa.org/books/supp/mena). These include a PowerPoint presentation that covers topics from this chapter, a sample multicultural research methods course description, classroom exercises that encourage students to critique research methods, and a list of additional readings.

http://dx.doi.org/10.1037/0000137-021
Integrating Multiculturalism and Intersectionality Into the Psychology Curriculum: Strategies for Instructors, J. A. Mena and K. Quina (Editors)

PRINCIPLES OF MULTICULTURALLY SENSITIVE RESEARCH

Harding (2004) criticized the ideological underpinnings of traditional science, which seek universal laws and "truth," pointing out ways in which these assumptions have historically been sexist, androcentric, racist, and Eurocentric. Our goal is to help students develop a "critical consciousness," or informed critique, of psychological science through a reflexive examination of values and context. Reflexive practice, which is intended to result in self-change, has historically been a core value and competency of qualitative research (Lincoln, Lynham, & Guba, 2011); we suggest it should be applied by quantitative researchers as well. We often introduce students to the critique of the scientific method with an exercise that encourages students to question brief statements that reflect commonly held beliefs that are often misguided, such as "success breeds success."[2] Caution is advised, however, as students can become so focused on this critique they reject science entirely; we urge a balanced approach that examines the strengths and limitations of research designs.

Deconstructing Traditional Research Paradigms

Along with the traditional positivist and post-positivist paradigms, we introduce social construction (Holstein & Gubrium, 2007), critical race theory (Crenshaw, 1989; Wing, 2003), and participatory research (Minkler & Wallerstein, 2011). In small groups, students can summarize each paradigm, including its assumptions about ontology (nature of reality), epistemology (relationship of the knower to the known), axiology (the role of values), and methodology (how information is collected). Together, they can generate a list of the types of questions each paradigm might address; for example, whereas a positivist paradigm may ask, "How much?" and "What is the cause?" a constructivist paradigm may ask, "Why?" and "What is the lived experience?" (Anderson, 2013).

Instructors can assign a topic, break students up into groups, and ask half of the groups to design a research study using quantitative methods and the other half qualitative methods. Discussion questions may revolve around the advantages and disadvantages of various measurement approaches, such as surveys and interview guides. Together, the class can discuss the merits of a mixed methods approach (i.e., research that includes both quantitative and qualitative approaches). A rich history of attending to multicultural issues exists in the qualitative research literature (Ormston, Spencer, Barnard, & Snape, 2014). Students can also review recent issues of *Cultural Diversity and Ethnic Minority Psychology*, *Feminism in Psychology*, and *Qualitative Psychology* and identify the designs and their underlying paradigms.

Countering the Myth of Objectivity

Initially, students rarely question research findings, at least partly because research is often presented as if attitudes, beliefs, and values had no influence.

---

[2]Guidelines for conducting the "Success Breeds Success" exercise are available from this book's companion webpage (http://pubs.apa.org/books/supp/mena).

This obfuscates the subjective elements of research that inform and transform research (Finlay, 2002); in fact, research is value laden at every step (Howard, 1985; Prilleltensky, 1997). It is imperative to bring attention to potential influences across the spectrum of psychological research, from funding sources to reporting of results. For example, students should consider the power and privileges of researchers and funding sources along with the relative powerlessness and potential marginalization of research participants. After identifying threats to internal and external validity, instructors can provide a series of examples of problematic research designs and ask students to search for such threats, discussing in small groups the values informing those flawed decisions. Caplan and Caplan's (2016) readable, powerful examples of gender biases in research can supplement a traditional textbook; students can write reflection papers on topics such as the beliefs about men and women that might lead to such errors. We also encourage students to reflect on their perceptions about psychological research, as well as their personal research goals and experiences.[3]

Questioning the Search for Universality

Heine and Norenzayan (2006) stated, "Few people would dispute that culture is relevant to psychology. Yet for much of the history of their field, most psychologists have sought to discover and explain human thought and behavior in terms of universal principles" (p. 251). A great deal of psychological research has been based on the premise that people share a core set of traits and that certain principles are shared across animal and human species. In contrast, multiculturalism assumes that sociopolitical, historical, and cultural contexts influence individuals and communities (Pope-Davis, Liu, Toporek, & Brittan-Powell, 2001). To ignore these contexts risks producing fragmented knowledge that is not applicable to diverse people in the context of their lives (Stokols, 1996). Feminists and scholars of color have expounded on this view (see Moraga & Anzaldúa, 2015).

As a start, instructors can ask students to read a study conducted with college student participants in an on-campus laboratory and discuss whether the results might apply in other contexts with non–college students, identifying potential influences. More advanced students can discuss more complex examples, such as the impact that undocumented status (policy) has on Latina (culture) victims of intimate partner violence (interpersonal) and the barriers to social services (institutional; see O'Neal & Beckman, 2017). Together they can then create a list of design considerations for studying a broader topic such as well-being among Latinas.

Examples of controversial universal assertions include claims that girls lack the "math gene" (Ceci & Williams, 2010), that ethnoracial minority individuals and those with low socioeconomic status are less intelligent for biological reasons (Sternberg, Grigorenko, & Kidd, 2005), and that heterosexual parents

---

[3]Research reflection questions are available on this book's companion webpage (http://pubs.apa.org/books/supp/mena).

are superior to lesbian, gay, bisexual, and transgender parents (Patterson, 2006). As they read the research on these popular notions, students can engage in reflexive practices through journaling about their reactions to the flawed research behind these claims, as well as the impact such findings might have on individuals.

Ethical and Socially Responsible Conduct

Early in the course, students should read the American Psychological Association's (APA's) *Ethical Principles of Psychologists and Code of Conduct* (2017a) and *Multicultural Guidelines* (2017b) and their school's institutional review board (IRB) requirements. Emphasize that these are more than merely "dos and don'ts"; they offer ways to think about all aspects of their work and the work they read. Freyd and Quina (2000) provided an ethics-based critique of a popular research topic found in many introductory and research textbooks, recovered memories, including such challenges as multiple roles of researchers, conceptual biases, misuse of data, misinterpretations, and intentional misrepresentations. Suggestions for conducting an ethical critique are also offered.

Internal Validity

Shadish, Cook, and Campbell (2002) provided a wealth of valuable information on common errors of internal validity caused by poorly defined or selected independent and dependent variables, as well as situational, environmental, and cultural factors present in the conduct of a study. Students are often unaware of the possibility of such errors yet are quick to recognize these and other confounding factors once they are pointed out. The lesson is not, however, to assume that all research is invalid because of such flaws. Rather, through critical analysis, students can recognize the valuable information provided by research while acknowledging the limitations of any single study.

A useful exercise to help students understand important decision points in the scientific method and identify potential biases entails drawing a circle using clockwise arrows that depict unidirectional decision points. Starting with a theory (at the top of the circle), deductive reasoning is used to draw a hypothesis and design an empirical study (step by step) to test the theory using statistical tests (now at the bottom of the circle). Then, using inductive logic, the researcher must interpret the results and make conclusions about the theory (arriving full circle at the top). Rather than thinking of the scientific process as purely objective, students learn to identify researcher decision points, which can be heavily influenced by personal and societal biases as well as the decisions made in previous steps. We have added one final step, sharing the results with others, which is affected not only by active decisions but also by biases of the scholarly forums available.[4] This exercise lends itself well to discussing quantitative and

---

[4]A more detailed overview of these decision points and suggested classroom exercises for critiquing them are available on this book's companion webpage (http://pubs.apa.org/books/supp/mena).

qualitative methodologies and inductive versus deductive reasoning as well. In many cases, qualitative research may be the choice of methodology, given its potential to give voice to the concerns of marginalized populations (Madison, 2012; Wing, 2003).

Participant Selection

Students should understand that sociodemographic variables (e.g., race) do not have inherent conceptual meaning (Helms, Jernigan, & Mascher, 2005). That said, sociodemographic categories can serve as a proxy for structural oppression not easily measured by individual psychological processes (Schwartz & Meyer, 2010). Students can read published papers that demonstrate sociodemographic group differences and generate alternate explanations for those differences. For example, students might read a study that reports a purported sex difference in math achievement scores. A potential alternate explanation of these findings might include contextual factors such as *stereotype threat*, which refers to the observation that when placed in a situation where they face judgment based on societal stereotypes (e.g., math achievement tests), women tend to under-perform compared with conditions under which they are reassured there are no sex differences on the given test (Spencer, Steele, & Quinn, 1999). Alter-natively, with guidance, students might understand that the effect size for the observed group difference is small in magnitude and, thus, of questionable practical significance (Kirk, 1996).

Additional problems arise when groups are compared (e.g., male/female, White/non-White; heterosexual/sexual minority): (a) individuals are forced into categories, thus losing intersectional qualities; (b) individuals may not identify in either category (e.g., transgender, biracial, bisexual); and (c) the variability within a category is usually large, particularly when "all non-Whites" are grouped together. Such an approach might perpetuate bias and "encourage a deficit orientation" in which one group is compared with a "normative, 'well-adjusted' group" (Yali & Revenson, 2004, p. 150). Further, confounding or interacting influences are often ignored. Group differences are interpreted as categorical and typical of all members of that group rather than a mean differ-ence with substantial overlap across groups. Else-Quest & Hyde (2016a, 2016b) noted that more sophisticated multivariate techniques open up the possibility for group differences to be interpreted in an inherently value-laden framework even when the magnitude of the difference, as measured by an effect size esti-mate, for example, is minuscule and representative of "overlapping continuous dimensions" (Reis & Carothers, 2014, p. 19).

Concepts, Instruments, and Measurement

It is unethical to use a measure or assessment instrument with a population for which the measure has not been validated (APA, 2017a). Thus, researchers have often restricted their participant selection due to a lack of validation research with diverse populations on their measures, further limiting the accu-racy of the literature. Ideally, investigators should conduct such validation research to allow for wider applicability of their work. However, even when items appear to be applicable, participants may have different reactions to the measures, or *response sets*. Researchers have observed differential response sets among certain cultural groups that may pose a threat to the validity of quantitative studies (Matsumoto, 1994; van de Vijver & Leung, 2011). For example, Latinxs tend to use more extreme ratings in a 5-point Likert scale, but when the scale is increased to 10 points, that is no longer observed (Hui & Triandis, 1989). Students might discuss their experiences with tests and measures they felt were not appropriate to their response sets.

Another concern critical to the validity of research findings is *equivalence*, when a construct affects different populations similarly (Trimble & Vaughn, 2014). *Inequivalence* can confound results and interpretations of research with diverse populations. Students can ask: Are the concepts being measured cross-culturally equivalent? Are the study constructs measuring the same thing across participants of different cultures? An illustrative example comes from cross-cultural research on the Big Five personality model, which was created in English based primarily on U.S. participants. Although the model appears stable across cultures, examination of the constructs has led to critiques of their equivalencies (Cheung, van de Vijver, & Leong, 2011). Many excellent sources discuss measurement equivalence and bias as well as methods to examine and neutralize their effect (Cheung, van de Vijver, & Leong, 2011; Rogler, 1999).

Interpretation of Data

Statistical results may reflect "true" differences or relationships but may also represent mere artifact caused by biased measurement or inappropriate statistical technique. It is important for students to understand probability in statistical interpretation and to critically appraise the real-world significance and meaningfulness of any group difference. *Statistical power*, the probability of detecting a statistically significant effect, is helpful in this discussion (Cohen, 1992). Maxwell (2004) argued that attention to adequate statistical power can foster the development of a more accurate scientific knowledge base.

External Validity

Students should be able to examine the applicability of the research topic to diverse populations by considering the demographic characteristics of the participants. For example, students might perform a literature review to identify the variables related to corporate leadership (most of which has involved White men). Then they can identify groups that might have a completely different experience in the workforce, such as people of color, women, and individuals with disabilities, and discuss whether the original findings have external validity. Are these marginalized groups represented in key articles? This approach can help students uncover important gaps in the literature related to diverse populations that stem from bias, privilege, and power. Unfortunately, researchers continue to underreport sociodemographic characteristics in published studies (Cundiff, 2012), and many rely on college student participants (Henry, 2008). We recommend inviting students to examine the limitations of theory and research based on a narrow subset of the population (e.g., White, college students). Having students compare the demographic characteristics of the participants in a published study with census data of a diverse local community can be eye opening.

CONDUCTING MULTICULTURALLY INFORMED PSYCHOLOGICAL RESEARCH WITH STUDENTS

Increasingly, undergraduate students are engaging in research experiences. Such projects can stress the importance of culturally anchored research methods to the relevance and quality of psychological science (Zebian, Alamuddin, Maalouf, & Chatila, 2007). Instructors are encouraged to engage students in research that directly addresses community needs using principles of service learning (Bringle, Reeb, Brown, & Ruiz, 2016). Here, we recommend strategies to increase awareness of multicultural issues when students conduct research.

Developing a Strategy

A well-formulated research question will help determine many other aspects of a study, starting with the decision to use a quantitative, qualitative, or mixed-methods design. Regardless of the paradigm, there are myriad pitfalls to consider. Bowleg (2012) urged researchers to view the complexities of inter-sectionality research as an opportunity to develop creative research strategies. For example, asking, "Which of your identities do you believe was the source of discrimination?" forces a participant to choose from among many held identities, thus losing valuable information about the intersections among those identities. At present, the statistical options for quantitative data trail the theoretical understanding of intersectionality and might require advanced analyses of interaction effects or multilevel or hierarchical modeling (see Else-Quest & Hyde, 2016a, 2016b, and other articles in the same special issues of *Psychology of Women Quarterly*).

In some cases, a broadly representative sample is best, whereas in others, recruiting participants that share characteristics, culture, or experiences will best answer research questions (Shadish et al., 2002). For example, qualitative researchers often prefer to capture the lived experience of a culture-sharing group rather than generalizing the results to large populations (Carspecken, 2013). The selected recruitment strategy can impact the diversity of participants (Yali & Revenson, 2004; Yancey, Ortega, & Kumanyika, 2006). Instructors can review historical events contributing to the underrepresentation of ethnoracial and other minority participants and their mistrust of medical and public health research (Corbie-Smith, Thomas, & St. George, 2002).

Reinforcing Ethical and Socially Responsible Conduct

Ethical and socially responsible conduct is critical. If a research survey asks for sensitive information related to identities (e.g., sexual orientation, immigration status), safeguards to mitigate risks regarding confidentiality should be carefully planned, clearly specified, and conscientiously enacted. We require students to complete a mock or actual application to the IRB and/or have an IRB member deliver a guest lecture to discuss recommendations for conducting research, with an emphasis on protected groups.

Students are often interested in considering which demographic characteristics are relevant or necessary for a study and the cultural sensitivity of these questions. For example, what are the pros and cons of having participants select their race or sex from a checklist versus allowing participants to self-identify by writing or typing in responses? If written in, how will this information be transformed into useful quantitative data? Instructors can ask students to review instruments for gender neutral and unbiased phrasing (e.g., significant other vs. wife or husband). If the focus of the study exclusively includes a sample from an underrepresented group, within-group differences should be considered because they can impact the validity of the results and interpretation. For example, within an ethnic group, level of acculturation may moderate the results and lead to a new understanding of that sample.

Designing Multiculturally Sensitive Research

Procedures

Instructors should help students mitigate the impact of cultural differences that might threaten the validity of findings. Reviewing the proposed methodology step by step can reveal challenges to internal and external validity (Leong, Leung, & Cheung, 2010). Students may wish to conduct exploratory data analysis to provide preliminary validation for the measure with the diversity of the research sample in mind or seek out existing data sets that could allow for secondary data analysis. Throughout, stress the importance of anticipating cultural issues and perhaps asking participants questions that can uncover more complex variations associated with sociocultural variables, thus generating more nuanced knowledge.

Analyzing and Interpreting Data

Instructors can help students determine the approximate sample size needed to adequately power their study (Rossi, 2013) or, with qualitative research, the point at which they have reached saturation, the guiding principle to determine sample size (Patton, 2015). Also, the *Guidelines for Research in Ethnic Minority Communities* (Council of National Psychological Associations for the Advancement of Ethnic Minority Interests, 2000) are useful for discussions of data analytic and interpretive practices specific to various ethnoracial minority groups. If analyses of group differences are planned, we suggest a discussion about the risks of relying solely on group difference statistics, as described previously.

Interpreting and Presenting Results

As students discuss whether their results complement or counter previous findings, they should consider implications for marginalized groups. Limitations should include unaddressed cultural issues (e.g., sociodemographic generaliz-ability, psychometric properties of instruments). The class should read the sec-tion of the *Publication Manual of the American Psychological Association* (APA, 2010) on bias-free language, which provides guidelines to reduce bias in professional psychological writing. Including adherence to these guidelines in rubrics for research reports further emphasizes their importance.

CONCLUSION

Multiculturally informed research methods courses can enhance student schol-arly training and lead to a more accurate, nuanced, and culturally informed scientific knowledge base. Whether or not they choose to become researchers in their careers, students can become critical consumers of psychological sci-ence. Students' reactions to the misuse of psychological science can be trans-formed from their initial shock to the ability to tease apart biased research that perpetuates stereotypes and discrimination and a confidence that they can pro-duce methodologically rigorous and trustworthy results.

REFERENCES

American Psychological Association. (2010). *Publication manual of the American Psycho-logical Association*. Washington, DC: Author.

American Psychological Association. (2017a). *Ethical principles of psychologists and code of conduct* (2002, Amended June 1, 2010, and January 1, 2017). Retrieved from http://www.apa.org/ethics/code/index.aspx

American Psychological Association. (2017b). *Multicultural guidelines: An ecological approach to context, identity, and intersectionality*. Retrieved from http://www.apa.org/about/policy/multicultural-guidelines.pdf

Anderson, T. (2013). *Research paradigms: Ontologies, epistemologies, and methods*. Retrieved from http://www.slideshare.net/eLearnCenter/research-methods-uoc-2013

Bowleg, L. (2012). The problem with the phrase women and minorities: Intersectionality–an important theoretical framework for public health. *American Journal of Public Health, 102*, 1267–1273. http://dx.doi.org/10.2105/AJPH.2012.300750

Bringle, R. G., Reeb, R. N., Brown, M. A., & Ruiz, A. I. (2016). *Service learning in psychol-ogy: Enhancing undergraduate education for the public good*. Washington, DC: American Psychological Association. http://dx.doi.org/10.1037/14803-000

Caplan, P. J., & Caplan, J. (2016). *Thinking critically about research on sex and gender* (3rd ed.). New York, NY: Routledge.

Carspecken, F. P. (2013). *Critical ethnography in educational research: A theoretical and practical guide*. New York, NY: Routledge.

Ceci, S., & Williams, W. (2010). *The mathematics of sex: How biology and society conspire to limit talented women and girls*. New York, NY: Oxford University Press.

Cheung, F. M., van de Vijver, F. J., & Leong, F. T. (2011). Toward a new approach to the study of personality in culture. *American Psychologist, 66*, 593–603. http://dx.doi.org/10.1037/a0022389

Cohen, J. (1992). A power primer. *Psychological Bulletin, 112*, 155–159. http://dx.doi.org/10.1037/0033-2909.112.1.155

Corbie-Smith, G., Thomas, S. B., & St. George, D. M. M. (2002). Distrust, race, and research. *Archives of Internal Medicine, 162*, 2458–2463. http://dx.doi.org/10.1001/archinte.162.21.2458

Council of National Psychological Associations for the Advancement of Ethnic Minority Interests. (2000). *Guidelines for research in ethnic minority communities.* Washington, DC: American Psychological Association.

Crenshaw, K. (1989). Demarginalizing the intersection of race and sex: A Black feminist critique of antidiscrimination doctrine, feminist theory, and antiracist politics. *University of Chicago Legal Forum, 140,* 139–168.

Cundiff, J. L. (2012). Is mainstream psychological research "womanless" and "raceless"? An updated analysis. *Sex Roles, 67,* 158–173. http://dx.doi.org/10.1007/s11199-012-0141-7

Else-Quest, N. M., & Hyde, J. S. (2016a). Intersectionality in quantitative psychological research: I. Theoretical and epistemological issues. *Psychology of Women Quarterly, 40,* 155–170. http://dx.doi.org/10.1177/0361684316629797

Else-Quest, N. M., & Hyde, J. S. (2016b). Intersectionality in quantitative psychological research: II. Methods and techniques. *Psychology of Women Quarterly, 40,* 319–336. http://dx.doi.org/10.1177/0361684316647953

Finlay, L. (2002). Negotiating the swamp: The opportunity and challenge of reflexivity in research practice. *Qualitative Research, 2,* 209–230. http://dx.doi.org/10.1177/146879410200200205

Freyd, J. J., & Quina, K. (2000). Feminist ethics in the practice of science: The contested memory controversy as an example. In M. M. Brabeck (Ed.), *Practicing feminist ethics in psychology* (pp. 101–123). Washington, DC: American Psychological Association. http://dx.doi.org/10.1037/10343-005

Harding, S. (2004). A socially relevant philosophy of science? Resources from standpoint theory's controversiality. *Hypatia, 19,* 25–47. http://dx.doi.org/10.1111/j.1527-2001.2004.tb01267.x

Heine, S. J., & Norenzayan, A. (2006). Toward a psychological science for a cultural species. *Perspectives on Psychological Science, 1,* 251–269. http://dx.doi.org/10.1111/j.1745-6916.2006.00015.x

Helms, J. E., Jernigan, M., & Mascher, J. (2005). The meaning of race in psychology and how to change it: A methodological perspective. *American Psychologist, 60,* 27–36. http://dx.doi.org/10.1037/0003-066X.60.1.27

Henry, P. J. (2008). College sophomores in the laboratory redux: Influences of a narrow data base on social psychology's view of the nature of prejudice. *Psychological Inquiry, 19,* 49–71. http://dx.doi.org/10.1080/10478400802049936

Holstein, J. A., & Gubrium, J. F. (2007). Constructionist perspectives on the life course. *Sociology Compass, 1,* 335–352. http://dx.doi.org/10.1111/j.1751-9020.2007.00004.x

Howard, G. S. (1985). The role of values in the science of psychology. *American Psychologist, 40,* 255–265. http://dx.doi.org/10.1037/0003-066X.40.3.255

Hui, C., & Triandis, H. C. (1989). Effects of culture and response format on extreme response style. *Journal of Cross-Cultural Psychology, 20,* 296–309. http://dx.doi.org/10.1177/0022022189203004

Kirk, R. E. (1996). Practical significance: A concept whose time has come. *Educational and Psychological Measurement, 56,* 746–759. http://dx.doi.org/10.1177/0013164496056005002

Leong, F. T. L., Leung, K., & Cheung, F. M. (2010). Integrating cross-cultural psychology research methods into ethnic minority psychology. *Cultural Diversity and Ethnic Minority Psychology, 16,* 590–597. http://dx.doi.org/10.1037/a0020127

Lincoln, Y. S., Lynham, S. A., & Guba, E. G. (2011). Paradigmatic controversies, contradictions, and emerging confluences, revisited. In N. K. Denzin & Y. S. Lincoln (Eds.), *The Sage handbook of qualitative research* (4th ed., pp. 97–128). Thousand Oaks, CA: Sage.

Madison, D. S. (2012). *Critical ethnography: Method, ethics and performance.* Thousand Oaks, CA: Sage.

Matsumoto, D. (1994). *Cultural influences on research methods and statistics.* Pacific Grove, CA: Brooks/Cole.

Maxwell, S. E. (2004). The persistence of underpowered studies in psychological research: Causes, consequences, and remedies. *Psychological Methods, 9,* 147–163. http://dx.doi.org/10.1037/1082-989X.9.2.147

Minkler, M., & Wallerstein, N. (Eds.). (2011). *Community-based participatory research for health: From process to outcomes.* New York, NY: Wiley.

Moraga, C., & Anzaldúa, G. (Eds.). (2015). *This bridge called my back: Writings by radical Women of Color* (4th ed.). New York, NY: SUNY Press.

O'Neal, E. N., & Beckman, L. O. (2017). Intersections of race, ethnicity, and gender reframing knowledge surrounding barriers to social services among Latina intimate partner violence victims. *Violence Against Women, 23,* 643–665. http://dx.doi.org/10.1177/1077801216646223

Ormston, R., Spencer, L., Barnard, M., & Snape, D. (2014). The foundations of qualitative research. In J. Ritchie, J. Lewis, C. M. N. Nicholls, & R. Ormston (Eds.), *Qualitative research practice: A guide for social science students and researchers* (pp. 1–23). Thousand Oaks, CA: Sage.

Patterson, C. J. (2006). Children of lesbian and gay parents. *Current Directions in Psychological Science, 15,* 241–244. http://dx.doi.org/10.1111/j.1467-8721.2006.00444.x

Patton, M. Q. (2015). *Qualitative research and evaluation methods* (4th ed.). London, England: Sage.

Pope-Davis, D. B., Liu, W. M., Toporek, R. L., & Brittan-Powell, C. S. (2001). What's missing from multicultural competency research: Review, introspection, and recommendations. *Cultural Diversity and Ethnic Minority Psychology, 7,* 121–138. http://dx.doi.org/10.1037/1099-9809.7.2.121

Prilleltensky, I. (1997). Values, assumptions, and practices: Assessing the moral implications of psychological discourse and action. *American Psychologist, 52,* 517–535. http://dx.doi.org/10.1037/0003-066X.52.5.517

Reis, H. T., & Carothers, B. J. (2014). Black and white or shades of gray: Are gender differences categorical or dimensional? *Current Directions in Psychological Science, 23,* 19–26. http://dx.doi.org/10.1177/0963721413504105

Rogler, L. H. (1999). Methodological sources of cultural insensitivity in mental health research. *American Psychologist, 54,* 424–433. http://dx.doi.org/10.1037/0003-066X.54.6.424

Rossi, J. S. (2013). Statistical power analysis. In J. A. Schinka, W. F. Velicer, & I. B. Weiner (Eds.), *Handbook of psychology: Vol. 2. Research methods in psychology* (pp. 71–108). Hoboken, NJ: Wiley.

Schwartz, S., & Meyer, I. H. (2010). Mental health disparities research: The impact of within and between group analyses on tests of social stress hypotheses. *Social Science & Medicine, 70,* 1111–1118. http://dx.doi.org/10.1016/j.socscimed.2009.11.032

Shadish, W. R., Cook, T. D., & Campbell, D. T. (2002). *Experimental and quasi-experimental designs for generalized causal inference.* Boston, MA: Houghton Mifflin.

Spencer, S. J., Steele, C. M., & Quinn, D. M. (1999). Stereotype threat and women's math performance. *Journal of Experimental Social Psychology, 35,* 4–28. http://dx.doi.org/10.1006/jesp.1998.1373

Sternberg, R. J., Grigorenko, E. L., & Kidd, K. K. (2005). Intelligence, race, and genetics. *American Psychologist, 60,* 46–59. http://dx.doi.org/10.1037/0003-066X.60.1.46

Stokols, D. (1996). Translating social ecological theory into guidelines for community health promotion. *American Journal of Health Promotion, 10,* 282–298. http://dx.doi.org/10.4278/0890-1171-10.4.282

Trimble, J. E., & Vaughn, L. (2014). Cultural measurement equivalence. In K. Keith (Ed.), *Encyclopedia of Cross-Cultural Psychology* (p. 213). New York, NY: Wiley.

van de Vijver, F. J. R., & Leung, K. (2011). Equivalence and bias: A review of concepts, models, and data analytic procedures. In D. Matsumoto & F. J. R. van de Vijver (Eds.),

Cross-cultural research methods in psychology (pp. 17–45). New York, NY: Cambridge University Press. http://dx.doi.org/10.1017/CBO9780511779381.003

Wing, A. K. (2003). *Critical race feminism: A reader* (2nd ed.). New York, NY: New York University Press.

Yali, A. M., & Revenson, T. A. (2004). How changes in population demographics will impact health psychology: Incorporating a broader notion of cultural competence into the field. *Health Psychology, 23,* 147–155. http://dx.doi.org/ 10.1037/0278-6133.23.2.147

Yancey, A. K., Ortega, A. N., & Kumanyika, S. K. (2006). Effective recruitment and retention of minority research participants. *Annual Review of Public Health, 27,* 1–28. http://dx.doi.org/10.1146/annurev.publhealth.27.021405.102113

Zebian, S., Alamuddin, R., Maalouf, M., & Chatila, Y. (2007). Developing an appropriate psychology through culturally sensitive research practices in the Arabic-speaking world: A content analysis of psychological research published between 1950 and 2004. *Journal of Cross-Cultural Psychology, 38,* 91–122. http://dx.doi.org/10.1177/ 0022022106295442

21

Teaching Biopsychology

Multicultural Findings and Implications

Lisa Weyandt, Danielle R. Oster, Bergljot Gyda Gudmundsdottir, and Meghan Lamarre Rinaldi-Young

For most of the 20th century, popular psychological theories emphasized the role of emotional, environmental, and sociocultural factors in the development of behavior. More recently, the pendulum has swung back to a biological emphasis, with the emergence of cognitive psychology and cognitive neuroscience. Although great advances have been made with this resurgence, concerns have been raised that it is deterministic, neglecting the role of sociocultural factors, including multicultural factors.

One concern is that there may be a tendency to think less critically about neuroscience and biopsychology than other subfields of psychology. Weisberg, Keil, Goodstein, Rawson, and Gray (2008) revealed that when people were presented with poor psychological explanations combined with scientifically sounding but irrelevant neuroscience information, both laypeople and introductory neuroscience students rated them more favorably than the same explanations presented without neuroscientific information. Thus, even individuals with some training in the field may be swayed by the appeal of neuroscience. We discuss this tendency with students and provide frequent reminders of this precaution.

We refer to biological psychology as a subfield of psychology that attempts to understand, via scientific inquiry, the biological factors and processes involved in human cognition, affect, and behavior—a vast array. We have selected five major domains in which recent research is particularly compelling, offering practical implications for teaching about evolution and genetics,

http://dx.doi.org/10.1037/0000137-022
Integrating Multiculturalism and Intersectionality Into the Psychology Curriculum: Strategies for Instructors, J. A. Mena and K. Quina (Editors)

281

brain development and plasticity, hormones and sex, drug addiction, and psychiatric disorders.[1]

FOUNDATIONS OF BIOPSYCHOLOGY: GENETICS, EXPERIENCE, AND PLASTICITY

In 2013, President Obama unveiled the BRAIN Initiative to support collaboration among scientists to better understand the intricacies of the human brain. Although recent advances have led to remarkable discoveries in the study of human physiology and behavior, the mapping of the brain also has its limitations. In addition to commonly voiced concerns that brain mapping is simply modern phrenology and overly reductionist (Poldrack, 2010; Shimamura, 2010), it may also perpetuate the myth that the relationship between brain and behavior is unidirectional and unalterable. The deterministic view is commonly associated with the idea that different outcomes across cultural groups are biologically and/or genetically predetermined, which, in turn, has been associated with stereotyping and prejudice (Haslam, Bastian, Bain, & Kashima, 2006). Historically, this notion that various group differences are rooted in biology and genetics has been used to justify unequal treatment (Gould, 1996). As noted by Weyandt (2006) and others, however, a significant body of research reveals that the relationship between brain and behavior is, in fact, bidirectional and indeed malleable.

Research has shown that brain development is shaped by the interplay between genetics and experience throughout the lifespan (Li, 2003). A large body of research has indicated that environmental experience can lead to neurochemical and morphological brain changes, known as *neuroplasticity*. Neuroplastic changes can be adaptive (resulting in functional improvement) or maladaptive (resulting in a decline in function; Kennard, 1936; Kolb & Whishaw, 1989). Neuroplasticity in the human brain has been associated with environmental enrichment (e.g., Schlaug et al., 2009), deprivation (e.g., Bauer, Hanson, Pierson, Davidson, & Pollak, 2009), and brain injury (e.g., Serra-Grabulosa et al., 2005).

After presenting the research on these mechanisms, we encourage students to consider how the relationship between biological factors and behavior is mediated and moderated by cultural factors, including race, ethnicity, gender, sexual orientation, and socioeconomic status (SES), that have been shown to contribute to neuroplasticity. For example, SES can have profound effects on neurodevelopment, particularly linguistic ability and executive function (Hackman, Farah, & Meaney, 2010). Hanson and colleagues (2013) found that children from low-income families are at greater risk for smaller gray matter volumes in the frontal and parietal lobes and slower brain growth trajectories.

---

[1]A PowerPoint presentation that features the topics covered in this chapter, which instructors can use in their own classes, is available at the companion webpage for this book (http://pubs.apa.org/books/supp/mena).

Although studies are scant and controversial (Isamah et al., 2010), some studies have found differences in several aspects of brain morphology, including male and female volumes (Brain Development Cooperative Group, 2012), White and Chinese adults (Kochunov et al., 2003), and across ages in non-White adults (Carmichael et al., 2007). It is important to caution students that (a) "bigger does not mean better"; (b) these morphological differences are not causally related to functional brain differences or behavioral differences; (c) differences across cultural groups may be better explained by other variables, including socioeconomic disparities and stress; and (d) because cultural variables cannot be experimentally manipulated, statements regarding causal effects are scientifically inappropriate. To increase critical thinking, students can share examples of misuse found in popular media.

SEX, GENDER, AND SEXUAL ORIENTATION

Sex and Sexuality

Sex and sexuality are often viewed as fixed and fundamental to our lives. Recent issues in legislation, health care practices, and various media have led to questions about the influence of biopsychology in gender formation and sexual orientation, underscoring the need for culturally sensitive discussions. Research has suggested that sexual development and behavior are greatly influenced by the glands and hormones of the endocrine system, including the gonads, the male testes and the female ovaries, which develop during gestation and produce sperm and ova. Although adult ovaries release greater estrogen and adult testes release more androgen, the assumption that males and females have distinct sex hormones is incorrect. In fact, males and females experience many similar pubertal changes, including the growth of pubic and axillary hair, which develop from the release of androgens (Bain, 2007; Hiort, 2013).

Students can discuss these physiological similarities, providing support for their answers, with a prompt such as, "What makes an individual male or female; is it our chromosomes, hormones, genitalia, how we are brought up to think about ourselves, or all of the above?" They should also be mindful of potential exceptions—for example, is an individual with Turner syndrome any less of a woman because of her XO chromosomal abnormality?

Gender

Hormones influence sex by (a) shaping sexual development through the anatomical, physiological, and behavioral characteristics differentiating male, female, and intersex individuals and (b) activating reproductive behaviors in sexually mature individuals. External synthetic doses of hormones have been implicated in sexuality since the 1960s, suggesting that hormones in the environment may shape how sex is manifested (Ehrhardt & Money, 1967; Wilkins, Jones, Holman, & Stempfel, 1958). For example, Money and Mathews (1982) reported that approximately 92% of young women with a history of prenatal synthetic progestin exposure had induced virilization of the external genitalia, attributed to not only progestogenic but also androgenic effects of the hormone. Money and Ehrhardt (1982) reported that women with progestin-induced prenatal androgenization demonstrated a greater IQ score and more sexual experiences, implying that male hormones, even in a female body, may increase an individual's IQ and sexual behavior. Despite such claims, a number of limitations invalidated the conclusions of the study.

This early research provides an excellent forum for discussions about leaping to biologically based explanations without considering alternatives such as SES or repeated contact with the medical system. Students can read Fausto-Sterling's (2000) arguments against selecting a gender for an intersexual newborn and discuss whether it is appropriate that when sex abnormalities are identified at birth, the vast majority of parents are advised to suppress male traits through surgery and hormonal treatment. The Intersex Society of North America (n.d.) offers several key frequently asked questions that can provide a springboard for interesting discussions or reflection papers.

Sexual Orientation

Sexual attraction typically begins around 10 years of age, regardless of the child's sexuality (Quinsey, 2003). A simple determinant of sexual orientation does not exist; rather, research has substantiated that a combination of genes, hormones, and environmental factors (Långström, Rahman, Carlström, & Lichtenstein, 2010) are influential. Given the current social and political issues surrounding sexual orientation, a class debate challenging stereotypes (e.g., the "gay gene"; gay men are feminine; in each relationship, there is a "man/butch" and a "woman/femme") may be appropriate. Caplan and Caplan (2016) offered additional resources and class exercises.

Gender variant college students have become more visible in the last decade, and yet they remain one of the most underserved populations and are largely ignored in literature. Even multiculturally minded researchers and instructors often lack basic knowledge, resulting in practices that continue to marginalize gender variant students. There is a common belief that most transgender students are lesbian, gay, or bisexual or are planning to undergo sex reassignment surgery; however, this view fails to acknowledge heterosexual trans and gender-queer students who do not classify themselves as "male" or "female" (Grant et al., 2010). In addition, gender identity may change over time and across race, gender, class, and sexual identities (Scheim & Bauer, 2015).

POPULAR BIOPSYCHOLOGY TOPICS

Drug Addiction

Students are often surprised to learn that Sigmund Freud was addicted to cocaine and nicotine and that even after recurring oral cancer caused the removal of his entire jaw, he refused to stop smoking (World History Project, n.d.). Given the high rates of drug-related injuries and deaths among youth, students need to know what factors lead to addiction, how drugs affect their health and behavior, and the gender and cultural variables that might affect drug use and abuse. Students can review a list of substances and their impacts at the National Institute on Drug Abuse website (https://www.drugabuse.gov/).

A variety of brain regions are believed to be involved in addiction, most notably the mesolimbic region that includes dopamine-rich pathways extending from the limbic structures, substantia nigra, and nucleus accumbens and projecting to the prefrontal cortex. We ask students to locate these areas on a brain map, thus reinforcing identification of brain regions as well as the extent of brain involvement when a drug is ingested.

It is important to stress that the route of administration influences the rate and degree of drug effects. Repeated exposure decreases the body's sensitivity to a drug (*tolerance*), whereas increasing sensitivity to a drug is known as *drug sensitization*. Although not everyone who uses drugs becomes physically dependent, once physical dependence has occurred, sudden elimination of that drug will result in withdrawal symptoms, with severity depending on the type of drug, duration of use, and rapidity of elimination from the body. The desire to avoid withdrawal and drug cravings maintain addiction and, along with environmental stressors and triggers, contribute to relapse (Robinson, Fischer, Ahuja, Lesser, & Maniates, 2015). Students can locate addiction recovery approaches online and evaluate their awareness of these biopsychological mechanisms.

Early studies suggested that racial and ethnic minorities were at increased risk for substance use, abuse, and addiction (e.g., Hubbard et al., 1986). Recently, more methodologically sound research has indicated that relationship is complex, and sociocultural factors also play a significant role. For example, Jamal et al. (2014) reported that Whites have a higher rate of cigarette smoking than Hispanics, Blacks, and Asians, and men have a higher rate than women. Individuals who are younger, of ethnic minority status, and/or diagnosed with a serious mental illness are also at higher risk for cigarette smoking (Prochaska, Grossman, Young-Wolff, & Benowitz, 2015). Among college students, racial and ethnic minority males are at greater risk for polytobacco use (Butler, Ickes, Rayens, Wiggins, & Hahn, 2016). Clark, Nguyen, and Coman (2015), however, found that cigarette smoking trajectories among adolescents and young adults differed across SES levels among White, Black, and biracial respondents. This underscores that a number of interacting variables influence the onset of cigarette smoking, dispelling the myth that minority status alone predicts the difference.

What factors predict adolescent smoking? Kandel, Griesler, and Hu (2015) examined a number of factors and reported the strongest predictor of adolescent smoking was parental smoking, regardless of race or ethnicity. Interestingly, analyses of cigarette advertising in magazines from 1998 to 2002 found that Black and Latinx magazines contained significantly more ads for brands that targeted women (Landrine et al., 2005) and were 9.8 times more likely than White magazines to contain ads for menthol cigarettes, which may be more addictive than nonmentholated cigarettes (Garten & Falkner, 2004). As a group or class project, students can locate a variety of magazines and analyze smoking-related advertisements with respect to gender, race, and ethnicity.

Alcohol use is associated with increased smoking, and this relationship can vary across cultural factors. For example, Hispanics who smoke tend to be younger and report greater alcohol use intensity than Whites (e.g., Webb Hooper, Baker, & McNutt, 2014). However, studies also consistently find an association between smoking, alcohol use, and neighborhood racial, ethnic, and socioeconomic composition, including greater presence of tobacco advertisements (John, Cheney, & Azad, 2009) and a higher density of liquor stores (Moore & Diez Roux, 2006) in lower income and minority neighborhoods. Romley, Cohen, Ringel, and Sturm (2007) suggested that, considering the adverse consequences of alcohol, this disparity "may represent an important kind of environmental injustice" (p. 54). Indeed, research suggests that minority groups in the United States tend to have greater rates of heavy drinking, alcohol-related mortality, homicide, and health effects (Witbrodt, Mulia, Zemore, & Kerr, 2014).

Other drug use is also a concern for racial and ethnic minorities. Wu, Brady, Mannelli, and Killeen (2014) examined cannabis use disorder prevalence rates in respondents 12 years and older from seven racial and ethnic groups. In all groups, adolescents showed the highest rates; mixed-race, Native American, Asian American, and Black individuals had higher odds of cannabis use disorder compared with Whites. Similar patterns have been found with stimulants; for example, rates for admission to treatment for methamphetamine abuse are increasing overall, whereas admissions among Whites appear to be decreasing (Brecht, Greenwell, & Anglin, 2005). Bolanos et al. (2012) reported that minority populations are at increased risk for adverse methamphetamine-related health consequences (e.g., weapons injuries, sexually transmitted diseases, dental problems). Bernstein and colleagues (2006) found that rates of cocaine use were higher among African Americans enrolled in substance abuse treatment programs compared with Hispanic and Whites. African American and Latino men who use sexual networks to find male partners are at even higher risk for stimulant use, including cocaine and methamphetamine (Young & Shoptaw, 2013), suggesting additional contextual factors should be considered. Interestingly, prescription stimulant misuse (e.g., Adderall) tends to be higher in White males and females (Weyandt et al., 2013). A similar trend is found with other prescription medications; racial minorities report less misuse of tranquilizers and opioids than Whites. Bisexual, heterosexual, or other-identified participants, however, have been more likely than lesbian and gay participants to report higher misuse of prescription drugs (Kecojevic, Wong, Corliss, & Lankenau, 2015).

Gender differences also emerge in the literature: Overall, rates of substance abuse and dependence are higher among men; women typically begin to use substances later; women are less likely to seek treatment, but when they do, they enter earlier; and women report they are strongly influenced by their partners to use (Brady & Randall, 1999; Epstein, Fischer-Elber, & Al-Otaiba, 2007). Once in treatment, however, gender does not appear to be a significant predictor of treatment retention, completion, or outcome (Greenfield et al., 2007; Saloner & Karthikeyan, 2015). However, racial and ethnic minority women are less likely to remain in treatment, largely due to a lack of economic resources (Substance Abuse and Mental Health Services Administration, 2009), and women who have had a history of trauma are more likely to report negative relationships in the 12 months following treatment, perhaps placing them at greater risk for relapse (Min, Tracy, & Park, 2014).

Although a variety of brain regions are involved in addiction, structures and neurotransmitters within the mesocortical "reward" center of the brain are most often implicated. A large body of research supports that prolonged use of substances leading to addiction can alter the development of the brain in adolescents (De Bellis et al., 2000) and cause morphological changes in cells, including decreased density of receptors and dendrites as well as death of glial cells and neurons (e.g., Trantham-Davidson et al., 2014; Volkow, Fowler, & Wang, 2004). Students can view informative videos on the National Institute on Drug Abuse website and generate a list of questions to be discussed in class (National Institute on Drug Abuse, 2018; National Institute on Drug Abuse for Teens, 2014).

Whether ethnic and racial differences in biological systems contribute to, or protect from, problem drug use is an area that is under-investigated in biological psychology. What is clear is that biological factors alone are not deterministic of complex behavior such as substance abuse. Clark and colleagues (2015) provided an accessible study for students to read and discuss its implications for intervention.

Psychiatric Disorders

The diagnosis of psychiatric disorders is often guided by the *Diagnostic and Statistical Manual of Mental Disorders* (fifth ed. [*DSM*]; American Psychiatric Association, 2013). Use of the *DSM*, however, has been criticized due to evidence that (a) patients diagnosed with the same disorder often display different symptoms (Fried & Nesse, 2015); (b) patients experiencing different disorders may display similar symptoms, leading to different diagnoses among health care providers (Asherson et al., 2014); and (c) systematic biases have been demonstrated for some of the diagnoses and their applications to patients according to cultural stereotypes (e.g., Klonoff, Landrine, & Campbell, 2000). Students can read and reflect on these articles as well as Brown et al.'s (2000) "Being Black and Feeling Blue."

A majority of treatment studies across the spectrum of disorders are relational (not causal), lack diverse samples, and sometimes do not control for known differences between groups, impeding the generalizability of such findings (Weyandt, 2006). For example, although twin studies of affective disorders suggest a 60% concordance rate among identical twins and 15% among fraternal twins, regardless of upbringing environment (Otowa, Gardner, Kendler, & Hettema, 2013), stress and trauma, including major life losses, have also been implicated in episodes of depression (e.g., Hauschildt, Wittekind, Moritz, Kellner, & Jelinek, 2013; Schmidt, Murphy, Haq, Rubinow, & Danaceau, 2004). Harvey, Hitchcock, and Prior (2009) examined ovulation and mood across menstrual cycles of healthy women and found that reported mood change appeared to be amplifications of normal experiences. Students can read and discuss studies suggesting that media (Chrisler & Levy, 1990) and self-serving biases (Chrisler, Rose, Dutch, Sklarsky, & Grant, 2006) may contribute to the maintenance of cultural stereotypes of premenstrual and menopausal women.

Chung, Bemak, Ortiz, and Sandoval-Perez (2008) found that negative ethnic identity is associated with a greater risk for schizophrenia. Approximately 6.4% of Whites, 4.2% of African Americans, and 7.2% of Hispanics have been diagnosed with depression (Akincigil et al., 2011); among these, 73% of Whites, 60% of African Americans, and 63.4% of Hispanics received treatment. White Americans are more likely than minority groups to be diagnosed with an anxiety disorder, with the exception of posttraumatic stress disorder, which is more prevalent among African Americans (Asnaani, Richey, Dimaite, Hinton, & Hofmann, 2010). Asian Americans are least likely to meet the diagnostic criteria for anxiety disorders, compared with other racial groups. These findings underscore the importance of race, ethnicity, and environmental variables in diagnosis and treatment.

CONCLUSION

These materials can help instructors and students alike better understand that the relationship between brain and behavior is not unidirectional and deterministic but, in fact, is bidirectional and malleable by a wide array of environmental factors; that more research is needed with diverse populations; that future studies improve methodological rigor, statistical power, and sample size; and that studies approach multicultural populations with a strengths-based perspective rather than a negative-difference perspective.

REFERENCES

Akincigil, A., Olfson, M., Walkup, J. T., Siegel, M. J., Kalay, E., Amin, S., . . . Crystal, S. (2011). Diagnosis and treatment of depression in older community-dwelling adults: 1992–2005. *Journal of the American Geriatrics Society, 59,* 1042–1051. http://dx.doi.org/10.1111/j.1532-5415.2011.03447.x

American Psychiatric Association. (2013). *Diagnostic and statistical manual of mental disorders* (5th ed.). Arlington, VA: Author.

Asherson, P., Young, A. H., Eich-Höchli, D., Moran, P., Porsdal, V., & Deberdt, W. (2014). Differential diagnosis, comorbidity, and treatment of attention-deficit/ hyperactivity disorder in relation to bipolar disorder or borderline personality disorder in adults. *Current Medical Research and Opinion, 30,* 1657–1672. http://dx.doi.org/10.1185/03007995.2014.915800

Asnaani, A., Richey, J. A., Dimaite, R., Hinton, D. E., & Hofmann, S. G. (2010). A cross-ethnic comparison of lifetime prevalence rates of anxiety disorders. *Journal of Nervous and Mental Disease, 198,* 551–555. http://dx.doi.org/10.1097/NMD.0b013e3181ea169f

Bain, J. (2007). The many faces of testosterone. *Clinical Interventions in Aging, 2,* 567–576.

Bauer, P. M., Hanson, J. L., Pierson, R. K., Davidson, R. J., & Pollak, S. D. (2009). Cerebellar volume and cognitive functioning in children who experienced early deprivation. *Biological Psychiatry, 66,* 1100–1106. http://dx.doi.org/10.1016/j.biopsych.2009.06.014

Bernstein, E., Bernstein, J., Tassiopoulos, K., Valentine, A., Heeren, T., Levenson, S., & Hingson, R. (2006). Racial and ethnic diversity among a heroin and cocaine using population: Treatment system utilization. *Journal of Addictive Diseases, 24,* 43–63. http://dx.doi.org/10.1300/J069v24n04_04

Bolanos, F., Herbeck, D., Christou, D., Lovinger, K., Pham, A., Raihan, A., . . . Brecht, M. L. (2012). Using facebook to maximize follow-up response rates in a longitudinal study of adults who use methamphetamine. *Substance Abuse: Research and Treatment, 6.* http://dx.doi.org/10.4137/SART.S8485

Brady, K. T., & Randall, C. L. (1999). Gender differences in substance use disorders. *Psychiatric Clinics of North America, 22,* 241–252. http://dx.doi.org/10.1016/S0193-953X(05)70074-5

Brain Development Cooperative Group. (2012). Total and regional brain volumes in a population-based normative sample from 4 to 18 years: The NIH MRI Study of Normal Brain Development. *Cerebral Cortex, 22,* 1–12. http://dx.doi.org/10.1093/cercor/bhr018

Brecht, M. L., Greenwell, L., & Anglin, M. D. (2005). Methamphetamine treatment: Trends and predictors of retention and completion in a large state treatment system (1992–2002). *Journal of Substance Abuse Treatment, 29,* 295–306. http://dx.doi.org/10.1016/j.jsat.2005.08.012

Brown, T. N., Williams, D. R., Jackson, J. S., Neighbors, H. W., Torres, M., Sellers, S. L., & Brown, K. T. (2000). "Being Black and feeling blue": The mental health consequences of racial discrimination. *Race and Society, 2,* 117–131. http://dx.doi.org/10.1016/S1090-9524(00)00010-3

Butler, K. M., Ickes, M. J., Rayens, M. K., Wiggins, A. T., & Hahn, E. J. (2016). Polytobacco use among college students. *Nicotine & Tobacco Research, 18,* 163–169. http://dx.doi.org/10.1093/ntr/ntv056

Caplan, P. J., & Caplan, J. (2016). *Thinking critically about research on sex and gender* (3rd ed.). New York, NY: Routledge.

Carmichael, O. T., Kuller, L. H., Lopez, O. L., Thompson, P. M., Dutton, R. A., Lu, A., . . . Becker, J. T. (2007). Acceleration of cerebral ventricular expansion in the Cardiovascular Health Study. *Neurobiology of Aging, 28,* 1316–1321. http://dx.doi.org/10.1016/j.neurobiolaging.2006.06.016

Chrisler, J. C., & Levy, K. B. (1990). The media construct a menstrual monster: A content analysis of PMS articles in the popular press. *Women & Health, 16,* 89–104. http://dx.doi.org/10.1300/J013v16n02_07

Chrisler, J. C., Rose, J. G., Dutch, S. E., Sklarsky, K. G., & Grant, M. C. (2006). The PMS illusion: Social cognition maintains social construction. *Sex Roles, 54,* 371–376. http://dx.doi.org/10.1007/s11199-006-9005-3

Chung, R., Bemak, F., Ortiz, D., & Sandoval-Perez, P. A. (2008). Promoting the mental health of migrants: A multicultural/social justice perspective. *Journal of Counseling & Development, 86,* 310–317. http://dx.doi.org/10.1002/j.1556-6678.2008.tb00514.x

Clark, T. T., Nguyen, A. B., & Coman, E. (2015). Smoking trajectories among mono-racial and biracial Black adolescents and young adults. *Journal of Drug Issues, 45,* 22–37. http://dx.doi.org/10.1177/0022042614542511

De Bellis, M. D., Clark, D. B., Beers, S. R., Soloff, P. H., Boring, A. M., Hall, J., . . . Keshavan, M. S. (2000). Hippocampal volume in adolescent-onset alcohol use disorders. *The American Journal of Psychiatry, 157,* 737–744. http://dx.doi.org/10.1176/appi.ajp.157.5.737

Ehrhardt, A. A., & Money, J. (1967). Progestin-induced hermaphroditism: IQ and psychosexual identity in a study of ten girls. *Journal of Sex Research, 3,* 83–100. http://dx.doi.org/10.1080/00224496709550517

Epstein, E. E., Fischer-Elber, K., & Al-Otaiba, Z. (2007). Women, aging, and alcohol use disorders. *Journal of Women & Aging, 19,* 31–48. http://dx.doi.org/10.1300/J074v19n01_03

Fausto-Sterling, A. (2000). *Sexing the body: Gender politics and the construction of sexuality.* New York, NY: Basic Books.

Fried, E. I., & Nesse, R. M. (2015). Depression is not a consistent syndrome: An investigation of unique symptom patterns in the STAR*D study. *Journal of Affective Disorders, 172,* 96–102. http://dx.doi.org/10.1016/j.jad.2014.10.010

Garten, S., & Falkner, R. V. (2004). Role of mentholated cigarettes in increased nicotine dependence and greater risk of tobacco-attributable disease. *Preventive Medicine, 38,* 793–798. http://dx.doi.org/10.1016/j.ypmed.2004.01.019

Gould, S. J. (1996). *The mismeasure of man* (Rev. ed.). New York, NY: Norton.

Grant, J. M., Mottet, L. A., Tanis, J., Herman, J. L., Harrison, J., & Keisling, M. (2010, October). *National transgender discrimination survey report on health and health care.* Retrieved from http://nursingstudentsforsexualandreproductivehealth.org/resources/Pictures/Trans-Health-Supplements.pdf

Greenfield, S. F., Brooks, A. J., Gordon, S. M., Green, C. A., Kropp, F., McHugh, R. K., . . . Miele, G. M. (2007). Substance abuse treatment entry, retention, and outcome in women: A review of the literature. *Drug and Alcohol Dependence, 86,* 1–21. http://dx.doi.org/10.1016/j.drugalcdep.2006.05.012

Hackman, D. A., Farah, M. J., & Meaney, M. J. (2010). Socioeconomic status and the brain: Mechanistic insights from human and animal research. *Nature Reviews Neuroscience, 11,* 651–659. http://dx.doi.org/10.1038/nrn2897

Hanson, J. L., Hair, N., Shen, D. G., Shi, F., Gilmore, J. H., Wolfe, B. L., & Pollak, S. D. (2013). Family poverty affects the rate of human infant brain growth. *PLoS One, 8*(12), e80954. http://dx.doi.org/10.1371/journal.pone.0080954

Harvey, A. T., Hitchcock, C. L., & Prior, J. C. (2009). Ovulation disturbances and mood across the menstrual cycles of healthy women. *Journal of Psychosomatic Obstetrics & Gynaecology, 30,* 207–214. http://dx.doi.org/10.3109/01674820903276438

Haslam, N., Bastian, B., Bain, P., & Kashima, Y. (2006). Psychological essentialism, implicit theories, and intergroup relations. *Group Processes & Intergroup Relations, 9,* 63–76. http://dx.doi.org/10.1177/1368430206059861

Hauschildt, M., Wittekind, C., Moritz, S., Kellner, M., & Jelinek, L. (2013). Attentional bias for affective visual stimuli in posttraumatic stress disorder and the role of depression. *Psychiatry Research, 207,* 73–79. http://dx.doi.org/10.1016/j.psychres.2012.11.024

Hiort, O. (2013). The differential role of androgens in early human sex development. *BMC Medicine, 11,* 152. http://dx.doi.org/10.1186/1741-7015-11-152

Hubbard, R. L., Schlenger, W. E., Rachal, J. V., Bray, R. M., Craddock, S. G., Cavanaugh, E. R., & Ginzburg, H. M. (1986). Patterns of alcohol and drug abuse in drug treatment clients from different ethnic backgrounds. *Annals of the New York Academy of Sciences, 472,* 60–74. http://dx.doi.org/10.1111/j.1749-6632.1986.tb29611.x

Intersex Society of North America. (n.d.). *What is intersex?* Retrieved from http://www.isna.org/faq/what_is_intersex

Isamah, N., Faison, W., Payne, M. E., MacFall, J., Steffens, D. C., Beyer, J. L., . . . Taylor, W. D. (2010). Variability in frontotemporal brain structure: The importance of recruitment of African Americans in neuroscience research. *PLoS One, 5*(10), e13642. http://dx.doi.org/10.1371/journal.pone.0013642

Jamal, A., Agaku, I. T., O'Connor, E., King, B. A., Kenemer, J. B., & Neff, L. (2014). Current cigarette smoking among adults—United States, 2005–2013. *Morbidity and Mortality Weekly Report, 63,* 1108–1112.

John, R., Cheney, M. K., & Azad, M. R. (2009). Point-of-sale marketing of tobacco products: Taking advantage of the socially disadvantaged? *Journal of Health Care for the Poor and Underserved, 20,* 489–506. http://dx.doi.org/10.1353/hpu.0.0147

Kandel, D. B., Griesler, P. C., & Hu, M. C. (2015). Intergenerational patterns of smoking and nicotine dependence among US adolescents. *American Journal of Public Health, 105,* e63–e72. http://dx.doi.org/10.2105/AJPH.2015.302775

Kecojevic, A., Wong, C. F., Corliss, H. L., & Lankenau, S. E. (2015). Risk factors for high levels of prescription drug misuse and illicit drug use among substance-using young men who have sex with men (YMSM). *Drug and Alcohol Dependence, 150,* 156–163. http://dx.doi.org/10.1016/j.drugalcdep.2015.02.031

Kennard, M. A. (1936). Age and other factors in motor recovery from precentral lesions in monkeys. *American Journal of Physiology, 115,* 138–146. http://dx.doi.org/10.1152/ajplegacy.1936.115.1.138

Klonoff, E. A., Landrine, H., & Campbell, R. (2000). Sexist discrimination may account for well-known gender differences in psychiatric symptoms. *Psychology of Women Quarterly, 24,* 93–99. http://dx.doi.org/10.1111/j.1471-6402.2000.tb01025.x

Kochunov, P., Fox, P., Lancaster, J., Tan, L. H., Amunts, K., Zilles, K., . . . Gao, J. H. (2003). Localized morphological brain differences between English-speaking Caucasians and Chinese-speaking Asians: New evidence of anatomical plasticity. *Neuroreport, 14,* 961–964. http://dx.doi.org/10.1097/01.wnr.0000075417.59944.00

Kolb, B., & Whishaw, I. Q. (1989). Plasticity in the neocortex: Mechanisms underlying recovery from early brain damage. *Progress in Neurobiology, 32,* 235–276. http://dx.doi.org/10.1016/0301-0082(89)90023-3

Landrine, H., Klonoff, E. A., Fernandez, S., Hickman, N., Kashima, K., Parekh, B., . . . Weslowski, Z. (2005). Cigarette advertising in Black, Latino, and White magazines, 1998–2002: An exploratory investigation. *Ethnicity & Disease, 15,* 63–67.

Långström, N., Rahman, Q., Carlström, E., & Lichtenstein, P. (2010). Genetic and environmental effects on same-sex sexual behavior: A population study of twins in Sweden. *Archives of Sexual Behavior, 39,* 75–80. http://dx.doi.org/10.1007/s10508-008-9386-1

Li, S. C. (2003). Biocultural orchestration of developmental plasticity across levels: The interplay of biology and culture in shaping the mind and behavior across the life span. *Psychological Bulletin, 129,* 171–194. http://dx.doi.org/10.1037/0033-2909.129.2.171

Min, M. O., Tracy, E. M., & Park, H. (2014). Impact of trauma symptomatology on personal networks among substance using women. *Drug and Alcohol Dependence, 142,* 277–282. http://dx.doi.org/10.1016/j.drugalcdep.2014.06.032

Money, J., & Ehrhardt, A. A. (1982). *Man & woman, boy & girl: The differentiation and dimorphism of gender identity from conception to maturity.* Baltimore, MD: Hopkins University Press.

Money, J., & Mathews, D. (1982). Prenatal exposure to virilizing progestins: An adult follow-up study of twelve women. *Archives of Sexual Behavior, 11,* 73–83. http://dx.doi.org/10.1007/BF01541367

Moore, L. V., & Diez Roux, A. V. (2006). Associations of neighborhood characteristics with the location and type of food stores. *American Journal of Public Health, 96,* 325–331. http://dx.doi.org/10.2105/AJPH.2004.058040

National Institute on Drug Abuse. (2018, July). *Drugs and the brain*. Retrieved from https://www.drugabuse.gov/publications/drugs-brains-behavior-science-addiction/drugs-brain

National Institute on Drug Abuse for Teens. (2014, December). *Brain and addiction*. Retrieved from https://teens.drugabuse.gov/drug-facts/brain-and-addiction

Obama, B. H. (2013). *Brain research through advancing innovative neurotechnologies*. Retrieved from https://obamawhitehouse.archives.gov/the-press-office/2013/04/02/remarks-president-brain-initiative-and-american-innovation

Otowa, T., Gardner, C. O., Kendler, K. S., & Hettema, J. M. (2013). Parenting and risk for mood, anxiety and substance use disorders: A study in population-based male twins. *Social Psychiatry and Psychiatric Epidemiology, 48*, 1841–1849. http://dx.doi.org/10.1007/s00127-013-0656-4

Poldrack, R. A. (2010). Mapping mental function to brain structure: How can cognitive neuroimaging succeed? *Perspectives on Psychological Science, 5*, 753–761. http://dx.doi.org/10.1177/1745691610388777

Prochaska, J. J., Grossman, W., Young-Wolff, K. C., & Benowitz, N. L. (2015). Validity of self-reported adult secondhand smoke exposure. *Tobacco Control, 24*, 48–53. http://dx.doi.org/10.1136/tobaccocontrol-2013-051174

Quinsey, V. L. (2003). The etiology of anomalous sexual preferences in men. *Annals of the New York Academy of Sciences, 989*, 105–117. http://dx.doi.org/10.1111/j.1749-6632.2003.tb07297.x

Robinson, M. J. F., Fischer, A. M., Ahuja, A., Lesser, E. N., & Maniates, H. (2015). Roles of "wanting" and "liking" in motivating behavior: Gambling, food, and drug addictions. *Current Topics in Behavioral Neurosciences, 27*, 105–136. http://dx.doi.org/10.1007/7854_2015_387

Romley, J. A., Cohen, D., Ringel, J., & Sturm, R. (2007). Alcohol and environmental justice: The density of liquor stores and bars in urban neighborhoods in the United States. *Journal of Studies on Alcohol and Drugs, 68*, 48–55. http://dx.doi.org/10.15288/jsad.2007.68.48

Saloner, B., & Karthikeyan, S. (2015, October 13). Changes in substance abuse treatment use among individuals with opioid use disorders in the United States, 2004–2013. *JAMA, 314*, 1515–1517. http://dx.doi.org/10.1001/jama.2015.10345

Scheim, A. I., & Bauer, G. R. (2015). Sex and gender diversity among transgender persons in Ontario, Canada: Results from a respondent-driven sampling survey. *Journal of Sex Research, 52*, 1–14. http://dx.doi.org/10.1080/00224499.2014.893553

Schlaug, G., Forgeard, M., Zhu, L., Norton, A., Norton, A., & Winner, E. (2009). Training-induced neuroplasticity in young children. *Annals of the New York Academy of Sciences, 1169*, 205–208. http://dx.doi.org/10.1111/j.1749-6632.2009.04842.x

Schmidt, P. J., Murphy, J. H., Haq, N., Rubinow, D. R., & Danaceau, M. A. (2004). Stressful life events, personal losses, and perimenopause-related depression. *Archives of Women's Mental Health, 7*, 19–26. http://dx.doi.org/10.1007/s00737-003-0036-2

Serra-Grabulosa, J. M., Junqué, C., Verger, K., Salgado-Pineda, P., Mañeru, C., & Mercader, J. M. (2005). Cerebral correlates of declarative memory dysfunctions in early traumatic brain injury. *Journal of Neurology, Neurosurgery & Psychiatry, 76*, 129–131. http://dx.doi.org/10.1136/jnnp.2004.027631

Shimamura, A. P. (2010). Bridging psychological and biological science: The good, bad, and ugly. *Perspectives on Psychological Science, 5*, 772–775. http://dx.doi.org/10.1177/1745691610388781

Substance Abuse and Mental Health Services Administration. (2009). *Substance abuse treatment: Addressing the specific needs of women* (Report No. SMA 09-4426). Retrieved from http://www.ncbi.nlm.nih.gov/books/NBK83252/

Trantham-Davidson, H., Burnett, E. J., Gass, J. T., Lopez, M. F., Mulholland, P. J., Centanni, S. W., . . . Chandler, L. J. (2014). Chronic alcohol disrupts dopamine receptor activity and the cognitive function of the medial prefrontal cortex. *The Journal of Neuroscience, 34,* 3706–3718. http://dx.doi.org/10.1523/JNEUROSCI.0623-13.2014

Volkow, N. D., Fowler, J. S., & Wang, G. J. (2004). The addicted human brain viewed in the light of imaging studies: Brain circuits and treatment strategies. *Neuropharmacology, 47,* 3–13. http://dx.doi.org/10.1016/j.neuropharm.2004.07.019

Webb Hooper, M., Baker, E. A., & McNutt, M. D. (2014). Racial/ethnic differences among smokers: Revisited and expanded to help seekers. *Nicotine & Tobacco Research, 16,* 621–625. http://dx.doi.org/10.1093/ntr/ntt206

Weisberg, D. S., Keil, F. C., Goodstein, J., Rawson, E., & Gray, J. R. (2008). The seductive allure of neuroscience explanations. *Journal of Cognitive Neuroscience, 20,* 470–477. http://dx.doi.org/10.1162/jocn.2008.20040

Weyandt, L. L. (2006). *The physiological bases of cognitive and behavioral disorders.* Mahwah, NJ: Erlbaum.

Weyandt, L. L., Marraccini, M. E., Gudmundsdottir, B. G., Zavras, B. M., Turcotte, K. D., Munro, B. A., & Amoroso, A. J. (2013). Misuse of prescription stimulants among college students: A review of the literature and implications for morphological and cognitive effects on brain functioning. *Experimental and Clinical Psychopharmacology, 21,* 385–407. http://dx.doi.org/10.1037/a0034013

Wilkins, L., Jones, H. W., Jr., Holman, G. H., Jr., & Stempfel, R. S., Jr. (1958). Masculinization of the female fetus associated with administration of oral and intramuscular progestins during gestation: Non-adrenal female pseudohermaphrodism. *The Journal of Clinical Endocrinology and Metabolism, 18,* 559–585. http://dx.doi.org/10.1210/jcem-18-6-559

Witbrodt, J., Mulia, N., Zemore, S. E., & Kerr, W. C. (2014). Racial/ethnic disparities in alcohol-related problems: Differences by gender and level of heavy drinking. *Alcoholism: Clinical and Experimental Research, 38,* 1662–1670. http://dx.doi.org/10.1111/acer.12398

World History Project. (n.d.). *Death of Sigmund Freud.* Retrieved from https://worldhistoryproject.org/1939/9/23/death-of-sigmund-freud

Wu, L. T., Brady, K. T., Mannelli, P., & Killeen, T. K. (2014). Cannabis use disorders are comparatively prevalent among nonwhite racial/ethnic groups and adolescents: A national study. *Journal of Psychiatric Research, 50,* 26–35. http://dx.doi.org/10.1016/j.jpsychires.2013.11.010

Young, S. D., & Shoptaw, S. (2013). Stimulant use among African American and Latino MSM social networking users. *Journal of Addictive Diseases, 32,* 39–45. http://dx.doi.org/10.1080/10550887.2012.759859

22

Teaching Critical, Multivocal Histories of Psychology

Uncovering Diversity

Kelli Vaughn-Johnson and Alexandra Rutherford

For 30 years, psychologist–historians have reexamined the histories we provide in light of historiographic challenges (e.g., Bohan, 1995; Danziger, 1990; Furumoto, 1989; Guthrie, 1976/1998). Yet, the purposeful inclusion of multiple voices and diverse origins has not become a staple in the standard classroom. History of psychology courses continue to vary only minimally from traditional Western male celebratory centered perspectives about the development of psychology, without acknowledging that these narratives are the products of particular viewpoints and privileged voices.

We argue that the History of Psychology course can be an exciting opportunity for students to critically engage with the ways both history and psychology are constructed. Historians of psychology analyze how psychology has developed over time in particular contexts, including whose voices get heard, whose remain muted, and how these dynamics shape the construction of psychological knowledge (see Rutherford, 2014). This requires addressing gender, race and ethnicity, sociocultural and political contexts, and other factors that have affected the field's disciplinary practices, knowledge production, and social impact. A critical historical perspective requires, in part, asking, "Who made the knowledge, for what purpose, and to what ends?" (Rutherford & Pickren, 2015, p. 523). Injecting these kinds of questions and encouraging historical thinking as a method in the course can increase capacities for critical reflection on psychology as a whole. To facilitate this process, in this chapter we curate a selection of resources and provide guidance for their use, but we emphasize

http://dx.doi.org/10.1037/0000137-023
Integrating Multiculturalism and Intersectionality Into the Psychology Curriculum:
Strategies for Instructors, J. A. Mena and K. Quina (Editors)

that teaching critical reflection and active learning as specific objectives of the History of Psychology course.[1]

UNCOVERING HISTORY THROUGH ACTIVE, CRITICAL INQUIRY

Students often enter the course expecting a story of psychology's greatest achievements, from mythic origins to triumphant endings. Students expect traditional histories that are based entirely on schools or primarily on the contributions of the so-called "great White men" (Ball, 2012; Beins, 2011). Although these do reflect a certain standpoint, it has come to be recognized as a standpoint that is partial, privileged, and incomplete. Such stories also serve little pedagogical purpose; psychology is not static, and its historical narratives are not fixed. Mezirow (1981) proposed that active learning should include a social interaction component that helps students construct meaning from information they encounter, an immersion pedagogy of "perspective transformation within learning" (p. 6). History can facilitate such transformation (e.g., Grim, Pace, & Shopkow, 2004; Lo, Chang, Tu, & Yeh, 2009).

Van Drie and van Boxtel (2008) defined *historical reasoning* as a process whereby students not only acquire knowledge of history but also use it to interpret the past and present. Thinking historically requires that a student "become comfortable with abstractions whose meaning changes over time. . . . to exercise their imagination, which plays an important role in establishing the relationship between disconnected historical facts" (Lo et al., 2009, p. 155). Student-centered active learning environments increase retention and expand conceptions of historical reasoning (Abramson, Burke-Bergmann, Nolf, & Swift, 2009; Yang, 2009).

This transformational learning environment allows students to explore what Calder (2006) called the "uncoverage" of history, exploring

> the very things hidden away by traditional survey instruction: the linchpin ideas of historical inquiry that are not obvious or easily comprehended; the inquiries, arguments, assumptions, and points of view that make knowledge what it is for practitioners of our discipline; the cognitive contours of history as an epistemological domain. (p. 1363)

In other words, we need to help students uncover how knowledge is conceived, conceptualized, and disseminated from certain viewpoints and within larger contexts. A historical perspective thus becomes a highly effective method for providing a multicultural focus (Young, Rodkey, & Rutherford, 2015). Goodwin (2013) reminded us that when taught well, the History of Psychology course allows students to "understand the intellectual and cultural foundations of the

---

[1]The companion webpage for this book also includes additional recommended resources that instructors can incorporate in their classes (http://pubs.apa.org/books/supp/mena).

discipline . . . and appreciate the interconnectedness among the various fragments of knowledge they have accumulated in other courses" (p. 349).

THREE EXAMPLES: UNCOVERING ALTERNATIVES

Instructors often have to take what students already know in some form, such as a theory of personality or a classic experiment, and provide a different way to understand and contextualize it. One strategy is to attend to the gendered, racialized, "classed," heteronormative, and religious contexts in which theory and experimentation almost always occur. Eleanor Gibson's visual cliff experiment provides an example (Gibson & Walk, 1960). Students generally enter the History of Psychology class with some knowledge of this experiment. To further their historical understanding, students could read a short biography of Gibson, along with the original study. In the traditional approach, that might be the end of the story, but there is more to uncover. Rodkey (2015) wrote, "Reconstruction of the visual cliff research began with the classic . . . photograph" (p. 135). The iconic photograph showing the baby on the cliff receiving encouragement from its mother was only one of dozens depicting a variety of animal species as they navigated the cliff. The mythic narrative that followed suggested that the study focused mainly on human babies and was inspired by Gibson's children. Rodkey's detailed analysis of the reception and communication of Gibson's studies argued that not only was the comparative context lost but also that a distinctly gendered process was applied that generated and perpetuated the mythic narrative about the experiment's conception, execution, and results.

Students can examine Rodkey's (2015) evidence and respond to questions such as: How might Gibson's race and class have affected her access to training and resources as well as choices about what to study? How might these have been different if she had been a Woman of Color? Alberta Banner Turner was an African American developmental psychologist and activist working in this same period (Vaughn, 2011). Although both are technically members of the second generation of women psychologists in the United States, Turner is part of the first generation of Black women. The first generation of White women had been much more inclined to participate in activism than those of Gibson's generation (Johnston & Johnson, 2008). How did not only race but also generational establishment impact their career trajectories? How might Gibson's or Turner's research or advocacy have been alternatively conceived and received if conducted by a prominent White male such as their contemporary, Arnold Gesell (Bergen, 2017)?

Comparing two models of identity development provides another opportunity to learn how historical, cultural, and personal contexts affect psychological theory from a male-centered storyline. G. Stanley Hall's (1904) *Adolescence: Its Psychology and Its Relations to Physiology, Anthropology, Sociology, Sex, Crime and Religion*, for example, reflects his pronounced Christian-based orthodoxy, eugenic ideologies, and beliefs about sex differences that were widely held in early 20th century America (see Arnett, 2006; Bederman, 1995). Hall's work can be compared with Erikson's (1968) *Identity, Youth, and Crisis*. Erikson was a German Jewish immigrant to the United States, and his developmental theory was affected by political contexts and his identity crises. Primary documents alongside biographical information can help students uncover highly specific personal factors that impacted supposedly universal theories of development (for Hall, see Ross, 1972; for Erikson, see Friedman, 2004, and Marcia, 1966).

For example, Mamie Phipps Clark's work on racial self-identification in children and her famous "doll studies," published with her husband Kenneth B. Clark, were submitted to the U.S. Supreme Court in the *Brown v. Board* case that led to the desegregation of U.S. public schools. Students can read the original studies (e.g., M. P. Clark, 1939; K. B. Clark & Clark, 1939) and historical resources that unpack their context and significance (Jackson, 2001; Keppel, 2002; Lal, 2002; Rutherford, 2012). How and why did Mamie Clark design the studies? How might the Clarks' integrationist commitments have shaped their interpretation and mobilization of their results? How did her race and class affect the trajectory of her career and her convictions about how to help children? How has her legacy been portrayed compared with that of her husband? Uncovering each layer reveals the complex dynamics that shape psychology and its social impact.

INTEGRATING CONSIDERATIONS OF INDIGENIZATION

A critical history of psychology has the duty to uncover and restore the voices of those marginalized or omitted in the dominant narrative. To that end, critical historians of psychology place attention on how knowledge generated in local contexts circulates through and is modified by other contexts, a process known as *indigenization*. Arnett (2008) reminded us that research undertaken by and on U.S. populations, although "indigenous" as any other, continues to "stand in" for a universal psychology and is resistant to contributions from non-North American psychologists and psychologies. Teo (2013) described *indigenization* as

> a general process, by which theories and concepts from outside of a particular cultural setting are accommodated into any local context. . . . Yet, if indigenous psychologies refer to the study of the psyche of native humans and are used for and derived from particular groups of people, then American (or German) psychology needs to be included as an indigenous psychology. (pp. 1–2)

There are debates over the influence of American-centered norms, gendered approaches, and lack of racial diversity in presentations of psychology's history (see Rutherford & Pickren, 2015). Historians of psychology are now entering these debates because history offers unique insights into the question of how psychological knowledge relates to its cultural contexts (see Pickren, 2011; Shams, 2002; Sher & Long, 2012). Engaging students in dialogues about the ways psychological knowledge and practice are rooted in local norms and cultures can expand their capacity for critical reflection on knowledge claims.

In *Re-Examining Psychology: Critical Perspectives and African Insights,* Holdstock (2013) argued that a move from an atomistic, ethnocentric approach to one of critical awareness requires that we place how we regard our roles and specializations as psychologists in the forefront. This requires an openness to indigenous practices as constructions of self. Asking students "to fit themselves into the world about them, and to understand themselves as part of that world," provides a foundation on which to build an exploratory learning environment (Harcum, 1988, p. 231). Self-bias identification and examination of the instructor at the beginning of a course can assist students in understanding how we as individual researchers engage with the evidence and develop hypotheses.

FROM UNCOVERING TO INFUSING: INCORPORATING DIVERSE VOICES INTO HISTORIES OF PSYCHOLOGY

Providing opportunities for exploration of multiple cultures and identities can help destabilize traditional historical narratives and help students develop critical thinking skills (Gone, 2011; Okazaki, David, & Abelmann, 2008; Pickren, 2009). Amplifying and integrating diverse voices throughout is arguably more effective than a special unit; for example, when exploring the development of laboratory work, instructors can include laboratories in Mexico (Escobar, 2014) and Lithuania (Bagdonas, Pociūtė, Rimkutė, & Valickas, 2008). Pickren (2011) offered guidance for such cultural integration. The 2009 special issue of *Cultural Diversity and Ethnic Minority Psychology* introduced the history of the myriad cultures and ethnicities within American psychology (Leong, 2009).

Articles providing Indigenous and critical approaches to historical pedagogy can also be helpful. *History and Philosophy of Psychology* devoted a special issue to innovative teaching from a primarily British perspective (Hegarty, Hubbard, & Nyatanga, 2015); Brock (2013) offered a Canadian perspective. A virtual issue of *History of Psychology* provided examples of using history to promote critical engagement with diversity, including gender, race, and the intersections of disability and sexuality (Rutherford, 2013). For more applied courses, see Clegg (2012) on teaching the history of the *Diagnostic and Statistical Manual of Mental Disorders* and Carson (2014) on internationalizing the history of mental testing. Helpful teaching guides are found in de Freitas Campos (2010), Faye and Baker (2011), and Stock (2010).

The historiography of psychology in multiple countries and regions can open students' eyes not only to different theories but also to the diverse and varied methodologies used by psychologists throughout the world (Baker, 2012; Gross, Abrams, & Enns, 2016). A 2010 special issue of *History of Psychology* reviews such historiography in Brazil, the Czech Republic, Italy, and Spain (Pickren, 2010). Winston, Butzer, and Ferris (2004) analyzed how psychology has historically constructed concepts of racial difference; Glucksmann (2008) examined issues of power within subjugated groups (e.g., feminists of varied classes and ethnicities).

WOMEN AND FEMINISM IN THE HISTORY OF PSYCHOLOGY

There is a sizeable literature on women's contributions to psychology (Furumoto, 2003), although there remains room for much more work, especially on non–North American or European women. *Psychology's Feminist Voices* (http://www.feministvoices.com), a multimedia digital archive dedicated to capturing, preserving, writing, and disseminating the history of women and feminism in psychology, provides global stories of women in psychology and their contributions, feminist movements, and social activism. The archive is continually updated with oral histories, historical profiles, teaching resources, research options, and class activities (Ball et al., 2013). Feminists tell their stories in their own words, thus complementing traditional, depoliticized, and depersonalized narratives of psychology's past. A special issue of *History of Psychology* examined the intertwined histories of feminism and psychology (Rutherford & Pettit, 2015), from female sexologists in Germany and Austria in the early 1900s to the traffic between feminist grassroots activism and the feminist academy in 1970s Canada.

GENDER AND SEXUALITY

Gender is not synonymous with women or sex; however, historically, the two have been linked, as illustrated in Basow's (2010) survey of textbook portrayals between 1975 and 2010. Combining different approaches helps students to understand that the perception of a gendered historical narrative depends as much on the perspective of the narrator as it does on the purview of its subject. The *Handbook of Gender Research in Psychology* (Chrisler & McCreary, 2010) is a strong springboard for discussions on gender from multiple perspectives. Cochran (2010) invited us to ask what considerations of and concentrations on masculinity might mean for broader conceptualizations of gender. Hegarty's (2007) article on the gendering of intelligence by Lewis Terman also offered an alternative historical framework for concepts of gender. Minton's (2000) study of gender and psychology during the early 20th century provided a useful contrast to Hegarty both in its historiographic approach and content. Students can also explore gender as a social justice narrative when told from a psychologist–activist standpoint (see Loss, 2011; Russo, Pirlott, & Cohen, 2011).

Pettit and Hegarty's (2014) chapter in the American Psychological Association *Handbook of Sexuality and Psychology* excavated underground histories of sexuality in psychology and, in doing so, provided new historical narratives. It offered not only a history of the topic but also articulated the complexity of writing any narrative about sexuality. In their words,

> history of sexuality is not a narrative of greater enlightenment and universal emancipation, but an uneven and event-filled terrain featuring surprising reversals. Furthermore, the object of the psychology of sexuality is not historically stable because sexual subjects interact in complicated ways with the knowledge produced about them. (p. 75)

Combining Hegarty's (2012) analysis of the Committee for Research on Problems of Sex and Rutherford's (2012) commentary with Pettit, Serykh, and Green's (2015) visualization of the funding choices of that committee through "multispecies networks" provides students with several ways of looking at a single history. Other histories focus on lesbian feminisms (Ellis & Peel, 2011), same-sex politics in psychology (Hammack & Windell, 2011), and queer theory (Hancock & Greenspan, 2010; Minton, 1997). For an interesting class discussion that will refocus students' gaze on how psychologists have projected their biased assumptions about race and sex onto their nonhuman subjects, explore Guthrie's (1976/1998) *Even the Rat Was White*, along with Pettit's (2012) *The Queer Life of a Lab Rat*.

MULTIPLE VOICES IN HISTORY OF PSYCHOLOGY TEXTBOOKS

History textbooks, like any teaching tool, are influenced by both the author(s) perspective and available scholarship (Bazar, 2015). However, students may also approach their history texts as containing established "truths." Although we advocate teaching through active historiographical methods and challenging the notion of any single story of psychology's past, there are a few texts that can help the student uncover the multivocality of history, including Pickren and Rutherford (2010); Walsh, Teo, and Baydala (2014); and Goodwin (2012). The first two offer strong introductory chapters on historiographic approaches and incorporate in-depth coverage of non-North American psychologies. Walsh and colleagues provided an intensive critical theory focus on premodern psychological thought and its philosophical origins. Pickren and Rutherford focused more on modern psychology using a social-constructionist framework, addressing the rise of feminism and the psychology of gender. Goodwin took a more traditional approach to teaching the History of Psychology with broader coverage of gender and culture from a seasoned psychologist–historian. All touch on developments in studies of sexuality, disability, and religious history, although these topics continue to warrant supplemental readings.

CONCLUSION

Teaching psychology's complex history affords diverse opportunities for active learning and critical reflections on the field. The proliferation of historiography in recent years can help facilitate thoughtful dialogue about psychological constructions of gender, race, ethnicity, culture, sexuality, and many other axes of difference. As scholarship in the history of psychology has changed, the way it is taught must also change. This offers unique opportunities to teach our students that psychology is shaped as much by historical, cultural, personal, and political forces as by statistical results and intake assessments. We instructors have to give ourselves permission to teach these complex narrations of knowledge, to not only challenge but also build tenable disciplinary identities: To distinguish who we are, we must be conscious of who and what we have been and how that changes over time and location.

These kinds of inquiries need not be limited to the History of Psychology classroom. Applying historical reasoning as a way of thinking about knowing will help students in all aspects of their educations, practice, and research. For the psychological scientist particularly, it is no longer sufficient to ask only whether a question is measurable, they must also be prepared to deconstruct it, before experimentation, to see whether it is meaningful. Critical historiography provides a framework to ask what our lens (or bias) is—and what is theirs. Uncovering and engaging history, with its multiple voices, competing narratives, and critical inquiries, diversifies both the lessons we teach and the kinds of questions students learn to ask.

REFERENCES

Abramson, C. I., Burke-Bergmann, A. L., Nolf, S. L., & Swift, K. (2009). Use of board games, historical calendars, and trading cards in a history of psychology class. *Psychological Reports, 104*, 529–544. http://dx.doi.org/10.2466/PR0.104.2.529-544

Arnett, J. J. (2006). G. Stanley Hall's *Adolescence*: Brilliance and nonsense. *History of Psychology, 9*, 186–197. http://dx.doi.org/10.1037/1093-4510.9.3.186

Arnett, J. J. (2008). The neglected 95%: Why American psychology needs to become less American. *American Psychologist, 63*, 602–614. http://dx.doi.org/10.1037/0003-066X.63.7.602

Bagdonas, A., Pociūtė, B., Rimkutė, E., & Valickas, G. (2008). The history of Lithuanian psychology. *European Psychologist, 13*, 227–237. http://dx.doi.org/10.1027/1016-9040.13.3.227

Baker, D. B. (Ed.). (2012). *The Oxford handbook on the history of psychology: Global perspectives*. New York, NY: Oxford University. http://dx.doi.org/10.1093/oxfordhb/9780195366556.001.0001

Ball, L. C. (2012). Genius without the "Great Man": New possibilities for the historian of psychology. *History of Psychology, 15*, 72–83. http://dx.doi.org/10.1037/a0023247

Ball, L. C., Bazar, J. L., MacKay, J., Rodkey, E. N., Rutherford, A., & Young, J. L. (2013). Using psychology's feminist voices in the classroom. *Psychology of Women Quarterly, 37*, 261–266. http://dx.doi.org/10.1177/0361684313480484

Basow, S. A. (2010). Changes in psychology of women and psychology of gender textbooks (1975–2010). *Sex Roles, 62*, 151–152. http://dx.doi.org/10.1007/s11199-010-9744-z

Bazar, J. L. (2015). Origins of teaching psychology in America. In D. S. Dunn (Ed.), *Oxford handbook of undergraduate psychology education* (pp. 1–10). New York, NY: Oxford University Press.

Bederman, G. (1995). *Manliness and civilization: A cultural history of gender and race in the United States, 1880–1917*. Chicago, IL: University of Chicago. http://dx.doi.org/10.7208/chicago/9780226041490.001.0001

Beins, B. C. (2011). Using history to teach contemporary psychology. *Teaching of Psychology, 38*, 309–313. http://dx.doi.org/10.1177/0098628311421338

Bergen, D. (2017). What Arnold Gesell would advocate today. *Childhood Education, 93*, 199–203. http://dx.doi.org/10.1080/00094056.2017.1325229

Bohan, J. S. (1995). *Re-placing women in psychology: Readings toward a more inclusive history* (2nd ed.). Dubuque, IA: Kendall/Hunt.

Brock, A. C. (2013). Introduction to the special issue on the history of psychology in Canada. *Canadian Psychology/Psychologie canadienne, 54*, 87–93. http://dx.doi.org/10.1037/a0032546

Calder, L. (2006). Uncoverage: Toward a signature pedagogy for the history survey. *The Journal of American History, 92*, 1358–1370. http://dx.doi.org/10.2307/4485896

Carson, J. (2014). Mental testing in the early twentieth century: Internationalizing the mental testing story. *History of Psychology, 17*, 249–255. http://dx.doi.org/10.1037/a0037475

Chrisler, J. C., & McCreary, D. R. (2010). *Handbook of gender research in psychology.* New York, NY: Springer.

Clark, K. B., & Clark, M. P. (1939). Segregation as a factor in the racial identification of Negro pre-school children: A preliminary report. *Journal of Experimental Education, 8*, 161–163. http://dx.doi.org/10.1080/00220973.1939.11010160

Clark, M. P. (1939). The development of the consciousness of self in Negro pre-school children. *Archives of Psychology.* Washington, DC: Howard University.

Clegg, J. W. (2012). Teaching about mental health and illness through the history of the *DSM. History of Psychology, 15*, 364–370. http://dx.doi.org/10.1037/a0027249

Cochran, S. V. (2010). Emergence and development of the psychology of men and masculinity. In J. C. Chrisler & D. R. McCreary (Eds.), *Handbook of gender research in psychology* (pp. 43–58). New York, NY: Springer New York. http://dx.doi.org/10.1007/978-1-4419-1465-1_3

Danziger, K. (1990). *Constructing the subject: Historical origins of psychological research.* Cambridge, MA: Cambridge University Press. http://dx.doi.org/10.1017/CBO9780511524059

de Freitas Campos, R. H. (2010). Sources: The UFMG archives of the history of psychology in Brazil. *History of Psychology, 13*, 201–205. http://dx.doi.org/10.1037/a0019381a

Ellis, S. J., & Peel, E. (2011). Lesbian feminisms: Historical and present possibilities. *Feminism & Psychology, 21*, 198–204. http://dx.doi.org/10.1177/0959353510370178

Erikson, E. H. (1968). *Identity: Youth and crisis.* New York, NY: Norton.

Escobar, R. (2014). The instruments in the first psychological laboratory in Mexico: Antecedents, influence, and methods. *History of Psychology, 17*, 296–311. http://dx.doi.org/10.1037/a0038038

Faye, C., & Baker, D. (2011). Sources: The Center for the History of Psychology at the University of Akron. *History of Psychology, 14*, 204–209. http://dx.doi.org/10.1037/a0023481a

Friedman, L. (2004). Erik Erikson: A biographer's reflection on a decade-long process. In K. Hoover (Ed.), *The future of identity: Centennial reflections on the legacy of Erik Erickson* (pp. 23–42). Lanham, MD: Lexington Books.

Furumoto, L. (1989). The new history of psychology. In I. S. Cohen (Ed.), *The G. Stanley Hall Lecture Series* (Vol. 9, pp. 9–34). Washington, DC: American Psychological Association. http://dx.doi.org/10.1037/10090-001

Furumoto, L. (2003). Beyond great men and great ideas: History of psychology in sociocultural context. In P. E. Bronstein & K. Quina (Eds.), *Teaching gender and multicultural awareness: Resources for the psychology classroom* (pp. 113–124). Washington, DC: American Psychological Association. http://dx.doi.org/10.1037/10570-008

Gibson, E. J., & Walk, R. D. (1960). The "visual cliff". *Scientific American, 202*, 64–71. http://dx.doi.org/10.1038/scientificamerican0460-64

Glucksmann, M. (2008). V. Airbrushing the history of feminism: 'Race' and ethnicity. *Feminism & Psychology, 18*, 405–409. http://dx.doi.org/10.1177/0959353508092096

Gone, J. P. (2011). Is psychological science a-cultural? *Cultural Diversity and Ethnic Minority Psychology, 17*, 234–242. http://dx.doi.org/10.1037/a0023805

Goodwin, C. J. (2012). *A history of modern psychology.* Hoboken, NJ: Wiley.

Goodwin, C. J. (2013). Teaching the history of psychology. In S. F. Davis & W. Buskist (Eds.), *The teaching of psychology: Essays in honor of Wilbert J. McKeachie and Charles L. Brewer* (pp. 349–360). New York, NY: Taylor & Francis.

Grim, V., Pace, D., & Shopkow, L. (2004). Learning to use evidence in the study of history. *New Directions for Teaching and Learning, 2004*, 57–65. http://dx.doi.org/10.1002/tl.147

Gross, D., Abrams, K., & Enns, C. Z. (Eds.). (2016). *Internationalizing the undergraduate psychology curriculum: Practical lessons learned at home and abroad.* Washington, DC: American Psychological Association. http://dx.doi.org/10.1037/14840-001

Guthrie, R. V. (1998). *Even the rat was white: A historical view of psychology.* Boston, MA: Allyn & Bacon. (Original work published 1976)

Hall, G. S. (1904). *Adolescence: Its psychology and its relations to physiology, anthropology, sociology, sex, crime, religion and education* (Vol. 1 & 2). Englewood Cliffs, NJ: Prentice-Hall.

Hammack, P. L., & Windell, E. P. (2011). Psychology and the politics of same-sex desire in the United States: An analysis of three cases. *History of Psychology, 14,* 220–248. http://dx.doi.org/10.1037/a0024541

Hancock, K. A., & Greenspan, K. (2010). Emergence and development of the psychological study of lesbian, gay, bisexual, and transgender Issues. In J. C. Chrisler & D. R. McCreary (Eds.), *Handbook of gender research in psychology* (pp. 59–78). New York, NY: Springer. http://dx.doi.org/10.1007/978-1-4419-1465-1_4

Harcum, R. E. (1988). Defensive reactance of psychologists to a metaphysical foundation for integrating different psychologies. *The Journal of Psychology: Interdisciplinary and Applied, 122,* 217–235. http://dx.doi.org/10.1080/00223980.1988.9915509

Hegarty, P. (2007). From genius inverts to gendered intelligence: Lewis Terman and the power of the norm. *History of Psychology, 10,* 132–155. http://dx.doi.org/10.1037/1093-4510.10.2.132

Hegarty, P. (2012). Beyond Kinsey: The committee for research on problems of sex and American psychology. *History of Psychology, 15,* 197–200. http://dx.doi.org/10.1037/a0027270

Hegarty, P., Hubbard, K., & Nyatanga, L. (Eds.). (2015). Innovative approaches to teaching CHIP [Special issue]. *History & Philosophy of Psychology, 16*(1).

Holdstock, T. L. (2013). *Re-examining psychology: Critical perspectives and African insights.* Philadelphia, PA: Routledge.

Jackson, J. P. (2001). *Social scientists for social justice: Making the case against segregation.* New York, NY: New York University Press.

Johnston, E., & Johnson, A. (2008). Searching for the second generation of American women psychologists. *History of Psychology, 11,* 40–72. http://dx.doi.org/10.1037/1093-4510.11.1.40

Keppel, B. (2002). Kenneth B. Clark in the patterns of American culture. *American Psychologist, 57,* 29–37. http://dx.doi.org/10.1037/0003-066X.57.1.29

Lal, S. (2002). Giving children security: Mamie Phipps Clark and the racialization of child psychology. *American Psychologist, 57,* 20–28. http://dx.doi.org/10.1037/0003-066X.57.1.20

Leong, F. T. L. (2009). Guest editor's introduction: History of racial and ethnic minority psychology. *Cultural Diversity and Ethnic Minority Psychology, 15,* 315–316. http://dx.doi.org/10.1037/a0017556

Lo, J.-J., Chang, C.-J., Tu, H.-H., & Yeh, S.-W. (2009). Applying GIS to develop a web-based spatial-person-temporal history educational system. *Computers & Education, 53,* 155–168. http://dx.doi.org/10.1016/j.compedu.2009.01.016

Loss, C. P. (2011). "Women's studies is in a lot of ways—consciousness raising": The educational origins of identity politics. *History of Psychology, 14,* 287–310. http://dx.doi.org/10.1037/a0024799

Marcia, J. E. (1966). Development and validation of ego-identity status. *Journal of Personality and Social Psychology, 3,* 551–558. http://dx.doi.org/10.1037/h0023281

Mezirow, J. (1981). A critical theory of adult learning and education. *Adult Education Quarterly, 32,* 3–24. http://dx.doi.org/10.1177/074171368103200101

Minton, H. L. (1997). Queer theory: Historical roots and implications for psychology. *Theory & Psychology, 7,* 337–353. http://dx.doi.org/10.1177/0959354397073003

Minton, H. L. (2000). Psychology and gender at the turn of the century. *American Psychologist, 55,* 613–615. http://dx.doi.org/10.1037/0003-066X.55.6.613

Okazaki, S., David, E. J. R., & Abelmann, N. (2008). Colonialism and psychology of culture. *Social and Personality Psychology Compass, 2,* 90–106. http://dx.doi.org/10.1111/j.1751-9004.2007.00046.x

Pettit, M. (2012). The queer life of a lab rat. *History of Psychology, 15,* 217–227. http://dx.doi.org/10.1037/a0027269

Pettit, M., & Hegarty, P. (2014). Psychology and sexuality in historical time. In D. L. Tolman, L. M. Diamond, J. A. Bauermeister, W. H. George, J. G. Pfaus, & L. M. Ward (Eds.), *APA handbook of sexuality and psychology: Vol. 1. Person-based approaches* (pp. 63–78). Washington, DC: American Psychological Association. http://dx.doi.org/10.1037/14193-003

Pettit, M., Serykh, D., & Green, C. D. (2015). Multispecies networks: Visualizing the psychological research of the Committee for Research in Problems of Sex. *Isis, 106,* 121–149. http://dx.doi.org/10.1086/681039

Pickren, W. E. (2009). Liberating history: The context of the challenge of psychologists of color to American psychology. *Cultural Diversity and Ethnic Minority Psychology, 15,* 425–433. http://dx.doi.org/10.1037/a0017561

Pickren, W. E. (Ed.). (2010). International historiography of psychology [Special issue]. *History of Psychology, 13*(3).

Pickren, W. E. (2011). Internationalizing the history of psychology course in the USA. In F. T. L. Leong, W. E. Pickren, M. M. Leach, & A. J. Marsella (Eds.), *Internationalizing the psychology curriculum in the United States* (pp. 11–28). New York, NY: Springer. http://dx.doi.org/10.1007/978-1-4614-0073-8_2

Pickren, W. E., & Rutherford, A. (2010). *A history of modern psychology in context.* Hoboken, NJ: Wiley.

Rodkey, E. N. (2015). The visual cliff's forgotten menagerie: Rats, goats, babies, and myth-making in the history of psychology. *Journal of the History of the Behavioral Sciences, 51,* 113–140. http://dx.doi.org/10.1002/jhbs.21712

Ross, D. (1972). *G. Stanley Hall: The psychologist as prophet.* Chicago, IL: University of Chicago.

Russo, N. F., Pirlott, A. G., & Cohen, A. B. (2011). The psychology of women and gender in international perspective: Issues and challenges. In F. T. L. Leong, W. E. Pickren, M. M. Leach, & A. J. Marsella (Eds.), *Internationalizing the psychology curriculum in the United States* (pp. 157–178). New York, NY: Springer. http://dx.doi.org/10.1007/978-1-4614-0073-8_8

Rutherford, A. (2012). Problems of sex and the problem with nature: A commentary on "Beyond Kinsey". *History of Psychology, 15,* 228–232. http://dx.doi.org/10.1037/a0027668

Rutherford, A. (2013). Teaching diversity: What can history offer? *History of Psychology, 16,* 1–5. http://dx.doi.org/10.1037/a0034368

Rutherford, A. (2014). Historiography. In T. Teo (Ed.), *Encyclopedia of critical psychology* (Vol. 2, pp. 866–872). New York, NY: Springer. http://dx.doi.org/10.1007/978-1-4614-5583-7_136

Rutherford, A., & Pettit, M. (2015). Feminism and/in/as psychology: The public sciences of sex and gender. *History of Psychology, 18,* 223–237. http://dx.doi.org/10.1037/a0039533

Rutherford, A., & Pickren, W. E. (2015). Teaching history of psychology: Aims, approaches, and debates. In D. Dunn (Ed.), *Oxford handbook of undergraduate psychology education* (pp. 521–531). London, England: Oxford University Press.

Shams, M. (2002). Issues in the study of indigenous psychologies: Historical perspectives, cultural interdependence and institutional regulations. *Asian Journal of Social Psychology, 5,* 79–91. http://dx.doi.org/10.1111/1467-839X.00096

Sher, D., & Long, W. (2012). Historicising the relevance debate: South African and American psychology in context. *South African Journal of Psychology, 42,* 564–575. http://dx.doi.org/10.1177/008124631204200410

Stock, A. (2010). The Adolf-Würth-Center for the History of Psychology at the University of Würzburg: Its history, present, and future. *History of Psychology, 13*, 335–339. http://dx.doi.org/10.1037/a0020320a

Teo, T. (2013). Backlash against American psychology: An indigenous reconstruction of the history of German critical psychology. *History of Psychology, 16*, 1–18. http://dx.doi.org/10.1037/a0030286

van Drie, J., & van Boxtel, C. (2008). Historical reasoning: Towards a framework for analyzing students' reasoning about the past. *Educational Psychology Review, 20*, 87–110. http://dx.doi.org/10.1007/s10648-007-9056-1

Vaughn, K. (2011). Alberta Banner Turner (1909–2008). *The Feminist Psychologist, 38*(1). Retrieved from https://www.apadivisions.org/division-35/about/heritage/ alberta-turner-biography.aspx

Walsh, R. T., Teo, T., & Baydala, A. (2014). *A critical history and philosophy of psychology: Diversity of context, thought, and practice*. New York, NY: Cambridge University Press. http://dx.doi.org/10.1017/CBO9781139046831

Winston, A. S., Butzer, B., & Ferris, M. D. (2004). Constructing difference: Heredity, intelligence, and race in textbooks, 1930–1970. In A. S. Winston (Ed.), *Defining difference: Race and racism in the history of psychology* (pp. 199–229). Washington, DC: American Psychological Association. http://dx.doi.org/10.1037/10625-008

Yang, S. C. (2009). A case study of technology-enhanced historical inquiry. *Innovations in Education and Teaching International, 46*, 237–248. http://dx.doi.org/10.1080/ 14703290902844040

Young, J. L., Rodkey, E. N., & Rutherford, A. (2015). Sparking the historical imagination: Strategies for teaching conceptual and historical issues in psychology. *History & Philosophy of Psychology, 16*, 61–68.

23

Including Social Determinants of Health Disparities in Health Psychology

Colleen A. Redding and Miryam Yusufov

ealth Psychology courses encompass a vast and growing arena that includes health disparities. Such courses can help students recognize that many health disparities are preventable and that psychology and health professionals can play important roles in addressing these problems in culturally competent ways (Carter-Pokras & Baquet, 2002; Hardeman, Medina, & Kozhimannil, 2016; Robillard, Annang, & Buchanan, 2015). We offer resources[1] and strategies for exploring the social determinants of health as primary drivers of health disparities in Health Psychology courses.

Some definitions of health disparities reflect differences between subgroups in prevalence and incidence of health conditions or diseases, whereas others are broad and inclusive (Carter-Pokras & Baquet, 2002). We use a more inclusive definition informed by the population health, sustainability, and social justice values consistent with the World Health Organization's (2017) *Sustainable Development Goals*, in which structural and social inequities drive important differences in health outcomes across gender, ethno-racial, and sociocultural subgroups.

Striking health disparities are evident for many health conditions and diseases across various subgroups at all life stages both within the United States (Braveman, Cubbin, Egerter, Williams, & Pamuk, 2010; Chetty et al., 2016; C. J. L. Murray et al., 2006) and worldwide (Engle et al., 2007; Global Burden

---

[1]Additional recommended resources can be found on the companion webpage for this book (http://pubs.apa.org/books/supp/mena).

Authorship is fully shared and collaborative.

http://dx.doi.org/10.1037/0000137-024
Integrating Multiculturalism and Intersectionality Into the Psychology Curriculum: Strategies for Instructors, J. A. Mena and K. Quina (Editors)

of Disease 2015 Risk Factors Collaborators, 2016; Palafox et al., 2016). Increasing health equity by reducing preventable disparities is an important goal integrated into U.S. (National Center for Health Statistics, 2016) and worldwide (World Health Organization, 2017) policies.

CAUSES OF DISPARITIES

Merely reporting U.S. racial disparities can have unintended negative consequences, such as reifying racial categories, erroneously inferring that health is mainly caused by biomedical or genetic causes, or even "blaming the victim" (Carter-Pokras & Baquet, 2002). Although our understanding of their many interactions with environmental and behavioral influences on health is growing, genetics are estimated to account for only about 10% of overall health variance and even less for most health disparities. Indeed, individual behaviors (e.g., smoking, physical activity, eating behaviors, alcohol intake) have at least 3 times more influence than genetics. Rather, health disparities are most influenced by the uneven distribution of social, environmental, and socioeconomic resources, including income, education, and health care (Braveman et al., 2010; Marmot, Friel, Bell, Houweling, & Taylor, 2008; National Center for Health Statistics, 2016).

The relationships can be complex. For example, education is strongly related to socioeconomic class and mobility, yet in many parts of the world, education is only expected of or provided for males (Kim & Evans, 2015; Subrahmanian, 2005) according to cultural tradition or religious beliefs and enforced by labor and economic inequities and even violence. Sexist expectations are associated with higher levels of gender inequity and create limiting environments for too many women (Brandt, 2011).

EXPLORING SOCIAL DETERMINANTS OF HEALTH AS MECHANISMS OF HEALTH DISPARITIES

Racial Health Disparities

Within the U.S., racial health disparities are evident across a wide range of diseases and conditions (Kimmel, Fwu, Abbott, Ratner, & Eggers, 2016). First, it is important to define the word *race* itself. The American construct of race reflects false ideas about skin color and historically and sociologically constructed categories rooted in justifications of our shared racist history of slavery (Gravlee, 2009; Smedley, 2012; Yudell, Roberts, DeSalle, & Tishkoff, 2016). Racial categories are marker variables that appear to describe differences observed across a range of other more causally relevant variables, including income, education, socioeconomic status (SES), health care access, culture, and ancestry, but are rarely causal themselves. Exploring mechanisms for differences can reveal the layers of privilege, ancestry, and class that intersect to form our current ideas about race, whereas failing to do so can support deterministic arguments, unfairly blaming those in low-resource environments for their health problems.

Cancer

Prominent racial disparities exist in U.S. cancer incidence, prevalence, mortality, and survivorship (National Cancer Institute, 2016). Blacks exhibit the highest mortality rates for all cancers, with rates 25% higher than Whites. Although White women have the highest incidence rate for breast cancer, Black women have higher death rates, likely because among Black women, breast cancers are diagnosed later when fewer treatment options are successful. In a research review, Landrine et al. (2017) found evidence that segregation influenced cancer incidence and mortality, independent of insurance rates and SES. More research is needed on possible reasons for these effects, particularly neighborhood influences (e.g., air quality, toxic exposures, safety) and obesity, smoking, and lack of physical activity, all known to affect breast cancer incidence and survival (Landrine et al., 2017). Though specific cancers (e.g., breast, colon) do have a partially genetic basis, most cancers are not associated with specific genes, and genetics research has found that only 5% to 10% of cancer cases are hereditary (American Cancer Society, 2016). Rather, contextual, environmental, and behavioral factors account for most cancer disparities. Such factors include living conditions (e.g., presence of environmental toxins), stressors, health insurance, access to health care and cancer screenings, and health behaviors (e.g., physical inactivity, smoking, diet, alcohol use). Across a range of cancers, individuals from medically underserved and/or marginalized populations (e.g., poor, no health insurance, minority) are more likely to be diagnosed with later-stage cancers that have fewer successful treatment options, leading to lower survival rates (National Cancer Institute, 2016).

Sexual Health

Worldwide, rates of human immunodeficiency virus (HIV) are highest in countries with high poverty levels and are mainly driven by heterosexual behaviors that disproportionately affect women and children, especially when women are poor, lack access to contraception, and have lower social status (Adimora, 2016; Campbell & Cornish, 2012; Johnson et al., 2010). Some behaviors that transmit HIV remain stigmatized (e.g., sex work, injection drug use, same-sex behaviors), making accurate assessment difficult. Improved access to life-saving treatments has changed the face of HIV from a death sentence to a more chronic, manageable condition, and improvements in access to effective antiviral medication, condoms and contraception, health education, and medical male circumcision are reducing the spread of HIV worldwide (Krishnaratne, Hensen, Cordes, Enstone, Hargreaves, 2016), although effective population prevention strategies are needed to prevent resurgence and spread of the virus

(Cornish, Priego-Hernandez, Campbell, Mburu, & McLean, 2014; Isbell, Kilonzo, Mugurungi, & Bekker, 2016).

In the U.S., although HIV emerged first as mainly sexually transmitted between men having sex with men, many transmission routes, especially heterosexual transmission, have increased and remain highest in racial minority groups, especially African Americans (Adimora, Schoenbach, & Floris-Moore, 2009; Friedman, Cooper, & Osborne, 2009; Kraut-Becher et al., 2008). Poverty, disparate rates of incarceration, and injection drug use are some of the factors considered possible as drivers of the racial disparities in U.S. HIV rates (Adimora et al., 2009; Friedman et al., 2009; Kraut-Becher et al., 2008).

Also, in the U.S., marked regional and racial disparities are found in adolescent pregnancy and sexually transmitted infection among females (Kraut-Becher et al., 2008; Lindberg, Santelli, & Desai, 2016; Schalet et al., 2014). Historically, pregnancy prevention efforts focused almost exclusively on females. Regional rates of teen pregnancy have been highest in the South, where abstinence-only sex education is still taught in many high schools (Kohler, Manhart, & Lafferty, 2008; Santelli, Ott, Lyon, Rogers, & Summers, 2006; Schalet et al., 2014). Access to comprehensive, medically accurate sexual health information and effective contraception lower rates of teen pregnancy (Lindberg et al., 2016). Goodman, Onwumere, Milam, and Peipert (2017) reduced rates of adolescent pregnancy in Colorado by removing contraceptive cost, access, and knowledge barriers; ultimately these structural interventions eliminated racial differences in pregnancy rates. This is a good example of how attending to structural drivers—contraceptive access, cost, and knowledge—can reduce adolescent pregnancy, in spite of past regional and racial disparities.

Obesity

U.S. obesity rates have increased in all subgroups, but some are disproportionately affected. Non-Hispanic Blacks have the highest rates of obesity, followed by Hispanics, non-Hispanic Whites, and Asians (Hales, Carroll, Fryar, & Ogden, 2017). Although obesity also has a partially genetic basis, primary drivers of obesity disparities include differential access to education, transportation, safe recreation, health care, segregation, and healthy food choices (Corral et al., 2015). Overweight and obesity are major contributors to increasing rates of diabetes, cardiovascular diseases, cancer, and all-cause mortality (Flegal, Kit, Orpana, & Graubard, 2013). Clearly, addressing obesity-related health disparities by increasing access to health-promoting resources would benefit all.

Stress

Early life adverse experiences can have profound and lasting negative effects on physical and emotional health and well-being that linger into adulthood (Adler, 2011; Taylor, 2010). Using the Adverse Childhood Experiences (ACE) scale, which evaluates exposure to events such as physical and/or sexual abuse and parental absence, mental illness, death, divorce, and so forth, a strong, graded relationship has been observed between degree of ACE exposure and adult risk for many leading causes of death (Felitti et al., 1998) and premature mortality (Brown et al., 2009). A large Centers for Disease Control and Prevention study found that at least one ACE was reported by nearly 60% of adults and that ACE exposure was associated with a range of adult physical and emotional health problems across all racial and ethnic, age, gender, and educational subgroups (Bynum et al., 2010). Such events were also related to cardiovascular diseases, cancers, and premature mortality.

How might adverse experiences get into the genes and body, causing inflammatory, immune, and/or stress-related reactions that ultimately contribute to disease states, such as cardiovascular disease or cancer or chronic pain? Our understanding of these multifaceted biopsychosocial processes is growing. For example, telomeres are microscopic caps that protect chromosomes and shorten naturally with age and in response to stress. Telomere length may be an important marker of cellular aging that can correspond well to natural age or can accelerate when other stresses are present (Adler, 2011). Evidence of social disadvantage in 9-year-old children's telomere lengths was found in another study (Mitchell et al., 2014). Early adverse events have been found to affect the physiology and function of the brain, cardiovascular, immune, and nervous systems, creating potentially chronic stress reactivity and systemic inflammation that can have a cascade of negative health impacts over time (see Figure 23.1; Carroll et al., 2013; Taylor, 2010).

Stress perception and physiology can also explain how adverse experiences can affect psychobiology (Andersen, Zou, & Blosnich, 2015; Dunkel Schetter et al., 2013; Levy, Heissel, Richeson, & Adam, 2016; Taylor, Karlamangla, Friedman, & Seeman, 2011). Stress can reflect acute and chronic experiences, from minimally upsetting experiences that end quickly (e.g., irritation while waiting in line) to more upsetting events (e.g., bullying, discrimination) to ACEs. In general, the number and severity of stresses increase with both poverty (financial stresses) and minority status (discrimination, stigma). For example, compared with rural or suburban settings, urban environments often are more crowded, noisy, polluted, and violent; leave residents with low levels of control; have more convenience stores and liquor stores and fast food options but fewer affordable markets selling fresh, healthy foods; and lack safe "green spaces" in which to walk or play. Early environments shape learning, nervous systems, and subsequent stress responses. Social capital—that is, supportive relationships—can buffer some of the negative influences of stressful experiences (Carroll et al., 2013; Evans & Kim, 2012; Taylor, 2010; Taylor et al., 2011).

Life Expectancy

In the U.S., income is strongly associated with life expectancy (Braveman et al., 2010; Chetty et al., 2016), and early life income inequality is predictive of later health (Lillard, Burkhauser, Hahn, & Wilkins, 2015). New research is demonstrating critical developmental periods, notably early childhood and adolescence, during which evidence-based supportive and/or

FIGURE 23.1. Potential Pathways Between Early Life Stress and Adult Health

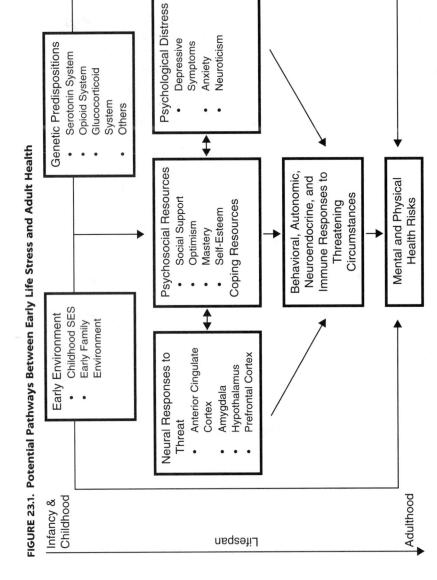

SES = socioeconomic status. From "Mechanisms Linking Early Life Stress to Adult Health Outcomes," by S. E. Taylor, 2010, *Proceedings of the National Academy of Sciences, 107*(19), p. 8508. Copyright 2010 by the National Academy of Sciences. Reprinted with permission.

preventive interventions can have a positive effect on health, not only during that time frame but also well beyond it into adulthood (Blair & Raver, 2014; Farrell, Simpson, Carlson, Englund, & Sung, 2017; Patton et al., 2016). This has led public health experts to call for worldwide investments in early childhood education and prevention programs to reduce inequalities perpetuated by poverty, poor nutrition, and restricted learning opportunities (Engle et al., 2007; Fritze, Doblhammer, & van den Berg, 2014; Wise, 2016). They assert that these investments are cost-effective and warn of wasted generational resources without such interventions. Many studies have found that supportive, nurturing parental relationships can buffer some of the health effects of childhood poverty (Brody, Miller, Yu, Beach, & Chen, 2016; Evans & Kutcher, 2011; Miller et al., 2011; Prinz, Sanders, Shapiro, Whitaker, & Lutzker, 2009). Sesame Street has produced a television series for young children with educational, engaging characters, and scientific publications demonstrate how their media programs around the world have increased social skills and learning, especially among the most vulnerable youngsters (Mares & Pan, 2013; Sesame Workshop, n.d.).

Population Health

Improving the health of a large population by definition means health equity and requires addressing social determinants of health. Interventions should provide higher levels of preventive and supportive services for those with higher needs and multiple social determinants of poor health, including poverty and low education.

There are reasons for optimism, in spite of discouragingly high rates of health and income inequality in the U.S. and worldwide. Better investments in supportive early childhood and adolescent educational programs could build resilience in many children and young adults that could maintain adult health and well-being (Sznitman, Reisel, & Romer, 2011; Wise, 2016). Improving basic education and early educational environments may improve not only knowledge but also health outcomes (Goldman & Smith, 2011; Kaplan, 2014). Effective stress management techniques (e.g., mindfulness) are available as well to improve resilience and thriving. Health disparities result from the inequitable social distribution of resources, and we can play a role in improving the distribution of those resources to reduce these disparities.

THINKING CRITICALLY ABOUT HEALTH DISPARITY MECHANISMS

Instructors may use metaphors and examples to illustrate health disparity mechanisms. Jones (2000) described the "Gardener's Tale," in which a gardener separated seeds into two separate boxes, one with rich soil and one with poor soil, and found that students attributed the resulting flowers to the flowers themselves, rather than the nourishment available in the different types of soil. This underscores that attributing responsibility to the individual alone is inaccurate, unfair, and reductionist, and it is crucial to consider available environmental supports. Robillard et al. (2015) offered methods for discussing how health disparities result from a complex interplay of environment and institutionalized racism, including how such metaphors may serve to attenuate individualistic assumptions and underscore race as a sociohistorical, rather than a biological construct.

Numerous resources can illustrate the impact of inequality on health disparities. The seven-part documentary series "Unnatural Causes: Is Inequality Making Us Sick?" highlights the extent to which the social circumstances into which we are born predict our health outcomes (Silverman, 2008). Instructors may facilitate a class discussion on this series and have students write reflections. Relatedly, instructors can play a brief video, "Does Where You Live Affect How Long You Live?" and then engage students in an interactive activity in which they enter different ZIP codes and see predicted life expectancies for men and women (http://www.rwjf.org/en/library/interactives/whereyouliveaffectshow longyoulive.html). For more global or worldwide perspectives on inequitable distribution of resources leading to health disparities, view one of several TED talks by Hans Rosling (e.g., Rosling, 2007) or documentaries (Gapminder, n.d.), or read papers (Heckman, n.d.).

Experiential teaching approaches can further solidify understanding of mechanisms of health disparities. Instructors can give student groups a list of neighborhoods (preferably a list that includes low SES, middle class, and affluent neighborhoods) and ask them to use Google Maps to find nearby health-related resources, including clinics, hospitals, and supermarkets. Students can then compare and contrast resources. This activity may be followed by a discussion of differential access to resources, based on neighborhoods and ZIP codes.

A hands-on activity illustrates the role of poverty as it affects food choices, producing health disparities. Each student brings in copies of a circular or flyer from a nearby supermarket. The instructor tells the students that they are single parents with three children and have only $40 a week available to feed their family. The rules for this activity are that (a) each family member must have three meals per day, and (b) the students may only select items from the circular for weekly food shopping. The instructor can encourage the students to work in pairs and time them for completing this activity. Students then discuss the difficulty of this activity and the quantity, health, and nutritional value of the foods that students selected; if time permits, they can refer back to the location of supermarkets and the differential availability of healthy foods, based on the SES of different neighborhoods.

Two additional activities illustrate health disparities mechanisms. Either individually or in small groups, students may choose a specific disease (e.g., diabetes) or health behavior (e.g., drug addiction) and research the differential rates in minority groups. They can then present these data and propose causes of the differences between the groups to the class, perhaps in a class wiki or similar format. An extension of this activity is a classroom discussion on the causes of health problems. Instructors may select a disease or behavior (e.g., obesity, HIV/AIDS, drug addiction) and pose the question of why people have such issues, asking students to make a list of reasons for each disease or behavior and classify each cause as internal (dispositional) or external (sociocultural). The number of dispositional versus sociocultural causes generated can be used to guide a classroom discussion on attributions for health disparities.

A perhaps more influential activity may be conducted outside the classroom. Students may analyze a personal medical visit (e.g., annual physical) and take notes, noting the neighborhood and/or ZIP code of the clinic or office they visited. Then, as a class, students may compare their notes to identify differences in experiences across neighborhoods. In addition, students may locate information about, and then visit, two different clinics or hospital waiting rooms: one in an affluent area and one in a low SES area. They can then compare and contrast differences in waiting times, staff-to-patient ratios, facilities, availability of services, and how staff seems to treat patients. Instructors are encouraged to advise students against making recordings or taking notes on protected health information because this would violate patient confidentiality. Rather, the exercise should be focused on students' perceptions and experiences with their own medical visits, as well as observations of the facilities.

PEDAGOGICAL CHALLENGES IN HEALTH PSYCHOLOGY COURSES

An overarching challenge for the instructor may be inherent socioeconomic differences within the classroom. For instance, students may have different experiences with personal or familial sacrifices, work lives, or debt, especially to cover the rising costs of college. Such differences may parallel health disparities and might make it challenging for some students to fully grasp the extent to which environment can be predictive of health outcomes. Another difference may be whether students are living on campus. Most college campuses have at least one fitness facility with regularly scheduled classes, and all residential college campuses have a health center or clinic to which students are granted access. Thus, it may be challenging for them to relate to the struggles in many underresourced environments and neighborhoods. Nonetheless, students may be engaged by activities and discussions on health disparities using several other methods. For example, in the wake of actions to repeal the Affordable Care Act, many individuals have shared their stories of living with a disability or chronic illness without insurance (e.g., ObamaCareFacts.com, 2015; PBS, n.d.).

To make the concept of health disparities clear and personally relevant, instructors may have students select an unhealthy behavior from their lives (Mio, Barker-Hackett, & Tumambing, 2006), such as physical inactivity, poor sleep, or cigarette smoking. First, they can describe the behavior and then write a plan to address it, such as creating an exercise schedule, setting a regular bedtime, or developing a smoking cessation plan. Next, students can explore potential barriers to implementing their plans, including sociocultural and environmental factors. For instance, they may decide they have trouble with regular and healthy sleep because their residence hall is often noisy, or they may cite unhealthy choices on campus as a barrier to more healthy eating. Students without a means of transportation may have no way of accessing healthy food at a supermarket, an issue pervasive across many communities. Instructors can engage students in a discussion on how their environment can be a barrier to health behavior change and then direct them to online resources (e.g., http://www.healthpowerforminorities.com) to supplement the afore-mentioned classroom activities and discussions.

Finally, one experiential exercise can demonstrate how hard manual field work can be. Have students stand up, circle the classroom, and then bend at the waist. Then, have them walk, snaking around the classroom, like a cater-pillar, for a minute and a half. At the end of this exercise, students are often out of breath. Instructors can discuss how, before 1975, Mexican farm workers requested long-handled hoes to till the fields, but the farm owners only pro-vided them with short-handled hoes (less than 18 inches long), because they were thought to be more accurate (D. Murray, 2004; The National Museum of American History, n.d.). Then, ask students to imagine how they would feel if they had to do this for 12 to 14 hours a day in the hot sun. Another important point is that bending over places their noses right next to the freshly tilled soil, increasing their exposure to breathing in not only dirt but also any fertilizers or pesticides in use.

CONCLUSION

Health disparities are commonly attributed to biomedical, genetic, or individual-level factors, and simple reporting of health disparity rates for various condi-tions in Health Psychology classes can unwittingly reinforce this perspective. In contrast, social and environmental differences in resource allocation account for much of the variance and offer a more comprehensive explanation for the mechanisms, as well as ways to address health disparities. It is important that instructors underscore these contextual, interrelated, and complex factors to offer a more thorough explanation for the many striking health disparities in the U.S. and around the world.

REFERENCES

Adimora, A. A. (2016). Preventing HIV among women—a step forward, but much farther to go. *The New England Journal of Medicine, 375*, 2195–2196. http://dx.doi.org/10.1056/NEJMe1613661

Adimora, A. A., Schoenbach, V. J., & Floris-Moore, M. A. (2009). Ending the epidemic of heterosexual HIV transmission among African Americans. *American Journal of Preventive Medicine, 37*, 468–471. http://dx.doi.org/10.1016/j.amepre.2009.06.020

Adler, N. E. (2011). Cell aging and social disadvantage: Perspectives on mechanisms underlying health disparities from "across the pond". *Brain, Behavior, and Immunity, 25*, 1290–1291. http://dx.doi.org/10.1016/j.bbi.2011.06.013

American Cancer Society. (2016). *What causes cancer?* Retrieved from https://www.cancer.org/cancer/cancer-causes.html

Andersen, J. P., Zou, C., & Blosnich, J. (2015). Multiple early victimization experiences as a pathway to explain physical health disparities among sexual minority and heterosexual individuals. *Social Science & Medicine, 133*, 111–119. http://dx.doi.org/10.1016/j.socscimed.2015.03.043

Blair, C., & Raver, C. C. (2014). Closing the achievement gap through modification of neurocognitive and neuroendocrine function: Results from a cluster randomized controlled trial of an innovative approach to the education of children in kindergarten. *PLoS ONE, 9*(11), e112393. http://dx.doi.org/10.1371/journal.pone.0112393

Brandt, M. J. (2011). Sexism and gender inequality across 57 societies. *Psychological Science, 22*, 1413–1418. http://dx.doi.org/10.1177/0956797611420445

Braveman, P. A., Cubbin, C., Egerter, S., Williams, D. R., & Pamuk, E. (2010). Socioeconomic disparities in health in the United States: What the patterns tell us. *American Journal of Public Health, 100*, S186–S196. http://dx.doi.org/10.2105/AJPH.2009.166082

Brody, G. H., Miller, G. E., Yu, T., Beach, S. R. H., & Chen, E. (2016). Supportive family environments ameliorate the link between racial discrimination and epigenetic aging: A replication across two longitudinal cohorts. *Psychological Science, 27*, 530–541. http://dx.doi.org/10.1177/0956797615626703

Brown, D. W., Anda, R. F., Tiemeier, H., Felitti, V. J., Edwards, V. J., Croft, J. B., & Giles, W. H. (2009). Adverse childhood experiences and the risk of premature mortality. *American Journal of Preventive Medicine, 37*, 389–396. http://dx.doi.org/10.1016/j.amepre.2009.06.021

Bynum, L., Griffin, T., Riding, D. L., Wynkoop, K. S., Anda, R. F., Edwards, V. J., . . . Croft, J. B. (2010). Adverse childhood experiences reported by adults—five states, 2009. *Morbidity and Mortality Weekly Report, 59*, 1609–1613.

Campbell, C., & Cornish, F. (2012). How can community health programmes build enabling environments for transformative communication? Experiences from India and South Africa. *AIDS and Behavior, 16*, 847–857. http://dx.doi.org/10.1007/s10461-011-9966-2

Carroll, J. E., Gruenewald, T. L., Taylor, S. E., Janicki-Deverts, D., Matthews, K. A., & Seeman, T. E. (2013). Childhood abuse, parental warmth, and adult multisystem biological risk in the Coronary Artery Risk Development in Young Adults study. *PNAS, 110*, 17149–17153. http://dx.doi.org/10.1073/pnas.1315458110

Carter-Pokras, O., & Baquet, C. (2002). What is a "health disparity"? *Public Health Reports, 117*, 426–434. http://dx.doi.org/10.1016/S0033-3549(04)50182-6

Chetty, R., Stepner, M., Abraham, S., Lin, S., Scuderi, B., Turner, N., . . . Cutler, D. (2016). The association between income and life expectancy in the United States, 2001–2014. *JAMA, 315*, 1750–1766. http://dx.doi.org/10.1001/jama.2016.4226

Cornish, F., Priego-Hernandez, J., Campbell, C., Mburu, G., & McLean, S. (2014). The impact of community mobilisation on HIV prevention in middle and low income countries: A systematic review and critique. *AIDS and Behavior, 18*, 2110–2134. http://dx.doi.org/10.1007/s10461-014-0748-5

Corral, I., Landrine, H., Hall, M. B., Bess, J. J., Mills, K. R., & Efird, J. T. (2015). Residential segregation and overweight/obesity among African-American adults: A critical review. *Frontiers in Public Health, 3*, 169. http://dx.doi.org/10.3389/fpubh.2015.00169

Dunkel Schetter, C., Schafer, P., Lanzi, R. G., Clark-Kauffman, E., Raju, T. N., & Hillemeier, M. M. (2013). Shedding light on the mechanisms underlying health disparities through community participatory methods: The stress pathway. *Perspectives on Psychological Science, 8*, 613–633. http://dx.doi.org/10.1177/1745691613506016

Engle, P. L., Black, M. M., Behrman, J. R., Cabral de Mello, M., Gertler, P. J., Kapiriri, L., . . . the International Child Development Steering Group. (2007). Strategies to avoid the loss of developmental potential in more than 200 million children in the developing world. *The Lancet, 369*, 229–242. http://dx.doi.org/10.1016/S0140-6736(07)60112-3

Evans, G. W., & Kim, P. (2012). Childhood poverty and young adults' allostatic load: The mediating role of childhood cumulative risk exposure. *Psychological Science, 23,* 979–983. http://dx.doi.org/10.1177/0956797612441218

Evans, G. W., & Kutcher, R. (2011). Loosening the link between childhood poverty and adolescent smoking and obesity: The protective effects of social capital. *Psychological Science, 22,* 3–7. http://dx.doi.org/10.1177/0956797610390387

Farrell, A. K., Simpson, J. A., Carlson, E. A., Englund, M. M., & Sung, S. (2017). The impact of stress at different life stages on physical health and the buffering effects of maternal sensitivity. *Health Psychology, 36,* 35–44. http://dx.doi.org/10.1037/hea0000424

Felitti, V. J., Anda, R. F., Nordenberg, D., Williamson, D. F., Spitz, A. M., Edwards, V., . . . Marks, J. S. (1998). Relationship of childhood abuse and household dysfunction to many of the leading causes of death in adults. The Adverse Childhood Experiences (ACE) Study. *American Journal of Preventive Medicine, 14,* 245–258. http://dx.doi.org/10.1016/S0749-3797(98)00017-8

Flegal, K. M., Kit, B. K., Orpana, H., & Graubard, B. I. (2013). Association of all-cause mortality with overweight and obesity using standard body mass index categories: A systematic review and meta-analysis. *JAMA, 309,* 71–82. http://dx.doi.org/10.1001/jama.2012.113905

Friedman, S. R., Cooper, H. L., & Osborne, A. H. (2009). Structural and social contexts of HIV risk Among African Americans. *American Journal of Public Health, 99,* 1002–1008. http://dx.doi.org/10.2105/AJPH.2008.140327

Fritze, T., Doblhammer, G., & van den Berg, G. J. (2014). Can individual conditions during childhood mediate or moderate the long-term cognitive effects of poor economic environments at birth? *Social Science & Medicine, 119,* 240–248. http://dx.doi.org/10.1016/j.socscimed.2014.07.011

Gapminder. (n.d.). *Videos.* Retrieved from https://www.gapminder.org/videos/

Global Burden of Disease 2015 Risk Factors Collaborators. (2016). Global, regional, and national comparative risk assessment of 79 behavioural, environmental and occupational, and metabolic risks or clusters of risks, 1990–2015: A systematic analysis for the Global Burden of Disease Study 2015. *The Lancet, 388,* 1659–1724. http://dx.doi.org/10.1016/S0140-6736(16)31679-8

Goldman, D., & Smith, J. P. (2011). The increasing value of education to health. *Social Science & Medicine, 72,* 1728–1737. http://dx.doi.org/10.1016/j.socscimed.2011.02.047

Goodman, M., Onwumere, O., Milam, L., & Peipert, J. F. (2017). Reducing health disparities by removing cost, access, and knowledge barriers. *American Journal of Obstetrics and Gynecology, 216,* 382.e1–382.e5. http://dx.doi.org/10.1016/j.ajog.2016.12.015

Gravlee, C. C. (2009). How race becomes biology: Embodiment of social inequality. *American Journal of Physical Anthropology, 139,* 47–57. http://dx.doi.org/10.1002/ajpa.20983

Hales, C. M., Carroll, M. D., Fryar, C. D., & Ogden, C. L. (2017). *Prevalence of obesity among adults and youth: United States, 2015–2016* (NCHS Data Brief, No. 288). Retrieved from https://www.cdc.gov/nchs/data/databriefs/db288.pdf

Hardeman, R. R., Medina, E. M., & Kozhimannil, K. B. (2016). Structural racism and supporting Black lives—the role of health professionals. *The New England Journal of Medicine, 375,* 2113–2115. http://dx.doi.org/10.1056/NEJMp1609535

Heckman. (n.d.). *Academic papers.* Retrieved from https://heckmanequation.org/resource-type/academic-papers/

Isbell, M. T., Kilonzo, N., Mugurungi, O., & Bekker, L. G. (2016). We neglect primary HIV prevention at our peril. *The Lancet. HIV, 3,* e284–e285. http://dx.doi.org/10.1016/S2352-3018(16)30058-3

Johnson, B. T., Redding, C. A., DiClemente, R. J., Mustanski, B. S., Dodge, B., Sheeran, P., . . . Fishbein, M. (2010). A network-individual-resource model for HIV prevention. *AIDS and Behavior, 14,* 204–221. http://dx.doi.org/10.1007/s10461-010-9803-z

Jones, C. P. (2000). Levels of racism: A theoretic framework and a gardener's tale. *American Journal of Public Health, 90,* 1212–1215. http://dx.doi.org/10.2105/AJPH.90.8.1212

Kaplan, R. M. (2014). Behavior change and reducing health disparities. *Preventive Medicine, 68,* 5–10. http://dx.doi.org/10.1016/j.ypmed.2014.04.014

Kim, J. Y., & Evans, T. (2015). Promoting women's health for sustainable development. *The Lancet, 386,* e9–e10. http://dx.doi.org/10.1016/S0140-6736(15)60942-4

Kimmel, P. L., Fwu, C. W., Abbott, K. C., Ratner, J., & Eggers, P. W. (2016). Racial disparities in poverty account for mortality differences in U.S. medicare beneficiaries. *SSM - Population Health, 2,* 123–129. http://dx.doi.org/10.1016/j.ssmph.2016.02.003

Kohler, P. K., Manhart, L. E., & Lafferty, W. E. (2008). Abstinence-only and comprehensive sex education and the initiation of sexual activity and teen pregnancy. *Journal of Adolescent Health, 42,* 344–351. http://dx.doi.org/10.1016/j.jadohealth.2007.08.026

Kraut-Becher, J., Eisenberg, M., Voytek, C., Brown, T., Metzger, D. S., & Aral, S. (2008). Examining racial disparities in HIV: Lessons from sexually transmitted infections research. *JAIDS Journal of Acquired Immune Deficiency Syndromes, 47,* S20–S27.

Krishnaratne, S., Hensen, B., Cordes, J., Enstone, J., & Hargreaves, J. R. (2016). Interventions to strengthen the HIV prevention cascade: A systematic review of reviews. *The Lancet. HIV, 3,* e307–e317. http://dx.doi.org/10.1016/S2352-3018(16)30038-8

Landrine, H., Corral, I., Lee, J. G., Efird, J. T., Hall, M. B., & Bess, J. J. (2017). Residential segregation and racial cancer disparities: A systematic review. *Journal of Racial and Ethnic Health Disparities, 4,* 1195–1205. http://dx.doi.org/10.1007/s40615-016-0326-9

Levy, D. J., Heissel, J. A., Richeson, J. A., & Adam, E. K. (2016). Psychological and biological responses to race-based social stress as pathways to disparities in educational outcomes. *American Psychologist, 71,* 455–473. http://dx.doi.org/10.1037/a0040322

Lillard, D. R., Burkhauser, R. V., Hahn, M. H., & Wilkins, R. (2015). Does early-life income inequality predict self-reported health in later life? Evidence from the United States. *Social Science & Medicine, 128,* 347–355. http://dx.doi.org/10.1016/j.socscimed.2014.12.026

Lindberg, L., Santelli, J., & Desai, S. (2016). Understanding the decline in adolescent fertility in the United States, 2007–2012. *Journal of Adolescent Health, 59,* 577–583. http://dx.doi.org/10.1016/j.jadohealth.2016.06.024

Mares, M. L., & Pan, Z. (2013). Effects of Sesame Street: A meta-analysis of children's learning in 15 countries. *Journal of Applied Developmental Psychology, 34,* 140–151. http://dx.doi.org/10.1016/j.appdev.2013.01.001

Marmot, M., Friel, S., Bell, R., Houweling, T. A. J., & Taylor, S. (2008). Closing the gap in a generation: Health equity through action on the social determinants of health. *The Lancet, 372,* 1661–1669. http://dx.doi.org/10.1016/S0140-6736(08)61690-6

Miller, G. E., Lachman, M. E., Chen, E., Gruenewald, T. L., Karlamangla, A. S., & Seeman, T. E. (2011). Pathways to resilience: Maternal nurturance as a buffer against the effects of childhood poverty on metabolic syndrome at midlife. *Psychological Science, 22,* 1591–1599. http://dx.doi.org/10.1177/0956797611419170

Mio, J. S., Barker-Hackett, L., & Tumambing, J. (2006). *Multicultural psychology: Understanding our diverse communities.* Boston, MA: McGraw-Hill.

Mitchell, C., Hobcraft, J., McLanahan, S. S., Siegel, S. R., Berg, A., Brooks-Gunn, J., . . . Notterman, D. (2014). Social disadvantage, genetic sensitivity, and children's telomere length. *PNAS, 111,* 5944–5949. http://dx.doi.org/10.1073/pnas.1404293111

Murray, C. J. L., Kulkarni, S. C., Michaud, C., Tomijima, N., Bulzacchelli, M. T., Iandiorio, T. J., & Ezzati, M. (2006). Eight Americas: Investigating mortality disparities across races, counties, and race-counties in the United States. *PLoS Medicine, 3*(9), e260. http://dx.doi.org/10.1371/journal.pmed.0030260

Murray, D. (2004). The abolition of the short-handled hoe. In D. M. Newman (Ed.), *Sociology: Exploring the architecture of everyday life* (5th ed.). Retrieved from https://studysites.sagepub.com/newman5study/resources/murray1.htm

National Cancer Institute. (2016). *Cancer statistics.* https://www.cancer.gov/about-cancer/understanding/statistics

National Center for Health Statistics. (2016). *Social determinants of health.* Retrieved from https://www.cdc.gov/nchs/data/hpdata2020/HP2020MCR-C39-SDOH.pdf

The National Museum of American History. (n.d.). *Short-handled hoe, 1950s and 1960s.* Retrieved from http://americanhistory.si.edu/collections/search/object/nmah_1352222

ObamaCareFacts.com. (2015, July 17). ObamaCare stories: Real life stories on ObamaCare. Retrieved from https://obamacarefacts.com/obamacare-stories/

Palafox, B., McKee, M., Balabanova, D., AlHabib, K. F., Avezum, A. J., Bahonar, A., . . . Yusuf, S. (2016). Wealth and cardiovascular health: A cross-sectional study of wealth-related inequalities in the awareness, treatment and control of hypertension in high-, middle- and low-income countries. *International Journal for Equity in Health, 15,* 199. http://dx.doi.org/10.1186/s12939-016-0478-6

Patton, G. C., Sawyer, S. M., Santelli, J. S., Ross, D. A., Afifi, R., Allen, N. B., . . . Viner, R. M. (2016). Our future: A *Lancet* commission on adolescent health and wellbeing. *The Lancet, 387,* 2423–2478. http://dx.doi.org/10.1016/S0140-6736(16)00579-1

PBS. (n.d.). *The uninsured.* Retrieved from http://www.pbs.org/healthcarecrisis/uninsured.html

Prinz, R. J., Sanders, M. R., Shapiro, C. J., Whitaker, D. J., & Lutzker, J. R. (2009). Population-based prevention of child maltreatment: The U.S. Triple P System Population Trial. *Prevention Science, 10,* 1–12. http://dx.doi.org/10.1007/s11121-009-0123-3

Robillard, A. G., Annang, L., & Buchanan, K. L. (2015). Talking about race an important first step in undergraduate pedagogy: Addressing African American health disparities. *Pedagogy in Health Promotion, 1,* 18–23. http://dx.doi.org/10.1177/2373379914559218

Rosling, H. (2007). New insights on poverty [Video file]. *TED2007.* Retrieved from https://www.ted.com/talks/hans_rosling_reveals_new_insights_on_poverty

Santelli, J., Ott, M. A., Lyon, M., Rogers, J., & Summers, D. (2006). Abstinence-only education policies and programs: A position paper of the Society for Adolescent Medicine. *Journal of Adolescent Health, 38,* 83–87. http://dx.doi.org/10.1016/j.jadohealth.2005.06.002

Schalet, A. T., Santelli, J. S., Russell, S. T., Halpern, C. T., Miller, S. A., Pickering, S. S., . . . Hoenig, J. M. (2014). Invited commentary: Broadening the evidence for adolescent sexual and reproductive health and education in the United States. *Journal of Youth and Adolescence, 43,* 1595–1610. http://dx.doi.org/10.1007/s10964-014-0178-8

Sesame Workshop. (n.d.). *Our results.* Retrieved from http://www.sesameworkshop.org/what-we-do/our-results/

Silverman, F. (Producer & Director). (2008). *Unnatural causes: Is inequality making us sick?* [Video file]. Retrieved from http://www.unnaturalcauses.org/

Smedley, B. D. (2012). The lived experience of race and its health consequences. *American Journal of Public Health, 102,* 933–935. http://dx.doi.org/10.2105/AJPH.2011.300643

Subrahmanian, R. (2005). Gender equality in education: Definitions and measurements. *International Journal of Educational Development, 25,* 395–407. http://dx.doi.org/10.1016/j.ijedudev.2005.04.003

Sznitman, S. R., Reisel, L., & Romer, D. (2011). The neglected role of adolescent emotional well-being in national educational achievement: Bridging the gap between education and mental health policies. *Journal of Adolescent Health, 48,* 135–142. http://dx.doi.org/10.1016/j.jadohealth.2010.06.013

Taylor, S. E. (2010). Mechanisms linking early life stress to adult health outcomes. *PNAS, 107,* 8507–8512. http://dx.doi.org/10.1073/pnas.1003890107

Taylor, S. E., Karlamangla, A. S., Friedman, E. M., & Seeman, T. E. (2011). Early environment affects neuroendocrine regulation in adulthood. *Social Cognitive and Affective Neuroscience, 6,* 244–251. http://dx.doi.org/10.1093/scan/nsq037

Wise, P. H. (2016). Child poverty and the promise of human capacity: Childhood as a foundation for healthy aging. *Academic Pediatrics, 16,* S37–S45. http://dx.doi.org/10.1016/j.acap.2016.01.014

World Health Organization. (2017). *Sustainable development goals for 2030.* Retrieved from http://www.who.int/topics/sustainable-development-goals/test/sdg-banner.jpg?ua=1

Yudell, M., Roberts, D., DeSalle, R., & Tishkoff, S. (2016). Taking race out of human genetics. *Science, 351,* 564–565. http://dx.doi.org/10.1126/science.aac4951

24

Diversity Education in Professional Psychology

Kathleen A. Malloy, Julie L. Williams, LaTrelle D. Jackson,
Janeece R. Warfield, and Steven Kniffley

The American Psychological Association (APA; 2017) has deemed that the provision of multiculturally competent services is an ethical mandate, and research has shown that client perception of therapist multicultural competence has strong, positive effects on therapeutic processes and moderate effects on therapy outcome (Tao, Owen, Pace, & Imel, 2015). To meet this mandate and assure that diversity competent services are provided, we must consider how we train aspiring professional psychologists. In this chapter, we describe work from our diversity classes offered in the Wright State University School of Professional Psychology clinical psychology doctoral program. Our students take three team-taught diversity classes throughout their training—their first course in their beginning semester and the last in their final semester. This chapter focuses on the first semester beginning training, in which we help our students learn how to have productive dialogues to explore socially constructed identities and the resulting experiences of privilege and oppression and how those experiences impact both the providers and recipients of psychological services and scholarship. In later courses, they learn the skills necessary to apply what they are learning to all aspects of their professional work (described in Malloy, Dobbins, Williams, Allen, & Warfield, 2009).

Two prominent models attempt to define competencies that must be attained by future psychologists in their professional training: APA's Competency Benchmarks in Professional Psychology (Fouad et al., 2009) and the National Council of Schools and Programs of Professional Psychology's Developmental Achievement Levels (Roysircar, Dobbins, & Malloy, 2010). Each diversity domain reflects

http://dx.doi.org/10.1037/0000137-025
Integrating Multiculturalism and Intersectionality Into the Psychology Curriculum:
Strategies for Instructors, J. A. Mena and K. Quina (Editors)

a core competency underlying performance in all areas of professional psychology, and training programs must help their students begin a journey toward achieving that competence. Programs should provide the opportunity for students to explore their attitudes, expand their knowledge base regarding diversity, and develop a diversity-sensitive skill set (Sue, Arredondo, & McDavis, 1992). Although all three of these components are essential in diversity training, a willingness to explore one's experiences and attitudes allows one to understand better the knowledge one has acquired and skills one has developed. This chapter focuses on how to help psychologists-in-training develop the attitudes necessary to become competent in working with diverse individuals and communities.

Multicultural competence is often used in the literature to refer to working with diverse peoples. We use the term *diversity competence* instead; we find that when the term *multicultural* is used, it is easy to drift toward a focus on culture as defined by race and ethnicity with less emphasis on other identity variables. Although race and ethnicity indeed impact how we understand all diversity variables (e.g., disability status, gender, socioeconomic status, sexual orientation, spirituality), these other identity variables also impact how one experiences race and ethnicity. For example, a gay Latinx may experience Latinx culture differently than a heterosexual Latinx. Given the complexity of human experience, it is impossible to understand the impact of one identity variable without exploring the intersectionality of all aspects of identity (Vaccaro, 2017; see also Chapter 2, this volume). Our use of the term *diversity competence* is our attempt to maintain awareness of that complexity.

INTRAPERSONAL ASSESSMENT: ADDRESSING ATTITUDES FROM WITHIN

We guide students in exploring their identities, social contexts, and life experiences that have impacted their understanding of themselves, others, and the world. This reflective process includes the ways in which cultures allocate various levels of unearned privilege and power to identity variables and how these relate to oppression. For example, in most cultures, White, male, able-bodied, heterosexual people are granted more privilege, resulting in oppression of non-privileged groups (i.e., non-White, female, disabled, gay people; Malloy et al., 2009). All students possess multiple identities; thus, they have experienced varying levels of privilege and oppression throughout their lives, often without their awareness. We encourage students to see cultural influences that impact them, including those often invisible to them. It also helps them to understand how social context and experiences impact others. It is important to explore how those differences play out in their therapeutic work: what it means to have both more and less privileged identities when working as a professional psychologist. For example, when a White student is working with an African American client, or vice versa, each can explore how stimulus value and/or oppression affects the therapeutic relationship.

The assumption that one can achieve complete diversity competence puts significant pressure on both students and instructors to reach that "peak." Students have to understand that moving toward diversity competence differs from achieving competence in most other academic areas; one does not learn the concepts and then take a test, hoping to get an *A* and thus prove that one has mastered diversity competence. The literature supports the concept of diversity competency existing on a continuum, where individuals fluctuate between periods of greater competency and lesser competency depending on the context and identity saliency (Pernell-Arnold, Finley, Sands, Bourjolly, & Stanhope, 2012). For example, a White male may be aware of racism and work hard to maintain an awareness of White privilege and to eradicate his racist attitudes. However, he may be more successful when interacting with individuals of other races who are also middle class than when trying to understand the impact of racist attitudes on low-income incarcerated African American men, or he may be unaware of how his beliefs toward culturally sanctioned gender roles may result in the oppression of women.

Students begin diversity training at various points on the continuum. Expecting students to be at a certain place at a given time or to progress in a linear fashion is frustrating for both instructors and students. Student success must be measured by noting incremental changes in a student's behavior, thinking, emotional expression, and willingness to remain engaged in the learning process. These incremental changes can include a growing awareness of the impact of their behavior and words, being willing to share their process in class, developing a posture of seeking first to understand rather than being understood, and a growing acknowledgment of the role their intersecting identities have played in their experiences of power, privilege, and oppression.

Many students exhibit significant challenges related to diversity training (Pernell-Arnold et al., 2012). For many, a diversity class is their first exposure to issues of power, privilege, and oppression and can bring up challenging emotional experiences such as anxiety, anger, sadness, shame, and guilt (Roysircar et al., 2010). A growing awareness of one's intersecting points of power and privilege can exacerbate these emotional states and prompt the use of resistance-based coping strategies (e.g., denial, avoidance, silence).

Jackson (1999) quantified three forms of resistance that diversity educators can expect when working with students beginning to explore diversity: character, content, and transference. Students exhibiting *character resistance* will demonstrate a limited ability to assess and evaluate anxiety-related topics discussed in the classroom due to inherent personality functioning. The experience is a reminder for diversity educators that students' personal narratives of power, privilege, and oppression may be filled with painful stories that impact how they perceive and interpret issues of diversity. Students experiencing *content resistance* feel comfortable discussing diversity knowledge but become defensive when confronted with their limited self-awareness in relation to experiences of power and privilege. Often these students will cope through expressions of anger and resentment. *Transference* resistance describes challenges in the relationship between the student and diversity instructors as difficult cultural dialogues manifest. Both present with identity variables that vary in salience, and their intersecting identities can lead to conflict or overidentification on the part of the student (Jackson, 1999). For example, if both the student and instructor are female, the student may make assumptions of similarity or difference about the instructor's experience of being female. The student's assumptions may hamper communication with the instructor and lead to a disruption in their relationship. Such disruptions must be addressed with the student in a sensitive manner, using some of the techniques suggested in the next section.

DEVELOPING A POSITIVE LEARNING ENVIRONMENT

When teaching attitude development, instructors are responsible for guiding students in exploring their beliefs and developing an awareness of how their experiences and social contexts have affected their worldviews. Such insights will help them separate their worldviews from those of others and understand the role that context plays in how others experience the world. Deconstructing their belief systems can help them to help others navigate that same process and be better prepared to conceptualize client cases and their communities in a diversity-competent manner.

A primary tool that serves as a fundamental mechanism for increasing awareness and deconstructing attitudes is open and honest dialogue. Discussion becomes central in their classroom experience. We emphasize facilitating students' ability to "lean into" difficult and emotionally laden dialogues rather than merely demonstrating content acquisition.

For growth-producing dialogue to occur, it is essential to create a safe learning climate. Without a firm foundation of trust, it is difficult for students to engage in the challenging processes of self-examination, mutual reflection, and paradigm exploration. Instructors must establish clear parameters for effective communication, interpersonal respect, and trust that instructors will handle process factors that arise, ability to deal with vulnerabilities, and willingness to consider other perspectives (Corey, Corey, & Corey, 2014).

Given differences in personality, social norms in one's upbringing, and degree of comfort with challenge, engaging in difficult dialogue can be an intimidating expectation. Some students freely express opinions, whereas others may be more reserved. Although individuals cannot always predict the impact their words will have, it remains important to invite students to reflect on that impact before speaking. Words have power and, if used well, purposeful influence. To build a climate of social responsibility as narratives are unpacked in daily class discussions, students can ask themselves, What do I hope to achieve by sharing these thoughts? Who is the true target of this observation (self vs. other)? What effect might my comments have on others? Reflecting on their answers fosters respectful, responsible engagement, whereas not addressing responsibility for personal discourse can lead to interpersonal rifts and process blocks.

Students are often afraid they will appear insensitive even after considering the possible consequences of their words. The difference between impact and intent can help students when they take risks. *Intent* is defined as what the speaker "means" to say or ask; the impact on the listener can be different than what the speaker intends. A student may have questions about the cultural practices of a racial group different than his or her own but may be afraid that by asking he or she will come across as racist. Indeed, others' responses may be colored by their biases or understanding. The goals go beyond learning the content of the discussion: to help students sit with discomfort, improve their ability to remain engaged, and further the discussion. Listeners are tasked with letting a speaker know when they are feeling offended by what is being said, with an understanding that the intent of the speaker may be different than what is perceived. The responsibility of speakers is to remain in discussion and explore why the listener is experiencing what they are saying or how they are saying it as painful. This dimension of self-reflection is an important aspect of the engagement and growth process.

In addition to reflection, there is a need to distinguish between being "safe" and being "comfortable" in this process. Exploring one's attitudes can lead to discomfort; however, working through that discomfort can lead to growth. Safety, however, involves the fear of harm. Fear by students that they will be ostracized outside of class or will be in danger of being expelled from the program because of what they say are examples of feeling unsafe. For productive dialogue to occur, students are expected to sit with discomfort but to inform instructors when they feel unsafe.

All class members should be included in developing ground rules; those rules will vary across classes. We suggest, however, that the following are uniformly considered for inclusion: (a) Repeat back what others say before offering points (conveys respect for hearing what has been said), (b) be prepared to experience and perceive others' affect (people tend to get emotional when discussing oppression and privilege, especially their own; both taking the risk to share feelings and experiences and being able to sit with the emotions being expressed should be valued), (c) sit with the difficult moments in discussion (allow the inner work to be done in those silent times), (d) adopt an attitude of puzzlement (by taking an open and curious stance, one can avoid the pitfalls of arguing—there is no right or wrong answer—and move forward through engaged dialogue), (e) if a break is needed from the discussion, ask for one (it is important not to let students go to a place of being unable to recompose themselves), and (f) accept that each person is the expert on his or her experiences, even when a classmate feels he or she would have understood the experience differently (telling another that he or she simply misunderstood a situation invalidates that person's reactions to his or her experiences).

Remain aware that the journey toward diversity competence is a process that can sometimes be rocky but also can be helpful. Pushing students to progress while allowing space for individuals to be at different places and respond in different manners allows students to feel proud of movement rather than judging themselves and others for not reaching perfection. Supporting students in staying engaged when they are feeling stressed helps them to move forward.

We acknowledge that even the best-intentioned instructor and student can make a cultural faux pas. Sharing techniques and modeling how to address cross-cultural, interpersonal mistakes will help students learn what to do when they occur. Taking the time to address this issue supports the students' trust-building processes and relieves the pressure to demonstrate diversity competence at all times. This strategy validates our human side, while also encouraging interpersonal responsibility to address mistakes when they occur. *Anticipatory strategizing* suggests that mistakes do not have to lead to shutdowns, relationship severances, or dismissal of previous conceptualizations of the other person. When serious breakdowns occur (e.g., rupture), instructors can reframe them as relationship injuries that serve as building blocks for growth, both intrapersonal and interpersonal.

Conflict, anxiety, anger, and injury can come about not only from the discourse between students but also as a result of interactions between students and instructors and even between co-instructors. Instructors can inadvertently misunderstand and/or use power to silence a student or each other. They must own and address any missteps that occur, via class discussion as well as journal feedback provided to students. In the event conflict arises between cofacilitating instructors, it is vital that the instructors model conflict as normal and inevitable. Such conflict is not catastrophic, and instructors can help students learn to manage the conflict without letting it derail ongoing dialogue or stop participants from progressing on the journey toward increased diversity competence. In our experience, modeling humility is the ultimate strategy for promoting healthy, productive, and yet at times, painful dialogues. These moments are opportunities to practice, model, and normalize the reparative power of "calling out" and "calling in," as illustrated by Williams and Kniffley's (2017) TEDxDayton talk, *Meeting in the Middle.*

Power differentials between instructors and students may also hinder the diversity dialogue. When instructors represent the diversity variable being discussed, they should be able to remain open to students' level of exposure to and understanding of their salient diversity variable, particularly those struggling to understand the impact it may have on the instructor's life experiences.

Clarifying the appropriate venues for processing the learning points and emotional flow that come with diversity training (e.g., journals, class discussions), as well as how the data will be evaluated, will facilitate a sense of safety and trust. Knowing how information will be used decreases anxiety and prevents wounded feelings that can come from misperceptions. For example, instructors who have multiple roles in student training, including evaluation of progress in the training program, should be clear about what information will be shared with others. Specific information offered by students should not be shared; rather, share students' willingness to participate in the diversity training process. Likewise, instructors must address anxiety about grading. Students may feel a need to meet instructor expectations even when they are not conducive to their growth (e.g., some share beyond their comfort levels so that they will be evaluated positively). Others may try to determine the "politically correct" thing to say. Grading should be based on students' readiness to participate in discussions, exercises, and assignments in a way that challenges them to grow and is sensitive to the needs of classmates. Guidelines should be made clear at the beginning of class and feedback regarding their progress provided frequently. One suggestion is to identify ways students may earn or lose points based on specific behavioral markers (e.g., losing points for refusing to participate in discussion or rolling their eyes at other students' comments, gaining points by listening actively or sharing their thoughts). Students should be assured that if an instructor feels they are not performing in a constructive manner, the instructor will inform them as soon as possible and work with them to understand expectations.

Ultimately, the instructor is the best resource for facilitating safety. Authentically representing commitment to the learning process, value for each student, and appreciation for and belief in multicultural work is essential to forming a safe environment. Once this is demonstrated, the platform for exploration, support, challenge, and learning is established. The instructor's role is not to promise safety, but to help a student through unsafe territory.

Deconstruction and Dialogue

Diversity courses are as much about unlearning as about learning. Students must revisit what they have been taught to believe to be true about life, others, and perhaps most painfully, fairness. This evaluation can only come about as a function of dialogue. The most powerful dialogues are generally with people who hold different worldviews and who are willing to challenge the validity of learned belief systems. For example, if a student who has been taught to believe that disability means deficiency, pity, and/or burden is placed in a room with classmates and/or instructors who have disabilities, and that student is confronted with disability pride, competency, and value, he or she not only must sit with cognitive dissonance but also actually engage with the object of his or her beliefs. These can become transformative learning experiences, especially as feelings of guilt or shame turn to feelings of relief and liberation when the object becomes a real person.

Instructors may consider inviting diverse individuals to discuss their experiences. Continuing the earlier example, guests with a disability who can share their experiences in a world that does not privilege those with disabilities can broaden awareness, foster sensitive understanding, and assist in perspective sharing. Describing how they were able to develop their sense of pride and self-value challenges students to both view disability in the social context that currently exists and explore how individuals can challenge and change the ways that oppressive beliefs affect their understanding of themselves. Readings and videos to help students explore life experiences that may be different from their own include *Lives Worth Living* (Neudel, 2011), which presents the history and context of the disability rights movement, and *Sins Invalid* (Berne, 2013), which addresses taboos and stigma about people with disabilities and sexuality. Readings on Crip theory (e.g., McRuer, 2006) challenge students to explore cultural and individual beliefs about disability, most importantly locating "suffering" at the intersections in society (see Chapter 12, this volume). Whether or not a person who lives a given identity variable is present, instructors must be prepared to facilitate discussions that challenge students to think "out of the box" and explore the impact of privilege and oppression on people living that identity.

A number of exercises can promote effective dialogue. Select an exercise on the basis of level of intended intensity and students' developmental readiness; for instance, a low level of intensity might include a progressive revealing exercise or the "shield" exercise, both of which promote introductions to one another without the expectation of deep discussion, inviting students to contextualize themselves for their classmates in limited doses. In the progressive revealing exercise, each student is given 1 minute to speak of a diversity experience they had that was positive and then a diversity experience they had that was negative. In the shield exercise, students create and then discuss a shield that reflects valued elements of their family, social, ethnic, and cultural worldviews. Each shield is divided into six sections with a designated topic. Students draw a picture of what that topic represents to them and then present the shield to the class, discussing the meaning each picture has. Examples of topics include your family, a favorite holiday, a she/hero, something representing your ethnicity, your favorite season, and a student choice category. Both exercises are followed by class discussion to explore the experience and the understanding gained.

As the course develops, strategies should focus on deeper exploration. Students are asked to sit with experiences that differ from their own (brought into the room via self-disclosure, guests, exercises, readings, and/or videos) and the emotions that arise. One such exercise is the diversity walk. All students stand on one side of the room. An identity variable (e.g., White, Black, gay or lesbian, heterosexual, woman, man) is then spoken and all students who identify with that variable move to the other side of the room. Students in the identifying group express what they never want to hear again about the identity variable they are claiming. Students who do not identify as a member of the given group (the listening group) stand at the opposite end of the room facing the identifying group. They are to listen and are then challenged to reflect what they heard without questioning the accuracy and/or validity of what they are hearing. Students who are in the listening group are instructed to reflect the affect and/or the content heard, whereas the students who spoke are asked to provide feedback as to whether they have been accurately heard. This activity is a critical exercise in that students are asked to suspend judgment and hear their classmates on both cognitive and emotional levels.

We have developed an immersion exercise that fosters deeper exploration. Instructors arrange for students to participate in events within communities whose identity variables differ from their own, and all are asked to engage meaningfully. For example, able-bodied students can attend training at a local Independent Living Center for individuals with disabilities, heterosexual students may attend events with the university lesbian, gay, bisexual, transgender, and queer or questioning (LGBTQ) center, and White students can attend an event in the African American community. It is important that the events are open to the public or attended with the permission of the host group. After the event, students meet to process their reactions. The key to this exercise is that students are to focus primarily on their experiences, not those of the group they are joining: how they felt being a numerical minority, how that affected their sense of privilege, and how they understand the occurrence of oppression. An instructor participates in the event and facilitates the discussion afterward to assure that the discussion remains focused on students exploring their attitudes and biases. Students then each write an individual paper incorporating the experience of the event and the discussion, thus allowing them to discuss their experiences with the instructor privately. This exercise allows students to explore with others their experience of privilege.

Self-Care

Students have to care for themselves throughout diversity training. One way is to seek individual conversations with instructors, through journals or in person, to help them find ways to stay engaged in a healthy way that allows them to continue their development. Support systems outside of class can also help. Instructors should also consider ways to facilitate and implement their own self-care; educating students about diversity and social justice can be intellectually and emotionally challenging (Vaughn & Krutka, 2013). We have co-instructors in diversity classes, especially those with a strong focus on exploring attitude-related issues. Like students, instructors are raised in a context that affects their experiences and their understanding of the world, and what happens in class can be triggering for them as well. For example, a gay or lesbian instructor may have to sit with students addressing religious beliefs that support heterosexist thinking. Instructors can also feel emotionally and intellectually threatened by examining their privileged identities, resulting in feeling guilt, shame, and discomfort. Having a co-instructor to process those reactions with is helpful; furthermore, a co-instructor can take the lead in managing a class discussion to allow the other instructor to manage his or her reactions.

Having co-instructors is also helpful in managing workload. In attitude-based classes, it is important to have real discussions with students, not only in class but also through journals and other assignments. Thus, instructors spend a lot of time reviewing those assignments. Sharing that task can allow instructors to spend the time needed to engage students.

An issue closely related to self-care relates to whether the administration sees the pedagogical value in training in diversity. Administrators decide whether resources can be spent on providing co-instructors; whether issues related to diversity, including issues of power, privilege, and oppression, are addressed throughout training and not only in diversity classes; and how to deal with diversity course instructor evaluations, which may be harsher than in other classes. This is especially true when instructors are individuals of color, women, disabled and/or LGBTQ individuals because they are not only more likely to teach diversity classes but also more likely to be confronted and evaluated negatively by students (Vaccaro, 2017). An understanding administration is especially helpful when strong and favorable course evaluations are needed for promotion.

CONCLUSION

Exploring attitudes and biases plays a pivotal role in diversity training. Self-awareness and an understanding of the impact of privilege, power, and oppression allow students to form strong therapeutic relationships and better understand the knowledge and skills that are necessary for diversity-competent practice. It is important for instructors to understand the ongoing nature of the journey toward cultural competence. Further, instructors should be prepared to normalize and productively address the emotions and resulting defenses that are triggered and to establish an environment that fosters honest, safe, and respectful dialogue. The journey toward diversity competence can be challenging for every participant, making it beneficial for instructors to treat themselves with the same respect, honesty, and acceptance with which they treat students.

REFERENCES

American Psychological Association. (2017). *Multicultural guidelines: An ecological approach to context, identity, and intersectionality*. Retrieved from http://www.apa.org/about/policy/multicultural-guidelines.pdf

Berne, P. (Director). (2013). *Sins invalid: An unshamed claim to beauty in the face of invisibility* [Motion Picture]. United States: New Day Films.

Corey, M. S., Corey, G., & Corey, C. (2014). *Groups: Process and practice*. Belmont, CA: Brooks/Cole–Cengage Learning.

Fouad, N. A., Grus, C. L., Hatcher, R. L., Kaslow, N. J., Hutchings, P. S., Madson, M. B., . . . Crossman, R. E. (2009). Competency benchmarks: A model for understanding and measuring competence in professional psychology across training levels. *Training and Education in Professional Psychology, 3*, S5–S26. http://dx.doi.org/10.1037/a0015832

Jackson, L. C. (1999). Ethnocultural resistance to multicultural training: Students and faculty. *Cultural Diversity and Ethnic Minority Psychology, 5*, 27–36. http://dx.doi.org/10.1037/1099-9809.5.1.27

Malloy, K. A., Dobbins, J. E., Williams, J. L., Allen, J. B., & Warfield, J. R. (2009). In J. L. Chin (Ed.), *Diversity in mind and in action: Vol 2. Disparities and competence* (pp. 107–127). New York, NY: Praeger.

McRuer, R. (2006). *Crip theory: Cultural signs of queerness and disability*. New York, NY: New York University Press.

Neudel, E. (Producer & Director). (2011). *Lives worth living* [Motion picture]. United States: Storyline Motion Pictures.

Pernell-Arnold, A., Finley, L., Sands, R. G., Bourjolly, J., & Stanhope, V. (2012). Training mental health providers in cultural competence: A transformative learning process. *American Journal of Psychiatric Rehabilitation, 15*, 334–356. http://dx.doi.org/10.1080/ 15487768.2012.733287

Roysircar, G., Dobbins, J. E., & Malloy, K. A. (2010). Diversity competence in training and clinical practice. In M. B. Kenkel & R. L. Peterson (Eds.), *Competency-based education for professional psychology* (pp. 179–197). Washington, DC: American Psychological Association. http://dx.doi.org/10.1037/12068-010

Sue, D. W., Arredondo, P., & McDavis, R. J. (1992). Multicultural counseling competencies and standards: A call to the profession. *Journal of Multicultural Counseling and Development, 20*, 64–88. http://dx.doi.org/10.1002/j.2161-1912.1992.tb00563.x

Tao, K. W., Owen, J., Pace, B. T., & Imel, Z. E. (2015). A meta-analysis of multicultural competencies and psychotherapy process and outcome. *Journal of Counseling Psychology, 62*, 337–350. http://dx.doi.org/10.1037/cou0000086

Vaccaro, A. (2017). Does my story belong? An intersectional critical race feminist analysis of student silence in a diverse classroom. *NASPA Journal About Women in Higher Education, 10*, 27–44. http://dx.doi.org/10.1080/19407882.2016.1268538

Vaughn, C. A., & Krutka, D. G. (2013). Self-reflections, teaching, and learning in a graduate cultural pluralism course. *International Journal of Action Research, 9*, 300–332.

Williams, J., & Kniffley, S. (2017). *Meeting in the middle* [Video file]. *TEDxDayton.* Retrieved from https://www.youtube.com/watch?v=5trvm6-18F0

INDEX

ABOUT THE EDITORS

Jasmine A. Mena, PhD, is an assistant professor of psychology and Latin American Studies Program affiliate at Bucknell University. She received her doctorate in clinical psychology from the University of Rhode Island. Her research examines the influence of culture and discrimination on mental and physical health and wellness. She has numerous publications that center on her research interests and use qualitative, quantitative, and mixed methods in community settings. She is the recipient of various honors, including an Association for Academic and University Women Postdoctoral Research Leave Fellowship, Emerging Professional—Contributions to Service Award (American Psychological Association Division 45), and Association for Women in Psychology Annual Women of Color Psychologies Award. As a licensed clinical psychologist, the ultimate goal of her research is to develop and implement interventions to improve the health and wellness of marginalized populations.

Kathryn ("Kat") Quina, PhD, is Emerita Associate Dean and professor of psychology and gender and women's studies at the University of Rhode Island. She received her doctorate in experimental psychophysics from the University of Georgia, but soon after entering academia, she discovered feminist psychology and left the literally dark world of her vision lab to shed light on issues of gender and trauma. For most of her academic career, her research has related to women and gender, with a primary focus on the sequelae of sexual abuse, including funded research on women's HIV risk and incarceration. As psychology coordinator and advisor, and subsequently associate dean, of the University of Rhode Island's College of Continuing Education, she studied and championed adult and nontraditional students, directing programs and funded projects that enhance minority and immigrant success in adult education. Dr. Quina has coauthored or coedited six books and numerous articles, including coediting two previous volumes on teaching psychology from a multicultural perspective, and has received local and national awards for her mentorship, teaching, research, and service in feminist and multicultural psychology.